NEW TESTAMENT MESSAGE

A Biblical-Theological Commentary

Wilfrid Harrington, O.P. and Donald Senior, C.P.

EDITORS

New Testament Message, Volume 3

MATTHEW

John P. Meier

Michael Glazier, Inc.
Wilmington, Delaware

MICHAEL GLAZIER, INC.
1723 Delaware Avenue
Wilmington, Delaware 19806

First printing 1980
Second printing (with revisions) 1981

Library of Congress Catalog Card Number: 79-55807
International Standard Book Number:
    New Testament Message series: 0-89453-123-9
    MATTHEW: 0-89453-126-3

Nihil Obstat: Myles M. Bourke, S.S.L., S.T.D.
Imprimatur: Joseph T. O'Keefe, Vicar General, Archdiocese of New York.

Cover Illustration:
"Christ in Majesty" — mediaeval stained glass from Canterbury Cathedral, Kent.

Printed in the United States of America

To His Eminence

TERENCE CARDINAL COOKE

Archbishop of New York

*in thanks for his encouragement
and support of this work*

Contents

BOOK FIVE
THE MESSIAH AND HIS CHURCH ON THE
WAY TO THE PASSION

THE CLIMAX
THE DEATH-RESURRECTION

EDITORS' PREFACE

New Testament Message is a commentary series designed to bring the best of biblical scholarship to a wide audience. Anyone who is sensitive to the mood of the church today is aware of a deep craving for the Word of God. This interest in reading and praying the scriptures is not confined to a religious elite. The desire to strengthen one's faith and to mature in prayer has brought Christians of all types and all ages to discover the beauty of the biblical message. Our age has also been heir to an avalanche of biblical scholarship. Recent archaeological finds, new manuscript evidence, and the increasing volume of specialized studies on the Bible have made possible a much more profound penetration of the biblical message. But the flood of information and its technical nature keeps much of this scholarship out of the hands of the Christian who is eager to learn but is not a specialist. *New Testament Message* is a response to this need.

The subtitle of the series is significant: "A Biblical-Theological Commentary." Each volume in the series, while drawing on up-to-date scholarship, concentrates on bringing to the fore in understandable terms the specific message of each biblical author. The essay-format (rather than a word-by-word commentary) helps the reader savor the beauty and power of the biblical message and, at the same time, understand the sensitive task of responsible biblical interpretation.

A distinctive feature of the series is the amount of space given to the "neglected" New Testament writings, such as Colossians, James, Jude, the Pastoral Letters, the Letters of Peter and John. These briefer biblical books make a significant but often overlooked contribution to the richness of the New Testament. By assigning larger than normal coverage to these books, the series hopes to give these parts of Scripture the attention they deserve.

Because *New Testament Message* is aimed at the entire English speaking world, it is a collaborative effort of international proportions. The twenty-two contributors represent biblical scholarship in North America, Ireland, Britain and Australia. Each of the contributors is a recognized expert in his or her field, has published widely, and has been chosen because of a proven ability to communicate at a popular level. And, while all of the contributors are Roman Catholic, their work is addressed to the Christian community as a whole. The New Testament is the patrimony of all Christians.It is the hope of all concerned with this series that it will bring a fuller appreciation of God's saving Word to his people.

Wilfrid Harrington, O.P.
Donald Senior, C.P.

INTRODUCTION

AT SOME TIME around A.D. 80-90, a learned Christian, perhaps a Jew, perhaps a Gentile Semite, recast and combined the two major liturgical and catechetical documents of his church: the gospel of Mark and a collection of Jesus' sayings which scholars call "Q." These two documents were already steeped in the oral traditions of the author's church, traditions which we globally label "M." It was by skillfully combining and editing these three sources that the author created the theological masterpiece we call the gospel of Matthew. In the commentary which follows we will seek to understand the author's own thought by carefully tracing the process by which he welded disparate sources into an original and meaningful unity. Comparing what the author says with what his sources said will be the main way by which we will enter into the author's mind.

This new synthesis of Mark, Q, and M was necessitated by a severe crisis in the author's church. Stringently Jewish in origins, it had experienced the trauma of separation from the synagogue and a great influx of Gentiles into its ranks. This shift in its Christian existence demanded a new interpretation of old traditions, a new way of looking at Christ and his church, at the Old Testament and salvation history, at discipleship and morality. To achieve this new synthesis, the author divided salvation history into three periods: "all the prophets and the Law" up to the Baptist (Mt 11:13); the public ministry of Jesus, restricted to the land and people of Israel (10:5-6; 15:24); and the mission to all nations, a mission made possible by the great turning point, the death-resurrection of Jesus (27:51-54; 28:2-3; 28:16-20). Narrow, exclusivistic Jewish-Christian statements could thus be retained by being referred to the unique period of Jesus' public ministry, while the evangelist could view his own time as under the final, universal mandate of 28:16-20. This flow of salvation history shows that the church, not Judaism, is the true people of God because it is the people formed by God's Son, Jesus Christ, the fulfiller of the Law and the prophets. The author's solution to his theological problem is a pattern of discontinuity within a large framework of continuity.

Who the author of this gospel is we cannot say, though he is probably not the apostle Matthew. Writing in a Greek better than Mark's and addressing a large urban church ca. A.D. 80-90, Matthew—as we shall continue to call him—labored in Syria, probably at Antioch. As Luke is a verbal portrait-painter, Matthew is a verbal architect. The public ministry is welded into five books, each book composed of first narrative and then discourse. Five great discourses, put together by Matthew, form the five pillars of the gospel: the sermon on the mount (chaps. 5-7), the missionary discourse (chap. 10), the parables (chap. 13), the church-life discourse (chap. 18), and the discourse on the end (chaps. 24-25). The climax comes in the death-resurrection (chaps. 26-28), a climax which is foreshadowed by the introductory infancy narrative (chaps. 1-2).

Since Matthew is using Mark as the backbone of his narrative, I refer the reader to the Mark volume in this series for a detailed consideration of the material also found in Mark. Here we shall concentrate on the new message Matthew conveys by his "remodeling" of the good news. For arguments in favor of the positions espoused in this commentary, I refer the reader to two other works of mine: *Law and History in Matthew's Gospel* (Rome: Biblical Institute Press, 1976) and *The Vision of Matthew: Christ, Church, and Morality in the First Gospel* (New York: Paulist Press, 1979).

ABBREVIATIONS

OT – Old Testament; NT – New Testament; v(v) – verse(s); chap(s). – chapter(s); Mt – Matthew; Mk – Mark; Lk – Luke; Jn – John.

THE PROLOGUE
Mt 1-2:
THE INFANCY ANTICIPATES
THE PASSION

THE PROLOGUE of Mt's gospel must not be dismissed as a collection of warm-hearted Christmas stories with no substantial theological message, and therefore with no essential connection to the body of the gospel. Like the prologue of John's gospel, Mt 1-2 form an "overture" to the whole work, weaving together in miniature a number of significant themes which will be played out at length as the gospel progresses. Like Jn's prologue, Mt 1-2 seek to define the significance of Jesus (1) by applying a string of titles to him; and (2) by defining his origin and goal, his "whence" and his "whither." In Jn's gospel, this "whence" and "whither" are defined in terms of the Son's preexistence with the Father and his return to the Father *via* his exaltation on the cross. In Mt, the "whence" is defined in terms of (1) continuity with OT salvation history (the genealogy), (2) discontinuity with that history as the end-time breaks in (the eschatological miracle of virginal conception), and (3) by the fulfillment of the "eschatological geography" mapped out for the Messiah in the OT (birth in David's city of Bethlehem, pilgrimage of the Gentiles of Jerusalem, flight into and exodus from Egypt, residence of the "Nazirite" in Nazareth). The "whither" consists of hints concerning the ultimate fate of this child: rejection by the Jews, acceptance by the Gentiles, persecution unto death, restoration to life through the Father's intervention on behalf of his Son. The passion narrative at the end of the gospel is mirrored in miniature especially in chap. 2.

A. GENEALOGY: JESUS THE SON OF DAVID, THE GOAL OF ISRAEL'S HISTORY.
1:1-17.
[Lk 3:23-38].

1. The book of the genealogy of Jesus Christ, the Son of David, the son of Abraham.

[2]Abraham was the father of Isaac, and Isaac the father of Jacob, and Jacob the father of Judah and his brothers, [3]and Judah the father of Perez and Zerah by Tamar, and Perez the father of Hezron, and Hezron the father of Ram, [4]and Ram the father of Amminadab, and Amminadab the father of Nahshon, and Nahshon the father of Salmon, [5]and Salmon the father of Boaz by Rahab, and Boaz the father of Obed by Ruth, and Obed the father of Jesse, [6]and Jesse the father of David the king.

And David was the father of Solomon by the wife of Uriah, [7]and Solomon the father of Rehoboam, and Rehoboam the father of Abijah and Abijah the father of Asa, [8] and Asa the father of Jehoshaphat, and Jehoshaphat the father of Joram, and Joram the father of Uzziah, [9]and Uzziah the father of Jotham, and Jotham the father of Ahaz, and Ahaz the father of Hezekiah, [10]and Hezekiah the father of Manasseh, and Manasseh the father of Amos, and Amos the father of Josiah, [11]and Josiah the father of Jechoniah and his brothers, at the time of the deportation to Babylon.

[12]And after the deportation to Babylon; Jechoniah was the father of Shealtiel, and Shealtiel the father of Zerubbabel, [13]and Zerubbabel the father of Abiud, and Abiud the father of Eliakim, and Eliakim the father of

Azor, [14]and Azor the father of Zadok, and Zadok the father of Achim, and Achim the father of Eliud, [15]and Eliud the father of Eleazar, and Eleazar the father of Matthan, and Matthan the father of Jacob, [16]and Jacob the father of Joseph the husband of Mary, of whom Jesus was born, who is called Christ.

[17]So all the generations from Abraham to David were fourteen generations, and from David to the deportation to Babylon fourteen generations, and from the deportation to Babylon to the Christ fourteen generations.

The basic affirmation of the genealogy is two-fold: (1) Jesus' origins lie in the old people of God, Israel; and (2) Jesus is the fulfillment of Israel's history, a history carefully guided by God to its goal. Mt emphasizes Jesus' status as messianic King by tracing his line through David and the kings of Judah. By contrast, Lk traces Jesus' lineage backwards, through non-reigning sons of David, to Adam, the father of the whole human race, who was, in virtue of his direct creation, something of a "son of God." Mt may be using Jewish-Christian sources which in turn draw upon Ruth 4:18-22 and 1 Chr 1-3. Most of the names in the third part of the list are not paralleled elsewhere in the bible's genealogical lists, and so the historical accuracy of this part of the genealogy cannot be determined. Since Mt and Lk disagree for most of the time after the exile, at least one of them, and possibly both, do not report Jesus' actual genealogy. The genealogies in Mt and Lk are to be understood as theological statements, not biological reports.

Mt underlines the fact that his genealogy is carefully divided into three sets of fourteen generations. Why does Mt cast Israel's history into this artificial mold, even to the point of arbitrarily dropping names of Judean kings? Around the time of Mt, Jewish apocalyptic thought was greatly concerned with dividing the world's history into neat periods of seven's, consisting of so many "weeks" of years. Mt sums up Israel's rollercoaster history by counting two "weeks" of generations (2 x 7 = 14 generations) from

Israel's beginnings in Abraham to its high point in *King* David, two more weeks from its high point to its low point in the disaster of the Babylonian exile, and two further weeks during its ascent to its goal, Jesus the Messiah. Jesus Christ thus begins the seventh period, the period of perfection and fulfillment (cf. Daniel's seventy weeks of years in Dan 9). Hence Mt uses an apocalyptic convention to proclaim that God has secretly ordered the economy of salvation so that all of Israel's history moves smoothly towards the Messiah. Also, Mt may be playing with the numerical values given Hebrew letters (a technique called "gemetria"). The consonants in the Hebrew name David add up to fourteen (D + W + D = 4 + 6 + 4). When you "add up" the meaning of Israel's history, the bottom line is Jesus Christ, the Son of David.

The first verse of this section acts as a title, but a title to what? The RSV translates *geneseōs* as genealogy, thus supplying a title for 1:2-17, or at most 1:2-25. Also possible, however, is the translation "origin" or "birth"; the word would thus introduce the whole of the infancy narrative. Some would even translate *geneseōs* as "story" or "history," which would sum up the whole of the gospel; but *geneseōs* cannot bear so wide a meaning. Two titles are immediately added to Jesus Christ in v.1. Jesus is son of David, and thus the promised Messianic King. But he is also son of Abraham, and thus the fulfillment of the promise that in Abraham's seed "all the nations" of the earth would be blessed (cf. Gen 22:18). Jesus fulfills this promise at the end of the gospel when he sends the eleven to make disciples of "all the nations" (Mt 28:19). This universal blessing is already prefigured in the Magi of chap. 2.

One startling feature of Mt's genealogy is that four women are mentioned: Tamar, Rahab, Ruth, and indirectly, Bathsheba ("the wife of Uriah"). Instead of being the great patriarchesses of Israel, they form a very strange sorority. Some think Mt has introduced them to stress that Christ's salvation is offered even to sinners and/or Gentiles. But the most likely explanation is that they represent "holy irregularities" in God's orderly plan; they represent discontinuities within the continuity of salvation history. God writes straight with crooked lines. All four women point ahead to the supreme holy irregularity, the supreme discontinuity: the virginal conception of Jesus by Mary.

The genealogy thus shows us Mt's basic approach to solving the relationship of the OT to Jesus. On the one hand, there is an underlying continuity. Indeed, Mt even includes the psalmist Asaph and the prophet Amos among the kings of Judah to emphasize that Jesus is the fulfillment of all the Scriptures. Yet, on the other hand, there is also a rupture as the final age breaks into Israel's history. This is symbolized by the four women as well as by the virginal conception in v.16, where the genealogical pattern is broken and the "of whom" properly refers to Mary. There may also be a hint of discontinuity-within-continuity in the fact that the third part of the genealogy contains only thirteen generations (i.e., pairs of begetter and begotten). If we do not allow for a slip on the part of Mt or a later scribe, we may have here an indication that "Jesus" and "Christ" are to be counted separately. Jesus is born of the royal line within the flow of history, but as Messiah he not only concludes the old dispensation but also opens up a new age (just as David both concludes one part of the genealogy and begins another). In this sense, Mt is quite correct in claiming that up to "the Christ" (not "up to Jesus") there are fourteen generations (v.17). The Messiah closes out the sixth and final period of the old Israel and introduces the seventh period, the period of fulfillment, the period of the Messiah.

B. JESUS, VIRGINALLY CONCEIVED YET SON OF DAVID. 1:18-25.

[18]Now the birth of Jesus Christ took place in this way. When his mother Mary had been betrothed to Joseph, before they came together she was found to be with child

of the Holy Spirit; [19]and her husband Joseph, being a just man and unwilling to put her to shame, resolved to divorce her quietly. [20]But as he considered this, behold, an angel of the Lord appeared to him in a dream, saying, "Joseph, son of David, do not fear to take Mary your wife, for that which is conceived in her is of the Holy Spirit; [21]she will bear a son, and you shall call his name Jesus, for he will save his people from their sins." [22]All this took place to fulfil what the Lord had spoken by the prophet:

[23]"Behold, a virgin shall conceive and bear a son,
    and his name shall be called Emmanuel"
(which means, God with us).

[24]When Joseph woke from sleep, he did as the angel of the Lord commanded him; he took his wife, [25]but knew her not until she had borne a son; and he called his name Jesus.

The theme of discontinuity-within-continuity proceeds as Jesus is defined both by his virginal conception (discontinuity) and by legal paternity from Joseph (continuity). The Davidic Messiah (continuity) is more than a mere Messiah; he is God with us (discontinuity). Verses 18-25 act as an extended footnote to v.16, which has already hinted at a virginal conception. This conception is understood not in terms of some promiscuous god of Greek mythology. The "Holy Spirit" (feminine in Hebrew, neuter in Greek) betokens not sexual union but God's life-giving power. In apocalyptic circles, a fresh outburst of activity by the Holy Spirit was awaited as a sign of the last days. The virginal conception is thus not just another miracle but an eschatological event. Eschatological events, however, usually disturb things. They certainly disturb Joseph. Joseph was already betrothed to Mary; consequently, even before he took her into his home for regular sexual relations, he counted as her "husband" and had legal rights over her. If found pregnant by another man, Mary could, according to the strict letter of the Law, be put to death.

Joseph is in a dilemma. He is "just" in a double sense: he wishes to show loyalty and kindness to Mary, yet he must satisfy the requirement of the Law not to countenance adultery. He seeks to satisfy both desires by giving Mary the prescribed document of divorce privately. (As Mt adapts the tradition he has received, he apparently does not ask himself how this act would protect Mary from public shame when she must soon bear a son without benefit of husband. Actually, the only way Joseph could save Mary from disgrace would be to marry her. All this reminds us that Mt is writing theology, not giving an eyewitness report.)

The human calculations of Joseph are cut short by a sudden divine intervention. An angel appears in a dream and makes known God's mysterious plan to his elect. While there is a certain apocalyptic flavor here, the dream-motif is more reminiscent of the dreams granted to the patriarchs in Genesis. We remember especially that the patriarch *Joseph* was a dreamer, as well as a compassionate and just man. The words of the "angel of the Lord" (in the OT, the Lord himself in visible form) fall into a neat pattern of command (v.20a) and explanation (20b), command (21a) and explanation (21b). Joseph, "the son of *David*," is to take Mary into his house, not so much to protect her as to confer *Davidic* paternity on her child and so insert her child into its proper place in salvation history. Joseph need have no scruples, for the real origins of the child lie not with Davidic or any human lineage, but with the creative power of God's Spirit. This eschatological birth far surpasses the miraculous births in the OT. Joseph's key role is therefore to act as the child's father by giving it the name God has already chosen, a name not mentioned in Joseph's genealogy. God chooses the common but significant name Jesus, a later form of the biblical Joshua. Originally it meant "Yahweh helps," but by the first century A.D. the popular explanation of the name was "Yahweh saves." The angel, in true Genesis style, makes a pun on the popular meaning by declaring that Jesus will *save* his people from their sins (cf. Ps 130:8). The Jews were indeed expecting a national liberator like David, but Jesus the Davidic liberator will grant his people a spiritual liberation in almost priestly fashion. The liberation Jesus offers will not be acceptable to most of the people of Israel. The people who actually accept Jesus' saving act, *his* people, will be the group Jesus calls "*my* church" (Mt 16:18). They form the "other people" (21:43), Gentiles included, who accept the life-giving death of Jesus (27:51-54), a death which Jesus declares at the Last Supper to be "for the remission of sins" (26:28), a death whose saving power is ever available to "his people" in the church's celebration of the eucharist. The church is the people Jesus the Messiah creates by achieving forgiveness of sins through his death.

As is his custom, Mt pauses for a moment, steps back, and looks at the event he is narrating, and reflects on how perfectly this episode of Jesus' life fulfills OT prophecy. In v.22, he introduces the first of about twelve "reflection citations" or "formula quotations" which comment on his "life" of Jesus. Each quotation shows that, in Jesus' life, God is carefully ordering history towards the fulfillment of his prophetic word. In this citation of Is 7:14, Mt reworks the original text to underline the eschatological fulfillment in Christ. Isaiah spoke of a young woman who would conceive; Mt adopts the standard Greek translation, "a virgin shall conceive." But Mt is more interested in the name Jesus bears and in the fact that Joseph as well as Mary confers it. (The text of Mt 1:23 reads literally: "*they* shall call . . . .," although the standard Hebrew text mentions only the woman.)

At first it seems strange that a story about the name Jesus should have as its foundation in the prophets a verse which speaks of "Emmanuel" rather than "Joshua." What connection does Mt see between the personal name Jesus and the "throne name" Emmanuel? In Jesus, we find fulfilled the great promise of God to the patriarchs and prophets: "I shall be with you." It is Jesus, "God-with-us" in person, who concludes Mt's gospel by promising his church: "Lo, *I am with you* always, to the close of the age."

But what has prevented this saving presence till now? The great divide which has separated God from man is sin. It is precisely by removing sin from his people that *Jesus* ("he shall save from sin") removes the accursed distance and makes God present among his people. Thus he makes good the promise of his throne-name, Emmanuel.

In v.24 Mt returns to his narrative: Joseph, being just, obeys God's command immediately, as he also does in chap 2. Mt uses here the pattern of command-and-execution-of-command ("he did as commanded"—followed by the action commanded). This pattern appears a number of times in the gospel to stress that a true disciple obeys immediately and perfectly. To this obedience belongs, in Joseph's case, the waiving of marital intercourse ("he *knew* her not") "until" she bore the miraculous child. In Hebrew and Greek, "until" need not mean that there was a change in the situation after Jesus' birth. On the other hand, the author who wrote Mt 1:25 also wrote in 13:55 that Jesus' mother is Mary and his brothers (not "cousins") are James, Joseph, Simon, and Judas. Historically, these verses have created difficulties for the later church tradition about the perpetual virginity of Mary, a doctrine which becomes common in the fourth century A.D. However, the main concern for Mt at the end of this story is not the virginity of Mary but the function of Joseph, who places Jesus in the Davidic line by adoption.

C. JESUS THE KING, THE HOPE OF THE GENTILES.
2:1-12.

2 Now when Jesus was born in Bethlehem of Judea in the days of Herod the king, behold, wise men from the East came to Jerusalem, saying, [2]"Where is he who has been born king of the Jews? For we have seen his star in the East, and have come to worship him." [3]When Herod the king heard this, he was troubled, and all Jerusalem with him; [4]and assembling all the chief priests

and scribes of the people, he inquired of them where the Christ was to be born. [5]They told him, "In Bethlehem of Judea; for so it is written by the prophet:
[6]'And you, O Bethlehem, in the land of Judah,
   are by no means least among the rulers of Judah;
   for from you shall come a ruler
   who will govern my people Israel.'"
[7]Then Herod summoned the wise men secretly and ascertained from them what time the star appeared; [8]and he sent them to Bethlehem, saying, "Go and search diligently for the child, and when you have found him bring me word, that I too may come and worship him." [9]When they had heard the king they went their way; and lo, the star which they had seen in the East went before them, till it came to rest over the place where the child was. [10]When they saw the star, they rejoiced exceedingly with great joy; [11]and going into the house they saw the child with Mary his mother, and they fell down and worshiped him. Then, opening their treasures, they offered him gifts, gold and frankincense and myrrh. [12]And being warned in a dream not to return to Herod, they departed to their own country by another way.

Chapter 2 turns more to the question of the "whither," the destiny of Jesus: adored by Gentiles, yet persecuted unto death by his own people. Mt indicates this somber "whither" by using motifs from stories about Jacob (Israel) and Moses. Some have labeled Mt's creative reworking of OT narratives to illumine the birth of Christ "haggadic midrash," comparable to the imaginative retelling of the OT in Jewish homilies.

With precision, Mt places Jesus' birth in Bethlehem of *Judea* (as opposed to another Bethlehem in Galilee). Herod the Great reigned over a Jewish Kingdom as large as David's from 37 to 4 B.C. Herod's whole reign was a bloody struggle to maintain his throne in the face of opposition from the Hasmoneans (Jewish priestly rulers) and from messianic movements. With his frequently used "behold" (signaling a new divine intervention), Mt introduces the Magi, translated here as "wise men." Magi were originally members of the Persian priestly caste, but the word came to mean any possessor of supernatural knowledge and power—often with a pejorative nuance. Here they are astrologers. Like other Gentiles, they speak of the King of the *Jews*; the title occurs again only in the passion narrative (cf. especially 27:37). It was a common motif in antiquity that a new star marked the birth of a ruler. Mt takes the motif from the OT story of Balaam, a "magus" *from the east*, who is supposed to curse Israel but instead blesses it: "A star shall rise from Jacob, and a scepter [or 'man,' in the Greek] from Israel" (Num 24:17). One should not seek out astrological phenomena of the time, e.g., the conjunction of Jupiter and Saturn in 7 B.C., to explain what is a literary and theological motif. The Magi come to worship the king by prostration (*proskyneō,* a favorite verb of Mt's, which indicates an activity properly rendered only to God or Jesus). Worship of Jesus will be the last physical act of the disciples (28:17). Since the star does *not* move before them at this point, the Magi must find out the place of birth. Observing the proper course of salvation history, the Gentiles go to the Jews for instruction about messianic prophecy.

The question about the new King of the Jews frightens Herod the King of the Jews *and all Jerusalem with him.* Mt is intent on presenting an official Judaism united against Jesus; actually, most Jews, including the priests, hated Herod and would have gladly seen him go. Herod calls together the priestly nobility and the professional scholars (scribes); thus, the future enemies of Jesus ironically witness to the truth about the birth of Jesus and his messiahship. Mt adapts Micah 5:1,3 (putting in "by no means"), joins it to 2 Sam 5:2 ("my people Israel"), and puts it into the mouth of the experts, without the usual introduction of a "formula quotation." The eschatological good shepherd of Israel is to be born in the city from which the shepherd-King David came. Herod then finds out the time of the star's appearance, so that he can gauge the age of the child. The massacre of 2:16-18 is thus prepared for. Mt often rails against the sin of hypocrisy throughout his gospel; here we meet it for the first time. After the Magi leave the murderer and the murderous city (cf. 23:37), the star reappears and now acts as a guide, perhaps like the pillar of fire in Exodus. The astrological sign will lead the Magi out of pagan superstition and worship. The eschatological great joy of the Magi is reminiscent of Lk's infancy narrative; Mt on the whole is more somber.

The center of attention becomes the child and his mother (vv.11,13,14,20,21). Joseph is not even mentioned in this story; he appears only when needed. In the ancient world, one never visited a god or king without gifts. The Magi offer the three gifts of gold (Ps 72:10-15), frankincense (Is 60:6) and myrrh (another type of aromatic gum, like frankincense). The *three* gifts later gave rise to the idea of *three* Magi, who still later became kings with specific names. A dream, the regular form of revelation in the infancy narrative, prevents the Magi from being Herod's accomplices. God guides the course of history to save his Son and his people.

D. JESUS THE SON OF GOD, REJECTED BY ISRAEL. 2:13-18.

> [13]Now when they had departed, behold, an angel of the Lord appeared to Joseph in a dream and said, "Rise, take the child and his mother, and flee to Egypt, and remain there till I tell you; for Herod is about to search for the child, to destroy him." [14]And he rose and took the child and his mother by night, and departed to Egypt, [15]and remained there until the death of Herod. This was to fulfil what the Lord had spoken by the prophet, "Out of Egypt have I called my son."
>
> [16]Then Herod, when he saw that he had been tricked by the wise men, was in a furious rage, and he sent and

killed all the male children in Bethlehem and in all that region who were two years old or under, according to the time which he had ascertained from the wise men. [17]Then was fulfilled what was spoken by the prophet Jeremiah:

[18]"A voice was heard in Ramah,
   wailing and loud lamentation,
   Rachel weeping for her children;
   she refused to be consoled,
   because they were no more."

Two ancient traditions contribute to this story. (1) In a legend about Moses, Josephus, the Jewish historian, narrates how astrologers warned Pharaoh that a liberator would be born for Israel. Frightened, Pharaoh commanded the murder of all male Israelite children; but in a dream the father of Moses is forewarned. (2) In a passover narrative (haggada), Jacob (= Israel) and his family are said to have been persecuted by Laban and forced to flee into Egypt. Mt uses these traditions to affirm that Jesus, the new Moses and the new Israel, recapitulates in himself the history of his people.

The contrast is stark: the divine child, just presented with royal gifts, must flee for his life. The appearance of the "angel of the Lord" (an OT phrase for God in visible form) is described by the same stereotyped formula in 1:20 and 2:13,19. In each case a command is given, and then a reason for the command. Here the command is to flee into Egypt, the traditional OT place of refuge (1 Kings 11:40; Jer 26:21). Note that God does not reveal his full plan to Joseph now; he prefers to indicate only the immediately necessary step. The reason for the flight recalls Ex 2:15: "Pharaoh . . . sought to slay Moses." Mt then uses his typical command-execution pattern: obedient compliance is described in the same words as the command. The anticipatory reference to the death of Herod in v.15 links up with v.19, after the narrative of the slaughter of the innocents. The formula quotation in v.15, tacked on immediately to the narrative, is from Hos 11:1. This citation is the theological highpoint of the infancy narrative, because here Jesus receives his most exalted definition. While certainly son of David, son of Abraham, son of Mary, son of Joseph, Jesus the true Israel is above all "my son," i.e., Son of God. Like Israel, God's Son, Jesus the true Son undergoes an exodus from Egypt, passes through the waters of the Jordan, and is tempted in the desert (cf. especially 4:1-11). Of course, in fulfilling Hos 11:1 Jesus transcends the text's original meaning. The text no longer speaks of a collectivity with an adoptive sonship, but of a unique individual with true, divine sonship. The eschatological fulfillment Jesus brings goes beyond the letter of the OT (cf. 5:17-48).

For the moment, innocent children die so that Jesus may be saved, but only so that the innocent Jesus may later die to save his people from their sins. While the massacre is in keeping with Herod's character, we have no record of it from Josephus, who was hostile to Herod. The story itself could be legendary. Herod takes no chances; his orders are exact as to number (*all* the children; cf. Ex 1:22), area, and age (with very broad limits, so that, humanly speaking, there is no escape). Mt spares the reader the actual account of the slaughter by drawing the curtain of a formula quotation in front of the events. He pointedly does not introduce the quotation in v. 17 with the usual "in order that . . . ." He narrates the fact of fulfillment, but shrinks from saying that this is God's direct intention. Sin is directly willed by man, though God's wisdom can encompass even man's sin and insert it into the divine plan for salvation. Interestingly, Mt avoids the phrase "in order that" in only one other formula quotation: the suicide of Judas (27:9). The quotation in v. 18 is from Jer 31:15, in which Rachel, the wife of Jacob-Israel, is imagined to be weeping at Ramah, five miles north of Jerusalem. Ramah was both the place of her death and also the place where, centuries later, the Israelites were gathered for the march into the Babylonian exile. Later tradition placed Rachel's tomb on the road to

Bethelehem, and this tradition may have influenced Mt's choice of this OT text. As Jesus, the new Israel, goes into exile, Rachel bewails her slaughtered children of a later age.

E. JESUS THE LOWLY NAZOREAN, THE HOLY ONE OF GOD. 2:19-23.

> [19]But when Herod died, behold, an angel of the Lord appeared in a dream to Joseph in Egypt, saying, [20]"Rise, take the child and his mother, and go to the land of Israel, for those who sought the child's life are dead." [21]And he rose and took the child and his mother, and went to the land of Israel. [22]But when he heard that Archelaus reigned over Judea in place of his father Herod, he was afraid to go there, and being warned in a dream he withdrew to the district of Galilee. [23]And he went and dwelt in a city called Nazareth, that what was spoken by the prophets might be fulfilled, "He shall be called a Nazarene."

Now the infancy narrative comes to rest with a final answer to "whence": Nazareth. Thus does Mt link his special material to the common Synoptic tradition, in which Nazareth is the only home of Jesus. V. 19 harks back to v. 15, and indeed vv. 19-21 have the very same structure as vv. 13-14. Joseph is to take the child into the *land of Israel*, an OT phrase conjuring up a state of captivity or exile from the promised land. The reason for the return recalls Ex 4:19, where God tells Moses to return to Egypt, "for all those who sought your life are dead." As always Joseph obeys perfectly. Mt cannot, however, end his story here. His tradition presupposed that Joseph and Mary came from Bethlehem; there was no need to explain how Jesus came to be born there (contrast the Lukan census). But everyone knew that Jesus grew up at Nazareth and was called a Nazarene. Therefore Mt must find a reason for a final shift in sacred geography. While fear of Archelaus would be a good reason for leaving Judea, it is strange that safety would be sought in Galilee, which was ruled by Herod's other son, Herod Antipas, who later killed the Baptist. But Mt must get the family to Nazareth, in which Joseph now settles for the first time (compare 2:23 and 4:13). Lk takes the opposite tack in his infancy story: Mary and Joseph came from Nazareth, and a special reason (the historically dubious census) must be found for Jesus' birth in Bethlehem. Lk naturally needs no reason for a return to Nazareth. This causes a further difference between Mt and Lk. Since Bethlehem was Jesus' home town according to Mt, Galilee is a place of exile. It is in exile that Jesus will exercise his ministry. He will come home to Judea only to die.

Nazareth presented Mt with another, more theological problem. If various names and places in the infancy narrative had been prophesied, then certainly the key event of settling at Nazareth, the town which gives Jesus his "second name," must have been prophesied. Yet Nazareth is never mentioned in the OT (nor in Josephus or the early rabbis). Accordingly, Mt can speak only vaguely of "the prophets" in v.23; he knows there is no single text which mentions Nazareth. This is the only time the vague plural "prophets" introduces a formula quotation. What texts might Mt include under this general rubric? (1) Most probable is a reference to Judg 13:5,7, where Samson's birth is announced and he is designated as a Nazir, i.e., an ascetic who is set apart ("made holy") to lead a consecrated life and *to save Israel*. In some Greek texts the Hebrew *nāzir* is translated as *Naziraion*, which for Mt would be close enough to *Nazōraios*, Nazorean (not "Nazarene," as the RSV has at the end of v.23). (2) With reference to Jesus' lowly, contemptible origins, Mt may also be thinking of Is 11:1, where the Davidic offspring is called a *nēṣer*, a branch or shoot from the stump of Jesse. (3) Mt may also have in mind the various prophets he is going to cite during the public ministry, especially those referring to Jesus as the servant of the Lord (8:17; 12:17-21).

A final word on historicity. Since Mt and Lk seem to be independent of each other in their infancy narratives, we can be fairly sure that Jesus was born in Bethlehem towards the end of the reign of King Herod, that his mother was Mary and his putative father Joseph, and that he was brought up in Nazareth. Further, Jesus' Davidic descent and virginal conception are two theological affirmations which clearly existed before Mt or Lk. But since the two evangelists diverge sharply on other matters, the rest of Mt's infancy narrative may come from scribal use of OT traditions to illumine the full meaning of Christ's birth.

Book One
The Son Begins to Proclaim
the Kingdom.
3:1-7:29.

For the division of the public ministry of Jesus (chaps. 3-25) into five "books," each subdivided into narrative and discourse, please see the Introduction.

I. THE NARRATIVE OF BOOK ONE: BEGINNINGS OF THE MINISTRY 3:1-4:25

A. THE BAPTIST: DEMAND AND PROMISE.
3:1-12.
[Mk 1:2-8; Lk 3:1-9,15-18]

3 In those days came John the Baptist, preaching in the wilderness of Judea, ²"Repent, for the kingdom of heaven is at hand." ³For this is he who was spoken of by the prophet Isaiah when he said,

"The voice of one crying in the wilderness:
Prepare the way of the Lord,
make his paths straight."

⁴Now John wore a garment of camel's hair, and a leather girdle around his waist; and his food was locusts and wild honey. ⁵Then went out to him Jerusalem and all Judea and all the region about the Jordan, ⁶and they were baptized by him in the river Jordan, confessing their sins.

⁷But when he saw many of the Pharisees and Sadducees coming for baptism, he said to them, "You brood of vipers! Who warned you to flee from the wrath to come? ⁸Bear fruit that befits repentance, ⁹and do not presume to say to yourselves, 'We have Abraham as our father';

for I tell you, God is able from these stones to raise up children to Abraham. [10]Even now the axe is laid to the root of the trees; every tree therefore that does not bear good fruit is cut down and thrown into the fire.

[11]"I baptize you with water for repentance, but he who is coming after me is mightier than I, whose sandals I am not worthy to carry; he will baptize you with the Holy Spirit and with fire. [12]His winnowing fork is in his hand, and he will clear his threshing floor and gather his wheat into the granary, but the chaff he will burn with unquenchable fire."

MESHING ELEMENTS of Mk and Q, Mt creates a tripartite pericope: (1) appearance of the Baptist (vv.1-6); (2) call to repentance (vv.7-10); (3) promise of the one to come (vv.11-12).

(1) Mt makes John the great preacher of repentance for Mt's church as well as for the Jews of John's time. John's moral earnestness fits perfectly with Mt's concern that Jesus' disciples *do* the will of the Father. Mt begins solemnly ("now in those days"), indicating both that he views the past time of Jesus as something sacred, finished, and unique (Mt's "historicizing" tendency) and also that the period of eschatological revelation is dawning. Since this period, according to the standard Christian kerygma, began with Jesus' baptism, Mt must first deal with the Baptist. Mt does not stress baptism as the object of John's preaching (contrast Mk 1:4). Rather, in the desert of Judea, where the Qumran community also awaited eschatological deliverance, John preaches primarily repentance. Mt makes John proclaim the very words that Jesus will later pronounce (4:17). Mt at times makes John and Jesus parallel figures, while of course maintaining John's subordinate position. Since the time of salvation has in some sense already come with the birth of Jesus, the Baptist necessarily stands within this privileged time and must speak accordingly. Mt's high Christology (Jesus is *the* Son) precludes any equating of John with Jesus.

John's preaching (literally, "heralding") of repentance resumes the cry of the great OT prophets. Repentance is not emotional and often fruitless remorse over the past. It is a determined turning away from a sinful past and full-hearted turning to God. "Repent" means basically: change your heart and mind about what is important in life, and then change your life accordingly. But repentance is not primarily any external act betokening the internal change; repentance is the internal change itself. Repentance can never be based on human initiative. It is always one's reponse to the prior act of God, who, in Jesus, comes to assume his rightful and full rule over a rebellious world (="for the kingdom of heaven is at hand"). This is the heart of Synoptic eschatology. The concept of kingdom is thus a dynamic one. It is the NT equivalent of the triumphant cry of the psalms: "Yahweh has become king!" Mt usually prefers the reverent Semitic circumlocution "kingdom of heaven" for Mk's and Lk's "kingdom of God." For Mt, the coming of the kingdom is a "process event." To a degree it was present in the OT (21:43), comes in the person of Jesus (infancy narrative), impinges even more forcefully during the ministry, breaks in definitively at the death-resurrection of Jesus, and matures in the field of the world until the parousia.

Mt takes over the citation of Is 40:3 ("a voice" etc.) from Mk. But, like a true scholar, Mt makes sure the attribution is correct by dropping that part of the Markan citation which comes from the prophet Malachi. Is 40:3 was a key text for the desert community of Qumran as well. Qumran prepared the way of the Lord in the desert by study and punctilious observance of the Law. For the NT, however, it is the voice of the Baptist that is specified as being in the desert; the kingdom itself was not to be restricted to a secluded monastery. That John is a prophetic figure is then illustrated by his clothing which recalls Elijah (2 Kings 1:18). Mt repeats the equation of Elijah and John in 11:14 and 17:11-13. The asceticism of eating locusts and wild honey recalls the desert period after the exodus and expresses a tense expectation of God's final deliverance. When Mt describes

John's baptizing activity, he notes that the baptized confessed their sins; but he pointedly omits Mk's designation
of the baptism itself as being "unto the remission of sins"
(cf. Mk 1:4). Mt instead has the phrase joined to the consecration of the wine at the Last Supper (26:28). For Mt,
forgiveness of sins is possible only through Jesus the Savior
(1:21), whose atoning death (20:28) is appropriated by
believers in the eucharist.

(2) While Lk has John's sermon on repentance addressed
to the crowds, Mt has John attack the Jewish authorities,
represented by the historically unlikely alliance of the
Pharisees and Sadducees. The fact that historically the
Pharisees (pious laymen zealous for the written and oral
law) and the Sadducees (the priestly nobility and their
followers) were politically and doctrinally opposed to each
other is either unknown or irrelevant to Mt. Writing after
the bitter experience of the gospel's rejection by the Jews,
Mt portrays Jewish leaders as one front, united against
Jesus and his emissaries. The opposition Jesus will meet is
felt already by Jesus' precursor-yet-parallel-figure. John
utters the very epithet Jesus will use of the scribes and
Pharisees (23:33). The enmity of this brood of vipers, aimed
now at John, will bring Jesus to the cross. Jesus' continuity
with John and his separation from Judaism are already
intimated. John asks ironically if the leaders think that
baptism will save them from God's fiery judgment. Actually,
his baptism, like any ritual, is useless unless it is accompanied both by inner renewal ("repentance") and the
external action which fits and flows naturally from that
renewal ("fruits worthy of repentance"). This "fruit imagery"
is common in Christian moral exhortation in the NT,
especially in baptismal passages. For Mt, the Baptist has
become a Christian preacher. But no preacher can make
headway with professionally religious people who are
proud of and secure in their self-righteousness. The leaders
think God is bound by blood-ties; but, in his inexhaustible
creative power, God can turn stones into the children of
Abraham—and Gentiles into disciples, as the end of the

gospel will show (28:16-20). We should remember that Mt wants his fellow Christians to hear these warnings aimed at the Jewish leaders because Mt sees the same spiritual dangers besetting *Christians,* especially Christian leaders. What the Jewish leaders were, they might become. Christians might likewise become a hopelessly hardened group to whom no oracle can be spoken except that of imminent judgment. It is no accident that the fate with which the Baptist threatens the Jewish leaders (3:10) is the fate with which Jesus threatens false disciples (7:19).

(3) Turning from threat to promise, the Baptist shows his own humility vis-à-vis the pride of the leaders as he promises the one to come. The Baptist proclaims his inferiority on three counts: (1) his baptism is merely a material rite meant to lead people to repentance, while the promised one will plunge men into the fiery, purifying experience of God's holy spirit, poured out on the last days. (2) Paradoxically, the one who *comes after* John (with a pun on the idea of being a disciple of someone?) is the stronger of the two. Indeed, Jesus will prove to be stronger even than the devil, whose power he will break definitively (12:29). (3) The one to come is the master; John is but the slave (one of whose duties was to carry the master's sandals). John concludes with a final warning concerning the separation which the last judgment brings. The theme of the final punishment of the wicked is a firm element in Q, and Mt gladly takes it over. He concludes most of his discourses with similar stark warnings to Christians. As the time of the parousia became more indefinite, Mt compensates by stressing the stringent criteria of final judgment and the terrible penalty for failing. The theme of the final separation of the good and the bad is a favorite of Mt's, and it is graphically portrayed here by a farmer using a "winnowing fork" to separate the edible wheat from the inedible chaff. Chaff was indeed used for heating, but the eschatological reality peeps through the parable when the fire is called "unquenchable."

B. THE REVELATION OF THE SON IN BAPTISM.
3:13-17.
[Mk 1:9-11; Lk 3:21-22]

> [13]Then Jesus came from Galilee to the Jordan to John, to be baptized by him. [14]John would have prevented him, saying, "I need to be baptized by you, and do you come to me?" [15]But Jesus answered him, "Let it be so now; for thus it is fitting for us to fulfil all righteousness." Then he consented. [16]And when Jesus was baptized, he went up immediately from the water, and behold, the heavens were opened and he saw the Spirit of God descending like a dove, and alighting on him; [17]and lo, a voice from heaven, saying, "This is my beloved Son, with whom I am well pleased."

Mt reworks Mk, with possible touches from Q. The emphasis is on the revelation of Jesus as Son of God, not on his baptism as such, which is narrated only in passing by a participle. Jesus' coming is described with the verb that was used of John in 3:1; again, Mt draws a parallel. Since Jesus is coming *from* Galilee, the baptism is probably pictured as taking place in Judea, at the southern end of the Jordan. John expresses both his prophetic insight and his humility when he recognizes Jesus before his baptism. Mt alone among the Synoptics has John realize before the baptism that Jesus is the one he has been prophesying. John keeps trying to prevent Jesus from undergoing this baptism of repentance meant for sinners. John rather needs the eschatological baptism by the Spirit which the Coming One can give (v.11). What Jesus wants contradicts all John's fiery apocalyptic images of the final judge. The Coming One turns out to be an ordinary man who humbly and voluntarily associates himself with sinners. The Baptist objects to this reversal of the proper roles and order of salvation history. Jesus rejects the Baptist's objection. But, instead of stressing his superiority over John, Jesus associates himself with the Baptist ("it is fitting *for us*"— again, parallelism). Speaking for the first time in the gospel, Jesus points to the fittingness of God's plan for salvation. It befits both John and Jesus to fulfill in this critical hour the roles mapped out beforetime by prophecy. This seems to be the sense of the pregnant phrase "to fulfill all righteousness." In Mt, "to fulfill" (*plēroō*) usually refers to fulfillment of prophecy. It means more than simply "to do" or "to obey." And, while "righteousness" in Mt can mean moral conduct in keeping with the Father's will (so 5:10; 5:20; 6:1), that sense is usually applied to the disciples, not Jesus. Here "righteousness" seems to mean the saving activity of God (so 5:6; 6:33). Especially since the theophany which follows alludes to OT prophecies now being fulfilled, "to fulfill all righteousness" seems to refer to prophetic fulfillment. The Baptist accedes to the request (notice the command-execution formula: "let it be for now . . . then he let it be"). Thus, in vv. 14-15, inserted bodily into the Markan narrative, Mt. shows a mature theological reflection on the problem of the baptismal narrative, especially the problem of the superior's being baptized by the inferior.

Passing over the baptism with one word, Mt narrates the theophany which follows. The opening of the heavens may allude to Ezekiel's inaugural vision, also by a river (Ezek 1:1). Is 63:11-64:1 deals with the themes of exodus, passage through the divided waters, the Spirit descending from the Lord and being put on the Israelites, and God as Father—all ending with the cry: "O that you would rend the heavens and come down!" The promised eschatological theophany is now occurring. (Why the Spirit is represented as a dove has never been satisfactorily explained. This is the only time the symbolism occurs in the NT. Possibly it is connected with the ancient idea of birds as messengers of the gods.) This is not a vision given to Jesus alone, as in Mk, but is seen by others, as is clear from the accompanying message. As opposed to Mk's secrecy motif, revelation "goes public" in Mt. Accordingly, the Father himself speaks from heaven, and not only to Jesus. Mk has "*you* are my beloved Son," indicating that Jesus is informed of this or is designated as Son for the first time. Mt has pointedly moved back the source of Jesus' sonship to the virginal conception. Thus, it makes no sense in Mt's mind to have Jesus told that he is Son for the first time at his baptism. Hence, the message is directed to others: "*This* is my beloved Son." "Beloved," carrying a strong note of election, may reflect the Hebrew *yāhid*, which may also stand behind the adjective *monogenēs* ("only" Son) in the fourth gospel. Since Mt has changed the voice from the second to the third person, the allusion to Ps 2:7 (royal enthronement of the king as God's Son) is less clear. But, on the other hand, the reference to God's chosen servant, to whom God gives his spirit (Is 42:1), is clearer. Some would also see a reference to the Jewish tradition about the sacrifice of Isaac, Abraham's "beloved son" (Gen 22). Mt probably sees in this narrative a lesson on what baptism means for Christians (the Father grants sonship by bestowing his Spirit), especially since Mt, alone among the gospels, attaches a "trinitarian" formula to baptism (28:19).

C. THE TESTING OF JESUS' SONSHIP.
4:1-11.
[Mk 1:12-13; Lk 4:1-13]

> **4** Then Jesus was led up by the Spirit into the wilderness to be tempted by the devil. [2]And he fasted forty days and forty nights, and afterward he was hungry. [3]And the tempter came and said to him, "If you are the Son of God, command these stones to become loaves of bread." [4]But he answered, "It is written,
>
> > 'Man shall not live by bread alone,
> > but by every word that proceeds from the mouth of God.'"
>
> [5]Then the devil took him to the holy city, and set him on the pinnacle of the temple, [6]and said to him, "If you are

the Son of God, throw yourself down; for it is written,
  'He will give you his angels charge of you,'
and
  'On their hands they will bear you up,
  lest you strike your foot against a stone.'"
[7]Jesus said to him, "Again it is written, 'You shall not tempt the Lord your God.'" [8]Again, the devil took him to a very high mountain, and showed him all the kingdoms of the world and the glory of them; [9]and he said to him, "All these I will give you, if you will fall down and worship me." [10]Then Jesus said to him, "Begone, Satan! for it is written,
  'You shall worship the Lord your God
  and him only shall you serve.'"
[11]Then the devil left him, and behold, angels came and ministered to him.

The pericope comes from Q, but Mt ties it into the Markan narrative at the beginning and end. After Jesus' sonship is proclaimed in the baptismal theophany, it is tested by the devil in the wilderness. Jesus is "taken up by the Spirit" (better than "was led up") into an apocalyptic vision. Jesus is to experience what Israel, God's son in the OT, experienced in the desert. But, Jesus, the true Israel and true Son, will conquer and prove his sonship where the old Israel failed (cf. Dt 8:2-5). As in the infancy narrative, he recapitulates the history of Israel and its leaders. The Spirit miraculously sustains Jesus during his fast; only "afterward" does he feel hunger. The fast is thus not a sign of penance. Mt adds "and forty nights" to recall Moses' sojourn on Sinai (Ex 34:28).

Only after the forty days does "the tempter" *par excellence* suddenly appear (contrast Mk and Lk). He immediately takes up the question of Jesus' sonship (note "if you are the Son of God" in vv. 3 and 6). The baptism was Jesus' surrender to the Father's will, as marked out in prophecy (3:15). Now that surrender, which is at the heart of true sonship, is put to the test three times (with three citations from Dt involved in Jesus' replies). Will Jesus misuse his sonship for his own advantage? The temptation of bread is expressed in the plural ("stones" and "loaves of bread"— contrast Lk); this may hint at a temptation to play a political and social Messiah by feeding a hungry mankind. Jesus replies by citing Dt 8:3, referring to the manna. The mark of the Son is that he trustfully waits for God's help. He is nourished by total surrender to God's word, which creates and sustains humanity in all its needs.

For the second temptation, the devil (Mt uses this designation more often than "Satan") takes Jesus into the "holy city" (among the evangelists, Mt alone so names Jerusalem). Standing on the "pinnacle" of the Temple (a lintel of a high gate, or a balcony?), the devil shows that he too can quote Scripture for his purpose; the temptations turn into a rabbinic debate on the nature of true sonship. He cleverly seizes upon Jesus' main concern in the first temptation; trust in God. Quoting Ps 91:11-12, the devil urges Jesus to undertake a presumptuous show of pseudo-trust; the devil's real purpose is to have Jesus destroy himself. Jesus refuses to misuse God's gift of protection. He fights Scripture with Scripture (Dt 6:16): true trust includes an obedience which does not try to force God's hand, as Israel did at Massah. Instead of revealing his filial power to perform miracles, Jesus reveals his filial authority to interpret Scripture correctly. Finally, the devil takes Jesus to the top of the cosmic mountain of ancient myths and apocalyptic—symbolic mountains being a favorite of Mt. One is also reminded of Moses' viewing of the whole promised land from Mt. Nebo (Dt 34:1-4); as in the infancy narrative, so here the basic Israel typology is supplemented by a Moses typology. But the devil is especially interested in the OT promise that God would give his Messiah-Son the nations for an inheritance (Ps 2:6-8). Here the apocalyptic vision reaches its highpoint of horror. The cosmic struggle between God and Satan reaches its climax when Satan presents himself as a god to be worshipped (cf. 2

Thess 2:4; Rev 13). No further debate is possible, for the issue is now clear: Who is God, and therefore who is to be worshiped? The temptation is the basic temptation of Israel to idolatry, to putting a creature in the place of God. And so Jesus dismisses Satan with the fundamental commandment given to Israel: monotheism (Dt 6:13). With the authority that flows from the Son's unshaken union with the Father, Jesus sends Satan packing. This rough dismissal has a special meaning for Mt, because it links up with Jesus' rebuke to Peter at Caesarea Philippi: "Get behind me, Satan" (16:23). Peter unwittingly continues Satan's attempt to deflect the Son from the path of the cross, the only true way to the glory of the Kingdom. The temptation to false sonship will be taken up at the cross (27:40: "If you are the Son of God, come down from the cross"). But precisely by taking the road of the cross, Jesus will gain "all authority" at the resurrection (28:18). What the Son would not take from Satan's hands at the cheap price of idolatry he has won for himself at the cost of the cross. Satan obeys the command (command-execution pattern), angels take the devil's place, and the mount of temptation becomes the mount of paradise.

The message to Mt's church is that, as she is beset with hypocrites, miracle-workers, false prophets, and false teachers, she must remember that divine sonship is not primarily a matter of working wonders but of understanding God's will in Scripture and carrying it out in trust and obedience.

D. THE MOVE TO CAPERNAUM AND THE FIRST PROCLAMATION OF THE KINGDOM. 4:12-17.
[Mk 1:14-15; Lk 4:14-15]

> [12]Now when he heard that John had been arrested, he withdrew into Galilee; [13]and leaving Nazareth he went and dwelt in Capernaum by the sea, in the territory

of Zebulun and Naphtali, [14]that what was spoken by the
prophet Isaiah might be fulfilled:
[15]"The land of Zebulun and the land of Naphtali,
  toward the sea, across the Jordan,
  Galilee of the Gentiles—
[16]the people who sat in darkness
  have seen a great light,
  and for those who sat in the region and shadow of death
  light has dawned."
[17]From that time Jesus began to preach, saying, "Repent,
for the kingdom of heaven is at hand."

Between Mk 1:14a and 1:14b-15 Mt sandwiches Jesus'
removal to Capernaum and a formula quotation explaining
Jesus' action. A minor point of geography becomes a
major theological statement.

Mt tightens the causal connection between John's arrest
and Jesus' return to Galilee by adding "when he heard . . . ."
"He withdrew" is not the best translation of *anechōrēsen*
here. Jesus can hardly be seeking refuge as he marches into
Galilee, the territory of Herod Antipas, who has just
imprisoned John. Jesus is consciously taking up John's
fallen banner and continuing in the teeth of opposition.
It would likewise be better to translate *paredothē* not as
"arrested" but as "handed over," to underline the parallel
between John and Jesus, who will later be handed over to his
passion. Jesus leaves Nazareth definitively and makes
Capernaum his home town. Set on the northwest corner
of the Lake of Galilee, Capernaum lay in the old territory
of Naphtali—and *not* Zebulon. Mt is playing loose with
geography in v.13; he already has his eye on the OT citation.
Since Mt wants to see this move to Capernaum prophesied
in Is 8:23-9:1, he carefully notes the city is "by the sea,"
to correspond to "toward the sea" in the prophecy. Indeed,
Mt arranges a neat chiastic correspondence between the
place-designations in vv.12-13 and those of v.15. The
narrative has grown mainly out of the OT text, though this

kind of assimilation between narrative and citation can flow both ways in Mt.

There may be an apologetic or polemic note in this appeal to the OT. Jews might find it scandalous that the Messiah forsook Jerusalem and Judea to ply his ministry in Gentile-ridden, rebellious Galilee, which was infamous for its lax observance of the Law. Deliverance was to come from Zion and Jerusalem, or perhaps from the desert. But Galilee? Mt justifies Jesus' choice and explains its theological significance with a formula quotation (Is 8:23-9:1). Mt reworks the Hebrew text, with a nod to the Greek, for his own purposes. By "toward the sea" Isaiah meant the Mediterranean; Mt refers it to the Sea of Galilee. Isaiah's "circle of the Gentiles" referred to the Northern Kingdom of Israel, encircled and devastated by foreigners. In the Greek OT and in Mt it becomes the official name of the district, Galilee. "Of the Gentiles" brings out its lowly, oppressed, religiously darkened state. There may be a hint of the future mission to the Gentiles, starting from Galilee (28:19). But Jesus' ministry is restricted to Israel, and so the reference here to Gentiles is a negative one, stressing Galilee's religiously impoverished state. It is precisely to Jews living in this spiritual shadow-land, an earthly Sheol, that the eschatological light of Jesus the Messiah is now shining (cf. Lk 1:78-79; Jn 8:12). Jesus' coming to Capernaum is the dawning of the eschatological day in the Jewish land darkened by paganism. It is no accident that the formula quotation about Nazareth (2:23) is followed by a formula quotation about Galilee.

Mt now emphasizes the formal inauguration of Jesus' ministry with the solemn phrase, *"from that time Jesus began* to preach" (cf. the parallel in Mt 16:21, the first prediction of the passion; but here the sentence goes with what precedes). Jesus' proclamation is a repetition of John's (3:2). Jesus the herald continues the work of John the herald and brings it to fulfillment. Again, Mt inverts Mk's order to bring the imperative moral cry of "Repent!" to the fore. Then follows the kerygmatic basis for the demand: God is coming to assume his definitive rule over the world. Thus, the nexus between imperative and indicative, human response to God's prior saving act, is not lost in Mt.

E. THE CALL OF THE FIRST DISCIPLES.
4:18-22.
[Mk 1:16-20; Lk 5:1-11]

> [18] As he walked by the Sea of Galilee, he saw two brothers, Simon who is called Peter and Andrew his brother, casting a net into the sea; for they were fishermen. [19] And he said to them, "Follow me, and I will make you fishers of men." [20] Immediately they left their nets and followed him. [21] And going on from there he saw two other brothers, James the son of Zebedee and John his brother, in the boat with Zebedee their father, mending their nets, and he called them. [22] Immediately they left the boat and their father, and followed him.

Mt simply streamlines and schematizes Mk; he places the call between two of his own summaries (4:12-17 and 4:23-25). The call-story is needed at this point, since Mt wants disciples around Jesus for the sermon on the mount (cf. 5:1). The emphasis is on the authority of the Lord who calls and the immediate obedience of those called. Unlike Jn 1, our pericope mentions no psychological preparation for the disciples. The creative word of God simply meets them in their everyday world, lays hold of them, and changes their lives forever. This unmerited, unexpected grace of Jesus' call carries its own cost: total, permanent abandonment of livelihood and family. Peter, James, and John were to form the inner circle of witnesses at the transfiguration and in Gethsemane. Unlike Mk, Mt mentions Simon's title of Peter (Rock) at the call, thus pointing forward to Mt 16:18.

F. SUMMARY OF THE MINISTRY.
4:23-25.
[Mk 1:39; 3:7-12; Lk 4:44; 8:1; 6:17-19]

23And he went about all Galilee, teaching in their synagogues and preaching the gospel of the kingdom and healing every disease and every infirmity among the people. 24So his fame spread throughout all Syria, and they brought him all the sick, those afflicted with various diseases and pains, demoniacs, epileptics, and paralytics, and he healed them. 25And great crowds followed him from Galilee and the Decapolis and Jerusalem and Judea and from beyond the Jordan.

The summary has a double structural function: (1) it concludes the narrative of the first book; and (2) it acts as a bracket for the "diptych" of Jesus as Messiah of the Word (5:3-7:27, the sermon on the mount) and Messiah of the Deed (8:1-9:34, nine miracle stories). In 9:35, the summary of 4:23 is repeated, thus forming an inclusion. The summaries in Mt help to create a sense of a lengthy ministry and also alert the reader to some new major unit which is about to begin. Despite his settlement at Capernaum, Jesus is now presented as the itinerant messenger of Is 52:7, bearing the good news to *all Galilee* (thus fulfilling Is 8:23-9:1). His ministry is described with three participles. (1) He *teaches*, and only Jesus teaches authoritatively during the public ministry. The apostles are commissioned to preach and heal in chap. 10, but they are commissioned to teach only in 28:20. The verb "teaching" has no object; that will be supplied by the sermon on the mount and the other four discourses. Mt consistently speaks of the Jewish synagogues as *their* synagogues; he writes after his church's break with the synagogue. (2) He *preaches* (better: heralds or proclaims) the gospel (the good news) of the kingdom. While the teacher speaks of what a man is to do, the herald proclaims what God has done; he has seized power and begun his definitive rule over the world. Mt emphasizes the need for moral response to this good news. Hence, teaching is mentioned before proclaiming (cf. the order of imperative and indicative in 4:17). (3) He *heals*, for the power of the coming kingdom reaches into the present of Jesus' activity.

Jesus' work becomes known throughout Syria, the Roman province to which Palestine belonged. Mt alone mentions Syria in a summary, probably because he writes for a Syrian church (Antioch?) and so wishes to put his church into relationship with the unique sacred past of Jesus' ministry. Chaps. 8-9 are anticipated in a short description of Jesus' healing activity. His fame causes crowds to *follow* him. "Follow" here indicates more than mere motion and less than full discipleship. During the ministry, the oscillating crowds symbolize potential disciples, but stand at a farther distance than do the disciples (cf. 5:1). Out of these crowds the eschatological community will be formed. The crowds come from five specific areas, mentioned in the pattern of northwest, northeast, south-west, and southeast.

II. THE DISCOURSE OF BOOK ONE: THE SERMON ON THE MOUNT. 5:1-7:29.

A. INTRODUCTION AND BEATITUDES.
5:1-12.
[Mk 3:13a; Lk 6:20-23]

5 Seeing the crowds, he went up on the mountain, and when he sat down his disciples came to him. [2]And he opened his mouth and taught them, saying:

[3]"Blessed are the poor in spirit, for theirs is the kingdom of heaven.

[4]"Blessed are those who mourn, for they shall be comforted.

[5]"Blessed are the meek, for they shall inherit the earth.

[6]"Blessed are those who hunger and thirst for righteousness, for they shall be satisfied,

[7]"Blessed are the merciful, for they shall obtain mercy,.

[8]"Blessed are the pure in heart, for they shall see God.

[9]"Blessed are the peacemakers, for they shall be called sons of God.

[10]"Blessed are those who are persecuted for righteousness' sake, for theirs is the kingdom of heaven.

[11]"Blessed are you when men revile you and persecute you and utter all kinds of evil against you falsely on my account. [12]Rejoice and be glad, for your reward is great in heaven, for so men persecuted the prophets who were before you.

THE SIGHT of the vast crowds following him causes Jesus to go up "the mountain." This mountain is neither a mountain range nor some individual mount which can be located. The mountain in Mt is the special place of divine action and revelation, a fitting place for the sermon which lays out the "charter of the kingdom," "the law of discipleship." While there may be an allusion to Mt Sinai and the giving of the Law, Jesus is not the new Moses here. He is the one who speaks revelation and gives Law on the mount; he speaks in the place of God ("it was said [by God] . . . but *I* say to you . . . ."). The disciples who come up to receive Jesus' instruction stand in the place of Moses and his close companions, while the crowds at a distance might represent Israel of old. Jesus sits, for this was the ancient posture of teachers, a sign of their dignity and authority. The solemnity is increased by the hieratic formula, "and he opened his mouth."

The sermon on the mount was put together by Mt from a number of sources. The core comes from a sermon in Q, which can be seen in a more primitive form in Lk's sermon on the plain (Lk 6:20-49). Mt has woven into it many other Q and M sayings, producing a sermon almost four times as long as Lk's. While Lk's sermon emphasizes love, Mt's sermon, at least in its first half, emphasizes "justice" ("righteousness"), which can mean God's saving activity (5:6; 6:33) or man's response to God's activity, namely, moral action which does the Father's will (5:10,20; 6:1). This portrayal of Jesus as teaching righteousness has invited comparisons with the founder of Qumran, a great eschatological prophet called the Teacher of Righteousness. But, for Mt, there could be no comparison. Jesus is the Son of God and Son of Man. He shows sovereign freedom vis-à-vis the Law, at times abrogates its commands, becomes the friend of tax-collectors and sinners, and finally orders a universal mission.

When we read all the stringent moral demands in this sermon, we should remember that they follow, not precede, the basic proclamation of good news in 4:17,23, and in the beatitudes. What comes first is the gospel, the glad tidings of what God has done for us; all that follows is the fitting response of desperate people who have been surprised by joy. Mt composed his nine beatitudes from two sources. The beatitudes concerning the poor, the mourners, the hungry, and the longer one concerning the persecuted come from Q. The beatitudes concerning the meek, the merciful, the pure of heart, the peacemakers, and the shorter one concerning the persecuted come from M. Mt arranges two lists of beatitudes to create a chain of four beatitudes which emphasize passive attitudes, then four beatitudes which emphasize activity, and then a final long beatitude on persecution (4 + 4 + 1 = 9 beatitudes in all).

While Lk's four beatitudes in the second person plural (balanced by four woes) may reflect the original fiery apocalyptic address of Jesus to the literally poor and hungry, Mt has spiritualized and generalized the beatitudes, making them applicable to the spiritual needs and moral endeavor of every member of his church. By adopting the third person, he has assimilated them to the usual form found in OT wisdom (cf. Ps 1:1), where the happiness of some particular person or group is extolled, with a reason appended. But even in Mt, the eschatological paradox and reversal of values which Jesus proclaimed ring clear. The very people this world considers most miserable are the ones Jesus proclaims to be supremely happy ("blessed" here means "happy"), for with the full authority of the apocalyptic prophet he assures them of vindication on the last day. All the future verbs refer to God's final judgment, and the passive voice of the verbs points to God as the understood agent. Apocalyptic and wisdom often flow together in Mt.

The first beatitude harks back to the OT figure of the poor, the *anāwîm*, people who realize their own fragility and the illusory nature of human support, and who therefore look to Yahweh alone for safety. Yahweh's concern for the poor, the humble, and the contrite of spirit is extolled in the prophets (Is 57:15; 66:2), psalms (Ps 34:18), and wisdom literature (Prov 16:19; 29:23). The exact phrase "poor in spirit" does not occur in the OT, but is found in the War Scroll of Qumran. The Qumranites saw themselves as the poor whom God had redeemed by his grace. Mt has added "in spirit" (referring to man's spirit, his innermost being) to avoid a purely economic interpretation of poverty; such a spiritualization of the *anāwîm* had already occurred in the OT. The poor in spirit are those who bow humbly before God in total trust, who are willing to await everything at God's hand. They have seen through the false promise of wealth. As in each of the beatitudes, Jesus' declaration of happiness makes these people happy right now (cf. the present tense in v. 11). He gives them unshakable assurance that the future kingdom is already their possession ("theirs *is* the kingdom" in vv. 3 and 10).

The order of the first and second beatitudes may reflect Is 61:1-3, where the servant-prophet speaks of his mission to the poor and the mourners. The mourners could include both those who mourn over the power of evil in the world and those who mourn over sin in their own lives. Furthermore, Jews comforted the bereaved by praying that God would comfort them "amongst the mourners of Zion and Jerusalem." To the one who is, because of his very humanity and mortality, a mourner, Jesus promises comfort and strength from God on the last day (future tense).

Verse 5 is a citation of Ps 37:11: "The meek shall possess the earth." Today "meek" unfortunately conveys the idea of softness. The truly meek are, in the Bible, the considerate, the unassuming, the peaceable towards both God and man. They do not push their own plans to the detriment of God's saving plan. Jesus, the Wisdom of God, is the model of the meek man who gives rest to others (11:29), the meek King who brings salvation through his own sufferings (21:5), the Son who through meekness gains all authority (28:18). The "earth" (or better: "land") is no longer the land of Palestine promised to Abraham (Gen 17:8) or the poor (Ps 37:11), but the kingdom of heaven (cf. Jas 2:5). Ps 37:19 also promises that the poor will be "satisfied" (i.e., fed) in days of famine.

Mt adds thirst to the hunger and spiritualizes the whole by adding "for justice." Here justice means God's saving activity and the covenant-relationship which that activity sets up between God and man. The disorder of sin has broken that saving order, and now the Messiah promises the restoration of covenant-justice (cf. 26:28) under the image of being fed at the banquet in the kingdom. But God's justice demands that man also practice justice; hence, the other use of the term in v. 10.

Coming to the fifth beatitude (v. 7), we detect a more "activist" tone. Ps 37:21 speaks of the just man showing mercy. The rabbis praised mercy in terms similar to this beatitude; yet certain groups, especially the non-observant "people of the land" were excluded from mercy. Jesus rejects a legalistic piety that neglects mercy, one of the "weightier matters of the law" (23:23). Mt emphasizes mercy as the criterion for correct observance of the Law (cf. 9:13; 12:7) and fleshes out the fifth beatitude into a scene of final judgment (25:31-46). The sixth beatitude again emphasizes interior attitude ("pure—or better, "clean"—in heart). Already in the OT, ritual cleanness guaranteed access to the Temple only if one was also clean in his innermost being, in his heart, where he thought and decided (cf. Ps 24:3-5). The sinner had to beg God for inner cleansing (Is 6:5; Ps 51:4,12). Jesus warned the Pharisees not to become absorbed in questions of external cleanliness. For the human heart is the place where the real decisions about clean and unclean take place (Mt 15:16-18; 23:26). For Mt, purity of heart involves in particular a simple directness in one's intentions and attitudes, an undivided heart, a "one-track mind" when it comes to the things of God. It is close to Mt's idea of "perfect" (cf. 5:48; 19:21). Only such undivided hearts can "see God." This is not simply the OT metaphor for experiencing God in worship; it comes from the apocalyptic and rabbinic idea of the vision of God reserved for the just in paradise.

"Peacemakers" in the seventh beatitude recalls the great Hebrew word *shālôm*, literally, "wholeness," a perfect state of well-being and integration in the individual and in society on every level. Peacemaking was greatly esteemed among the rabbis, but there is no firm OT or rabbinic connection between peacemaking and being a son of God. The closest parallel would be Solomon, a peaceful man and an adopted son of God (1 Chron 22:9-10). The Hellenistic rulers claimed to be both peacemakers and sons of God, but the havoc they wrought belied their claim. Jesus the Son speaks the promise of divine sonship not to the great of this world but to the poor of Galilee, people whose simple act of making peace among themselves can lead them to becoming God's sons and daughters (cf. the promise in 5:44-45). "Shall be called" means "shall be declared sons by God on the last day." And what the Creator-God declares to be, is.

The eighth beatitude, the shorter one on persecution, comes from M and finds a parallel in 1 Pt 3:14. It holds a pivotal place in the structure, providing both an inclusion with the first and a transition to the ninth, the longer Q-beatitude on persecution. Mt uses the perfect participle to describe the persecuted: "Those who have been persecuted and still bear the scars." This may reflect the past history of Mt's church, which was formerly bound to the synagogue, but which, after various persecutions, broke with Judaism. The Christians of Mt's church probably saw themselves symbolized in the suffering just man of the OT (cf. Ps 22; Wis 5). The disciples of Jesus who practice justice, mercy, and peacemaking must expect the same fate, the fate of the persecuted prophets. This is made explicit in the last beatitude, which, by switching to the second person plural, facilitates the address to the disciples in vv. 13-16. Mt describes the persecution (which can include any type of harassment) in vaguer terms than Lk. Formal persecution by the synagogue is probably a thing of the past; the harassment seems largely a matter of reproach and calumny. One is "happy" in this situation only if the accusations are made "falsely" (perhaps a Matthean addition; cf. 1 Pt 2:19-20). Suffering for unjust acts must not have the pious cloak of suffering as a Christian thrown over it. Mt changes Q's "on account of the Son of Man" (cf Lk 6:22) to "on *my* account," to emphasize the personal attachment of the disciple to Jesus. To suffer for the sake of righteousness (v.10) is, for the Christian, to suffer for Jesus. Christians must constantly exult with the eschatological joy of the saved, who have learned to see in their sufferings the sign of their election. They stand in the noble succession of the martyred prophets, as do the Baptist (17:9-13) and Jesus (23:29-39). Ultimately, Jesus is the completely happy man of the beatitudes, the "happy attitudes." His beatitudes define his own being and call others to be what he is. This leads us to vv.13-16.

B. THE DISCIPLES ARE CALLED FOR THE WORLD. 5:13-16.
[Mk 9:49-50; 4:21; Lk 14:34-35; 8:16; 11:33]

> ¹³"You are the salt of the earth; but if salt has lost its taste, how shall its saltness be restored? It is no longer good for anything except to be thrown out and trodden under foot by men.
> ¹⁴"You are the light of the world. A city set on a hill cannot be hid. ¹⁵Nor do men light a lamp and put it under a bushel, but on a stand, and it gives light to all in the house. ¹⁶Let your light so shine before men, that they may see your good works and give glory to your Father who is in heaven.

The sayings in these verses originally circulated independently. The parable of the city is found both in the Oxyrhynchus papyri and in the Coptic Gospel of Thomas; the latter also contains the parable of the light. Mt's redaction consists in (1) reforming the Q-saying with a glance at Mk; (2) adding the emphatic headings, "*you* are" etc. in vv. 13 and 14 and the moral application in v.16. There is a stark contrast with what precedes. Those persecuted by the world are nevertheless the world's salvation. They exist for the world/against the world—but ultimately, for the greater glory of the Father (v.16).

For the ancients, salt was one of the most important necessities of human life, for everything from preserving and seasoning food to making covenants. The rabbis compared the Torah to salt, but the direct equation of men with salt is unusual. The parable should not be turned into an allegory. The point is that the disciples have an important, vital function to play in the world ("earth" here means "the world," as the parallel in v.14 shows). As v.16 shows, Mt is thinking of the positive action, the "good deeds" the disciples are to exhibit before the world. If the disciples lose their sense of moral fervor and stop witnessing to the world by their good deeds, they are as useless as the salt from the Dead Sea, which, because of chemical impurities, could decompose and lose its taste (literally: "become foolish"). The symbol of rejection is powerful, but hardly unusual in Mt. Mt is constantly warning his church: the rejection which befell Israel can befall you as well.

In the fourth gospel, Jesus says: "I am the light of the world" (8:12). Mt has already portrayed Jesus as the eschatological light of a darkened Galilee (4:12-17), and now that function of enlightening and guiding a morally confused humanity is shared with the disciples. The Jewish scribes and their disciples were similarly considered to be the lights of Israel. To stress the necessarily public nature of the disciples' function, Mt inserts a separate parable about a city set on a hill. The mission of these nondescript Galileans will be brought to the world's notice as surely as a town perched on a Galilean hill is visible from the surrounding countryside. There is probably no reference here to the pilgrimage of the nations to an exalted Mt Zion (Is 2:2-5); Jesus does not speak of *the* city set on *the* mountain. Returning to the light-image, Mt stresses that the disciples' light, which is meant to be seen by all ("all in the house"), can be smothered only by the disciples' own failure. The image is taken from a one-room, windowless house, where a lamp would be perched on a stand so that its rays could reach as far as possible. To extinguish the flame without dangerous sparks, a measuring vessel would be placed over the lamp. The confident image of the city is thus given a monitory proviso. The disciples can cause the failure of their mission if they ignore others and live only for themselves.

In v.16, Mt supplies the moral application of the salt and light parables, in language largely taken from the parables themselves. The good works are not specified; the rest of the sermon on the mount and the other discourses supply the details. As befits the salt and light *of the world*, the audience addressed is universal ("before men" in general, not just Jews or disciples). The ultimate goal, however, remains God-centered: the glory of the Father. This is the first time the name Father is used for God in Mt. With reference to the disciples, Mt often qualifies the name with "who is in heaven" or "heavenly." Mt carefully distinguishes between "my Father" (when Jesus speaks of or to God in relation to himself) and "your Father" (when Jesus speaks of God in relation to the disciples). The disciples are taught to pray "Our Father," but Jesus the Son never includes himself and the disciples under the one phrase, "Our Father." The call to action in vv.13-16 raises the question of the norms of moral action, which are treated in the rest of chap. 5.

C. JESUS AND THE LAW:
THE STATEMENT OF PRINCIPLE.
5:17-20.
[Lk 16:16-17]

> [17]"Think not that I have come to abolish the law and the prophets; I have come not to abolish them but to fulfil them. [18]For truly, I say to you, till heaven and earth pass away, not an iota, not a dot, will pass from the law until all is accomplished. [19]Whoever then relaxes one of the

least of these commandments and teaches men so, shall be
called least in the kingdom of heaven; but he who does
them and teaches them shall be called great in the kingdom of heaven. [20]For I tell you, unless your righteousness
exceeds that of the scribes and Pharisees, you will never
enter the kingdom of heaven.

Mt 5:17-20 is a dense statement of principle on the relation of the Mosaic Law to Jesus. V.20 has the Janus-like
function of both summing up vv. 17-19 and introducing six
concrete applications of the principle (vv.21-48, the "antitheses"). For detailed justification of the views espoused in
this commentary on 5:17-48, see Part III of my *The Vision
of Matthew* (New York: Paulist Press, 1979). As regards
sources, vv.17-19 may come from Q; v.20 is probably
Mt's creation.

In v.17 the disciples are warned that, despite the startling
new teaching they are about to hear in the antitheses, they
must not begin to think that Jesus' mission is to destroy the
Law or the prophets. Jesus' eschatological mission ("I have
come") is one of prophetic fulfillment. For Mt, to "fulfill"
Law is not the same as simply doing or obeying it. Mt does
not usually employ "to fulfill" with reference to the Law;
he uses it to express the fulfillment of prophecy (cf. the
formula quotations and 3:15). That Mt viewed even the
Law's relation to Christ in terms of prophetic fulfillment
is clear from Mt's reworking of a Q-saying in 11:13: "For
all the prophets and the Law *prophesied* until John"
(contrast Lk 16:16). Mt is turning the Jewish canon of Law
and prophets on its head. The touchstone becomes
prophecy, and the Law must be interpreted in analogy with
prophecy. Like the prophets, the Law pointed ahead to
Jesus the Messiah. And Jesus, when he comes, fulfills both
Law and prophets with an eschatological fulness that spills
over the top of the old vessel, that sometimes transcends
the old letter in the very process of fulfilling it. For Mt,
Jesus, not the Law, stands as the decisive center of his

religious universe. The key question is: what is the Law's relation to *the* center of our faith, Jesus?—and not vice versa. That is why Mt can end the sermon on the mount (7:24) and the entire gospel (28:20) with the accent on the words or commands of Jesus as *the* criterion of judgment, *the* norm to be taught. The Law question receives a Christological solution.

In v.18, with the solemn asseveration of an apocalyptic seer ("Amen I say to you"), Jesus assures his disciples that not the slightest commandment of the Law (= "not an iota, not a dot") will be abolished until a certain time point. The time point is expressed twice ("till . . . until"). The first clause ("till heaven and earth pass away") reflects, at first glance, the apocalyptic expectation that the old world was about to be dissolved (cf. Mt 24:35). But this apocalyptic event is reinterpreted by the last clause in v.18, which would be better translated: "until all things [prophesied] come to pass" (cf. the introductions to the formula quotations). As can be seen from Lk 16:17, Mt has added this last clause in v.18 to reinterpret a stringent statement about the Law's perdurance till the end of the world. Mt reinterprets the apocalyptic end of the world in terms of the fulfillment of all things prophesied. For Mt, the fulfillment of OT prophecies culminates in the earth-shaking, apocalyptic event of the death-resurrection of Jesus, which marks "the turning of the ages" (cf. the Introduction to this volume and the comments on 27:51-54; 28:2-3; 28:16-20). Before this great turning point, Jesus' mission remains within the land of Israel and within the framework of Jewish Law and institutions. The universal mission that will flow from the death-resurrection will break all these barriers, legal as well as geographic. What will bind post-Easter Christians will be the commands of Jesus, be they according to or contrary to the Mosaic Law—though in fact much of the content of Christian morality will remain Mosaic.

V.19 both draws a practical conclusion from v.18 and shifts the subject from Jesus the Fulfiller of the Law to human teachers of the Law. The abiding concern in both verses is the smallest part of the Law: "the least of these commandments" picks up the "iota" and "dot" of v. 18. Lax teachers will receive the lowest place in the kingdom at the last judgment. Those who *do* the commandments (Mt's great concern) and teach accordingly will be rewarded with a high place. Therefore, Jesus' prophetic fulfillment, which at times rescinds the Law, must not lead mere human teachers into a blasé attitude towards the Law. The Christian teacher must be scrupulous in doing and teaching the commandments of the Law, as reinterpreted by the Fulfiller of the Law.

V.20 shifts the focus firmly to the disciples in general, to whom the subsequent antitheses will be addressed. What the antitheses and all of Christ's moral teaching demand of them is "justice" (RSV: "righteousness"), here in the sense of moral activity which does God's will. In the life of a true disciple justice must overflow ("exceeds") with an abundance befitting the definitive salvation Jesus brings. This abundance is not a bigger and better Pharisaism, an ever more precise observance of legal niceties. It is radical gift of self to God and neighbor in both inner thought and outward action. It pursues the Law to its ultimate intention, even if that means abrogation of the letter. This justice far surpasses the legalistic approach of "the scribes and Pharisees" (Mt's stock phrase for official Judaism). Mt implies that Jewish moral standards will not be sufficient for entrance into the kingdom on the last day. His rejection of the Pharisees' doctrine will become even clearer as the gospel proceeds (cf. 15:12-20; 16:12). But Mt is equally unsparing when it comes to Christian disciples. No half-measures are permissible. If they do not practice the radical, eschatological morality Christ proclaims, they will be excluded too. In Mt's moral exhortation, the stringency of the last judgment replaces the imminence of judgment as the main motivation.

D. JESUS AND THE LAW:
THE PRINCIPLE APPLIED.
5:21-48.
[Lk 12:57-59; Mk 9:43-48; 10:3-4,11-12;
Lk 16:18; 6:27-36]

[21]"You have heard that it was said to the men of old, 'You shall not kill; and whoever kills shall be liable to judgment.' [22]But I say to you that every one who is angry with his brother shall be liable to judgment; whoever insults his brother shall be liable to the council, and whoever says, 'You fool!' shall be liable to the hell of fire. [23]So if you are offering your gift at the altar, and there remember that your brother has something against you, [24]leave your gift there before the altar and go; first be reconciled to your brother, and then come and offer your gift. [25]Make friends quickly with your accuser, while you are going with him to court, lest your accuser hand you over to the judge, and the judge to the guard, and you be put in prison; [26]truly, I say to you, you will never get out till you have paid the last penny.

[27]"You have heard that it was said, 'You shall not commit adultery.' [28]But I say to you that every one who looks at a woman lustfully has already committed adultery with her in his heart. [29]If your right eye causes you to sin, pluck it out and throw it away; it is better that you lose one of your members than that your whole body be thrown into hell. [30]And if your right hand causes you to sin, cut it off and throw it away; it is better that you lose one of your members than that your whole body go into hell.

[31]"It was also said, 'Whoever divorces his wife, let him give her a certificate of divorce.' [32]But I say to you that every one who divorces his wife, except on the ground of unchastity, makes her an adulteress; and whoever marries a divorced woman commits adultery.

³³"Again you have heard that it was said to the men of old, 'You shall not swear falsely, but shall perform to the Lord what you have sworn.' ³⁴But I say to you, Do not swear at all, either by heaven, for it is the throne of God, ³⁵or by the earth, for it is his footstool, or by Jerusalem, for it is the city of the great King. ³⁶And do not swear by your head, for you cannot make one hair white or black. ³⁷Let what you say be simply 'Yes' or 'No'; anything more than this comes from evil.

³⁸"You have heard that it was said, 'An eye for an eye and a tooth for a tooth.' ³⁹But I say to you, Do not resist one who is evil. But if any one strikes you on the right cheek, turn to him the other also; ⁴⁰and if any one would sue you and take your coat, let him have your cloak as well; ⁴¹and if any one forces you to go one mile, go with him two miles. ⁴²Give to him who begs from you, and do not refuse him who would borrow from you.

⁴³"You have heard that it was said, 'You shall love your neighbor and hate your enemy.' ⁴⁴But I say to you, Love your enemies and pray for those who persecute you, ⁴⁵so that you may be sons of your Father who is in heaven; for he makes his sun rise on the evil and on the good, and sends rain on the just and on the unjust. ⁴⁶For if you love those who love you, what reward have you? Do not even the tax collectors do the same? ⁴⁷And if you salute only your brethren, what more are you doing than others? Do not even the Gentiles do the same? ⁴⁸You, therefore, must be perfect, as your heavenly Father is perfect.

Christian justice (v. 20) is now made explicit in six concrete examples. Called "antitheses" because of the opposition between what God once said and what Jesus now says, they treat questions of murder, adultery, divorce, oaths and vows, retaliation, and hatred of enemies. The sources are Q and M, with a glance at Mk. The content is quite diverse, ranging from church discipline (divorce) to purely internal morality (impure thoughts). The antithetical formula ("it was said . . . but I say") may have been inherited from the tradition, but its six-fold repetition to order the material is Mt's contribution. The antithetical formula varies in length; not all the formulas contain "you have heard" (referring to the reading of Scripture in the synagogue and its explanation by Jewish teachers). As vv. 31-32 show, the basic opposition is between what was said and what Jesus says. "It was said" refers to what *God* said (the divine passive voice) to the desert generation at Sinai ("the men of old") when he gave the Law (almost all the quotations which follow are citations or paraphrases from the Pentateuch). To this is boldly opposed what Jesus now says. The opposition may take a mild form of deepening, spiritualizing, or radicalizing the Torah. This is the case with murder, adultery, and love of neighbor; the pattern is "not only . . . but also." But the radicalizing can be pushed so far that the letter of the Torah (some important command, permission, or institution) is revoked. This is the case with divorce, oaths and vows, and retaliation; the pattern is "not this . . . but that." When there is a conflict over what is the genuine will of God, the words of the Torah must cede to the word of Jesus.

The first antithesis declares that anger is as heinous as murder. The apparent heightening of crime and punishment (judgment [or "local court"]—council [or "Sanhedrin"]—hell) is simply a mocking parody of the moral casuistry of the Pharisees. The point is that, in the radical, eschatological morality of Jesus, insulting one's brother with the word "raka" (= "empty-headed"?) or "fool" betrays the same murderous heart that overt homicide displays. Mt would not seem comfortable with our neat, protective distinctions between mortal and venial sins. In the two parables which follow (vv. 23-26), Mt shifts the topic slightly to fraternal reconciliation. We dare not approach God in liturgy and, *a fortiori*, at the final judgment, unless we are first reconciled with our brother (cf. 6:12). An unreconciled brother means an unreconciled God, and no amount of liturgy can change that fact. We must be reconciled while we are still on the path of this life, before it is too late. Mt again uses the stringency of judgment to motivate morality.

The second antithesis puts lustful glances on a level with overt adultery (v.27). Sin is always committed first in the core of our free being (the heart). And the dignity of a woman can be violated by much more than simply illicit intercourse. Mt appends vv.29-30, which originally referred to avoiding all occasions of sin (cf. Mk 9:43-48). The harsh language is simply a strong metaphor, not to be taken literally: the salvation of the whole person at the last judgment is worth any sacrifice now. By adding vv.29-30 to the second antithesis, Mt gives eye and hand a sexual reference. The rabbis also warned against adultery of heart, hand (masturbation), and eye.

The third antithesis, on divorce, is the Q-form of the prohibition (cf. Lk 16:18); another, Markan form is found in Mk 10:2-4, 11-12 (cf. Mt 19:7,9). Paul gives a third, independent form in 1 Cor 7:10. From the variety of witnesses, it is clear that the historical Jesus forbade divorce without provisos. He thus revokes the Mosaic sanction of divorce. Mt's form, however, poses a special problem because of its "exceptive clauses" in 5:32 and 19:9. "Except on the ground of unchastity" has often been taken to refer to a dispute between the rabbinical schools of Shammai and Hillel. The former allowed divorce only when the woman was guilty of impurity or immodesty; the latter permitted divorce for practically any reason. Mt would be espousing the position of Shammai. Both on historical and philological grounds this interpretation is doubtful. "Unchastity" in v.32 translates *porneia*, a word which can mean almost any illicit sexual act. When Mt wants to speak of adultery he uses words like *moicheuō*, and he distinguishes adultery from *porneia* (cf. 15:19). *Porneia* in 5:32 refers rather to incestuous unions, i.e., marriages within prohibited degrees of consanguinity and affinity. All too common in the eastern Mediterranean, such marriages were forbidden by Lev. 18:6-18. Some rabbis allowed a Gentile to maintain the incestuous union when he entered Judaism, and similar problems about these unions arose when Gentiles became Christians. The problem is mentioned in Acts 15:20,29; 21:25; and 1 Cor 5:1. In all these texts *porneia* is used to describe the incestuous marriage. The "exceptive clause" is thus the exact opposite of a relaxation of Jesus' radical morality.

The fourth antithesis strictly forbids an esteemed institution of the Torah, namely, oaths and vows. The OT citation in v.33 sums up a number of prescriptions of the Pentateuch, while borrowing some words from Ps 49:14. At times the Torah even imposes oaths; and therefore, in such cases, Jesus would be directly revoking OT commands. Some commentators claim that Mt intends merely to substitute the mild oath of "yes, yes" or "no, no" (as the Greek of v.37 reads) for oaths that refer to God. The parallel text of Jas 5:12 is called upon to show that Jesus' original recommendation that we make our "yes" mean "yes" has been turned into an oath-formula: "yes,yes." But this ignores not only Mt's radicalizing tendencies but also his emphatic addition: "Do not swear *at all.*" "At all" is missing in Jas 5:12. As vv.34-37 indicate, Mt would find any oath, however mild, objectionable, because any kind of oath infringes on God's majesty and transcendence. Man is not to imagine that he can claim God as a witness or control God for his own purposes. With a twinkle in his otherwise stern eye, Mt adds: man cannot even control the color of his own graying hair, and so should not swear even by that— which brings us back to the point: not at all! It is difficult to reconcile Mt's absolute prohibition with later church practice.

The fifth antithesis clearly revokes the law of retaliation in Ex 21:24; Lev 24:20; and Dt 19:21. The Law firmly commanded proportionate retaliation to avoid unrestricted blood lust and feuds. In a sense, Jesus' prohibition brings the humanizing and moderating tendencies of the Torah to their logical conclusion. But in doing so he again revokes the letter of the Torah. In fact, what Jesus does is to prohibit any court action to obtain retribution or compensation. All human legal systems, which are necessarily based on a need to balance rights and redress injuries, are undermined by this antithesis. The "otherness" of the kingdom and of its justice could not be clearer. In the sermon on the mount, Jesus is not presenting a new program for human society; he is announcing the end of human society, the end of the world. That is what *eschatological* morality is all about. It is possible only for the believing disciple who through Jesus already lives in the end-time. After dealing with the more precise question of legal suits ("one who is evil" refers to one's opponent in court). Mt goes on to give more general examples of waiving our rights for the benefit of others, even those who have no strict claim on us (vv.41-42). This leads directly and logically to the final and climactic antithesis, on love.

Despite appearances, the sixth antithesis does not revoke the letter of the Torah. While love of neighbor was enjoined in Lev 19:18, hatred of enemies is not commanded in the Torah. It is true that certain OT passages presume the legitimacy of such hatred (cf. Ps 139:19-22), and the Manual of Discipline from Qumran commands hatred of the "sons of darkness" (the enemies of the community). Jesus is therefore addressing a widespread popular limitation on the love-command: the enemy of the just man or of the people of God is an enemy of God, and is to be treated accordingly. The obligation of loving one's neighbor (i.e., a fellow member of Israel's cultic community) was naturally interpreted as permission not to love the "non-neighbor." Jesus rejects all such limitations on love. Yet he does not base his rejection on a sentimental view that all people are neighbors or brothers and sisters. With the bracing realism of the bible, Jesus reaffirms the category of enemy, but demands love even of enemies simply because that is the way the Father acts. From sunrise to raindrops, the Father shows equal love towards good and bad, not because he is indifferent to morality but because he loves without limit. The disciples, the sons of this Father, must prove their "legitimacy" by showing the family likeness, which means loving with the all-embracing love their Father bestows. Otherwise, they do not rise above the tit-for-tat morality of those paradigms of the low life, tax collectors and Gentiles (note the Jewish viewpoint here). The "more" that true sons must exhibit is the eschatological morality of mercy without measure. This is the "more" (*perisson*, v.47) that manifests the all-exceeding (*perisseusē*) righteousness of 5:20. This sincere, single-hearted devotion to God and man is what Mt calls perfection. "To be perfect" (*teleios*, a word that, among the four gospels, occurs only in Mt, cf. 19:21) not only sums up the love-command, but also harks back to the beatitudes and the pure in heart (v.8) in particular. V.48 recapitulates the entire moral teaching of chap. 5. To be perfect is not the ideal of the monk; it is the obligation of every Christian.

E. THREE PIOUS PRACTICES: ALMSGIVING, PRAYER, AND FASTING. 6:1-18.
[Mk 11:25; Lk 11:1-4]

6 "Beware of practicing your piety before men in order to be seen by them; for then you will have no reward from your Father who is in heaven.

²"Thus, when you give alms, sound no trumpet before you, as the hypocrites do in the synagogues and in the streets, that they may be praised by men. Truly, I say to you, they have received their reward. ³But when you give alms, do not let your left hand know what your right hand is doing, ⁴so that your alms may be in secret; and your Father who sees in secret will reward you.

⁵"And when you pray, you must not be like the hypocrites; for they love to stand and pray in the synagogues and at the street corners, that they may be seen by men. Truly, I say to you, they have received their reward. ⁶But when you pray, go into your room and shut the door and pray to your Father who is in secret; and your Father who sees in secret will reward you.

⁷"And in praying do not heap up empty phrases as the Gentiles do; for they think that they will be heard for their many words. ⁸Do not be like them, for your Father knows what you need before you ask him. ⁹Pray then like this:

Our Father who art in heaven,
Hallowed be thy name.
¹⁰Thy kingdom come,
Thy will be done,
On earth as it is in heaven.
¹¹Give us this day our daily bread;
¹²And forgive us our debts,
As we also have forgiven our debtors;
¹³And lead us not into temptation,
But deliver us from evil.

¹⁴For if you forgive men their trespasses, your heavenly Father also will forgive you; ¹⁵but if you do not forgive men their trespasses, neither will your Father forgive your trespasses.

¹⁶"And when you fast, do not look dismal, like the hypocrites, for they disfigure their faces that their fasting may be seen by men. Truly, I say to you, they have received their reward. ¹⁷But when you fast, anoint your head and wash your face, ¹⁸that your fasting may not be seen by men but by your Father who is in secret; and your Father who sees in secret will reward you.

For pious Jews, justice (*ṣedāqâ*) meant more than observance of commands of the written Law. Justice also encompassed a number of pious practices, especially almsgiving (vv.2-4), prayer (vv.5-15), and fasting (16-18). The connection is already made in the OT, e.g., Tob 12:8. The source of Mt 6:1-18 is a catechetical tradition of Mt's church (M), carefully divided into three parallel sections. Mt adds 6:1 as a heading with the key word "justice" (RSV: "piety"), which harks back to 5:20. Mt has also broken the threefold schema by inserting a separate teaching on prayer: a warning against babbling like pagans (vv.7-8), which introduces the Our Father (vv. 9-13), followed by a final Markan saying on forgiveness (vv.14-15). The whole section betrays a double passion of Mt's: to *do* God's will and yet avoid Pharisaic display of virtue. Jesus affirms the basic value of these practices, but the value is put under the proviso of quiet, unobtrusive activity. The disciples should indeed practice their piety with an eye to their audience; but their true audience is their "Father who is in heaven," not their fellow men. All their activity must be aimed at God alone. The stress on the heavenly Father puts the reward idea—which is indeed part of Jesus' moral exhortation—into the context of a gift a Father gives his son, and not a strict wage an employer is bound to give his employee. The image of reward is to be understood in a context of personal relationship and dialogue; it stresses that God takes man seriously and reacts to man's acts. The whole point is that God cannot reply to man's actions in the dialogue of religion if man's actions do not speak to God but rather to other men.

Each of the three "practical antitheses on piety" has a fourfold structure: (1) the thesis, describing a hypocritical practice which aims at being seen and praised; (2) an Amen-word condemning the practice as exhausting its reward in this world; (3) the antithesis describing Christian justice ("but when *you* . . ."); (4) a concluding promise of reward. The first element corresponds to the third, the second to the fourth. Some ideas (modest conduct among men, tit-for-tat reward) stem from the wisdom tradition, but apocalyptic currents supply the idea of God's retribution on the last day, revealing what is secret in this life. Especially interesting is the phrase "they have their reward." The Greek verb (*apechousin*) is a set term for a receipt signifying receipt of payment in full; it expresses perfectly the crass commercial mentality of the hypocrites.

Jews maintained a regular system of relief for the poor. But besides that, individuals would vow sums to the poor during synagogue services or during a public fast. At times, such announcements could turn into bidding sessions. Some would even drop coins "in the streets" to attract the poor and so gain attention. Jesus caricatures this publicity-seeking by depicting a trumpet being blown. Such people are "hypocrites" (literally, "stage actors"). Out of a good deed which should be done in private they create a public spectacle, with themselves as director, producer, and star, bowing to the audience's applause. Hypocrisy is the split in a religious person between outward show and inner reality. It is one of the chief rebukes Mt aims at the Pharisees (cf. chap. 23), though he always has in mind the sad truth that Christians can fall into the same pit. Disciples must give alms in complete secrecy, which is expressed by the hyperbole of the ignorant left hand. By leaving the question of reward to God, one is set free for the concerns of others. As OT wisdom literature stresses, what is hidden to men is open to God. The Father sees "in secret"—be that the secret place where alms are given or the secret place of the heart. The idea of God's rewarding is expressed by the verb *apodidōmi*; interestingly, even Paul uses the same verb for the same idea (Rom 2:6).

The private prayer life of the pious Jew was nourished not only by the psalms and other prayers of the OT, but also by more recent compositions (e.g., the Thanksgiving Hymns for the Qumranites). Set times and set formulas arose; the set times in particular opened the way for ostentation. Some would make sure they were in the synagogue or on street corners when the set times came, so that they would have an audience. (Standing, however, does not indicate any

special ostentation; it was the usual posture for prayer).
Jesus points out that anyone who makes himself or others
the partner or object of his prayer loses the only important
partner. Using an image from Is 26:20 and 2 Kings 4:33,
Jesus says we must rather seek out a storeroom or shed
attached to a farmhouse and lock ourselves in. Again, the
metaphor bespeaks secrecy. At least for private prayer,
there is no consecrated place; the place receives its consecration from what happens there. Jesus certainly did not reject
group prayer, as is seen by his frequenting of synagogues
and the temple, and also by his promise in 18:19-20.

At this point, Mt inserts a separate catechesis on prayer,
which also has three parts: (1) admonition to terse prayer
(vv.7-8); (2) the Our Father (vv.9-13); (3) an admonition
to forgive (vv.14-15). Vv.7-8 are likewise antithetical, but
now the opposition is between Christians and Gentile
pagans (*ethnikoi*). Mt has a concept of Christians as a third
race, set over against both Jews and Gentiles. The Gentiles
babble on when they pray, reciting an endless list of divine
names, hoping they will hit on the secret name which will
force the god to act. Behind all long-winded prayer there
is a similar magical conception of man's relation to God.
Such religious marathons are an illusion: "They *think* they
will be heard . . . ." But God's hand is not forced by liturgical
rhetoric. True sons must concentrate on quality rather
than quantity in prayer, the chief quality being trust in
the Father's loving providence. The all-knowing God has
provided for our needs before we even knew them (cf.
6:25-34). There is only one rubric for Christian prayer:
trust, which makes for terse prayers. An example of—
though not the only formula for—such prayer is given in
the Our Father.

The Our Father stands in the middle of the sermon on
the mount; it is also the heart of the sermon. The themes
struck in the Our Father will provide whatever continuity
there is in the second, structurally looser half of the sermon.
Mt presents the form of the Lord's Prayer traditional in

his church, just as Lk represents the liturgical traditions of his church when he gives us the shorter form in Lk 11:1-4. On the whole, Lk's starker form probably reflects more accurately the words of Jesus, though Mt's version may be more original at certain points. Mt's Jewish-Christian church had "fleshed out" the Lord's prayer to give it the balanced shape and tolling cadences suitable for public worship. The words of Jesus themselves have parallels in ancient synagogue prayers (The Qaddish, the Eighteen Benedictions) and Mt's form is even more assimilated to liturgical usage. Mt's version is composed of (1) an initial address with modifiers; (2) a first half, made up of three "thou-petitions"; and (3) a second half, made up of three "we-petitions," the second and third petitions having two parts.

Instead of Lk's stark "Father," reflecting Jesus' *Abba,* Mt has the stately and more distanced address. We experience God's fatherhood not as isolated individuals but as members of the church, the family of Jesus the Son; hence, the "our." God is distinct from our earthly fathers ("in heaven," an addition common among the rabbis). Yet we must not confuse our relationship with him with that unique relationship possessed only by Jesus, who says simply "my Father" or "Father." But we are truly God's children, and so we are first concerned with the triumph of the Father's cause, not with our own petty concerns. The "thou-petitions" all aim at the Father's action and concerns, not ours; the passive voice has him, not ourselves as the understood agent (*You* hallow . . . *you* do). In the OT Yahweh promises his people that he will display his transcendent majesty, his holiness (= "otherness") before them, to save or judge. Ezek 36:23 declares: "I will sanctify [= hallow] my great name"— "name" being equivalent to the person of God as known through his revelation. For Jesus, the Father reveals his transcendent holiness precisely by bringing in his eschatological kingdom, by assuming his rightful rule over the world. Hence the second petition, which we might almost translate: "Sanctify your name by bringing in your kingdom." The resplendent theophany Jesus thinks of is the appearing of God on the last day; the "Our Father" is an eschatological prayer, a prayer that God will hasten the end-time.

This is also the intent of the third petition (not in Lk); "See that your will is done" by bringing to a climax the eschatological drama. When Mt places the third petition on the lips of Jesus in Gethsemane (26:42), he is doing more than making Jesus a model of prayer for us. The death-resurrection for Mt is the climax of the eschatological drama of Jesus; it is the turning of the ages. And so Jesus teaches his disciples to pray that God will bring this eschatological crisis to its consummation. All Christian disciples, as persons caught between the times, pray for the same saving resolution of their eschatological woes. Of course, Mt is not favoring quietism; the disciples must join in doing the Father's will. The three petitions are then bound neatly together by a short comparison; "as in heaven" forms an inclusion with "who are in heaven." The goods of salvation, already present in heaven, must be realized on earth: the basic apocalyptic vision.

Only after praying for the Father's concerns do we turn to our own: food, forgiveness, and freedom from evil. As in the first half, the imperative verbs are in the aorist tense (a single action) and may reflect the yearning for God's definitive, once-and-for-all act on the last day. If this is so, the bread refers to the final banquet, in the kingdom, which is urgently requested even for today. "Daily" translates a rare adjective which could also mean "for tomorrow," "for today," "coming," or "necessary." Prayed at the liturgy, the prayer would envision the eucharist as the anticipation of the final banquet. Lk changes the reference to God's continual giving of our physical sustenance every day.

The fifth petition looks to our need to be forgiven before the last judgment. God has made mutual forgiveness among the disciples a precondition of his own forgiveness on the last day (cf. 6:14-15; 18:23-35; 5:23-26). The rabbis also demanded reconciliation with one's brother before the Day of Atonement. Since "debt" was a metaphor for sin in Aramaic (*hôbâ*) but not usually in Greek, Lk clarifies the sentiment for Gentile readers by using "our sins."

The last double-petition looks forward to the terrible outbreak of moral chaos and violence just before the end, when the powers of evil would seem to gain the upper hand over the disciples. Knowing their fragility, the disciples pray that God will spare them the full impact of this final "test" (RSV: temptation). The semitic background of the prayer might allow us to translate: "And do not permit us to come to the test." But the biblical mind firmly held that God controlled all events, triumphant as well as tragic, and so "lead" or "bring" is perfectly acceptable. Mt's form, over against Lk's, clarifies this petition with a concluding, parallel one. To be spared the full horror of the apocalyptic clash between good and evil means to be snatched from the power of the Evil One (though *ponērou* could also be neuter: "from evil").

In our view, then, the Our Father is an eschatological prayer from start to finish; others, however, would refer the second half of the prayer to ordinary, daily food, forgiveness, temptations, and evil. The Matthean form soon triumphed over the Lukan in the church's liturgy, as can be seen as early as the Jewish-Christian document the *Didache,* which adds the doxology, "For thine is the kingdom," etc. The doxology, based on 1 Chron 29:11, was added to some manuscripts of Mt and entered into the liturgical practice of the Eastern churches, and through them into Protestant bibles and liturgies. An altered form now occurs in the Roman Catholic Mass, though not immediately after the Our Father.

In antithetical parallelism, vv. 14-15 develop the petition for forgiveness. Mt of course knows that God's forgiving act precedes any initiative of ours (18:23-35) but the very form of vv. 14-15 demands the order: our forgiveness, God's forgiveness. The verses reflect a set pattern called "Principles of Holy Law": the condition of each verse states man's action now, and the conclusion states the corresponding action of God on the last day. The main point is: God wills that human and divine forgiveness be inextricably bound together—a corollary of the double command of love (22:34-40).

In vv.16-18 Mt resumes and concludes the interrupted catechesis on almsgiving, prayer, and fasting. Fasting expressed intense longing for God's salvation; it was prayer in action and was naturally joined with prayer. Besides obligatory fasts, pious Jews would undertake private fasting as a pious work. Far from considering it a good work which forces God's hand, Mt sees fasting as a concrete expression of conversion to and dependence on "our Father." The prophets had rejected fasts which did not reflect an inner hunger for social justice (Is 58:3-9). Jesus attacks fasts which are turned into spectacles of religiosity. The hypocrites may be *sad* and dismal with their sad-sack looks, yet they are not really *serious* about fasting. Their play-acting is well expressed by Mt's play on words in v.16 ("they disfigure [*aphanizousin*] their faces that they may be seen [*phanōsin*]"). These people who fast are like dismal drug-addicts, hooked on the opium of men's approval. They get exactly what they crave, and nothing more. A true fast avoids the traditional signs of fasting, such as the omission of washing and of anointing oneself, actions performed to give a sense of well-being. This does not involve any new hypocrisy or deception with regard to one's fellows; the external appearance of joy and well-being is a true mirror of the disciple's inner state. In short: a genuine fast in the sight of God can never take place in the sight of men. Since the historical Jesus forbade his disciples to fast because the joyful time of salvation had come (Mt 9:14-15a), some think that the early church created this teaching on a proper fast when it took up the practice of fasting (as reflected in Mt 9:15b).

F. THE FUNDAMENTAL OPTION: SERVE GOD OR THIS WORLD. 6:19-34. [Lk 12:33-36; 16:13,22-32]

[19]"Do not lay up for yourselves treasures on earth, where moth and rust consume and where thieves break in and steal, [20]but lay up for yourselves treasures in heaven, where neither moth nor rust consumes and where thieves do not break in and steal. [21]For where your treasure is, there will your heart be also.

[22]"The eye is the lamp of the body. So, if your eye is sound, your whole body will be full of light; [23]but if your eye is not sound, your whole body will be full of darkness. If then the light in you is darkness, how great is the darkness!

[24]"No one can serve two masters; for either he will hate the one and love the other, or he will be devoted to the one and despise the other. You cannot serve God and mammon.

[25]"Therefore I tell you, do not be anxious about your life, what you shall eat or what you shall drink, nor about your body, what you shall put on. Is not life more than food, and the body more than clothing? [26]Look at the birds of the air: they neither sow nor reap nor gather into barns, and yet your heavenly Father feeds them. Are you not of more value than they? [27]And which of you by being anxious can add one cubit to his span of life? [28]And why are you anxious about clothing? Consider the lilies of the field, how they grow; they neither toil nor spin; [29]yet I tell you, even Solomon in all his glory was not arrayed like one of these. [30]But if God so clothes the grass of the field, which today is alive and tomorrow is thrown into the oven, will he not much more clothe you, O men of little faith? [31]Therefore do not be anxious, saying, 'What shall we eat?' or 'What shall we drink?' or 'What shall we wear?' [32]For the Gentiles seek all these things; and your heavenly Father knows that you need them all.

³³But seek first his kingdom and his righteousness, and all these things shall be yours as well.

³⁴"Therefore do not be anxious about tomorrow, for tomorrow will be anxious for itself. Let the day's own trouble be sufficient for the day.

After 6:1-18, Mt has exhausted his tight catechetical material, arranged in numerical patterns. The structure of the sermon becomes looser as Mt weaves together individual sayings, almost entirely from Q. The remainder of chap. 6 does have a controlling idea, summed up in v. 24: one must decide to worship either the true God, the Father in heaven, or the false god of worldly possessions. The single-hearted devotion of the disciple echoes the call to be "pure of heart" (5:8) and "perfect" (5:48), as well as the trusting, God-centered attitude of the Our Father. Although individual sayings are paralleled in the popular wisdom of the time, this spirit of trust in the Father places the sayings in a new, Christian context.

Mt apparently reorders Q to put vv. 19-23 first. His prime concern is the call to decide between the fragile security and illusory joy of earthly wealth and the true riches of possessing God. In the unsettled conditions of Palestine, peasants would hide coins and even clothing in the ground. but natural and human enemies could destroy it all ("break in" may refer either to digging up the treasure or digging into the mud walls of a house). Contrary to rabbinic Judaism, and closer to Qumran, Jesus disdains all earthly wealth. The disciple must pile up treasures in heaven—no doubt by heeding the demands of this sermon, especially 6:1-18. Mt does not understand this call for action in terms of a cross merit-system, as though one's heavenly treasure were payable on demand. As v. 21 shows, Mt's whole interest is one's basic choice for or against God; everything else flows from that. The person who makes the right choice experiences the riches of the heavenly kingdom already. Given this context, the mysterious parable in vv. 22-23 probably signifies for Mt the need for man to be illumined by Jesus' teaching on the transitory nature of earthly wealth, lest he fall into darkness and illusion. The problem is that this parable of the healthy and diseased eyes carries no interpretation, and may originally have referred to a kindly and generous spirit versus a mean and envious one. Mt, however, places the saying in the context of a call to single-minded service, which must be guided by the light Christ gives. The antithetic parable of v.24 makes this clear. One either worships the true God or adores the demonic power of *property* (the meaning of the Aramaic *māmôn*). Each disciple must face and pass the test Jesus withstood in 4:1-11, especially vv.8-9. All our apparently unimportant ethical choices answer one basic question: Who rightly claims to be God? The choice is unavoidable and the options are mutually exclusive ("hate . . . love").

The following verses apply this call to free oneself from the slavery of this world to the anxieties we feel about daily needs: food, clothing, and length of life. The whole passage can be seen as a commentary on the fourth petition of the Our Father. Jesus does not forbid all concern about physical needs, but rather that "anxiety" which expresses total absorption in the goods of this world. Discipleship frees one to trust in the only true Giver and Sustainer of life. The coming kingdom already shapes the present life of the disciple. His God does not simply dispense from the trials of this life, but grants him a higher security even in the midst of his trials. Free from anxiety, the disciple is free from confused priorities: one's life and body are the main gifts from God; food and clothing are just means to an end.

With natural poetic instinct Jesus directs the gaze of his fellow Galilean peasants to the lesson the Father gives in nature. God feeds the birds without the fierce effort of a farmer. He clothes the fields with flowers more glorious than Solomon's royal robes, yet neither men's farm labor nor women's spinning is required. Why then be anxious, when anxiety cannot add a single cubit (18-20 inches) to one's *height* (or, as the RSV takes it, one's span of life). Yet all these glories of nature which God lavishly supplies are burned up for fuel on the morrow. And here Mt hammers home his point: if such loving care is showered on this passing world by the Creator, *how much more* will your *Father* care for you, his own *children.*

Jesus surpasses popular faith in providence by stressing the special care the Father shows his very own, who stand under the protection of his kingdom. Jesus gently chides his disciples for their weak faith with an adjective that is a favorite of Mt's: *oligopistoi*, "O men of little faith." It designates not unbelievers or apostates, but true disciples who panic in a moment of crisis and act as though they did not believe. The disciples must stop being eaten up by anxious questions about physical needs; only pagans worship this world by giving it their full attention. It is the Father's part to take care of these needs, and he knows *all* of them.

Our seeking—the seeking, the commitment which defines us—must not be a pagan one. We must seek (not create or build!) the kingdom which God is bringing into the world, and we must likewise seek *his* saving action (his justice or "righteousness"). The qualification "first" after "seek" shows that Mt does not deny man's physical needs. It is a question of priorities, priorities set by the order of the "thou-" and "we-petitions" in the Our Father. Once the kingdom has invaded our lives, the Father will supply everything else that we need, our daily bread. Mt concludes with an enigmatic proverb from popular wisdom, which shifts the focus slightly from the present to the future. Each day has its own burden of problems; do not double them by considering tomorrow's as well. The disciple's present state must be formed not by the fleeting future of "tomorrow" but by the absolute future of the coming kingdom. The disciple therefore puts his future into the hands of God and modestly ask for his bread today.

G. THE KINDNESS OF MAN AND
THE KINDNESS OF THE FATHER.
7:1-12.
[Mk 4:24-25; Lk 6:37-42; 11:9-13; 6:31]

7 "Judge not, that you be not judged. ²For with the judgment you pronounce you will be judged, and the measure you give will be the measure you get. ³Why do you see the speck that is in your brother's eye, but do not notice the log that is in your own eye? ⁴Or how can you say to your brother, 'Let me take the speck out of your eye,' when there is the log in your own eye? ⁵You hypocrite, first take the log out of your own eye, and then you will see clearly to take the speck out of your brother's eye.

⁶"Do not give dogs what is holy; and do not throw your pearls before swine, lest they trample them under foot and turn to attack you.

⁷"Ask, and it will be given you; seek, and you will find; knock, and it will be opened to you. ⁸For every one who asks receives, and he who seeks finds, and to him who knocks it will be opened. ⁹Or what man of you, if his son asks him for bread, will give him a stone? ¹⁰Or if he asks for a fish, will give him a serpent? ¹¹If you then, who are evil, know how to give good gifts to your children, how much more will your Father who is in heaven give good things to those who ask him! ¹²So whatever you wish that men would do to you, do so to them; for this is the law and the prophets.

The structure of the sermon becomes still looser. Verbal links and the themes of the Our Father provide whatever connection exists between the various sayings, some of which were popular proverbs taken over by Jesus or the church and given a new application. The governing idea of 7:1-12 is the kindness or severity of man, and the corresponding attitudes in God. As the fifth petition of the Our Father stressed, our relationships with each other and with

God are intertwined. Almost all of chap. 7 is taken from Q. Indeed, with 7:1, Mt returns to the main thread of the traditional sermon also preserved in Lk 6.

Jesus forbids a *definitive condemnation* of another (this is the sense of "judge" here), for such an action arrogates to man the prerogative of God on the last day. Those who pass such a condemnation now will be correspondingly condemned by God (the sense of the passive voice). The proverb refers to condemnation, not to forming opinions, a process presupposed in vv.3-5. The "measure for measure" rule refers in Lk to merciful giving; Mt gives it a sterner application, to warn disciples against harsh judgments. While Mt knows the need for disciplinary procedures within the church (18:15-18), the supreme rule must always be mercy and forgiveness (18:21-35). Disciples are called to exercise not judgment, but fraternal correction. The latter demands that we be conscious of two things: (1) the one to be corrected is my brother; (2) my own faults (the log or the plank) are greater than his and require attention first. Self-righteous superiority dooms fraternal correction to failure; only self-correction makes fraternal correction credible and effective. Elsewhere in Mt the "hypocrites" are the scribes and the Pharisees; this saying may have originally been directed against them. Mt applies it to the disciples, because he knows all too well that Christians easily become guilty of all the failings he sees in the Pharisees.

V.6 is an enigmatic parable, present only in Mt. In a chiastic framework, we are warned not to give food offered in sacrifice ("what is holy") to dogs, lest they attack (literally, "tear") us, and not to give pearls to swine, lest they trample them. "What is holy" probably symbolizes the gospel of the *kingdom*, which is compared to a pearl in 13:45. Since the rabbis called the Gentiles dogs and swine, 7:6 may originally have expressed a strict Jewish-Christian prohibition of a Gentile mission (cf. 10:5). Mt may be applying the saying to apostate Christians (2 Pt 2:20-22) or to Christians who refuse to repent of sin (cf. Mt 18:17).

The *Didache* turns the saying into a prohibition against admitting the unbaptized or unrepentant to the eucharist.

The exhortation to constant prayer (vv.7-11) has little to do with the context, except for the verbal link "give." Interestingly, this exhortation in Lk 11 follows the Lord's Prayer. No precise object of petition is mentioned; for Mt the object may be the power to carry out all that Jesus commands in the sermon and throughout the gospel, in short, the power to do the Father's will. Ultimately, what the disciple seeks is God's kingdom and his justice (6:33); the disciple's seeking is the more abundant justice of 5:20. Christian morality is no human achievement generating merit; it is the gift of the Father. In this exhortation, the imperatives are in the present tense ("keep on asking"), and the passive voice refers to God as agent. The threefold repetition of verbs conveys both urgency and assurance. The disciples will be heard because they are children praying to the Father. Even human fathers, sinful and selfish ("evil") though they be, naturally delight in giving their children what they ask for, especially when it is a matter of basic food (cf. 6:11). The rhetorical questions may strike us as strange, but the Palestinian fish called "barbut" resembles a serpent, and a loaf of small round peasant bread looks like a stone. Mt's point here, as in 6:25-30, is *how much the more* will the all-good Father give the good things summed up in the Our Father.

Mt then closes this first part of chap. 7 with the "golden rule." This piece of common sense and popular morality goes back to Herodotus (fifth century B.C.). It spread among Greeks, Romans, and Jews in both positive and negative forms. There is nothing specifically Christian about it, and it does not rise above an enlightened self-interest. Rabbi Hillel considered the rule in negative form to be the essence of the Law; the rest was commentary. Mt adds to the Q-formulation his own tag, "this is the Law and the prophets." But this should not lead us to put 7:12 on a level with the loftier teaching of the double command of love

(22:34-40) simply because Mt also has "the Law and the prophets" there as well. Nor should 7:12 be called an inclusion with 5:17; 7:12 no more ends the sermon than 5:17 begins it. The weighty Christological statement of 5:17, a theological key to Mt's gospel, should not be put on the same level as sentiments from Herodotus. Still, the golden rule can serve Mt's purpose. By equating it with the Law and the prophets, Mt can cut through the Pharisaic casuistry which by its labyrinthine scholarship imprisons rather than frees the human soul.

H. THE FINAL DECISION:
PRETENDING OR DOING.
7:13-29
[Lk 13:23-24; 6:43-46; 13:25-27; 6:47-7:1]

[13]"Enter by the narrow gate; for the gate is wide and the way is easy, that leads to destruction, and those who enter by it are many. [14]For the gate is narrow and the way is hard, that leads to life, and those who find it are few.

[15]"Beware of false prophets, who come to you in sheep's clothing but inwardly are ravenous wolves. [16]You will know them by their fruits. Are grapes gathered from thorns, or figs from thistles? [17]So, every sound tree bears good fruit, but the bad tree bears evil fruit. [18]A sound tree cannot bear evil fruit, nor can a bad tree bear good fruit. [19]Every tree that does not bear good fruit is cut down and thrown into the fire. [20]Thus you will know them by their fruits.

[21]"Not every one who says to me, 'Lord, Lord,' shall enter the kingdom of heaven, but he who does the will of my Father who is in heaven. [22]On that day many will say to me, 'Lord, Lord, did we not prophesy in your name, and cast out demons in your name, and do many mighty works in your name?' [23]And then will I declare to them, 'I never knew you; depart from me, you evildoers.'

²⁴"Every one then who hears these words of mine and does them will be like a wise man who built his house upon the rock; ²⁵and the rain fell, and the floods came, and the winds blew and beat upon that house, but it did not fall, because it had been founded on the rock. ²⁶And every one who hears these words of mine and does not do them will be like a foolish man who built his house upon the sand; ²⁷and the rain fell, and the floods came, and the winds blew and beat against that house, and it fell; and great was the fall of it."

²⁸And when Jesus finished these sayings, the crowds were astonished at his teaching, ²⁹for he taught them as one who had authority, and not as their scribes.

Antithetical parallelism has run throughout the sermon. The sermon now ends with a series of such antitheses (two gates, two ways, sheep and wolves, two types of trees, two foundations). All the images describe two types of disciples, who, despite external similiarities, live totally different lives before God. Warnings of judgment become darker as Mt reminds the church that she, like Israel, is called to *do* God's will. If she fails, she, like Israel, will be rejected at the last judgment. Obedient, loving action, and not fair words or flashy miracles, will be the criterion on the day of judgment. Mt the pastor shows himself to be both an idealist and a realist. He proclaims the radical demands of Jesus as realizable for the true disciples; yet he recognizes that the church in this world is a "mixed bag" of true and false disciples. Only the final judgment will bring a definitive separation (cf. 13:36-43). This final section thus echoes the final double petition of the Our Father.

The two gates and the two roads are different metaphors for the same reality: the moral or immoral life between which each person must choose. Conduct in keeping with God's will leads to eternal life; sinful conduct leads to eternal doom. The image of the two ways was widespread in the OT and among pagan philosophers; it is found in the

Manual of Discipline at Qumran, the Didache, and the Epistle of Barnabas. For Mt, entrance into the kingdom is gained by obeying the commands of Jesus and therefore by practicing the exacting, overflowing justice (5:20) enunciated in this sermon. The hard demands of true discipleship attract only a few, while the comfortable path of false discipleship draws crowds.

The easy path is probably populated by the false Christian prophets of v.15. Christian prophets were very similar to Christian teachers and were probably equivalent to powerful preachers who might at times read men's hearts and predict the future. These prophets love the influence and power which leadership in the church brings them. They embrace that part of the gospel which makes life easy and exciting; they shun the commands of Christ which make life difficult and demanding. False prophets led Israel into idolatry and Judaism to the disaster of war with Rome; false prophets can lead the church to greater disaster still. They come into the sheepfold of Christ (cf. 9:36; 18:12-14) and give the appearance of being good disciples; but within they are seething with destructive self-centeredness. They are the wolves which will scatter and consume the flock (cf. Jn 10:12; Acts 20:28-30). To recognize them, ordinary Christians must test not how they look or what they say, but what they do. The healthy or diseased soul of each Christian is manifested by concrete action ("fruits"), either moral or immoral. Wild vines and wild fig trees look very much like the cultivated varieties, but the fruits show the difference. (Perhaps Mt calls the wild types thorns and thistles to recall the curse of Gen 3:18.) Repeating the threat of the Baptist, spoken to the Jews (3:10), Jesus threatens showy but empty Christians with the same fate of fiery damnation. The church, and especially her flashy leaders, are not exempt from judgment.

With v.21, Mt broadens the attack to all sorts of charismatic wonder-workers in the church. While Lk aims this saying at Jews who trust in their earthly acquaintance with

Jesus, Mt redirects the rebuke at Christian enthusiasts who imagine they have an "inside track" because of their special powers. These charismatics do not so much deny moral obligation as ignore it; they are laxists in practice, not antinomians in theory. In the church's worship, these charismatics are forever crying out in ecstasy to Jesus the Son with "Lord, Lord." (For Mt, this cultic exclamation is addressed to the risen Son who can speak simply of "my Father.") But "on that day" (the OT designation of the day of judgment) these enthusiasts will find that their prophecies, exorcisms, and miracles—all done by calling on Jesus' name and claiming his authority (cf. 10:8)—will not gain them admission to the kingdom. To their cultic cries Jesus will respond, in the words of Ps 6:8, with a formula of eternal excommunication (cf. 25:12). For all their presumed familiarity with the risen Christ and his Spirit, the charismatics are not even known by the real Jesus, who will judge in heaven according to the standards he taught on earth. All his standards simply explain the will of the Father, which is, in one word, love. The self-centered charismatics are too interested in their own power and glory to measure up to that exacting standard (cf. Paul's critique of charisms by the standard of love in 1 Cor 12-14 and the testing of the spirits in 1 Jn). The religion of the charismatics is an illusion; they say but they do not *do* (*poieō*, the verb also used for "bearing" fruit). Mt detects the same religious pathology in the scribes and Pharisees (23:3-5): either they speak but do not *practice* (literally, "do," *poieō*, v.3) or they practice (*poieō*), but only for the sake of external show (v.5). Both Christians and Jews can suffer the same basic split: the split between saying and doing, or between doing and being (cf. Rom 7). For Mt, this is the essence of hypocrisy, and it is the original sin of religious persons.

Mt follows the pattern of the primitive sermon (cf. Lk 6:47-49) by concluding with a parable written in strict antithetical parallelism. The opposition is now between hearing and doing, instead of saying and doing; and the application has been broadened out to "everyone who hears me," i.e., every Christian. Mt emphasizes the antithesis by adding that one man is wise, sensible, practical (i.e., he sees the needs of his situation and takes appropriate steps), while the other is foolish (i.e., he does not grasp the pressing demands of his situation and so fails to act). The wise disciple understands that he *will* face a stern judgment on the last day (hence the future: "will be like") and that the judgment will issue in life or death. The Torah of the OT ended with blessings and curses; so much the more, the "Torah" of Jesus! Hence the wise disciple acts decisively by building his whole life on the firm foundation of Jesus' words—more precisely, *these* words of mine, contained in the sermon on the mount (*these* is not in Lk). The wise disciple realizes that these words of Jesus the Son are identical with "the will of my Father" (v.21) and therefore will be the decisive criterion for the final judgment. Consequently the wise disciple forms his whole existence according to these words; he *does* them. On the other hand, the man who *merely* hears the teaching of Jesus does not *truly* understand it. The foolish disciple fails to grasp the essential connection between hearing Jesus' words, doing them, and being saved in the final crisis. And so his ruin will be complete ("great").

As regards the images used, Lk speaks of digging deep before laying the foundations, and then of a river overflowing its banks and dashing against the house. Mt thinks of a fierce rain and wind storm, perhaps in winter, accompanied by floods. In Mt, the strength of the house depends not on the deep foundation that was dug but on the rock on which it was built (cf. Mt 16:18); correspondingly, the weakness of the fool's house stems from the sand on which it was built. The references to "wise" and "foolish," and the depiction of the judgment in terms of a flood point ahead to the parables of crisis in the eschatological discourse (cf. 24:37-39; 25:1-13).

Mt signals the end of the first of the five discourses with a solemn formula, reminiscent of the OT: "and it came to pass when Jesus finished these words . . . ." The formula is used for each of the five discourses (cf. the Introduction to this volume), both to conclude the discourse and to provide a transition to the following narrative. The transitional function is lacking here. The sermon on the mount is so important to Mt that he pauses to recount the amazement of the crowds at Jesus' teaching (notice the return of the vocabulary of 5:1-2). They are astonished not at *what* he says but *how* he says it. The OT prophet had to legitimate his message by declaring: "The word of the Lord came to me, saying . . . ." The Jewish scribe had to legitimate his teaching by basing it on tradition. Jesus dares to confront the Torah of Moses and proclaim: "It was said . . . but *I* say . . . ." And he makes his teaching the criterion by which all will be saved or damned. He *has* authority.

Book Two
The Mission of Jesus and His
Disciples in Galilee.
8:1 - 11:1.

I. THE NARRATIVE OF BOOK TWO: THE CYCLE OF NINE MIRACLE STORIES.

8:1 - 9:38.

WITH CHAP. 8 Mt resumes the thread of Mk's narrative, which he left at 4:22 (though there are Markan elements in Mt 4:24-25). Most of the miracles in chap. 8-9 come from Mark, though they are not in the Markan order; only the stories of the centurion's servant and the dumb demoniac come from Q, which is also represented by some sayings.

Mt has undertaken a massive reordering of the Markan stories to set up neat numerical patterns. Often commentators speak of ten miracle stories in chaps. 8-9, and cite rabbinic traditions about Israel's experience of ten miracles in Egypt, ten at the Red Sea, and ten in the Sanctuary. But this is to misunderstand Mt's pattern. The stories of the healing of the woman with a hemorrhage and the raising of the dead girl were already woven together by Mk into one long pericope, and Mt cuts that pericope down to its bare bones. It is better to count nine miracle *stories* or pericopes, though there are admittedly more than nine miracles. In fact, there are really more than ten, since by common consent the healings at evening (8:16) are counted together with the healing of Peter's mother-in-law (8:14-15). As far as Mt's pattern goes, there are nine pericopes. Mt divides the nine stories into three sections, each with three stories. Between each section, there is some "buffer" pericope, containing sayings about the call to discipleship and the mercy of Jesus. A geographical unity is given by references to Capernaum and the environs of the Sea of Galilee; Capernaum, "his own city," stands at the center of the complex (9:1).

From the literary point of view, Mt streamlines the Markan narrative by dropping non-essential persons and actions, as well as Mk's colorful details. The stories are tied tightly together by short formulas and key words. The focus is on the encounter between Jesus and the petitioner, which almost becomes an encounter between words: the word of faith and prayer meets the healing word of Jesus. Yet it is an exaggeration to say that the miracle stories are transformed into pronouncement stories. From the theological point of view, Mt highlights four themes in his miracle stories: (1) At the center stands the majestic, all-powerful Christ. He fulfills the OT, acts as the mighty yet humble servant of God, gathers together and sustains his community, and shares his power with his community. (2) His community learns both the cost of following Jesus and also the power that flows from him. (3) The petitioner must have great faith, expressed in prayer; little faith is rebuked. (4) Some of the miracles point ahead to the mission to the Gentiles and the rejection of the Jews.

As for the place of chaps. 8-9 within the gospel, each unit of the gospel has a Janus-like quality; it looks both backwards and forwards. The sermon on the mount presented Jesus as "Messiah of the Word," the messianic teacher; chaps. 8-9 complement that portrait by presenting Jesus as "Messiah of the Deed," as messianic healer and wonderworker. The inclusion between 4:23-24 and 9:35 confirms this Christological diptych. Yet chaps. 8-9 also look forward to and belong with the missionary discourse in chap. 10. Book Two shows us the mission of Jesus in Galilee, which then becomes the mission of the disciples. The whole content of Book Two is well resumed at the beginning of Book Three (11:2) by the phrase "the deeds of the Christ," i.e., the messianic deeds performed by both Jesus and his disciples.

A. THE FIRST TRIO OF MIRACLE STORIES.
8:1-17.
[Mk 1:40-45; Lk 5:12-16; Lk 7:1-10; Jn 4:46b-54; Mk 1:29-34; Lk 4:38-41]

8 When he came down from the mountain, great crowds followed him; [2]and behold, a leper came to him and knelt before him, saying, "Lord, if you will, you can make me clean." [3]And he stretched out his hand and touched him, saying, "I will; be clean." And immediately his leprosy was cleansed. [4]And Jesus said to him, "See that you say nothing to any one; but go, show yourself to the priest, and offer the gift that Moses commanded, for a proof to the people."

[5]As he entered Capernaum, a centurion came forward to him, beseeching him [6]and saying, "Lord, my servant is lying paralyzed at home, in terrible distress." [7]And he said to him, "I will come and heal him." [8]But the centurion answered him, "Lord, I am not worthy to have you come under my roof; but only say the word, and my servant will be healed. [9]For I am a man under authority, with soldiers under me; and I say to one, 'Go,' and he goes, and to another, 'Come,' and he comes, and to my slave, 'Do this,' and he does it." [10]When Jesus heard him, he marveled, and said to those who followed him, "Truly, I say to you, not even in Israel have I found such faith. [11]I tell you, many will come from east and west and sit at table with Abraham, Isaac, and Jacob in the kingdom of heaven, [12]while the sons of the kingdom will be thrown into the outer darkness; there men will weep and gnash their teeth." [13]And to the centurion Jesus said, "Go; be

it done for you as you have believed." And the servant was healed at that very moment.

14And when Jesus entered Peter's house, he saw his mother-in-law lying sick with a fever; 15he touched her hand, and the fever left her, and she rose and served him. 16That evening they brought to him many who were possessed with demons; and he cast out the spirits with a word, and healed all who were sick. 17This was to fulfil what was spoken by the prophet Isaiah, "He took our infirmities and bore our diseases."

The first three miracle stories group three types of people who were excluded from or enjoyed diminished rights within the Israelite community: a leper, a Gentile soldier, and a woman.

A leper had to live alone, separated from any inhabited area (Lev 13:45-46); in the ancient world, many various skin diseases qualified as "leprosy." The story opens with Jesus moving from the mount of the sermon back to Capernaum. The crowds which follow Jesus throughout the gospel are not totally committed; yet they *follow* because they have been impressed by Jesus' words (7:28-29) and so are possible candidates for discipleship. They are vacillating, and so their following is ambiguous; more than physical motion yet less than discipleship. The approach of the leper—which contravenes the Law—is told in stereo-typed phrases: "behold," "came to," and "knelt before" [literally, "worshiped"] are favorite Matthean words. So also is the petitioner's address of "Lord," added to Mk; it is the title used by believers, as opposed to "teacher" or "Rabbi." The believer's faith and petition are expressed in a simple declaration: the cleansing of the leper depends only and totally on a simple act of will on Jesus' part. Mt omits Mk's reference to Jesus' feeling of mercy; in keeping with his portrait of the majestic Christ, Mt generally avoids references to Jesus' emotions. With great terseness the healing action and word of Jesus are narrated, using the leper's own formula. Note the use of "cleanse" as a key word: in the petition, the command, and the narration of the healing. Although Mt does not take over Mk's "messianic secret," he does keep the command of silence here, perhaps to stress the urgency of the command to go to the priest. The Markan command of silence stands in tension with the Matthean crowds following Jesus. Jesus, who fulfills the Law and prophets, demands that Lev 14:2-9 be observed. But the observance of the Law by Jesus does not guarantee his acceptance; the phrase "for a proof to the people" could also be translated: "as a witness against them." Mt omits Mk's statement that the leper spread the story: Jesus' command is not to be disobeyed.

Mt also reworks the story of the centurion, from Q, to emphasize the verbal interchange between petitioner and Lord and to show the power of faith, even in the case of a Gentile. The same story is also reflected in Jn 4:46-54— though there is no common literary source between Mt and Jn, only common oral tradition. The Q-story had already placed the event in Capernaum, so Mt uses it to complete Jesus' journey home. Being a strategic point, Capernaum had a military garrison made up of Syrian Gentiles; the centurion, a simple soldier who had made his way up through the ranks in the army of Herod Antipas, was probably Syrian too. His title indicates he was in charge of a hundred men, though in practice the number could be less. Again we have the address, "Lord," introducing a petition about his "servant" (*pais*), who is suffering from some sort of painful paralysis. Jesus' response is probably declarative, as the RSV reads. Some, however, stressing the many parallels this story has with that of the Canaanite woman in 15:21-28, understand v.7 as an ironic question and an indignant refusal. But the real parallel is with the preceding story, where Jesus immediately accedes to the plea of the outcast leper and even breaks the Law by touching him. Only because Jesus shows himself so ready to come does the centurion's response in v.8 receive its full weight. It is not a desperate attempt to bargain for a smaller favor after the greater has been refused. It is an astonishing refusal of so great a favor, a refusal based on total faith in the power of the mere word of Jesus. The centurion is a man used to both receiving and giving orders; he knows what a single word from a competent authority can make a slave do. A single word from Jesus can make this servant well.

Such humble faith causes Jesus to "marvel," the only time Mt uses this verb of Jesus. Jesus contrasts this belief with its lack in Israel. Actually this anticipates the later sections of the gospel from chap. 11 onward; so far Mt has not broached the theme of Israel's unbelief. Looking ahead to the tragedy to come, Mt inserts at this point a separate Q-saying (Lk 13:28-29). The Gentile is not only granted his wish; all Gentiles, symbolized by him, are granted the promise of entrance into the kingdom of heaven and a place at the eschatological banquet with the patriarchs of Israel. The only condition is faith in Jesus (cf. Mt 28:16-20). This universal vision (drawn from Is 25:6-8; 49:12; Mal 1:11) turns into a dire warning for the Israelites, the "sons of the kingdom," those who naturally belonged to it because of the covenants with the patriarchs. At this point, Jesus goes beyond the worst warnings of Jewish apocalyptic: the Israelites will be cast out of the kingdom, and in their futile rage they will have to watch the joy of the lighted festival hall from the "darkness outside." The references to darkness outside and to weeping and gnashing are tags Mt often uses to describe damnation (13:42,50; 22:13; 24:51; 25:30). Mt intends this warning to be heard by the members of his church, who now enjoy the status of "sons of the kingdom" (13:38), and who therefore are liable to imitate Israel's fall. The only true sons of the kingdom are those who believe; that is why the centurion receives his request forthwith. The conclusion in v.13 betrays Mt's hand (cf. 9:22; 15:28; 17:18).

Since Jesus has come home to Capernaum, Mt has an opportunity to insert a pericope from Mk 1 which he had omitted from the initial activity of Jesus. The cure of Peter's mother-in-law and the cures at evening are the only parts of Mk's initial day in Capernaum that Mt retains. But Mt has created a different "day," stretching from the beginning of the sermon (5:1) to the evening cures (8:16). The evening is no longer that of the sabbath (Mk 1:21), which explained the appearance of the sick after sundown in Mk. In Mt, Jesus does not arrive at the house until close to sundown; only then do the sick have a chance. As Mt omits the previous Markan scene in the synagogue, so in the healing of the mother-in-law, he omits all names except Peter's (Simon in Mk). Indeed, the cure is told with the fewest words possible. Only here, among Mt's miracle stories, does Jesus seize the initiative; there is no request as in Mk and no reference to faith, or even to the word of Jesus. This emphasis on Jesus' initiative fits in well with the citation of Is 53:4 in 8:17 ("*he* took . . . *he* bore"). The woman is raised up (an allusion to the theme of the Christian's being raised up from the sickness of sin by Jesus?) and in thanksgiving serves Jesus (*him*, not *them*, as in Mk). Again, the healer and the healed are profiled.

When the possessed and the sick (note the distinction) are brought in the evening, the omnipotence of Jesus is emphasized. While Mk says *all* the sick are brought to Jesus and he cures *many*, Mt reverses the statement: *many* possessed are brought and Jesus cures *all* the sick. And, pointedly, Jesus cures "with a word" (cf. 8:8). Instead of the typical Markan prohibition against speaking, Mt concludes the pericope, and the whole Matthean "day," with a formula quotation. Citing Is 53:4 according to the Hebrew Masoretic text rather than the Greek Septuagint, Mt shifts the meaning from vicarious, sacrificial death (he took our infirmities on himself and suffered them) to miraculous cure (he took away our infirmities). Mt certainly knows the concept of Jesus as the suffering servant who redeems us by his death (20:28; 26:28). But he extends the image of servanthood to include the powerful acts as well as the humble death of the servant. By his life and his death, Jesus the servant makes *us* whole (note *our* infirmities, *our* diseases). The healings thus become part of Jesus' saving of his people (1:21), part of the eschatological event prophesied in the OT. It is not that the miracles legitimate Jesus, as though he were some Hellenistic miracle-worker in need of legitimation. Rather, the miracles themselves need legtitimation or explanation, and this is what the OT supplies.

B. THE FIRST BUFFER: THE COST OF DISCIPLESHIP. 8:18-22. [Lk 9:57-62]

> [18]Now when Jesus saw great crowds around him, he gave orders to go over to the other side. [19]And a scribe came up and said to him, "Teacher, I will follow you wherever you go." [20]And Jesus said to him, "Foxes have holes, and birds of the air have nests; but the Son of man has nowhere to lay his head." [21]Another of the disciples said to him, "Lord, let me first go and bury my father." [22]But Jesus said to him, "Follow me, and leave the dead to bury their own dead."

This "buffer" pericope, from Q, separates the first and second trio of miracles and clearly looks forward to the second trio. Mt again creates a geographical unity by having Jesus leave Capernaum, cross the lake, and then recross it to return to Capernaum, where the last of the miracles of the second trio takes place. The buffer is closely attached to the stilling of the storm by the key words "follow" (vv. 19, 22, 23) and "go [over]" (vv. 18 and 19). The buffer is connected with the first trio more by contrast: to the radical grace of the miracles is counterposed the radical demand of discipleship; it is a demand spoken by the all-powerful healer, who is nevertheless a homeless wanderer.

In v.18, the reason for crossing the lake is probably to avoid the crowd's excessive enthusiasm, based on miracles; Jesus commands as the Lord of the disciples (v.25). The first of the two candidates for discipleship is said to be a scribe and addresses Jesus as "teacher," in Matthew an address used only by unbelievers who cannot see more deeply. He thinks of following in terms of local motion. Jesus replies that true discipleship is a matter of complete commitment that shatters one's former life, a matter of sharing the Son of Man's homelessness and wandering ministry. "Son of Man," which occurs twenty-nine times in Mt, appears here for the first time. In Mt, it has three meanings: (1) the powerful yet humble servant of the earthly ministry (seven times); (2) the suffering servant who dies and rises (nine times); (3) the key witness or judge who comes on the last day (thirteen times). The use here is obviously the first, though the dark note of having no place to rest, and therefore perhaps receiving no true welcome, may hint at the second meaning of Son of Man and the consequent terrible cost of discipleship. Mt may be implying that the cost is too much for the Jewish scribe, who is being contrasted unfavorably with the second candidate. But, since the latter is designated as "another of the disciples," it may be that the scribe does measure up to the challenge and becomes a disciple. If that is the case, he would be taking his first step toward discipleship, while the second candidate is already a disciple (he says "Lord") and is being called to renew and deepen his commitment in the face of competing demands. Piety towards dead parents was a duty highly esteemed by Jews, but Jesus affirms that his call into the new world of discipleship admits of no half measures or hesitations; the disciple must leave his old, dead world behind, including his family ties (contrast 1 Kgs 19:20).

C. THE SECOND TRIO OF MIRACLES.
8:23-9:8.
[Mk 4:35-41; 5:1-20; 2:1-12; Lk 8:22-25,26-39; 5:17-26]

23And when he got into the boat, his disciples followed him. 24And behold, there arose a great storm on the sea, so that the boat was being swamped by the waves; but he was asleep. 25And they went and woke him, saying, "Save, Lord; we are perishing." 26And he said to them, "Why are you afraid, O men of little faith?" Then he rose and rebuked the winds and the sea; and there was a great calm. 27And the men marveled, saying, "What sort of man is this, that even winds and sea obey him?"

28And when he came to the other side, to the country of the Gadarenes, two demoniacs met him, coming out of the tombs, so fierce that no one could pass that way. 29And behold, they cried out, "What have you to do with us, O Son of God? Have you come here to torment us before the time?" 30Now a herd of many swine was feeding at some distance from them. 31And the demons begged him, "If you cast us out, send us away into the herd of swine." 32And he said to them, "Go." So they came out and went into the swine; and behold, the whole herd rushed down the steep bank into the sea, and perished in the waters. 33The herdsmen fled, and going into the city they told everything, and what had happened to the demoniacs. 34And behold, all the city came out to meet Jesus; and when they saw him, they begged him to leave their neighborhood.

9 And getting into a boat he crossed over and came to his own city. 2And behold, they brought to him a paralytic, lying on his bed; and when Jesus saw their faith he said to the paralytic, "Take heart, my son; your sins are forgiven." 3And behold, some of the scribes said to themselves, "This man is blaspheming." 4But Jesus, knowing their thoughts, said, "Why do you think evil in your hearts? 5For which is easier, to say, 'Your sins are forgiven,' or to say, 'Rise and walk'? 6But that you may know

that the Son of man has authority on earth to forgive sins"—he then said to the paralytic—"Rise, take up your bed and go home." [7]And he rose and went home. [8]When the crowds saw it, they were afraid, and they glorified God, who had given such authority to men.

While the stilling of the storm does not cease to be a miracle story, Mt drops many concrete details and edits Mk to give the later church a lesson in the cost of discipleship. Contrary to Mk, Mt has Jesus take the initiative in getting into the boat; *his* disciples follow *him*, since following Jesus is the essence of discipleship. The ship may symbolize the church, which, despite the presence of Jesus, is a place of danger in this present age. Instead of a great windstorm, as in Mk, Mt has the ship and the sea shaken by a great earthquake (not the "great storm" of the RSV). The earthquake is a favorite symbol of apocalyptic for the shaking of the foundation of the old world as God brings in his kingdom, and Mt will insert earthquakes at both the death and the resurrection of Jesus to show that they constitute the turning of the ages. Here the idea is that the "messianic woes" of the end-time assail the church and threaten to overwhelm it.

The disciples reverently come to Jesus and beg him, as the majestic Lord of the church, to save them. The reader should contrast the rough complaint in Mk: "Teacher, are we to perish for all you care?" Mk then has Jesus perform the miracle of calming the sea; only after that does Jesus rebuke the disciples for having no faith. Mt reverses the agenda. Jesus, remaining where he lies, first rebukes the disciples for being men of little faith. While the disciples in Mk do not understand Jesus and do not have real faith, the Matthean disciples do understand and believe. But in times of crisis they panic and act as though they did not believe: this is the littleness of their faith. Only after this rebuke does Jesus arise and calm the winds and sea. Mt broadens out his conclusion to apply to the later church. "The men," i.e., all who hear this story and who have experienced similar acts of salvation, are called to marvel and ask themselves: "What sort of man [or better: how great a man] is this?" Mt writes his gospel to give an adequate answer.

Mt severely abbreviates Mk's story of the Gerasene demoniac. At the same time he speaks of *two* demoniacs (to make up for the omission of the possessed man in Mk 1:21-28?) and places them near the southeast shore at Gadara, which is closer to the lake than Gerasa. Mt concentrates totally on the person of Jesus; the demoniacs are so marginal that they disappear from the story as soon as the devils come out of them. The demoniacs have lived in tombs, the abode of unclean spirits. Since they cannot be controlled or bound, they are a permanent menace to travelers. Since they are supernatural beings, they, like God the Father and the devil, recognize Jesus as the Son of God. "What have you to do with us" expresses the total dissociation between themselves and Jesus, and may be an attempt to dismiss him. They know he will condemn them to endless torment in the abyss at the last judgment, but they protest that it is not fair for him to do this before that set "time" has come. Since they see Jesus is determined to cast them out of the men, they beg to be allowed to stay in this pagan region by entering into a herd of swine (the unclean swine indicating that the local population is Gentile). Without any exorcism-terminology, Jesus permits the transference with a single all-powerful word. The herd *rushes* (singular noun and verb) into the sea and *they* die (the plural perhaps indicating that the devils likewise perish). The victory of Jesus over evil is complete; he *has* destroyed the demonic powers "before the time" set by Jewish apocalyptic. With the coming of Jesus the powers of the kingdom are already at work. Even though she is "caught between the times," the church need fear no demonic power if she holds fast to the Son of God. The herdsmen testify to the reality of the event, which fills the pagans with superstitious fear. The conqueror of

demons might be a greater demon still (cf. the mistake of
the Pharisees in 9:34); so they beg the dangerous stranger
to leave. This fits Mt's outline of salvation history: while
Jesus' passing contacts with a few Gentiles point ahead to
the post-Easter mission (28:19), Jesus himself undertakes
no mission to the Gentiles during his earthly ministry.

Back in Capernaum, Jesus gives a paralytic both the
physical gift of healed limbs and the spiritual gift of a
healed, forgiven soul. The first gift (a miracle story) and
the second gift (tied to a dispute story) were already woven
together by Mk. Typically, Mt concentrates on the dispute
over Jesus' authority, with the physical cure as a subordinate
theme. Since Mt omits Mk's colorful story of how four
bearers of the bed lowered the paralytic through the roof,
Mt's statement about Jesus seeing "their" faith becomes
obscure. Jesus peers into the paralytic's soul and sees the
need for spiritual healing, and that is what he addresses first.
With an encouraging word that reminds us of Yahweh's
"Fear not!" in the OT, Jesus forgives the sins which, according to Jewish thought at the time, had caused or at
least were manifested in the illness. The scribes present
in Jesus' retinue see this claim to forgive sins as blasphemy—
no doubt for the reason given by Mk and omitted by Mt:
only God can forgive sins. We hear the first rumblings
of the opposition of official Judaism which will bring
Jesus to the cross. At his trial the high priest will repeat
the charge of blasphemy (26:65).

The all-powerful Lord sees the evil in the hearts of the
scribes as easily as he saw it in the heart of the paralytic.
In a sort of rabbinic debate, he counters their implicit question with another, on the relative difficulty of *saying* two
things: "your sins are forgiven," or "rise." While forgiving
sins might, from a metaphysical point of view, be the more
difficult deed (reserved to God alone), when it comes to
saying the words, forgiving sins is obviously easier. There
is no empirical way to check the inner change that is promised, while a promise of healing can be easily verified by

observation. To demonstrate the invisible wonder by a visible one, Jesus cures the paralytic. He does so as Son of Man, in the first sense of the title (the powerful yet humble servant of the public ministry—yet the hostility of the Pharisees may also hint at the second meaning, the servant put to death; cf. above, 8:20). The crowds provide the closing chorus of praise, in which Mt modifies Mk's general cry of amazement. In Mt, God is praised for having given such authority (to heal and forgive) to *men*, i.e., to the members of the later church (cf. 8:27). They are commissioned by their Lord to heal (10:8) and forgive sins (16:19; 18:18). Mt again brings together the Lord and his disciples, Christology and ecclesiology.

D. THE SECOND BUFFER:
THE JOY OF DISCIPLESHIP.
9:9-17.
[Mk 2:13-22; Lk 5:27-39]

⁹As Jesus passed on from there, he saw a man called Matthew sitting at the tax office; and he said to him, "Follow me." And he rose and followed him.

¹⁰And as he sat at table in the house, behold, many tax collectors and sinners came and sat down with Jesus and his disciples. ¹¹And when the Pharisees saw this, they said to his disciples, "Why does your teacher eat with tax collectors and sinners?" ¹²But when he heard it, he said, "Those who are well have no need of a physician, but those who are sick. ¹³Go and learn what this means, 'I desire mercy, and not sacrifice.' For I came not to call the righteous, but sinners."

¹⁴Then the disciples of John came to him, saying, "Why do we and the Pharisees fast, but your disciples do not fast?" ¹⁵And Jesus said to them, "Can the wedding guests mourn as long as the bridegroom is with them? The days will come, when the bridegroom is taken away from them, and then they will fast. ¹⁶And no one puts a

piece of unshrunk cloth on an old garment, for the patch tears away from the garment, and a worse tear is made. [17]Neither is new wine put into old wineskins; if it is, the skins burst, and the wine is spilled, and the skins are destroyed; but new wine is put into fresh wineskins, and so both are preserved."

The second buffer looks back to the last miracle in the second trio. After the forgiveness of sins is proclaimed to the paralytic, various sayings of Jesus emphasize the joy of mercy and forgiveness, the joy of this new age of salvation. The whole scene is fittingly set at a meal, one might guess a party. Mt has carefully lined up the various gloomy opponents of Jesus' joy: the scribes, who raise doctrinal objections (9:3); the Pharisees, who object to Jesus' practical behavior and companions (9:11); and the disciples of John, who object to Jesus' lack of asceticism (9:14).

Perhaps the healing of the paralytic is thought of as occurring while Jesus is still on his way to "his city." That would explain his passing a tax office. The call of a tax collector, despised both for his collaboration with the Romans and for his unjust exactions, is meant to be a model for Jesus' gratuitous call of those ostensibly unworthy of discipleship. It is radical grace enfleshed in the radical demand to follow, a demand which is immediately obeyed. The fact that we have here a general paradigm of discipleship may have encouraged our evangelist to change the tax collector's name from "Levi" (so Mk and Lk) to "Matthew," the name of an apostle. A further theological reason might be that our gospel tends to identify "disciples" in general with the twelve disciples in particular. Since Levi does not appear in any list of the twelve despite the fact that he receives a separate call, our evangelist prefers to substitute for "Levi" the name of one of the twelve disciples. Our evangelist picks Matthew, and then correspondingly notes in his list of the twelve that Matthew was a tax collector (a statement missing in Mk and Lk-Acts). It may be that our evangelist was moved to choose Matthew because that apostle was the source of special traditions in our evangelist's church. At any rate, there was no historical person who was named both Levi and Matthew; Jews understandably did not bear two first names that were both Hebrew ("Matthew" being a shortened form of Mattatiyah, "gift of Yahweh"). Since the present gospel was written in good Greek ca. A.D. 90, probably in Syrian Antioch, and since it would be strange for Matthew to depend on Mark for the story of his own call, it is highly unlikely that Matthew the apostle wrote "the gospel according to Matthew."

Since Jesus has shown special mercy to both sinners (the paralytic) and tax collectors (Matthew), both classes descend upon the house (Matthew's? Peter's? Jesus'?) to seek that table fellowship which is a means to and a foretaste of the eternal banquet (cf. 8:11-12). The Pharisees, who avoided table fellowship with such unclean types, ask the disciples, rather than Jesus directly, why "*your* teacher" (not *ours*!) risks living in a perpetual state of ritual uncleanness by sharing meals with these extortionists and non-observant Jews (the wide meaning of "sinners"). Jesus takes the initiative and answers the objection in three parts. (1) He quotes a proverb that it is the sick who need a doctor; the people despised by the spiritual elite are the spiritually sick, and Jesus is the spiritual as well as physical healer. (2) Mt then inserts into the Markan text a citation from Hosea 6:6, a verse he also inserts at 12:7. Using the rabbinic exhortation to appropriate a particular lesson from Scripture ("go and learn"), Jesus exalts mercy over sacrifice. The Hosea text was also used by rabbis after the destruction of Jerusalem to show that works of mercy had an atoning power, and so could substitute for the sacrifices of the temple. While the original sense of Hos 6:6 was comparative ("I desire mercy *more than* sacrifice"), Mt probably understands the verse as a complete rejection of temple sacrifices. Mercy, not sacrifice, is God's will. And, if mercy replaces the chief act of cult, how much more does it take precedence over Pharisaic rules of purity! (3) Mercy, then, determines the nature of Jesus' messianic mission ("I have come"). He comes to invite sinners, those who think they are excluded from the banquet of mercy. The "righteous" (perhaps with a note of sarcasm) surely do not need a special invitation, since they know the Scriptures so well. There is an unspoken warning here: if the "righteous" oppose Jesus' mission of mercy, they are opposing God's will, and may find themselves shut out from the banquet, having lost the invitation they thought they had.

In v.14, Mt edits Mk to have the disciples of John—and them alone—come to Jesus at the meal and ask him directly why they and the Pharisees fast but his disciples do not. Thus John's disciples are classed with the very group the Baptist himself opposed (3:7). Jesus replies that fasting is a sign of mourning. Now that he, the bridegroom, has come to claim his bride Israel, his disciples (the wedding guests) must join in the joy of the feast, symbolized by this meal. Fasting and mourning would be inappropriate for the visible presence of Jesus during the public ministry. Yet Mt knows that his own church fasts in this "in between time" in which the church, the true bride of Christ, is bereft of her bridegroom's visible presence and waits eagerly for the parousia. Fasting in this already/not-yet period reminds the church not to fall into the illusion of overrealized eschatology; "the end is not yet."

Two parables are added to stress that the new economy of salvation demands new ways, not just a patch-work adaptation to the old, and certainly not confusion with the old. A tailor who wishes to mend an old, torn garment does not use a patch of new, raw cloth; the new cloth would only cause a worse tear. The new, vibrant strength of the dispensation Christ brings cannot simply paper over the gaps in the old dispensation. Likewise, to pour new wine into old wine skins would cause the loss of both wine and skins, because the difference between new and old had not been respected. The effervescent good news of Christ demands new forms, new vehicles. The disciples of John, while joining Jesus in preaching repentance, do not recognize the radical newness, the dawning salvation, which Jesus brings. On the other hand, Mt the scribe who wants to preserve both new and old (13:52) in their proper place, who seeks to hold on to the older Jewish-Christian traditions of his church by placing them in proper perspective, exhorts his church not to lose its sense of balance. He adds to Mk's text a pointed warning against extremists of any stripe: both new and old should be preserved.

E. THE THIRD TRIO OF MIRACLES.
9:18-34.
[Mk 5:21-43; 10:46-52; 3:22; Lk 8:40-56; 18:35-43; 11:14-15]

¹⁸While he was thus speaking to them, behold, a ruler came in and knelt before him, saying, "My daughter has just died; but come and lay your hand on her, and she will live." ¹⁹And Jesus rose and followed him, with his disciples. ²⁰And behold, a woman who had suffered from a hemorrhage for twelve years came up behind him and touched the fringe of his garment; ²¹for she said to herself, "If I only touch his garment, I shall be made well." ²²Jesus turned, and seeing her he said, "Take heart, daughter; your faith has made you well." And instantly the woman was made well. ²³And when Jesus came to the ruler's house, and saw the flute players, and the crowd making a tumult, ²⁴he said, "Depart; for the girl is not dead but sleeping." And they laughed at him. ²⁵But when the crowd had been put outside, he went in and took her by the hand, and the girl arose. ²⁶And the report of this went through all that district.

²⁷And as Jesus passed on from there, two blind men followed him, crying aloud, "Have mercy on us, Son of David." ²⁸When he entered the house, the blind men came to him; and Jesus said to them, "Do you believe that

I am able to do this?" They said to him, "Yes, Lord."
²⁹Then he touched their eyes, saying, "According to your
faith be it done to you." ³⁰And their eyes opened. And
Jesus sternly charged them, "See that no one knows it."
³¹But they went away and spread his fame through all
that district.

³²As they were going away, behold, a dumb demoniac
was brought to him. ³³And when the demon had been
cast out, the dumb man spoke; and the crowds marveled,
saying, "Never was anything like this seen in Israel."
³⁴But the Pharisees said, "He casts out demons by the
prince of demons."

The life-giving newness Jesus brings is dramatized in
the raising of the ruler's daughter. Mt abbreviates Mk by
almost two-thirds to emphasize the word of faith meeting
the word of healing. While Jesus is still speaking of the new
wine, a Jewish ruler, a representative of the old, reverently
approaches and does him homage (typical Matthean
vocabulary). The ruler does not ask for the healing of a sick
daughter, as in Mk; the daughter is already dead. The ruler
dares to ask for a resuscitation, so great is his faith. Instead
of a great crowd following and pressing on Jesus, as in Mk,
his disciples *follow* him.

Mt omits Mk's colorful details about the woman's
illness. The important point is the daring of this woman,
whose flow of blood makes her perpetually unclean, who is
therefore cut off from normal participation in Jewish
worship. Nevertheless, she seeks to touch the tassels (better
than RSV's "fringe") of Jesus' cloak—the tassels being a
mark of a pious Jew (Num 15:37-39). She, like Mk, thinks
in terms of a quasi-magical cure from mere physical contact.
But it is personal encounter with Jesus and his word that
heals. Mt omits Mk's primitive idea of an instant cure by
a kind of "electric current" flowing from Jesus, as well as
the not very reverent portrait of Jesus looking around to
find the person who touched him, while his disciples rebuke

him. Instead, Jesus knows the woman and the problem instantly and declares that her faith is the source of the cure. The *word* of Jesus heals the woman at that moment. The Greek word for "made well" in vv.21 and 22 is *sǭzō*, literally, "to save." The church would see in the healing a symbol of the salvation of those spiritually unclean through the word of Jesus.

Mt naturally omits Mk's messenger announcing the daughter's death. He also omits the selection of Peter, James, and John as the inner group of disciples who witness the raising of the daugher. This idea of a few chosen witnesses belongs with Mk's messianic secret, which Mt usually drops. Mt adds the touch of the flute players to the crowd of professional mourners. Even a poor Jew would hire a few mourners for a funeral; the ruler is apparently quite rich. From this point of the story onward, the only direct statement of Jesus is the command that all of man's funeral trappings should depart; for what is death vis-à-vis mere men is only sleep vis-à-vis the word of Jesus. After the crowd is put out (Mt softens Mk's statement that Jesus threw them out), the miracle is narrated in the fewest words possible; Mt is not interested in the miraculous for its own sake. The Aramaic words in Mk are dropped, as they usually are by the supposedly Jewish Mt. Mt also omits Mk's awkwardly placed details of the girl's age and her walking about. The messianic-secret motif (amazement of the spectators, the—in this case—irrational command of silence) is also omitted. Instead, the report spreads throughout Galilee ("all that district," perhaps indicating that Mt writes from outside Palestine). In Mt, revelation goes public.

Mt needs two more miracles to round out his final trio. More specifically, he needs the healing of some blind and deaf persons, if Jesus' report in 11:5 is to reflect the foregoing narrative accurately and if the prophecy of Is 35:4-6 is to be fulfilled. Hence, in these last two miracles, Mt creates shadowy twins or "doublets" of more substantial miracle stories in Mk, stories Mt will give in fuller form later. Mt's story of the two blind men is a weak reflection of Bartimaeus' healing in Mk 10:46-52. The *two* men may come from Mt's meshing of the Bartimaeus story with the healing of another blind man in Mk 8:22-26, a story Mt otherwise omits. This may explain the presence of the command of silence (Mk 8:26), a messianic-secret motif Mt usually drops. Jesus, who has emphasized the centrality of mercy in his mission (Mt 9:9-13), is asked to show mercy by two blind men. They address him as "Son of David," thus appealing to him as the Davidic Messiah-King who should hear the cries of the poor among his own people Israel (cf. Ps 72:12-13). In Mt, "Son of David" indicates not only Jesus' Jewish and Davidic ties as Messiah (1:1-17, 20; 2:1-6) but also his special desire to heal poor or despised individuals. Jesus does not interrupt his journey back to the house in Capernaum, perhaps to test the two men's faith. When he arrives home, he receives the blind men, who have persevered in following him, and he pointedly questions them about their faith. His question about his power is reminiscent of 8:2-3 (the leper); his declaration of healing, of 8:13 (the centurion). Mt obviously wishes to stress faith in the power of Jesus as *the* condition for healing. The conclusion is curiously untypical of Mt. While he often concludes with the public proclamation of a miracle, this does not usually happen in contradiction of a prohibition from Jesus (a relic of Mk's messianic secret). Likewise Markan and un-Matthean is the rough description of Jesus' emotions ("sternly charged," literally, "snorted"). Perhaps Mt allows the silence-motif and the rough language here because the blind men have addressed Jesus as Son of David, a messianic title too easily interpreted in a political and nationalist sense. But at the end of the story, Mt's tendency to have revelation go public wins out.

Despite variations, the healing of the dumb demoniac seems parallel to Lk 11:14-15 and so derives from Q. Mt has a longer version about a dumb and blind demoniac in

12:22-24. There it introduces a dispute on Jesus and Beelzebul, as does the Lukan parallel. In 9:32-34 the demoniac is described as *kōphos*. The word can mean dumb and/or deaf. Here it certainly means dumb (v.33), and in the light of 11:5 ("the deaf [*kōphoi*] hear"), it probably also means "deaf." Most significant is the two-fold reaction to the miracle. The oscillating crowds are favorably impressed; they represent those not yet disciples but disposed towards faith. In their amazement they speak of an epiphany or revelation of God's power (*ephanē*) such as has never been seen before in the history of the chosen people Israel. On the other hand, the archenemies of Jesus, the Pharisees, explain that only by the power of the prince of devils could Jesus cast out this dumb devil. This blasphemy at the end of the narrative of the Second Book is meant to be an ominous pointer ahead. It foreshadows the predictions of rejection in the missionary discourse (chap. 10), the Beelzebul controversy in chap. 12, and the growing rejection of Jesus throughout Book Three.

F. THE THIRD BUFFER:
DISCIPLESHIP LEADS TO MISSION.
9:35-38.
[Mk 6:6b,34; Lk 8:1; 10:2]

> 35And Jesus went about all the cities and villages, teaching in their synagogues and preaching the gospel of the kingdom, and healing every disease and every infirmity. 36When he saw the crowds, he had compassion for them, because they were harassed and helpless, like sheep without a shepherd. 37Then he said to his disciples, "The harvest is plentiful, but the laborers are few; 38pray therefore the Lord of the harvest to send out laborers into his harvest."

The Janus-like quality of the buffer-sections is again clear. On the one hand, v.35 looks back, forming an inclusion with 4:23 (with a touch of Mk 6:6b) and binding together everything in between as the diptych of the Messiah of the Word and of the Deed. See 4:23 for comment. On the other hand, vv.36-38 look forward to the second half of Book Two, the missionary discourse (chap. 10).

Despite Mt's tendency to avoid references to Jesus' emotions, Mt stresses the sense of compassion Jesus feels for the crowds of ordinary Jews, dejected because they lack true leaders. They look like frightened sheep who simply fall helpless and exhausted to the ground (cf. Num 27:17; 1 Kings 22:17; Zech 10:2). Mk 6:34 mentions a similar sight, which moves Jesus to teach and feed the crowd of five thousand. Here the sight moves Jesus to think of the need for a mission by his disciples. Jesus himself is the true shepherd of Israel (2:6), but he desires his disciples to act as shepherds of his people in his place and after his manner (cf. 18:10-14). Even in this depressing scene Jesus intuits the possibility for a great harvest (Hos 6:11; Joel 3:13). Jesus declares that the mission of his disciples, bringing the good news to others and gathering believers into his community, is part of the eschatological event. That is why Mt will insert part of Mk's apocalyptic discourse into the missionary discourse of chap. 10. The mission not only forms part of the final drama; it also helps set it in motion. But the demands of this eschatological ingathering are great, while the laborers in the field, the missionaries bringing people into salvation, are few. Jesus produces no miracle or magic solution to solve this problem. Like the whole unfolding of the eschatological drama, this problem lies in the hands of the Father, the Lord of the harvest. All the disciples can do is beg him in prayer to send out more laborers on mission. In this vision, prayer itself becomes missionary and eschatological.

II. THE DISCOURSE OF BOOK TWO: THE MISSION, PAST AND FUTURE.
10:1 - 11:1.

BOTH MK (6:6b-13) AND Q (Lk 10:1-20) contained missionary discourses. Typically, Lk keeps Mk and Q separate by presenting two discourses, one to the Twelve in Lk 9:1-6, the other to seventy-two disciples (Lk 10:1-20). Mt just as typically meshes his sources into one large discourse, shorter than the sermon on the mount but slightly longer than the church-order discourse in chap. 18. After an introductory narrative (10:1-4), Mt presents the first part of the sermon, which concentrates on the major theme of mission (vv.5-16). He then inserts various pericopes from different sources, dealing with future opposition (vv.17-25), fearlessness in the face of opposition (vv.26-33), and the personal cost of discipleship (vv.37-39). Having inserted these various sayings, which are only loosely connected with the theme of mission, Mt repeats the pattern of the sermon on the mount: at the end of the discourse he returns to the thread of the primitive Q-discourse (vv. 40-42), with a promise of reward. This analysis is confirmed by the use of the key-word *apostellō* ("to send"). It occurs in 10:5 and 10:16, forming an inclusion for the truly missionary part of the discourse; it does not appear again until the conclusion (10:40). The strictly missionary part remains within the historical context of a limited mission to Galilee (cf. 10:5-6), while the subsequent parts widen the horizon to the future and the fate of the disciples after the resurrection (cf. vv.17-18). While the first part of the discourse focuses upon the mission *to* Israel, the second part emphasizes the rejection *by* Israel—and the Gentiles. Here Mt inserts elements of Mk's eschatological discourse, thus making the later mission of the church part of the cosmic, apocalyptic drama (cf. Mt 9:37-38). The cooption of the disciples for mission and the whole discourse reflect the basic gospel message: as goes the Master, so go his disciples. They share his mission and his fate.

A. THE TWELVE RECEIVE AUTHORITY
FOR THEIR MISSION.
10:1-4.
[Mk 6:7; 3:13-19; Lk 9:1; 6:12-16]

> **10** And he called to him his twelve disciples and gave them authority over unclean spirits, to cast them out, and to heal every disease and every infirmity. [2] The names of the twelve apostles are these: first, Simon, who is called Peter, and Andrew his brother; James the son of Zebedee, and John his brother; [3] Philip and Bartholomew; Thomas and Matthew the tax collector; James the son of Alphaeus, and Thaddaeus; [4] Simon the Cananaean, and Judas Iscariot, who betrayed him.

This short introductory narrative sets the stage for the discourse and sums up part of its content. V.1 may have originally led directly into the discourse. Since Mt, unlike Mk and Lk, has no separate story of the choice of the Twelve, he—rather awkwardly—inserts their names here (vv.2-4) and creates a second introduction to the discourse in v.5. Having commanded prayers for workers in the harvest (9:38), Jesus immediately supplies the initial answer to those prayers by summoning his twelve disciples and making them his coworkers. Deferring for the moment the mention of mission, Mt stresses the conferral of full authority to perform exorcisms and all kinds of healing (Mt adds to Mk 6:7 the mention of healing). What Jesus did in chaps. 8-9 the Twelve are now to do.

Mt has not previously mentioned the "twelve disciples"; up until now, only five have been called by name. But apparently Mt can presuppose knowledge about the Twelve in his church, which no doubt had been using Mk's gospel for some time. In v.2, Mt makes the intriguing identification of "his twelve disciples" with "the twelve apostles." In the early church of St. Paul's day (A.D. 40-60), "apostle" had a wide range of meanings. For Paul, apostle meant primarily one who had seen the risen Lord Jesus and who had received from the Lord a commission to preach the good news. Apostle could also be used in a looser sense of envoys of the churches, since all "apostle" means etymologically is "one sent." Mt reflects the usage of the church late in the first century, when a desire to legitimate the authentic tradition of the church against false teachers led to an emphasis on the original guardians of the tradition and their official successors. Lk mirrors such a development by equating the twelve disciples with the twelve apostles and by denying apostleship in the strict sense to anyone else, including Paul! Mt takes a slightly different route. He uses "apostle" only once in his gospel (10:2); elsewhere he speaks of the "Twelve" (10:5) or the "Twelve disciples" (10:1). In Mt's gospel, especially after chap. 10, there is a tendency to restrict the title "disciple" to the group of the Twelve. The Twelve, besides being the original followers of Jesus and the first leaders of the church, also acquire a double symbolic meaning. They represent all later disciples in general, and in a special way they represent the later leaders of the church.

The list of the Twelve in Mt is taken from Mk 3:13-19, with slight changes. Peter is specifically singled out as the "first" (the word in Greek is an adjective, not an adverb).

Actually, all the lists of the Twelve name Peter first; but Mt has a special interest in Peter's position, as Books Three and Four will make clear. Andrew is moved up to second place to be with his brother. Mt keeps the two-by-two order of the names, even though he drops Mk's statement that Jesus sent the apostles out two-by-two. The nickname for James and John, Boanerges ("Sons of Thunder") is also omitted (cf. Mk 3:17), in keeping with Mt's avoidance of Hebrew and Aramaic words when they are not necessary to his purpose. Matthew and Thomas exchange places, perhaps because it is less awkward to add "the tax collector" to the second name of the pair. On Matthew, see 9:9-13. Instead of Thaddaeus, some manuscripts have Lebbaeus, which is possibly the original reading. "Cananaean" probably reflects an Aramaic word for "Zealot," a member of the fiercely nationalistic Jewish group ready to resist Rome by force. The startling juxtaposition of this former Rome-hater with Matthew, a former lackey of Rome, shows that the new community of Jesus has embraced and transcended the tensions in the old community of Israel. Judas the betrayer is always mentioned last, with his terrible tag. The meaning of "Iscariot" is disputed; it may mean "from [the town of] Kerioth" in southern Judea. The number twelve symbolizes the twelve tribes of Israel (cf. 19:28); it is to gather in all Israel to the kingdom that the Twelve are now sent forth.

B. THE ESSENTIAL INSTRUCTIONS
FOR THE MISSIONARIES.
10:5-16.
[Mk 6:8-11; Lk 9:2-5; 10:3]

> [5]These twelve Jesus sent out, charging them, "Go nowhere among the Gentiles, and enter no town of the Samaritans, [6]but go rather to the lost sheep of the house of Israel. [7]And preach as you go, saying, 'The kingdom of heaven is at hand.' [8]Heal the sick, raise the dead,

cleanse lepers, cast out demons. You received without paying, give without pay. [9]Take no gold, nor silver, nor copper in your belts, [10]no bag for your journey, nor two tunics, nor sandals, nor a staff; for the laborer deserves his food. [11]And whatever town or village you enter, find out who is worthy in it, and stay with him until you depart. [12]As you enter the house, salute it. [13]And if the house is worthy, let your peace come upon it; but if it is not worthy, let your peace return to you. [14]And if any one will not receive you or listen to your words, shake off the dust from your feet as you leave that house or town. [15]Truly, I say to you, it shall be more tolerable on the day of judgment for the land of Sodom and Gomorrah than for that town.

[16]"Behold, I send you out as sheep in the midst of wolves; so be wise as serpents and innocent as doves.

Here we have the missionary discourse proper, an amalgam of Mk, Q, and M. The actual sending out occurs at v.5, so that the discourse can proceed unimpeded by further narrative and can expand its horizons to an apocalyptic future. Indeed, the discourse later becomes so general and future-oriented that neither the mission nor the return of the Twelve is narrated after the discourse (contrast Mk 6:12-13,30; Lk 9:6,10). By contrast, the first words of Mt's discourse, taken from M, are firmly anchored in the history of the earthly Jesus: the mission is strictly limited to the land and people of Israel, in fact, probably to Galilee. They are not to enter Gentile territory or any Samaritan "city" (though some suggest "city" is a mistranslation of the Aramaic word for "province"). This prohibition may very well stem from the historical Jesus, who commanded a short mission undertaken by his disciples in Galilee. In the early church, however, these words may have been used by conservative Jewish Christians to reject any formal mission to the Gentiles, perhaps to polemicize against the mission undertaken by the Hellenists and later by Paul. The conservatives would have felt that, in keeping with OT prophecy, it should be left to God to lead the Gentiles in pilgrimage to Zion on the last day. The conservative-yet-liberal Mt affirms vv.5-6 as venerable tradition of his Jewish-Christian church, yet modifies it by inserting it into a higher synthesis, namely his view of salvation history. The Twelve are sent only to the lost sheep which make up the house of Israel (a genitive of apposition; cf. Is 53:6; Ex 16:31). Jesus' prohibition stands during his public ministry; but, after the apocalyptic turning point of the death-resurrection, the exalted Son of Man, who now has all authority over the cosmos, commands the same group of disciples to undertake a *universal* mission (see the comments on 28:16-20). Thus does Mt preserve both the new and the old (cf. 9:17; 13:52).

The mission of the disciples mirrors that of Jesus in word and work. The proclamation of the kingdom is the same (4:17), though the command to repent is strangely lacking. More than Mk or Lk, Mt makes the work of the Twelve (v.8) reflect what Jesus has already been doing in chaps. 4-9. Notable by omission is the mandate to teach (contrast 4:23). Jesus still has three more discourses of teaching to give the Twelve; the mandate to teach "*all whatsoever* I commanded" can reasonably be given only at the end of the gospel (28:20), when the disciples are sent out definitively on their universal mission. All these powers are handed over by Jesus to the disciples at no price; in this they must also mirror their master and set no price for their use. Through their services they are to "acquire no gold" (better than the RSV's "take no gold") to put in their belts (the usual place for money). Mt's gold and silver coins may reflect a more affluent community than Mk's; Mk mentions only copper coins. The total radicalism of Mt's version of the discourse is also clear in the prohibition of a bag (for food and other necessities), a change of tunics (the inner garment under the cloak), sandals (slaves did not wear them), and a staff (to aid walking and for defense). The mission is urgent, limited to Galilee, and of short duration. Mk, thinking of future and more extensive journeys, allows a staff and sandals. The missionaries need only basic food and lodging, and that will be provided as their right by the ones they serve. (The RSV's "deserves" in v.10 is in Greek the adjective *axios*, "worthy"; it occurs again in v.11 and acts as a key-word for the discourse). Wherever they go they are to find out who would be a worthy host and are to remain with that person. They are not to seek out better lodgings later.

The worth of the host is no doubt to be judged by his acceptance of both the messenger (hospitality) and the message (faith); the two go together (cf. v.14). On entering the host's house, the plenipotentiary envoy of Jesus is to say: "Peace be to this house" (cf. Lk 10:5). As with the OT prophets, the word of the apostle has a dynamic force which accomplishes what it says. If the dynamic word of peace finds no fitting receiver, it will return to the speaker, who in turn will forsake the hostile house or town. The disciples are to shake off the dust from their feet to indicate total dissociation from the condemned town and to deny any responsibility for its dreadful fate. Pious Jews would knock off Gentile dust from themselves when they returned to the Holy Land. The apostles signify that the Jews who refuse the gospel are no better than pagans. Jesus, the apocalyptic seer ("Amen, I say"), assures his messengers that, at the last judgment, Sodom and Gomorrah, those infamous paradigms of wicked cities, will receive a lighter sentence than the Jewish town which rejects the gospel. Sodom and Gomorrah showed disrespect to the angels, the OT messengers of Yahweh; worse still is the disrespect shown to the apostles, the NT messengers of Christ.

Mt returns to a favorite theme: judgment is stringent for those who hear the good news and fail to act upon it. The situation is serious both for listeners and for messengers; the latter are sent by Jesus as defenseless sheep in the midst of hostile wolves. V.16a is a Q-saying which Lk places at the beginning of his second missionary discourse (10:3). Mt places it here to provide a transition to the second theme, persecution. Mt then adds from his M-traditions v.16b, urging the disciples to be as prudent and clever as serpents (cf. Gen 3:1) in dealing with enemies; they are not obliged to provoke or endure enmity unnecessarily. But their cleverness is to be only for self-protection; they are to harm no one and are thus to remain as innocent and free of malice as doves.

C. OPPOSITION TO THE DISCIPLES.
10:17-25.
[Mk 13:9-13; Lk 21:12-17; 12:11-12; 6:40]

> [17]Beware of men; for they will deliver you up to councils, and flog you in their synagogues, [18]and you will be dragged before governors and kings for my sake, to bear testimony before them and the Gentiles. [19]When they deliver you up, do not be anxious how you are to speak or what you are to say; for what you are to say will be given to you in that hour; [20]for it is not you who speak, but the Spirit of your Father speaking through you. [21]Brother will deliver up brother to death, and the father his child, and children will rise against parents and have them put to death; [22]and you will be hated by all for my name's sake. But he who endures to the end will be saved. [23]When they persecute you in one town, flee to the next; for truly, I say to you, you will not have gone through all the towns of Israel, before the Son of man comes.
>
> [24]"A disciple is not above his teacher, nor a servant above his master; [25]it is enough for the disciple to be like his teacher, and the servant like his master. If they have called the master of the house Beelzebul, how much more will they malign those of his household.

While vv.5-16 referred directly to the activity of traveling missionaries, most of the sayings on future persecution in vv.17-25 could apply to all disciples. In Mt's composition, the train of thought is: as the missionaries share the mission and authority of Jesus, so they will share his persecution and martyrdom (cf. especialy vv.24-25). Mt has inserted in this section verses from Mk's eschatological discourse (Mk 13), thus giving the future mission a cosmic scope and an apocalyptic coloration. Like Jesus, the disciples will be "delivered up" (the key verb *paradidōmi*) to councils (literally, "sanhedrins," local Jewish courts), where they will be flogged (though with the milder Jewish form of flogging, not the Roman scourging which led to crucifixion). And, like Jesus, they will then be brought before civil rulers. It is with the mention of governors and kings that the horizon widens beyond the immediate talk to the Twelve. These trials serve as a platform for witnessing to Jesus before both Jews and Gentiles. The disciples must be confident when they are put on public view, because the Holy Spirit is using them as mouthpieces. The proper words will be given them as a gift by the Spirit; they need not anxiously rehearse their defense. Their confidence befits sons of the Father who speak with the Father's Spirit (notice "the Spirit of *your* Father"). Their heavenly Father does not forsake them despite the fact that, in the terrible chaos of the last days, when all bonds of affection and loyalty are dissolved, the closest members of their own families will put them to death (cf. Micah 7:6). Hatred of disciples will become universal, a natural reason for despair. But the disciple who stands up under the pressure of the messianic woes will be saved. "To the end" can refer either to the individual's death or to the end of the world. If one connects it with v.23, the end is identical with the coming of the Son of Man to judge and reverse the false judgments and unjust persecutions of the disciples.

With a command that puts the discourse back into the framework of the Galilean mission of the Twelve, Jesus tells his disciples that they are not bound to remain in a hostile city and be martyred. The end is so soon that they will not exhaust places of refuge in Israel before Jesus comes as Son of Man. The saying in v.23 probably circulated in the early church as a word of comfort to persecuted Jewish-Christian missionaries, and was perhaps already

connected with vv.5-6. Mt, writing ca. A.D. 90, obviously
does not understand it in its original sense. Perhaps he
identifies the coming of the Son of Man with the "proleptic
parousia" in 28:16-20, when Jesus comes to his church as
Son of Man, with all authority in the cosmos, to remain with
it all days as its protector. In connection with the theme of
persecution, Mt adds in vv.24-25 two general proverbs
which remind the disciples that they as pupils and slaves
cannot expect an easier fate than that of their teacher and
master (cf. Lk 6:40; Jn 13:16). What they must aim at
instead is similarity with him. And the similarity will extend
to hostility and accusations of demonic possession (cf. 9:34;
12:24). If the name of the demonic prince Beelzebul means
"master of the dwelling (or house)," the original Aramaic
saying contained a wry pun, lost in translation.

D. THE FEARLESSNESS OF THE DISCIPLES.
10:26-33.
[Lk 12:2-9]

26"So have no fear of them; for nothing is covered that
will not be revealed, or hidden that will not be known.
27What I tell you in the dark, utter in the light; and what
you hear whispered, proclaim upon the housetops. 28And
do not fear those who kill the body but cannot kill the
soul; rather fear him who can destroy both soul and body
in hell. 29Are not two sparrows sold for a penny? And not
one of them will fall to the ground without your Father's
will. 30But even the hairs of your head are all numbered.
31Fear not, therefore; you are of more value than many
sparrows. 32So every one who acknowledges me before
men, I also will acknowledge before my Father who is in
heaven; 33but whoever denies me before men, I also will
deny before my Father who is in heaven.

Words about persecution are followed by words of exhortation to fearlessness. Mt makes his point clear by structuring these Q-statements with a threefold repetition of the OT command of Yahweh: Fear not! (vv.26,28,31). Despite imprisonments, their persecutors cannot keep the gospel hidden; revelation will out. What Jesus tells the disciples during periods of private instruction—Mt here anticipates the later Books of his gospel—must be given the greatest publicity by the disciples on mission. The consequent exposure to death must not frighten the disciples. Mere men can kill the body and no more. Fear is more properly directed to the Evil One, who destroys the whole person by eternal damnation. Some, however, take the "destroyer" to refer to God at the final judgment. (Note, by the way, how Mt adopts the Hellenistic distinction between body and soul, not present in the Lukan parallel.) But fear of final damnation is meant only to lead to complete trust in the Father, who lovingly watches over the life and death of even his smallest and least valuable creatures (sparrows being the cheapest edible birds). How much more will the Father watch over his children, wryly estimated as worth more than many sparrows! He knows and cares for the smallest details of their lives, down to the number of their hairs, something they themselves do not know or care about (cf. 6:25-34). This assurance will embolden the disciples to bear witness to the gospel before hostile tribunals. The disciples in turn will receive approving testimony from Jesus at the final tribunal. Jesus will be not only judge but also advocate for his own. The switch from "your Father" in v.29 to "my Father" in v.32 hints that it is through Jesus the Son that the disciples become sons and daughters. (Mk and Lk speak here of the "Son of Man" bearing witness on the last day; as in other places, Mt substitutes the personal pronoun for the title.) But failure to witness before the earthly tribunal will mean disgrace before the heavenly tribunal, where Jesus will disown the weak disciple as not being truly his brother and therefore not truly a son of the Father.

E. THE HIGH PRICE OF COMMITMENT.
10:34-39.
[Lk 12:51-53; 14:26-27; 17:33]

> 34"Do not think that I have come to bring peace on earth; I have not come to bring peace, but a sword. 35For I have come to set a man against his father, and a daughter against her mother, and a daughter-in-law against her mother-in-law; 36and a man's foes will be those of his own household. 37He who loves father or mother more than me is not worthy of me; and he who loves son or daughter more than me is not worthy of me; 38and he who does not take his cross and follow me is not worthy of me. 39He who finds his life will lose it, and he who loses his life for my sake will find it.

These Q-sayings return to the prospect of persecution and martydom. V.34 has the same form as 5:17; a comparison with Lk 12:51 shows Mt's creative hand at work. Jesus wards off a mistaken notion of his messianic mission. The Messiah was supposed to be a bringer of peace, and Jesus himself has declared his disciples peacemakers (5:9; 10:13). Yet, paradoxically, the challenge of Jesus occasions the strife and division within families ("the sword") which apocalyptic expectation assigned to the time preceding the Messiah, the time of the messianic woes. Such divisions proceed not from any malicious intent of Jesus, but from malicious rejection of his good news. The sad result is again depicted by citing Micah 7:6 (cf. Mt 10:21). Mt arranges the list of opposed parties to stress the division between the younger generation (answering the call of Christ?) and the older. The unity of natural families will be replaced by the unity of the family of Jesus (cf. 12:46-50).

The mention of the various relatives in the Micah citation attracts similarly worded sayings in vv.36-37. To be worthy of Jesus, one must place no one and nothing above him. Mt speaks in smoother Greek of "loving more," while Lk retains the harsh Semitic form, "hate." As Jesus forsook his home to begin his ministry, so must his disciples. And, adds Mt in a separate saying (v.38), as Jesus did not shrink before the cross, neither must his followers. The word "cross" occurs here for the first time in Mt. It was an Oriental form of torture and death, adopted by Rome for slaves and rebels, but not for Roman citizens. By holding before his disciples the most horrifying and shameful type of death, Jesus stresses that no sacrifice can be too great simply to "follow me." Jesus does not hesitate to say he is worth such a price. As goes the Master, so goes the disciple —even to martyrdom. Mt concludes this section with v.39, a proverb which expresses the paradox of loss and gain, the paradox of the cross. RSV's "life" might well be translated as "himself." A person who selfishly grasps at personal fulfillment will only see it slip through his fingers, while the person who surrenders his whole body for Christ will find his true being in Christ. It is the basic law of death-resurrection, which holds true for both master and disciple.

F. CONCLUSION:
THE REWARDS OF DISCIPLESHIP.
10:40-11:1.
[Mk 9:41,37; Lk 10:16; 9:48; Jn 13:20]

> [40]"He who receives you receives me, and he who receives me receives him who sent me. [41]He who receives a prophet because he is a prophet shall receive a prophet's reward, and he who receives a righteous man because he is a righteous man shall receive a righteous man's reward. [42]And whoever gives to one of these little ones even a cup of cold water because he is a disciple, truly, I say to you, he shall not lose his reward."
>
> [11] And when Jesus had finished instructing his twelve disciples, he went on from there to teach and preach in their cities.

Mt apparently concludes with the ending of the sermon found in Q, though parallels are also found in Mk and Jn. By carefully arranging the sayings, Mt creates the order: apostles ("you"), prophets, righteous man (an eminent member of the church) little ones (ordinary members of the church). This may reflect the structure of Mt's church. In v.40, the dynamic relation of the apostles to Jesus reflects the dynamic relation of Jesus to the Father ("the one who sent [*aposteilanta*] me," a favorite phrase in Jn). To offer hospitality and an obedient ear to the earthly envoys of Jesus is to receive *the* earthly envoy of the Father, and ultimately the Father himself. This apostle-concept is well expressed by rabbinic statements about a *shāliaḥ*, a messenger empowered to act for his sender: "The *shāliaḥ* of a man is as the man himself." Similar rewards await those hospitable to prophets and righteous men because of their dignity. The rewards due such holy men will be shared by those who shared their goods with them.

But God is concerned not only about these great men, but also with the little ones of the community, those ordinary disciples who could easily be overlooked. Originally v.42 may have referred to children, but Mt uses "little ones" to refer to disciples, especially those liable to be neglected or lost (cf 18:10). Not only full hospitality but even a glass of cold water (no mean gift in hot, water-scarce Palestine) will be duly noted and fittingly rewarded by the One who has an eye even for sparrows (cf. 25:31-46). On this encouraging note Mt ends his second discourse, concluding in 11:1 with the same formula as in 7:28. This time the sermon is summed up as a discourse "instructing his twelve disciples," which brings the reader, after these very general exhortations, back to the earthly ministry of Jesus. That ministry is again described in terms of teaching and preaching (cf. 4:23; 9:35). Healing is not mentioned because, as the Jews' hostility to Jesus increases, miracles become less frequent (cf. 13:58). But, as Book Four in particular will show, they do not cease entirely.

Book Three
Jesus Meets Opposition from Israel.
11:2 - 13:53.

The unbelief of the chosen people towards their own Messiah is the theme broached in Book Three, and it will continue until the end of the gospel (cf. 28:15). The struggle between belief and unbelief means that miracles decrease in number, the line between disciples and enemies hardens, and the narrative section is filled with questions, dispute stories, defenses, and counterattacks on the part of Jesus. This is why even the narrative section of Book Three is filled with sayings from Q. Unlike the other narrative sections in Mt, the Markan material, while present, is not prominent.

I. THE NARRATIVE OF BOOK THREE: JESUS DISPUTES WITH ISRAEL AND CONDEMNS IT.

11:2 - 12:50.

A. THE QUESTION OF THE BAPTIST AND THE ANSWER OF JESUS.
11:2-6.
[Lk 7:18-23]

> ²Now when John heard in prison about the deeds of the Christ, he sent word by his disciples ³and said to him, "Are you he who is to come, or shall we look for another?" ⁴And Jesus answered them, "Go and tell John what you hear and see: ⁵the blind receive their sight and the lame walk, lepers are cleansed and the deaf hear, and the dead are raised up, and the poor have good news preached to them. ⁶And blessed is he who takes no offense at me."

THE BAPTIST, whom Herod had put in prison (cf. 4:12; 14:1-12) hears of "the deeds of the Christ," i.e., the messianic works of preaching and healing performed by both Jesus (chaps. 5-7, 8-9) and his disciples (chap. 10). John had proclaimed the coming of a stringent judge and a fiery judgment (3:1-12). The merciful, healing mission he now hears of does not match his preconceptions. So John poses the central question: is Jesus "he who is to come"? Is Jesus the object and fulfillment of all prophecy, the Messiah?

(While the designation "he who is to come" does not appear
as a messianic title in the OT [cf. however Ps 118:26; Mal
3:1], the meaning is obvious enough.) Jesus replies not
with any theoretical argument but by pointing to all he
and his disciples have done in chaps. 5-10. Mt has carefully
arranged those chapters so that they correspond to and
verify Jesus' claim. The high point in Jesus' messianic
mission is not the series of healings (cf. Is 29:18-19; 35:5-6),
not even the raising of the dead (cf. Is 25:8), but rather the
preaching of good news to the poor (cf. Is 61:1-2). In these
messianic acts the prophecies are being fulfilled and the
time of salvation is at hand. But it is not as John had
conceived it. In a "beatitude" reminiscent of the nine
beatitudes of chap. 5, Jesus gently appeals to John not to
stumble and fall from faith (literally, "be scandalized")
because Jesus is a different type of Messiah from the one the
Baptist expected. Blessed is he who does not "look for
another" because in that case he is looking for the fulfillment
of his own dreams rather than of God's prophecies. The
alternative, faith or scandal, runs through the following
sections.

B. THE IMPORTANCE YET LIMITATIONS OF JOHN, COMPARED WITH JESUS.
11:7-19
[Lk 7:24-28; 16:16; 7:31-35]

> [7] As they went away, Jesus began to speak to the crowds
> concerning John: "What did you go out into the wilder-
> ness to behold? A reed shaken by the wind? [8] Why then
> did you go out? To see a man clothed in soft raiment?
> Behold, those who wear soft raiment are in kings' houses.
> [9] Why then did you go out? To see a prophet? Yes, I tell
> you, and more than a prophet. [10] This is he of whom it is
> written.
>
> > 'Behold, I send my messenger before thy face,
> > who shall prepare thy way before thee.'

[11]Truly, I say to you, among those born of women there has risen no one greater than John the Baptist; yet he who is least in the kingdom of heaven is greater than he. [12]From the days of John the Baptist until now the kingdom of heaven has suffered violence, and men of violence take it by force. [13]For all the prophets and the law prophesied until John; [14]and if you are willing to accept it, he is Elijah who is to come. [15]He who has ears to hear, let him hear.

[16]"But to what shall I compare this generation? It is like children sitting in the market places and calling to their playmates,

[17]'We piped to you, and you did not dance;

we wailed, and you did not mourn.'

[18]For John came neither eating nor drinking, and they say, 'He has a demon'; [19]the Son of man came eating and drinking, and they say, 'Behold, a glutton and a drunkard, a friend of tax collectors and sinners!' Yet wisdom is justified by her deeds."

After Jesus has answered John's disciples about who he (Jesus) is, he in turn asks the crowds who John is. More specifically, if Jesus is the Coming One, who is John in relation to Jesus? Jesus proceeds by rhetorical questions which one by one exclude various possibilities and leave the inquirer with only one conclusion. Large throngs were not drawn out to Jordan's banks to see a vacillating crowd-pleaser with his finger in the wind, a time-server fittingly symbolized by a reed on the banks of the Jordan. John was in prison precisely because he had the courage to denounce Herod's marriage (14:3-4). Nor did the crowds seek out some influential politician, a courtier of Herod clothed in fine linen. The Baptist is in Herod's prison, not Herod's palace; and his clothing was camel's hair and a leather belt. No, John was neither a weak nor an influential man, as this world counts influence. He was a prophet—and therefore the Spirit of prophecy, thought to have grown silent in Israel after the last canonical prophet, was speaking again.

But John was more than a mere prophet. He was a prophet allowed to see the age of fulfillment (cf. 13:17); indeed, he was part of the age he prophesied. He was the messenger of the covenant (Mal 3:1), the messenger God sent before his Messiah (cf. Ex 23:20). No mere human being ("those born of women") has ever appeared ("risen") who is greater than the Baptist. Yet—and Jesus' statements here are constantly balanced by an implied "yet"—the disciples of Jesus (and his later disciples in the church) enjoy a higher status. The kingdom has come in a new way in Jesus, and his death-resurrection will bring in that kingdom definitively. Any of Jesus' disciples, his "little ones" (cf. 10:42), could be counted least in this kingdom; and, indeed, in a spirit of servanthood, any disciple should so consider himself. Yet anyone who, by his commitment of discipleship and his close tie to Jesus, experiences this coming of the kingdom, has a privilege in salvation history beyond that even of the Baptist (who, of course, is not excluded from the final kingdom). One's status in the kingdom is not one's achievement, but a free gift from God, who assigns places as he wills (cf. 20:23).

Jesus continues the theme of the greatness yet limitations of John in v.12, a verse which could have two opposite meanings. More likely, the sense is: the violent opponents of the kingdom, the Herodians and the Pharisees, are trying to block the kingdom's coming and are trying to snatch the kingdom away from those who would receive it (cf. 23:13). But possibly, the sense is: the kingdom of God is entering the world with explosive power, and those who earnestly desire to enter it pay any price to become disciples. At any rate, John's importance is seen from the fact that his preaching of the kingdom (3:2) marked the beginning of its coming in Jesus. More than a prophet, John no longer belongs to the old age of prophecy but to the new age of the kingdom. That is why Mt often places John in parallel position to Jesus. (This is quite different from the view of Lk, who has John, with one foot in each age, acting as a link

between the two periods.) Most significant in v.13 is the
way Mt stands the canon of the OT on its head. The constant
order in Scripture and the rabbis is: the Law and the
prophets; the prophets' chief function, according to the
rabbis, was to guard and interpret the Law. Mt, instead,
subsumes Law under prophecy and has both *prophesy* up
until the age begun by John. The Law, like prophecy, finds
itself fulfilled—and, at times, transcended—in Christ (cf.
5:17-18). More than *a* prophet, John is *the* prophet who
was to prepare God's people before the coming of the
Messiah and the final judgment. He is the Elijah-figure
promised by Mal 4:5-6. The ironic "if you are willing to
accept it" is balanced by an urgent call for wisdom and
decision in v.15: listen attentively to this mysterious teaching about John and myself, and decide accordingly.

Jesus complains in vv.16-19 that, in general, his contemporaries ("this generation") have not listened and
decided wisely. The parable of the children in the market
place has been interpreted in three different ways. (1) The
rebuked generation is represented by the children who pipe
and wail; they are spoiled brats who want to set the tune
and tell everyone else how to play. John and Jesus have
refused to play by their rules and demands, which do not fit
this new day of salvation. (2) Others see "this generation"
represented by both groups of children, who in their spite
and self-will waste time and do nothing. (3) Others see
"this generation" represented by the moody, finicky children
who refused to be moved either by the piping (Jesus' joyful
style) or by the wailing (John's ascetic style). At any rate,
the point is that these contemporaries, self-willed, incon-
sistent, and never satisfied, have refused the offer of salvation both from the ascetic John and the expansive Jesus.
The asceticism of John challenged them, but the challenge
was neutralized by equating his forbidding manner with
diabolical possession. Jesus' free and easy table fellowship
with religious outcasts was an invitation to rejoice in God's
grace; but, in a sudden spirit of puritanism, the offer was

rejected by equating grace with license. Jesus the Son of Man, despite his great power on earth (9:6), is exposed to gibes, rejection, and unjust condemnation. The Son of Man is also the suffering servant.

Yet, in the face of this widespread rejection and apparent failure, God will see Jesus vindicated. Ostensibly, "wisdom" refers to God's plan for salvation; but there may also be a reference to Jesus as the embodiment of the Wisdom of God. Certainly, the *deeds* of Wisdom (11:19) which vindicate ("justifies") Wisdom are equated by Mt with the *deeds* of the Christ (11:2). Thus the first part of chap. 11 ends with an inclusion. Jesus and his disciples meet with rejection; yet their preaching and miracles prove who is in the right.

C. THE WOES UPON THE CITIES OF GALILEE.
11:20-24.
[Lk 10:12-15]

> 20 Then he began to upbraid the cities where most of his mighty works had been done, because they did not repent 21 "Woe to you, Chorazin! woe to you, Bethsaida! for if the mighty works done in you had been done in Tyre and Sidon, they would have repented long ago in sackcloth and ashes. 22 But I tell you, it shall be more tolerable on the day of judgment for Tyre and Sidon than for you. 23 And you, Capernaum, will you be exalted to heaven? You shall be brought down to Hades. For if the mighty works done in you had been done in Sodom, it would have remained until this day. 24 But I tell you that it shall be more tolerable on the day of judgment for the land of Sodom than for you."

Mt has expanded a Q-saying, adding the reference to Sodom in vv. 23b-24 to give the two woes a parallel structure. As Jesus has praised John, so now he condemns the cities who represent "this generation" (v. 16). Jesus has worked most of his "mighty works" (literally, "powers," deeds manifesting and communicating divine power) in certain privileged cities in and around Galilee. These miracles, like the proclamation they accompanied, were meant to point to the coming of the kingdom and to call people to repentance. The miracles as well as the proclamation fell on deaf ears, and so the cities' unrepentance in the face of such grace calls forth a stricter judgment than that due the unrepentant cities of the OT. Actually, Mt does not record any miracles worked in Chorazin and Bethsaida; he simply repeats early tradition, which is probably historically reliable. Chorazin was about two miles north of Capernaum, and Bethsaida was east of the Jordan on the northern shore of the Sea of Galilee. They are compared unfavorably with the Gentile cities of Tyre and Sidon, denounced by the OT for their pride; swift punishment is promised them (cf. Is 23; Ezek 26-28; Joel 3:4). Yet, if these pagan towns had seen the miracles of Christ, they would have imitated Nineveh's reaction to Jonah: they would have put on the signs of mourning and repentance, sackcloth and ashes (Jonah 3:6). Worse still is the case of Capernaum, Jesus' "own city" (9:1). Its position at the center of Jesus' ministry has given it delusions of grandeur similar to that of the king of Babylon, who is mocked in Is 14:13-15: "You said . . . 'I will ascend to heaven' . . . but you are brought down to Sheol." Mt pushes the condemnation to the extreme: Capernaum is worse than Sodom, the byword of depravity in the OT (cf. Is 1:9-10; Mt 10:15). In short: first in grace, first in judgment. On all these favored towns Jesus must cry "woe"—a word of lamentation pronounced over the dead. Like the prophets, Jesus uses the word to proclaim judgment over the spiritually dead.

D. THE REVELATION OF THE FATHER AND THE SON.
11:25-30.
[Lk 10:21-22]

> [25]At that time Jesus declared, "I thank thee, Father, Lord of heaven and earth, that thou hast hidden these

things from the wise and understanding and revealed them to babes; [26]yea, Father, for such was thy gracious will. [27]All things have been delivered to me by my Father; and no one knows the Son except the Father, and no one knows the Father except the Son and any one to whom the Son chooses to reveal him. [28]Come to me, all who labor and are heavy laden, and I will give you rest. [29]Take my yoke upon you, and learn from me; for I am gentle and lowly in heart, and you will find rest for your souls. [30]For my yoke is easy, and my burden is light."

Drawing on Q (vv.25-27) and M (vv.28-30), Mt concludes this chapter on belief and unbelief with a threefold saying: the Son's praise of the Father as Revealer (vv.25-26), the mutual knowledge of Father and Son, known by men only through revelation (v.27), and the invitation of the Son-Revealer to men (vv.28-30). The question about the identity of the Coming One, raised in v.3, receives its adequate answer here. While the darker tone of unbelief lingers in v.25, the rest of the pericope is suffused with joy that the revelation has been received. The pericope thus contrasts sharply with the denunciations in vv.16-24.

"At that time," i.e., at that critical time when Jesus finds his ministry largely rejected in Galilee, he nevertheless praises his Father, the Lord of heaven and earth (for this solemn introduction, cf. Sir 51:1: also Tob 7:18). The Father, in his mysterious plan, has hidden his saving revelation ("these things") from the "wise and understanding," i.e., proud religious experts such as the scribes and the Pharisees (cf. Is 29:14). Instead, he has granted his revelation to "babes" in the field of religion: the poor, the tax collectors, the sinners—those who lacked the knowledge or the means to obey the 613 precepts of the Law, together with all the complicated casuistry of the scribes. Belief or unbelief is tied up with the apocalyptic mystery of election or reprobation. It all ultimately depends on the Father's gracious will, which nevertheless takes into account the arrogance or openness of the ones in need of revelation.

This revelation has, both as its content and as its means of transmission, the direct and unique relationship between *the* Father and *the* Son. This is the summation of all the mysteries ("all things") given to the Son by the Father, and given by the Son to those whom he chooses. (Notice, the themes touched upon here will return in 28:16-20, though with a difference. There the Father will hand over to the risen Son of Man cosmic power; here the Father has handed over to the Son all apocalyptic mysteries, to be revealed even during the earthly ministry.) The exalted Christology contained in v.27 is reminiscent of the fourth gospel; yet it is equally at home in Mt. Mt himself expounds both a high Christology centered on the title "Son" and the importance of the Father's revelatory action in 16:16-17. One sees in 11:27 the central conception about the Father and the Son from which all of Mt's further statements about "Son of God" and "Son of Man" proceed. There is a mutual knowledge between Father and Son which puts them on a level of equality (cf. 28:19). It therefore belongs to the very nature of Jesus to possess a transcendent, divine sonship, which infinitely exceeds that adoptive sonship he grants as a grace to his disciples (cf. the comments on the Our Father).

It is precisely to a share in his relationship with the Father that Jesus invites his disciples in vv.28-30. Jesus speaks here in the stately, hieratic tones of personified Wisdom (Prov 8-9) and of the wisdom-teacher (Sir 51:23-27). Again we notice the meshing of the apocalyptic Son (of Man) and the figure of divine Wisdom (cf. 11:19). The Son's call is directed to all those who find the Pharisaic Law an insufferable burden. Jesus promises rest for these religious outcasts, the "people of the land" (*'am-hā'āretz*) who were despised by the Pharisees for not keeping the Law. The "rest" Jesus promises summons up the image of the eschatological rest in the days of the Messiah, of which the sabbath rest was a symbol and a foretaste. Paradoxically, Jesus' "rest" is also a kind of "yoke," a symbol used by the rabbis for the Mosaic Law. But there is a great difference. Central to the yoke or law of Jesus is Jesus himself. Since he embodies all he teaches and commands, the pupil must study him, his meekness towards men (cf. 9:5; 21:5), his lowly, obedient heart given to God. Thus, the spiritual rest Jesus gives (cf. Jer 6:16) comes not from practicing 613 commandments, but from assimilating and living Jesus' attitudes, indeed, his very person. In Jesus the Wisdom of God, the teacher and the subject taught are one and the same. Adherence to his person is the sum-total of the law, a yoke that proves most light to the true disciple.

E. THE FIRST SABBATH DISPUTE: PLUCKING GRAIN.
12:1-8.
[Mk 2:23-28; Lk 6:1-5]

12 At that time Jesus went through the grainfields on the sabbath; his disciples were hungry, and they began to pluck heads of grain and to eat. [2]But when the Pharisees saw it, they said to him, "Look, your disciples are doing what is not lawful to do on the sabbath." [3]He said to them, "Have you not read what David did, when he was hungry, and those who were with him: [4]how he entered the house of God and ate the bread of the Presence, which it was not lawful for him to eat nor for those who were with him, but only for the priests? [5]Or have you not read in the law how on the sabbath the priests in the temple profane the sabbath, and are guiltless? [6]I tell you, something greater than the temple is here. [7]And if you had known what this means, 'I desire mercy, and not sacrifice,' you would not have condemned the guiltless. [8]For the Son of man is lord of the sabbath."

In chap. 12, Mt develops the theme of the opposition mounted by Jesus' enemies. Mt follows the order of Mk 2-3, but inserts Q and M material as well. In 11:25-30 Jesus presented himself as the great wisdom-teacher who gives his pupil eschatological rest. It is Jesus' teaching about the sabbath-rest which forms the first dispute story in chap. 12. The story begins "at this time" of mounting opposition. Mt adds to Mk the mention of the disciples' hunger, thus making them clearly parallel to the case of David and all the more excusable. Both reaping and preparing food were among the thirty-nine works forbidden on the sabbath, and so the Pharisees object.

Jesus draws three counter-arguments from Scripture. (1) A "haggadic" argument drawn from the narrative of the "former prophets" (1 Sam 21:1-6): David and his companions were allowed to eat the holy bread placed before God in the tabernacle (cf. Lev 24:5-9) because they were hungry and no other bread was available. Actually, the restriction of the bread to priests did not hold at the time of David; but naturally rabbinical argumentation did not proceed according to our modern historical consciousness. Mt omits Mk's mention of the priest Abiathar, which is incorrect; the priest was Ahimelech. The point is that David and his companions, caught in dire need, could break a ritual ordinance without really offending God. How much more is this true of the companions of the Son of David, the Messiah, when they find themselves in similar need! (2) Mt adds to Mk a second, "halakic" argument, drawn from the Law: the priests can go about their ritual duties in the temple (including changing the bread of the Presence) even though these duties break the sabbath. The rabbis recognized that temple duties superseded the sabbath, and thus recognized that certain laws are subordinate to others. Jesus solemnly yet indirectly points to himself and his mission by declaring that "something" greater than the temple is here. Therefore, the disciples, while serving this "greater" reality, are exempt just as the priests are. (3) Mt adds to Mk a third argument drawn from the "latter prophets" (Hos 6:6; cf. Mt 9:13): the superiority of mercy to sacrifice creates the ascending hierarchy of values: sabbath law—temple law—law of love. If the unmerciful

Pharisees had understood their own Scriptures, especially Hosea, they would not have condemned Jesus' disciples, who are "guiltless," the word used in v.5 of the priests. Mercy is the yoke Jesus imposes on all, a yoke that brings true rest and freedom from Pharisaic casuistry about the sabbath-rest.

The clash between Jesus and the Pharisees is fundamentally over the essence of God: is God to be conceived of in terms of legalistic will or liberating mercy? The demand for mercy in the Hosea-citation replaces the general humanistic criterion of Mk 2:27; but the pericope still ends, as in Mk, with the ultimate appeal to the Son of Man. Mt no doubt interprets "lord of the Sabbath" as meaning the definitive interpreter and fulfiller of the Law and the prophets; Jesus interprets them with the hermeneutic of mercy. Once again, a legal question plaguing Mt's church receives a Christological solution.

F. THE SECOND SABBATH DISPUTE:
THE MAN WITH A WITHERED HAND.
12:9-14.
[Mk 3:1-6; Lk 6:6-11.

> 9And he went on from there, and entered their synagogue. 10And behold, there was a man with a withered hand. And they asked him, "Is it lawful to heal on the sabbath?" so that they might accuse him. 11He said to them, "What man of you, if he has one sheep and it falls into a pit on the sabbath, will not lay hold of it and lift it out? 12Of how much more value is a man than a sheep! So it is lawful to do good on the sabbath." 13Then he said to the man, "Stretch out your hand." And the man stretched it out, and it was restored, whole like the other. 14But the Pharisees went out and took counsel against him, how to destroy him.

Having passed through the grainfields, Jesus arrives at a synagogue on the same sabbath; events on two different sabbaths in Mk are thus closely connected in Mt. As often, Mt speaks of "their" synagogue, reflecting his own church's break with Judaism. Mt makes the miracle story more clearly a dispute story by having Jesus' enemies pose the central question: what is *lawful* or allowed on the sabbath (the key-word also occurs in vv. 2 and 12). The rabbis allowed aid for the sick on the sabbath only if there was a danger of death. The Pharisees already know Jesus' inclinations and even tacitly acknowledge his ability to heal. In their blind hatred all they are interested in is to accuse him. In good rabbinic form Jesus replies with a counter-question. He appeals to common sense rather than casuistry. A poor man with only one sheep would surely save him from a pit even on the sabbath. For Jesus, the *a fortiori* is obvious. A man is worth more than a sheep (cf. 6:26,30), and so human welfare takes precedence over sabbath rules (cf. Mk 2:27). Mercy is *lawful* on the sabbath. As in 9:6, Jesus then confirms his declaration by a miracle. The combination of teaching-and-miracle, both of which oppose the absoluteness of the sabbath, move the Pharisees (Mt omits Mk's "Herodians") to plot Jesus' death. This is the first mention of such a plot in Mt, and it is revelatory of the history of his own church that the sole conspirators are the Pharisees.

G. JESUS THE MEEK YET POWERFUL SERVANT. 12:15-21.
[Mk 3:7-12; Lk 6:17-19]

> [15]Jesus, aware of this, withdrew from there. And many followed him, and he healed them all, [16]and ordered them not to make him known. [17]This was to fulfil what was spoken by the prophet Isaiah:
> [18]"Behold, my servant whom I have chosen,
>   my beloved with whom my soul is well pleased.
>   I will put my Spirit upon him,
>   and he shall proclaim justice to the Gentiles.
> [19]He will not wrangle or cry aloud,
>   nor will any one hear his voice in the streets;

> ²⁰he will not break a bruised reed
> or quench a smoldering wick,
> till he brings justice to victory;
> ²¹and in his name will the Gentiles hope."

Mt, following the Markan thread, takes the two themes of withdrawal and healing and composes his own statement on servant-Christology, complete with a formula quotation. As opposed to Mk, Mt makes it clear that Jesus withdraws because he knows of the Pharisees' plot. Mt also changes Mk's "he healed many" to "he healed them all"; the power of Jesus cannot be limited to only some cases. Mt keeps Mk's command of silence, but not to preserve any messianic-secret theory. The silence rather goes with the motif of withdrawal: Jesus wishes to avoid unnecessary wrangling.

To show that this meekness proceeds not from weakness or fear but from Jesus' divine mandate to fulfill Scripture, Mt cites Is 42:1-4, the longest OT quotation in Mt. The text reflects neither the Masoretic nor the Septuagint forms perfectly. Mt is either borrowing from a collection of "testimonies to Christ" or fashioning the text-form himself, to suit his purposes. Jesus is the servant of the Lord; yet the themes of choice and love, along with reminiscences from the epiphany at Jesus' baptism (3:16-17), suggest that the Greek word for "servant" (*pais*) may also bear its other meaning here: "son." It is this servant-son who will proclaim God's just yet saving will (justice) to the pagans. Since Jesus has just been forced to withdraw from "their synagogue" because of the Pharisees' deadly hatred, the proleptic reference to the Gentile mission is fitting. Because Israel will fail to receive Jesus' proclamation of salvation, the gospel will be directed to the Gentiles. In the face of this hatred from his own people, Jesus does not reply with vengeful wrath or strident arguments (cf. 5:38-48). The meek servant seeks not publicity for himself but healing for others. Those broken in body or depressed in spirit (the reed and the wick) receive from him not the *coup de grâce* but recovery. In the teeth of opposition he will continue this mission, even on the sabbath, till he sees God's will victorious in the death-resurrection. From that moment on, the pagans will be able to place their hope in his name, i.e., in his person as revealed and preached to them (cf. "name" in 28:19). This triumph of Jesus will come about not through military might but through the meekness, even humiliation and death, of the servant who sacrifices himself to heal others.

H. JESUS REJECTS THE ACCUSATION OF DIABOLICAL COLLUSION.
12:22-37.
[Mt 9:32-34; 7:16-20; Mk 3:22-30; Lk 11:14-23; 12:10; 6:43-45]

[22]Then a blind and dumb demoniac was brought to him, and he healed him, so that the dumb man spoke and saw. [23]And all the people were amazed, and said, "Can this be the Son of David?" [24]But when the Pharisees heard it they said, "It is only by Beelzebul, the prince of demons, that this man casts out demons." [25]Knowing their thoughts, he said to them, "Every kingdom divided against itself is laid waste, and no city or house divided against itself will stand; [26]and if Satan casts out Satan, he is divided against himself; how then will his kingdom stand? [27]And if I cast out demons by Beelzebul, by whom do your sons cast them out? Therefore they shall be your judges. [28]But if it is by the Spirit of God that I cast out demons, then the kingdom of God has come upon you. [29]Or how can one enter a strong man's house and plunder his goods, unless he first binds the strong man? Then indeed he may plunder his house. [30]He who is not with me is against me, and he who does not gather with me scatters. [31]Therefore I tell you, every sin and blasphemy will be forgiven men, but the blasphemy against the Spirit will not be forgiven. [32]And whoever says a word against the Son of man will be forgiven; but whoever speaks against the Holy Spirit will not be forgiven, either in this age or in the age to come.

³³"Either make the tree good, and its fruit good; or make the tree bad, and its fruit bad; for the tree is known by its fruit. ³⁴You brood of vipers! how can you speak good, when you are evil? For out of the abundance of the heart the mouth speaks. ³⁵The good man out of his good treasure brings forth good, and the evil man out of his evil treasure brings forth evil. ³⁶I tell you, on the day of judgment men will render account for every careless word they utter; ³⁷for by your words you will be justified, and by your words you will be condemned."

The briefly narrated miracle comes from Q and indeed is one of Mt's "doublets" (cf. 9:32-34). The long discussion which follows is a mixture of Mk and Q. Here the miracle of exorcism is heightened: the deaf and dumb demoniac is also blind. Thus, the extraordinary healing (a concrete case of what Jesus is doing in 12:15) calls forth strong though divided reactions. The crowds are amazed (literally, "beside themselves," the only time this verb is used by Mt). With some hesitation they suggest that Jesus is the "Son of David" (on the title, cf. comments on 9:27). To deflect this dangerous opinion, the "Pharisees" (Mt's specification) seek to destroy Jesus' reputation so that they can destroy him (cf. the plot of 12:14). The exorcism is really done by the cooperation of the ruler of the devils—which is equivalent to accusing Jesus of magic, a capital offense (for Beelzebul, cf. comments on 10:25).

By his supernatural knowledge Jesus immediately knows what the Pharisees are saying to the crowds. Jesus gives a number of responses. First, any organization or movement (Mt adds "city" to Q's "kindgom" and "house") which fights against itself is doomed to destruction. That would be the case if the Pharisees' charge were true; if so, they should rejoice, because God's kingdom is breaking in and replacing Satan's. Actually, the kingdom *is* breaking in; but the triumph is being accomplished by a holy, not an evil, spirit (v.28). A second, *ad hominem* argument is that the

Pharisees also had exorcists among their members ("your sons"), and probably their exorcism-rituals looked much more like magic than Jesus' simple word and/or touch. They would be in no position to cast stones at Jesus. The truth is that Jesus' exorcisms are performed by God's spirit, i.e., by God himself visibly at work in the world—and that is practically the definition of God's kingdom coming in the last days, breaking Satan's evil hold over the world (cf. 4:8-9). To contrast the opposition of God and Satan, Mt keeps Q's more primitive "kingdom *of God*" instead of replacing it with his usual—though equivalent—"kingdom *of heaven*." This picture of the clash of two kingdoms is illustrated by a parable. Satan ("the strong man") holds all mankind captive ("his goods") in his palace or "house" (a pun on Beelzebul, "lord of the house"?). Only Jesus, the one who is stronger than Satan because he is equipped with God's Spirit (cf. 12:18), can defeat and bind Satan at the end-time (cf. Rev 20:2) and thus liberate mankind. Jesus' exorcism both prefigures this eschatological triumph and makes it a reality even now.

Having defended himself, Jesus now goes on the attack with a number of warnings to the Pharisees. First, in general, he warns them that, if they will not gather into his sheepfold of salvation (cf. 9:36), they will be scattered and lost. To refuse to decide positively for Jesus is already to have decided against him; no fence-straddling is allowed. Second, Jesus warns them against committing the unforgivable sin. While the concept of unforgivable sins was known in rabbinic theology, it was connected there with sins against the Law. Jesus means rather the basic sin against the light, the sin which calls good evil and attributes the manifest works of God's Spirit to the evil spirit. Since the Holy Spirit is the source of repentance and forgiveness, to blaspheme the Holy Spirit and to reject his clear operations within one's range of experience is to close oneself off from all hope of salvation. Early Jewish Christians, in their preaching to fellow Jews, probably made the distinction between blasphemy against the Son of Man and

blasphemy against the Spirit. The former was understandable in the days when Jesus acted as the lowly, hidden
servant, despite his power. The Jews can be forgiven their
former error regarding the mysterious Son of Man. But,
now that the Son of Man has been raised from the dead
and his Holy Spirit has been clearly poured out on all
believers, to persist in unbelief is the unforgivable sin
against the Spirit. The last days are upon us, and no further
chance for repentance will be possible.

A third warning is given in a parable on trees and
their fruits, reminiscent of the sermon on the mount (7:16-
20). There the Christian false prophets were attacked for
their evil deeds or "fruits." Here the Pharisees are rather
attacked for their malicious words, the fruits which inevitably
reveal the poisonous evil (cf. 3:7; 23:33) at the depths of
their being (the "heart" or "treasure," the seat of thinking
and willing). All the false accusations the Pharisees care-
lessly spew forth in this moment of confrontation and
polemic will have to be answered for in the sober court
of the last day. Acquittal ("justification") or condemnation
will hang on those words which reveal the depths of the
soul. And what holds true of the Pharisees in the Jewish
camp holds equally true of church leaders in the Christian
camp; Mt constantly holds up the one group as a warning
for the other group.

I. JESUS REJECTS THE REQUEST FOR A SIGN.
12:38-45.
[Mt 16:1-2,4; Mk 8:11-12; Lk 11:16,29-32,24-26]

> 38 Then some of the scribes and Pharisees said to him,
> "Teacher, we wish to see a sign from you." 39 But he
> answered them, "An evil and adulterous generation
> seeks for a sign; but no sign shall be given to it except
> the sign of the prophet Jonah. 40 For as Jonah was three
> days and three nights in the belly of the whale, so will
> the Son of man be three days and three nights in the heart

of the earth. [41]The men of Nineveh will arise at the judgment with this generation and condemn it; for they repented at the preaching of Jonah, and behold, something greater than Jonah is here. [42]The queen of the South will arise at the judgment with this generation and condemn it; for she came from the ends of the earth to hear the wisdom of Solomon, and behold, something greater than Solomon is here.

[43]"When the unclean spirit has gone out of a man, he passes through waterless places seeking rest, but he finds none. [44]Then he says, 'I will return to my house from which I came.' And when he comes he finds it empty, swept, and put in order. [45]Then he goes and brings with him seven other spirits more evil than himself, and they enter and dwell there; and the last state of that man becomes worse than the first. So shall it be also with this evil generation."

The pericope is from Q, with various Matthean alterations. The heretofore unmentioned scribes join the Pharisees in asking Jesus for a sign from heaven (cf. Is 7:11) which will legitimate the implicit messianic claims he has made in discussing his exorcisms. For his enemies, the miracles he has worked are not enough; they must have a clear sign from God himself, on their own terms (cf. 16:1-4). The truth is that, in their malice, they will never be satisfied, no matter how many signs Jesus performs. As Jesus has just said, their unbelief is betrayed by their words; "teacher" is the way unbelievers address Jesus. They are a generation that is "evil," ever resisting God's will, and "adulterous," ever breaking the covenant, which the prophets likened to a marriage bond (cf. Hos 2:2-13; Jer 3:6-10). Consequently no sign will be given by God ("divine passive") except the sign of Jonah (Mt pointedly designates him as "the prophet"). While Lk understands the sign of Jonah simply in terms of Jonah's preaching repentance (so too Mt 12:41), Mt adds an allegorical interpretation. The three days and three nights in the belly of the "whale" (better: "sea monster") prefigure the sojourn of the Son of Man in the depths ("heart") of the earth, i.e., Sheol, the abode of the dead, for the same time. The fact that Mt is citing Jonah 1:17 (from the Septuagint) and does not explicitly mention the resurrection occasions the poetic license of a three-day, three-night sojourn in the earth, despite the fact that Mt speaks of resurrection "on the third day" (16:21). The death-resurrection will be the great, cosmic sign given to all mankind. Yet Mt knows that the Jews will on the whole reject it (28:11-15) while the Gentiles, represented by the centurion and his soldiers, will accept it (27:54). This is the first time that Mt speaks of the Son of Man in the context of death (and implicitly, resurrection). The contours of the lowly-yet-powerful Son of Man during the earthly ministry are projected onto the larger screen of the murdered-yet-raised Son of Man. Mt's first use—and independent use—of the concept occurs pointedly in a context of prophetic fulfillment.

Since Mt has mentioned Jonah, he then reverses the order of sayings found in Lk 11:31-32. Following the theology of Q, Mt in v.41 portrays Jonah as a preacher of repentance. There is a double contrast: the pagan Ninevites repented while Israel now refuses to do so, and the preacher of repentance of Israel is greater than Jonah the prophet: he is the fulfiller of the Law and the prophets. Likewise, the pagan Queen of Sheba (from Arabia, the southern "ends of the earth") came to hear the wisdom of Solomon (1 Kings 10:1-13). Yet these Israelites, who have the Son of David, the Wisdom of God, before their eyes, refuse to come to him spiritually through faith. On the last day both Gentile groups—and indeed all Gentiles who have joined the church—will condemn faithless Israel.

Mt then concludes this passage of dire condemnation with another Q-passage (12:43-45). The catch-word "evil generation" forms an inclusion with v.39, while the theme of exorcism forms an inclusion with the larger unit (v.22).

Jesus' ministry, exorcisms included, has broken Satan's hold over Israel. But in a parable he warns Israel that worse still could befall it. An evil spirit is not content to be idle. His traditional haunt, the desert ("waterless places") offers no scope for his malicious, destructive tendencies. So, taking a full complement of devils, he returns to re-possess his former abode, the man from whom he was driven. When (or better, if) he finds that no positive good, no countervailing force, no Holy Spirit, has taken possession in his absence, he and his associates reclaim the man as their abode. The man's final state of diabolical possession is more aggravated than the first. So will it be with an Israel that refuses faith in its messianic deliverer from evil. Its final state will be worse than if Jesus had not come. For Mt, standing on the far side of the destruction of Jeru-salem and the break with the synagogue, this threat has already become history.

J. JESUS REJECTS BLOOD TIES.
12:46-50.
[Mk 3:31-35; Lk 8:19-21]

> [46]While he was still speaking to the people, behold, his mother and his brothers stood outside, asking to speak to him. [48]But he replied to the man who told him, "Who is my mother, and who are my brothers?" [49]And stretching out his hand toward his disciples, he said, "Here are my mother and my brothers! [50]For whoever does the will of my Father in heaven is my brother, and sister, and mother."

Mt follows the thread of Mk by having Jesus' saying about his true relatives follow the dispute about exorcism (though Mt has inserted much Q-material in between). On the basis of Mk 3:20-21,31, Mt presupposes that Jesus is inside a house (cf. Mt 13:1). Mt has avoided the idea of

outright hostility on the part of Jesus' family by omitting
the shocking statement that Jesus' relatives thought he was
insane (Mk 3:21). Yet a certain tone of opposition remains.
While Jesus is still speaking his condemnation of Israel, his
mother and brothers appear outside the house; their reason
for wanting to speak to him remains unspecified. While in
Mk Jesus states that those sitting in the circle around him
are his family, Mt has a much weightier theological statement. With a dramatic sweep of the hand, Jesus indicates
his disciples—and not the crowds or the people in general,
who for Mt are at best only potential believers. The disciples,
who have left their own families for Jesus (8:22; 10:37)
are his real mother and brothers. What Jesus asked of his
disciples—the breaking of family ties—he himself now
undertakes. For blood ties count for nothing in the kingdom
(cf. 3:9). What counts is being a disciple, which Jesus goes
on to define in terms of doing the will of "my Father."
The unique Son communicates the mysteries of the Father's
will to receptive disciples (cf. 11:27), who, by doing that will,
become sons and daughters of the Father, and brothers and
sisters—and yes, even the mother—of Jesus. For Mt, the
church is the family of God, incorporated into the communal life of the Godhead through baptism (cf. 28:19,10).
Indeed, the earthly family of Jesus, left cooling its heels
outside, may represent the unbelieving members of Israel,
cut off from the house where Jesus teaches, i.e., the church.
Yet it must be stressed that this is an inference from silence;
the brothers of Jesus are never explicitly said by Mt not to
believe in Jesus. Perhaps Mt's reverent treatment of Mary
in the infancy narrative keeps him from going as far as Mk.
On the brothers of Jesus, see the comments on 1:25 and
13:55.

II. THE DISCOURSE OF BOOK THREE: JESUS WITHDRAWS FROM ISRAEL INTO PARABOLIC SPEECH.

13:1-53.

THE THIRD GREAT discourse is made up of seven parables, a treatment of the reason why Jesus speaks in parables, allegorical interpretations of the parables of the sower and the parable of the weeds, and a concluding statement to the disciples. Mt follows the Markan outline, but he has increased Mk's three parables to seven, taking the other four from Q and M. The structure of the chapter may be viewed in different ways. If one divides the chapter into two halves at v.36, when Jesus leaves the crowds, the first half consists of the opening parable, the reason for parables and the allegorical explanation of the first parable, plus three parables closely tied together by the phrase "another parable" (vv.24,31,33). The second half consists of the explanation of the parable of the weeds plus three short parables, tied together by the phrase "(again) the kingdom of heaven is like . . . ." (vv.44,45,47).

For Mt, a main point of the parable chapter is that Jesus has met with resistance from obtuse people who refuse to understand, and so Jesus now responds to their lack of response first by withdrawing into the veiled speech of parables and then by withdrawing physically from the crowds. Jesus punishes his audience with parables. This may not have been the original purpose of the parables of the historical Jesus. A parable (Hebrew, *māshāl*) was a device of wisdom-teaching; a *māshāl* could be anything from a short axiom or proverb to a lengthy allegory or exemplary story. Jesus probably used short stories with one point of comparison to make his teaching concrete, and at the same time to tease and challenge the minds of his audience, indeed even to confront them with a radically new way of looking at God and man. The post-Easter church often adapted the parable to its new situation by turning the simple parables into elaborate allegories. Some parables were now seen to be mysterious messages in need of decoding. Finally, the evangelists inserted the parables into their own theological framework. In interpreting the parables, therefore, one has to distinguish between (1) the original message of Jesus, (2) the adaptations and applications made by the early church, and (3) the theological perspective of the evangelist. For more on parables, see the introductory volume in this series. For greater detail on the Markan parables, see the commentary on Mark.

A. INTRODUCTION AND THE PARABLE OF THE SOWER.
13:1-9.
[Mk 4:1-9; Lk 8:4-8]

13 That same day Jesus went out of the house and sat beside the sea. [2] And great crowds gathered about him, so that he got into a boat and sat there; and the whole crowd stood on the beach. [3] And he told them many things in parables, saying: "A sower went out to sow. [4] And as he sowed, some seeds fell along the path, and the birds came and devoured them. [5] Other seeds fell on rocky ground where they had not much soil, and immediately they sprang up, since they had no depth of soil, 6but when the sun rose they were scorched; and since they had no root they withered away. 7Other seeds fell upon thorns, and the thorns grew up and choked them. 8Other seeds fell on good soil and brought forth grain, some a hundredfold, some sixty, some thirty. 9He who has ears, let him hear."

On the same day as the dispute recorded in chap. 12, Jesus leaves the house to which he refused his relatives entrance. He "goes out" very much as the sower "goes out" to sow the seed of the word. As a teacher, Jesus again sits, recalling 5:1. Since the crowds are huge, Jesus gets into a fairly large boat (the disciples are with him) and delivers what is the first notably long parable in Mt, the parable of the sower. Mt takes over Mk's text with a few stylistic corrections; Mt does not abbreviate Mk as severely in the discourse material as in the narrative material. As for the original meaning of the parable: in Palestine, sowing often precedes ploughing; the sower prodigally casts his seed everywhere in the field, for he is unable to tell what may be under the thin topsoil. A great amount of seed may seem to be wasted, yet the success and abundance of the harvest is assured. In other words, despite so much opposition from officials and so little response from the people, Jesus expresses his confidence that God will see to the triumph of his kingdom and of its proclamation. The enormous success of Jesus' message is represented by the hundred-, sixty-, and thirty-fold—incredibly large yields even for a good harvest. Such oriental hyperbole is common in the parables of Jesus.

B. JESUS PUNISHES WITH PARABLES.
13:10-17.
[Mk 4:10-12,25; Lk 8:9-10,18b; 10:23-24]

10Then the disciples came and said to him, "Why do you speak to them in parables?" 11And he answered them, "To you it has been given to know the secrets of the kingdom of heaven, but to them it has not been given. [12]For to him who has will more be given, and he will have abundance; but from him who has not, even what he has will be taken away. [13]This is why I speak to them in parables, because seeing they do not see, and hearing they do not hear, nor do they understand. [14]With them indeed is fulfilled the prophecy of Isaiah which says:

'You shall indeed hear but never understand,
and you shall indeed see but never perceive.
[15]For this people's heart has grown dull,
and their ears are heavy of hearing,
and their eyes they have closed,
lest they should perceive with their eyes,
and hear with their ears,
and understand with their heart,
and turn for me to heal them.'

[16]But blessed are your eyes, for they see, and your ears, for they hear. [17]Truly, I say to you, many prophets and righteous men longed to see what you see, and did not see it, and to hear what your hear, and did not hear it.

At this point in Mk, the disciples, who understand no more than the crowds (Mk's messianic secret!) ask the meaning of the parables. In Mt, who drops the messianic secret, the disciples are by definition those who do understand and accept Jesus' message, as opposed to the crowds. In the boat with Jesus, they ask him why he speaks to the crowds in parables. Jesus replies by declaring the wall of division God has established between believers (the disciples) and nonbelievers (all others). The disciples have responded favorably to the grace God has given them through Jesus, and so God will give them even further grace and understanding. But Israel, which has failed to correspond to the offer of Jesus, will lose the special place it had under the old dispensation. In Mt, the problem of the parables has become the problem of Israel's unbelief.

Jesus speaks to the people in parables *because* they have refused to see and hear his clear message, which he has been offering them since chap. 4. This is the opposite of Mk's view, which has the mysterious Jesus speak in parables from the beginning of his ministry (chap. 4 in Mk) *in order that* the people may not understand. With a formula of introduction different from the usual one in Mt, Jesus himself speaks a formula quotation (Is 6:9-10). Isaiah, Mt, and the whole biblical tradition affirm both God's control over all events, even men's sins, and yet the full responsibility of men for their sins. No attempt is ever made in the bible to reconcile systematically the two poles of the grace/free-will paradox. While Mk has Jesus go on to berate the disciples for their lack of understanding (Mk 4:13), Mt inserts a Q-logion (Mt 13:16-17). This beatitude congratulates the disciples for being present as the age of fufillment dawns. The understanding disciples *see* and *hear* (note the contrast with Is 6:9-10) the object of all the prophecies and longings of the OT prophets and "just men" (Lk: "kings").

C. THE EXPLANATION OF THE PARABLE OF THE SOWER.
13:18-23.
[Mk 4:13-20; Lk 8:11-15]

[18]"Hear then the parable of the sower. [19]When any one hears the word of the kingdom and does not understand it, the evil one comes and snatches away what is sown in his heart; this is what was sown along the path. [20]As for what was sown on rocky ground, this is he who hears the word and immediately receives it with joy; [21]yet he has no root in himself, but endures for a while, and when tribulation or persecution arises on account of the word, immediately he falls away. [22]As for what was sown among thorns, this is he who hears the word, but the cares of the world and the delight in riches choke the word, and it proves unfruitful. [23]As for what was sown on good soil,

> this is he who hears the word and understands it; he
> indeed bears fruit, and yields, in one case a hundredfold,
> in another sixty, and in another thirty."

In keeping with the beatitude, the disciples receive the explanation of the parable, which Mt explicitly names "the parable of the sower"—though that hardly describes the thrust of the allegory which follows. This allegorical interpretation, which stems from the hard struggles and disillusioning defeats of early Christians, focuses upon the different dispositions with which people receive—or rather do not truly receive—the word proclaiming the kingdom. One can see the awkward imposition of the allegory on the original parable in v.19: 'what was sown," i.e., the *seed*, the *word* of the kingdom, is forced to represent the *person* who hears the word (clearly so in v.20). The first type hears but does not understand, i.e., never really becomes a disciple (cf. the opposition between hearing and understanding in v.14). Hence the devil, like a robber baron, carries off the word by force. The second type is the inconstant person who displays great joy in his Christian life until his faith proves inconvenient because of trouble or persecution. The third type has his faith either strangled by the silken cord of deceitful wealth or suffocated by a pile of anxieties over worldly success. The fourth type is the true disciple who both understands and *does* (Mt adds his favorite verb *poieō*, here translated "yields"). Mt encourages the members of his church to continue bearing fruit (doing God's will), despite the varying results they obtain, and despite the sad history of Jewish Christians or false teachers who apostatize.

D. THE PARABLE OF THE WHEAT AND THE WEEDS.
13:24-30.

> [24]Another parable he put before them, saying, "The
> kingdom of heaven may be compared to a man who

sowed good seed in his field; [25]but while men were sleeping, his enemy came and sowed weeds among the wheat, and went away. [26]So when the plants came up and bore grain, then the weeds appeared also. [27]And the servants of the householder came and said to him, 'Sir, did you not sow good seed in your field? How then has it weeds?' [28]He said to them, 'An enemy has done this.' The servants said to him, 'Then do you want us to go and gather them?' [29]But he said, 'No; lest in gathering the weeds you root up the wheat along with them. [30]Let both grow together until the harvest; and at harvest time I will tell the reapers, Gather the weeds first and bind them in bundles to be burned, but gather the wheat into my barn.'"

The three parables which follow are spoken to both the disciple and the crowds. Mt first presents a parable unique to his gospel, a parable created by his special tradition or by himself. No doubt, however, it reflects Jesus' rejection of the separatism and rigorism of the Pharisees, Qumranites, and Zealots. The words "may be compared" mean literally "was compared"; this may point back to the parable of the sower, or may simply reflect a semitic background (perfect tense with present meaning). Actually, the kingdom of heaven is not being compared simply to the man sowing good seed; the kingdom is compared to and illustrated by the situation narrated by the whole story. The sower, who is now a householder, has an enemy who secretly and maliciously sows among his wheat a type of poisonous weed known as darnel (*zizania*). At first the darnel looks very much like the wheat. By the time that the grain appears and the difference becomes obvious, the roots of the weeds are so entwined with those of the wheat that uprooting the one might endanger the other. The householder wisely tells his slaves to postpone the separation till harvest. The reapers first tie the weeds into bundles for fuel, and then they gather the wheat into the barns (cf. 3:12). Even without the allegorical interpretation, the main point is clear. Up until the parousia, the church will always be a mixed bag of good and evil; it should not play God by trying to purify itself completely through purges and Inquisitions. (Others interpret the wheat as the church and the weeds as the synagogue; both will endure until the end of time.) The definitive separation must be left to the last judgment; it is the church's part to preach repentance and practice patience.

E. THE PARABLES OF THE MUSTARD SEED AND THE LEAVEN; CONCLUSION OF THE PUBLIC TEACHING.
13:31-35.
[Mk 4:30-34; Lk 13:18-21]

³¹Another parable he put before them, saying, "The kingdom of heaven is like a grain of mustard seed which a man took and sowed in his field; ³²it is the smallest of all seeds, but when it has grown it is the greatest of shrubs and becomes a tree, so that the birds of the air come and make nests in its branches."

³³He told them another parable. "The kingdom of heaven is like leaven which a woman took and hid in three measures of flour, till it was all leavened."

³⁴All this Jesus said to the crowds in parables; indeed he said nothing to them without a parable. ³⁵This was to fulfil what was spoken by the prophet:

"I will open my mouth in parables,
I will utter what has been hidden since the foundation of the world."

Mt now presents two parables with the same message; the amazing contrast between the small, unpromising beginnings of the kingdom and its full, triumphant expansion. From Mk, Mt borrows the statement that the mustard seed is the smallest of seeds, and from Q he borrows the statement that the mustard seed becomes a tree. Neither statement is literally true, but the customary hyperbole serves to sharpen the point of the parable: contrast. The reference to the birds is an allusion to Dan 4:10-22, and shows that the tree is the universal kingdom of God which gives shelter to all the nations (cf. 28:19). The second parable uses a well-known symbol in an unusual way. Yeast or leaven was for Jews and Christians a symbol of corruption (cf. 1 Cor 5:6-8). Perhaps because Jesus gathers round him the unclean sinners of the land, he prefers to use yeast as a symbol of the kingdom which comes in small, hidden, and perhaps despised beginnings. The amount of flour is ridiculously large, another example of hyperbole to stress the vast success of the kingdom.

Mt concludes the public half of the discourse by paraphrasing Mk 4:33-34, the conclusion of the Markan discourse. Mk's conclusion fits this half-way point in Mt because in Mt Jesus is about to leave the crowds. Mt omits Mk's statement that Jesus spoke the word to the crowds in parables "as they were able to hear it"; that might imply that Jesus accommodated his message to the crowds' ability to understand. Mt adds a formula quotation, which, with his interest in prophecy, he assigns to "the prophet," even though it comes from Ps 78:2. Jesus is the perfect wisdom-teacher who speaks forth mysteries hidden from creation, i.e., the apocalyptic revelation of God's coming as king.

F. THE EXPLANATION OF THE PARABLE OF THE WHEAT AND THE WEEDS. 13:36-43.

> [36]Then he left the crowds and went into the house. And his disciples came to him, saying, "Explain to us the parable of the weeds of the field." [37]He answered, "He who sows the good seed is the Son of man; [38]the field is the world, and the good seed means the sons of the kingdom; the weeds are the sons of the evil one, [39]and the

enemy who sowed them is the devil; the harvest is the close of the age, and the reapers are angels. [40]Just as the weeds are gathered and burned with fire, so will it be at the close of the age. [41]The Son of man will send his angels, and they will gather out of his kingdom all causes of sin and all evildoers, [42]and throw them into the furnace of fire; there men will weep and gnash their teeth. [43]Then the righteous will shine like the sun in the kingdom of their Father. He who has ears, let him hear.

The return of Jesus to the house (cf. 13:1) signals his break with the crowds and symbolically his break with Israel. It is not an accident that this rupture occurs halfway through the gospel. Henceforth Israel will show greater and greater hostility, and Jesus will turn more and more to his disciples, to devote himself to their formation. The allegorical explanation, so filled with Matthean words and theology, is probably the evangelist's creation. He supplies a list of equivalencies to decode the parable. The picture of the Son of Man in the allegory is more Matthean than traditional. This Son of Man is the risen Jesus exercising his role as world-ruler and sower until the judgment, the role he assumes in 28:16-20. The field is defined as the *world*, not the *church*! The parable has a universal, and not merely an ecclesiological scope. The good seed symbolizes the "sons" of (i.e., citizens of, those belonging to and obedient to the kingdom). No doubt these "sons" of the kingdom are the true followers of Jesus, though Mt's appreciation of the mixed-up situation of the present age forbids a facile identification of true disciples with all the members of the church. Mt also called the Israelites the sons of the kingdom in 8:12, a reminder that no disciple can feel smug and confident about his final election (cf. 22:14). The sons of the devil are all who do evil and lead others to do evil (in v.41, "all causes of sin and all evildoers" is literally "all scandals and all who do iniquity"). This group exists inside as well as outside the church (cf. 7:15-23;

18:6-9; 24:5-12). Harvest-time is a frequent image for the last judgment in both the OT and the NT. Mt calls it "the close of the age," a phrase which, in this precise form, occurs only in Mt in the NT (cf. 13:40,49; 24:3; 28:20) and which signifies both the conclusion and the fulfillment of this world and its history. This present age constitutes the reign of the Son of Man, which will give way after the judgment to the kingdom of the Father (cf. 1 Cor 15:24-25). In Mt, the kingdom of God is a process-reality, which comes in stages. The angels, not the Son of Man, are the actual agents of judgment. All evildoers, including evil disciples, will suffer the same fate as unbelieving Israel (cf. 8:12), while the true disciples, designated by the great OT and Jewish title of honor, "the righteous," will share the divine glory, indeed, will be transformed into beings of light (cf. Dan 12:3). Both world and church are mixtures of good and evil in this present age; both stand under the threat of a stern judgment; and therefore both are called to repentance while there is still time. The allegorical interpretation seems to shift the parable's center of gravity from the need for patient tolerance now to the fearful judgment to come.

G. THE TWIN PARABLE OF THE TREASURE
AND THE PEARL.
13:44-46.

> [44]"The kingdom of heaven is like treasure hidden in a field, which a man found and covered up; then in his joy he goes and sells all that he has and buys that field.
> [45]"Again, the kingdom of heaven is like a merchant in search of fine pearls, [46]who, on finding one pearl of great value, went and sold all that he had and bought it."

Like the final parable of the fishnet, these two parables exist only in Mt and are tied together by the formula "(again) the kingdom of heaven is like . . . ." The parables of the treasure and the pearl (both are OT symbols for wisdom) have a common point: the genuine disciples respond joyfully to the discovery of the kingdom with total commitment. The first cameo-parable depicts a poor farm-laborer ploughing on another's land. Invasions and revolts often led the rich to bury their valuables in fields. If the rich were then killed, the treasures remained hidden until someone like this lucky laborer hit upon them. Overwhelmed with joy, he does not hesitate for a moment. He is a poor man; he has to sell everything to buy one field. But the treasure of the kingdom is worth any price. Such is the whole-hearted response of the disciple who is surprised by joy—the joy of finding Jesus Christ hidden in the subsoil of his ordinary life. Somewhat different is the well-to-do merchant who is on the look-out for the single most valuable substance in the ancient world: pearls, which some writers rated even above gold. Perhaps he has been thinking in terms of a number of pearls. But when he finds one pearl of supreme value, he sells all his holdings to possess it. His investment, his commitment, is total, because the pearl is beyond price.

H. THE CONCLUDING PARABLE OF THE FISHNET. 13:47-50.

> [47]"Again, the kingdom of heaven is like a net which was thrown into the sea and gathered fish of every kind; [48]when it was full, men drew it ashore and sat down and sorted the good into vessels but threw away the bad. [49]So it will be at the close of the age. The angels will come out and separate the evil from the righteous, [50]and throw them into the furnace of fire; there men will weep and gnash their teeth.

This parable does not have the same message as the other two before it. Rather it jumps back to the explanation of the parable of the wheat and the tares, thus forming an inclusion for the second half of the discourse. The themes of the temporary mixture of good and bad, a final separation, and fitting punishment not only recall vv. 36-43 but also point forward to the parables of judgment and the eschatological discourse spoken in Jerusalem. The image is that of a large dragnet, pulled by two boats or from the shore. All kinds of fish—clean and unclean from a Levitical point of view—are dragged along (there were about twenty-four types in the Sea of Galilee). Likewise, the "Jesus-movement," before and after the resurrection, embraced everyone from sincere observers of the Law to the worst sinners. "When it was *full (eplērōthē)*" signals "the close of the age"; notice how Matthean terms abound. The absence of the Son of Man, the devil, and the special reward of the good, focuses the point of the final parable on a grim reminder: the rejection and punishment of the evil. Again Mt substitutes the severity of judgment for the imminence of judgment as the basis of his moral exhortation.

I. THE CONCLUSION OF THE DISCOURSE.
  13:51-53.

> [51]"Have you understood all this?" They said to him, "Yes." [52]And he said to them, "Therefore every scribe who has been trained for the kingdom of heaven is like a householder who brings out of his treasure what is new and what is old."
> [53]And when Jesus had finished these parables, he went away from there.

It is typical of Mt, as opposed to Mk, that the disciples, the true sons of the kingdom, "understand" (and therefore accept) the message of the kingdom. Jesus replies to the joyful "yes" of his own by describing them in parabolic terms: the hearers of the parables are drawn into a parable. Every person learned in the Law and the prophets (i.e., a scribe) who also understands Jesus' announcement of the coming of the kingdom is like a householder who brings forth from his storeroom things new (the proclamation of Jesus the Fulfiller) and old (the Law and the prophets). Thus the third discourse ends with an allusion to 5:17 and 9:17. One should notice the telling order of words; contrary to natural expectations, the "new" is placed before the "old." Both shed light on each other; but the definitive norm is the new, the fulfillment. A scribe who has been so "trained" (or "instructed," *mathēteutheis*) for and in the kingdom has become a true disciple (*mathētēs*). Such Christian scribes may have been the leaders in Mt's church (cf. 23:34). At least, Mt presents such a scribe as his Christian ideal, and perhaps his self-portrait. Mt then ends the whole discourse with his usual formula of conclusion-and-transition, as Jesus himself makes a transition to another field of endeavor. He leaves Capernaum, "his city," and begins a more itinerant ministry throughout Galilee.

Book Four
The Messiah Forms His Church
and Prophesies His Passion.
13:54 - 18:35.

In Book Four, the breach between Jesus and Israel widens as Jesus extends his itinerant ministry around Galilee. On the one hand, Jesus transfers the "magisterium," the legitimate authority to teach, from the Jewish leaders to Peter and the disciples. On the other hand, against the background of increasing hostility, Jesus begins the formal prophecies of his passion, death, and resurrection, the shattering apocalyptic event which will bring his church to full birth. In a sense, one should not speak of Jesus' "founding the church" in Book Four. The founding of the church in the full sense takes place in 28:16-20. Book Four is rather the period of gestation. Starting with chap. 14 Mt adheres closely to the Markan thread of narrative, inserting little of major importance beyond pericopes about Peter (14:28-31; 16:16-19; 17:24-27) and the discourse on church life (chap. 18). These inserts manifest Mt's intention: to introduce or strengthen the ecclesiological dimension and to tie it closely to the christological dimension. As Jesus prepares to go to his passion, he forms his church and prepares it for a similar destiny. His disciples understand his message, yet their faith remains immature and easily shaken. Mt's theme of "little faith" allows him to take over from Mk some of the rebukes to the disciples, while rejecting Mk's basic theme that the disciples lack understanding. Since Mt follows the Markan order and matter so closely, the reader would do well to consult the volume on Mk in this series for further details on the Markan material.

I. THE NARRATIVE
OF BOOK FOUR:
THE ITINERANT JESUS
PREPARES FOR THE CHURCH
BY HIS DEEDS.
13:54 - 17:27

A. THE REJECTION AT NAZARETH.
13:54-58.
[Mk 6:1-6a; Lk 4:16-30]

> [54]And coming to his own country he taught them in their synagogue, so that they were astonished, and said, "Where did this man get this wisdom and these mighty works? [55]Is not this the carpenter's son? Is not his mother called Mary? And are not his brothers James and Joseph and Simon and Judas? [56]And are not all his sisters with us? Where then did this man get all this?" [57]And they took offense at him. But Jesus said to them, "A prophet is not without honor except in his own country and in his own house." [58]And he did not do many mighty works there, because of their unbelief.

AFTER HIS parable-discourse, Mk continues with a chain of miracle-stories (Mk 4:35-5:43) which Mt has already used (Mt 8:23-34 and 9:18-26). Mt logically moves to the

next Markan pericope, the rejection at Nazareth (Mk 6:1-
6a). From here on in, Mt will follow the Markan sequence
closely. Nazareth becomes the first stop on Jesus' itinerant
ministry around Galilee. Notice, however, that the name
of "his own country" is not mentioned; the reference may
be purposely vague and so paradigmatic of all Israel. The
Markan story is abbreviated: the sabbath is not mentioned,
and the disciples are omitted. Thus Mt focuses the narrative
entirely on Jesus. While the crowds hearing the sermon
on the mount were "astonished" in a positive way, the
astonishment of Nazareth turns out to be negative. By an
inclusion the first and last questions of the Nazarenes
(vv. 54 and 56) emphasize the basic question of the origin
of Jesus' wise teaching and powerful miracles (a perfect
summary of chaps. 5-9). In between the first and last
questions are the questions which explain why Jesus'
wisdom and power do not generate faith at Nazareth: the
Nazarenes know him too well. Familiarity breeds contempt,
even for the Messiah. The contempt can be felt in the "this
man" of vv. 54 and 56, which might be translated "this
fellow." The Nazarenes think they know all about Jesus
because they think they know his earthly origins and his
true family. He is the son of a "carpenter" (or "craftsman,"
"artisan"); they can name his mother and brothers; and
his sisters still live in the town. There is an irony in these
objections which reminds one of John's gospel: everything
the Nazarenes affirm is in one sense true and in another,
deeper sense false.

Mt carefully separates the question about Jesus' father
from the question about his mother and brothers. Those
who have read Mt's infancy narrative know that the unnamed Joseph is not the real father of Jesus the Son of God,
while the names in the second question do refer to Jesus'
mother and brothers (cf. comments on 1:25). Yet even
here the Nazarenes are mistaken: the true family of Jesus
is composed not of blood relatives but of obedient disciples
(12:46-50). As in Jn, the unbelieving audience is scandalized

by the "flesh," the ordinary earthly state of the revealer, and so fails to perceive the divine reality communicated by that flesh. Jesus the final prophet of God experiences the definitive rejection of Israel; thus does he recapitulate the rejection of all of the persecuted prophets before him. Mt reverentially corrects Mk, who probably shocked Mt by saying that Jesus *could* do no mighty work there. Impotence is changed to refusal, and the reference to Jesus' marveling at their unbelief is dropped. Similarly, the reverent Mt changes the Markan designation of Jesus as a "carpenter" to "the son of the carpenter." Neither impotence nor ignorance nor emotions nor social status must impugn Jesus' dignity. Mt also omits a reference to finding no acceptance among "his relatives" (cf. Mk 6:4); this may be an attempt to soften Mk's hostility towards Jesus' family, though the omission could also be explained by Mt's avoidance of needless repetition.

B. THE PROPHET'S DEATH:
JOHN THE BAPTIST AND JESUS.
14:1-12.
[Mk 6:14-29; Lk 9:7-9]

14 At that time Herod the tetrarch heard about the fame of Jesus; ²and he said to his servants, "This is John the Baptist, he has been raised from the dead; that is why these powers are at work in him." ³For Herod had seized John and bound him and put him in prison, for the sake of Herodias, his brother Philip's wife; ⁴because John said to him, "It is not lawful for you to have her." ⁵And though he wanted to put him to death, he feared the people, because they held him to be a prophet. ⁶But when Herod's birthday came, the daughter of Herodias danced before the company, and pleased Herod, ⁷so that he promised with an oath to give her whatever she might ask. ⁸Prompted by her mother, she said, "Give me the

head of John the Baptist here on a platter." [9]And the
king was sorry; but because of his oaths and his guests
he commanded it to be given; [10]he sent and had John
beheaded in the prison, [11]and his head was brought on a
platter and given to the girl, and she brought it to her
mother. [12]And his disciples came and took the body and
buried it; and they went and told Jesus.

In chap. 2 Herod the Great tried to murder the infant
Jesus; now his son, Herod Antipas, tetrarch of Galilee
and Perea, kills John the prophet. This in turn prefigures
the violent death of the final prophet, Jesus. Mk has the
narrative of John's death follow upon the mission of the
Twelve. Since Mt has anticipated the mission in chap. 10,
he has this martyrdom follow immediately upon the rejection at Nazareth; the rejection of both prophets by "this
generation" is thus profiled. In Mt, the murder of John
and Herod's concern about Jesus form the occasion for
Jesus' withdrawal (14:13); in Mk the reason was the return
of the Twelve and their need for rest.

"At that time," i.e., as Jesus is suffering rejection at
Nazareth, Herod hears about Jesus. Mt corrects Mk's
"King" to give Herod his proper title of tetrarch, though
Mt returns to the inexact "king" in v.9. Mt drops Mk's
report about what others thought of Jesus: he keeps only
Herod's opinions, spoken to his courtiers. The superstitious
and guilt-ridden Herod thinks that Jesus is John come back
from the dead; that is why Jesus is able to perform miracles
(something never reported of the Baptist). This estimation
provides a smooth bridge to the narrative of martyrdom,
which Mt severely abbreviates. Mt repeats Mk's error
about Herodias' being the wife of Philip; she was actually
the wife of another brother named Herod. Herod Antipas
is portrayed in darker tones by Mt. While Mk attributes
the murderous intentions to Herodias and claims that Herod
feared John because he was a *just* and *holy* man, Mt attributes the murderous intentions to Herod, who holds back

only because he *fears the crowds*, who consider John a *prophet* (a favorite theme of Mt). The theme of the fear of the crowds will return in Jesus' passion (26:3-5). Hence, Herod's sorrow in v.9 is nothing praiseworthy; he is afraid of political consequences. Herodias is not spared, however; despite his truncation of the story, Mt stresses that the daughter is "prompted" by her mother, who fittingly receives the head on the platter. For OT echoes of the story, cf. 1 Kings 19:2;21; Esther 5:2-3;7). The disciples *of John* tell Jesus what has happened, and it is at this point that Mt can rejoin Mk, who has the disciples *of Jesus* telling their master about their mission (Mk 6:30).

C. THE FEEDING OF FIVE THOUSAND.
14:13-21.
[Mk 6:32-44; Lk 9:10-17]

> [13]Now when Jesus heard this, he withdrew from there in a boat to a lonely place apart. But when the crowds heard it, they followed him on foot from the towns. [14]As he went ashore he saw a great throng; and he had compassion on them, and healed their sick. [15]When it was evening, the disciples came to him and said, "This is a lonely place, and the day is now over; send the crowds away to go into the villages and buy food for themselves." [16]Jesus said, "They need not go away; you give them something to eat." [17]They said to him, "We have only five loaves here and two fish." [18]And he said, "Bring them here to me." [19]Then he ordered the crowds to sit down on the grass; and taking the five loaves and the two fish he looked up to heaven, and blessed, and broke and gave the loaves to the disciples, and the disciples gave them to the crowds. [20]And they all ate and were satisfied. And they took up twelve baskets full of the broken pieces left over. [21]And those who ate were about five thousand men, besides women and children.

Mt follows Mk's wording closely, though as usual he abbreviates, omitting especially allusions to the Israel of the exodus-desert period. Obviously, the general allusions to the Ex 16 story of the manna in the "desert" (here in RSV: "lonely place") and to Elisha's feeding of a hundred men (2 Kings 4:42-44) remain. The reference to the sheep without a shepherd (Mk 6:34) was used in Mt 9:36 and is omitted here. This highlights the act of feeding itself, and gives a more solemn, cultic tone.

As the arrest of the Baptist signaled the beginning of Jesus' ministry in Galilee, so John's death marks a new stage and another act of "withdrawing" (cf. 4:12, as well as the withdrawal before the threat of Herod the Great, 2:14). The idea that Jesus withdraws from danger until the set time of the passion, when he knowingly goes to his death (26:1-2), is reminiscent of the "hour" of the fourth gospel. Perhaps for Mt this withdrawal means that Jesus sails away "alone" (RSV: "apart"); the disciples may come to him with the crowds who "follow" on foot. The RSV's "as he went ashore" might also mean: "When he came forth from his hiding place [to meet the crowds]." Although Mt usually avoids attributing emotions to Jesus, compassion (Mk 6:34; Mt 9:36) is mentioned. While Mk has the compassion issue in teaching, Mt has Jesus heal; Jesus stopped teaching the crowds openly at 13:36. Mt alters the dialogue between the disciples and Jesus to heighten the majesty of the latter. Jesus' initial reply indicates sovereign control: "They need not go away," for Jesus already knows what he will do; again, we approach the conception of the fourth gospel. There follows immediately the command which involves the disciples ("*you* give them . . . ."). The question of the disciples, and the counter-question of Jesus are dropped; the Master has no need to ask questions. The disciples supply the information about the loaves and fish (just enough for Jesus and themselves) as a direct reply and an objection to Jesus' command. Jesus ignores the objection and issues another order, also involving the disciples. But the main act is performed by Jesus alone. In a solemn, liturgical style, Mt describes the subordinate actions with participles (taking—looking up—breaking) and the main actions with main verbs (blessed—gave). "Blessed" means: "recited a prayer of praise to God for the bread," *not* "blessed the bread." The passage is so obviously Eucharistic that the gesture of looking up to heaven has passed into the consecration prayer of the Roman Canon, with no support from the narratives of the institution of the Eucharist. This miracle of Jesus, the prophet like Moses, anticipates the Eucharist, which in turn anticipates the final banquet in the kingdom (26:29). Mt then underscores the role of the disciples as mediators of the gifts to the crowds. Unlike Mk, Mt stresses the Eucharistic reference still further by simply omitting any action of Jesus as regards the fish. The crowds are "satisfied," as will be the blessed at the banquet in the kingdom (5:6). The twelve baskets left over underscore the abundance of the gift and recall Elisha's miracle. Mt likewise raises Mk's already hyperbolic number of participants by adding that women and children were not included in the count. Mt has thus begun Mk's "bread-section" (Mk 6-8); notice that most of the subsequent pericopes up until Caesarea Philippi will mention "bread," a key-word pointing to the messianic gift which Jesus offers the believer.

D. JESUS WALKS ON THE SEA AND RESCUES PETER.
14:22-36.
[Mk 6:45-56]

> ²²Then he made the disciples get into the boat and go before him to the other side, while he dismissed the crowds. ²³And after he had dismissed the crowds, he went up on the mountain by himself to pray. When evening came, he was there alone, ²⁴but the boat by this time was many furlongs distant from the land, beaten by the waves;

for the wind was against them. [25] And in the fourth watch of the night he came to them, walking on the sea. [26] But when the disciples saw him walking on the sea, they were terrified, saying, "It is a ghost!" And they cried out for fear. [27] But immediately he spoke to them, saying, "Take heart, it is I; have no fear."

[28] And Peter answered him, "Lord, if it is you, bid me come to you on the water." [29] He said, "Come." So Peter got out of the boat and walked on the water and came to Jesus; [30] but when he saw the wind, he was afraid, and beginning to sink he cried out, "Lord, save me." [31] Jesus immediately reached out his hand and caught him, saying to him, "O man of little faith, why did you doubt?" [32] And when they got into the boat, the wind ceased. [33] And those in the boat worshiped him, saying, "Truly you are the Son of God."

[34] And when they had crossed over, they came to land at Gennesaret. [35] And when the men of that place recognized him, they sent round to all that region and brought to him all that were sick, [36] and besought him that they might only touch the fringe of his garment; and as many as touched it were made well.

Mt follows Mk but inserts a separate tradition about the sinking Peter, which possibly stems from a story about Christ's first resurrection-appearance to Peter. This oral tradition has been rewritten with typically Matthean motifs. Here we begin the special Peter-traditions which dominate Book Four, the ecclesiastical Book *par excellence*.

Mt gives no reason why Jesus forces the disciples to leave; the idea of dangerous messianic fervor should not be imported from Jn 6:14-15. After dismissing the crowd, Jesus is again alone, as in v.13. What follows is a symbolic scene: the disciples in the boat (the church) are threatened by night (evil) and the waters of death, while Jesus is separated from them yet is praying to the Father (Mt mentions Jesus' praying only here and in Gethsemane,

26:36-44). In the church's direst need, when all seems lost, her Lord comes to save her, bestriding the waters of chaos like Yahweh or Wisdom in the OT (Ps 77:19; Job 9:8; 38:16; Is 43:16; Sir 24:5-6). In the darkness of the fourth watch (3 to 6 A.M.), the disciples think they see a ghost and panic. This is the definition of little faith: a faith that is still afraid. Jesus replies as does Yahweh when he appears in OT theophanies: "It is I, fear not." Indeed, the divine *egō eimi* ("I am" or "it is I") probably means here what it meant in Ex 3:14: I am here to save you. At this point Peter, with more daring than sense, addresses Jesus solemnly as "Lord" and asks permission to share his miraculous power. The "if it is you" expresses not doubt but confidence in Jesus' powerful presence. With a one-word command Jesus enables his disciple to imitate his miracle. But frightened by the power of nature, Peter begins to doubt the power of Jesus and so he sinks into death.

With the faith he has left he renews his cry to his Lord, repeating the cry of the church from 8:25. Like Yahweh Jesus stretches forth his saving hand to rescue the believer from the flood-waters of death (cf. Ps 18:16-17; Ps 144:7; there are similar motifs in pagan and Qumranite literature). In a quintessentially Matthean phrase, Jesus rebukes Peter for his little faith (a faith which panics when faced with crisis) and his doubt (practical hesitation rather than theoretical difficulties with doctrine). For Mt, the disciple in this life is always caught between faith and doubt (cf. 28:17!) and so must always struggle against his little faith. The rebuke of Jesus extends to every disciple who at first braves difficulties and then collapses (cf. Peter's following Jesus after his arrest, only to deny him).

While in Mk the blind disciples can respond to this theophany only with dumb amazement, the Matthean disciples ("those in the boat": the church) bow down in adoration and profess Jesus' divine sonship. The wording is very close to that of the profession of the centurion and his soldiers (=the Gentile church) at the cross (27:54), and partially anticipates Peter's profession at Caesarea Philippi. Mt adds a brief conclusion, from Mk. The land at Gennesaret is probably the plain on the northwest shore of the lake, south of Capernaum. Mt again stresses the unlimited power of Jesus: *all* the sick are brought to him, and *as many as* simply touched the tassels of his cloak (cf. 9:20-21) were healed. This is no mere miracle-worker; this is the Son of God.

E. THE DISPUTE OVER CLEAN AND UNCLEAN. 15.1-20.
[Mk 7:1-23; Lk 11:37-41; 6:39]

15 Then Pharisees and scribes came to Jesus from Jerusalem and said, ²"Why do your disciples transgress the tradition of the elders? For they do not wash their hands when they eat." ³He answered them, "And why do you transgress the commandment of God for the sake of your tradition? ⁴For God commanded, 'Honor your father and your mother,' and, 'He who speaks evil of father or mother, let him surely die.' ⁵But you say, 'If any one tells his father or his mother, What you would have gained from me is given to God, he need not honor his father.' ⁶So, for the sake of your tradition, you have made void the word of God. ⁷You hypocrites! Well did Isaiah prophesy of you, when he said:

⁸'This people honors me with their lips,
  but their heart is far from me;
⁹in vain do they worship me, teaching as doctrines the
  precepts of men.'"

¹⁰And he called the people to him and said to them, "Hear and understand: ¹¹not what goes into the mouth defiles a man, but what comes out of the mouth, this defiles a man." ¹²Then the disciples came and said to him, "Do you know that the Pharisees were offended when they heard this saying?" ¹³He answered, "Every plant which my heavenly Father has not planted will be rooted

up. [14]Let them alone; they are blind guides. And if a blind man leads a blind man, both will fall into a pit." [15]But Peter said to him, "Explain the parable to us." [16]And he said, "Are you also still without understanding? [17]Do you not see that whatever goes into the mouth passes into the stomach, and so passes on? [18]But what comes out of the mouth proceeds from the heart, and this defiles a man. [19]For out of the heart come evil thoughts, murder, adultery, fornication, theft, false witness, slander. [20]These are what defile a man; but to eat with unwashed hands does not defile a man."

Mt abbreviates, adds to, and inverts the Markan text. Mt omits Mk's explanation of Pharisaic customs, since his church, coming out of a Jewish-Christian matrix, knows the practices quite well. Mt places the Isaiah quotation at the end of the first half of the pericope, thus creating the order of Law (Ex) and prophets (Is). Mt's additions intensify Jesus' rejection of official Judaism, which is represented by a formal commission of Pharisees and scribes from Jerusalem. They immediately attack Jesus' disciples (i.e., the church) for *transgressing* (Mt's heightening of the charge) the oral law formulated and handed down by the early Pharisees (=the tradition of the elders). Specifically, the disciples, before they eat, do not wash their hands to purify themselves from any object that might be levitically unclean. Such rituals were very important to the Pharisees, the "separatists," because they maintained the wall of separation between Israel and the unclean Gentiles. Like a good rabbi, Jesus replies with a counter-question and a counter-attack, claiming that the Pharisees, in their zeal for their oral traditions, *transgress* (the verb used by the Pharisees) something much more serious: the commandment of God. To justify his accusation, Jesus shows how the rabbinic custom of dedicating property to the temple, and thus withdrawing it from "secular" use (even aid for one's parents), frustrates God's will in the fourth commandment

(Ex 20:12) and in the negative prohibition supporting the commandment (Ex 21:17). (As usual, Mt omits the Aramaic word used by Mk, in this case, "Corban.") Pharisaic sin arises out of a piety which ignores the teaching of the prophets: God wants not sacrifices for himself but compassion for a man's neighbors (cf. 9:13; 12:7). The gravity of their sin is underscored by changing Mk's "Moses said" to "God said." In v.6, Mt cleverly creates an inclusion and a chiasm by harking back to the terms of v.3, but now in reverse order: tradition versus the word (commandment) of God. These Pharisees are the hypocrites Isaiah spoke of when he prophesied (Is 29:13) that "this people" (the Jews, led by the Pharisees) *honor* God (the fourth commandment uses the same verb) with lipservice, but their mind and will ("heart") really do not obey him. Their worship is as useless as idolatry, because they elevate merely human commandments to the status of revealed doctrine. Their commandments honor neither their God nor their parents. Thus Mt concludes the first half of the pericope (vv.1-9, on oral traditions such as handwashing) with a round condemnation of the Pharisees from the prophets.

In the second half of the pericope (vv.10-19), Mt broadens the condemnation of the Pharisees to their teachings on defilement in general, and even includes a rejection of the food laws of the Pentateuch. The second half of v.2 supplies a good summary of the two halves of the whole pericope: "for they do not wash their hands [vv.1-9] when they eat bread [vv.10-19]." Emphasizing the new rule he now publicly gives his community, Jesus summons the crowds and informs them that it is not the food which goes into the mouth which defiles a man, but rather the evil words (and, by an awkward extension, the evil deeds) which come forth from the mouth. Thus is the levitical-ritual concept of defilement transformed into a moral one. Defilement means basically being unfit for fellowship with God and his people; only moral evil—and certainly, not food— can create such alienation. By abrogating the food laws of the Pentateuch, Jesus has given all people the freedom to eat together, both now and at the messianic banquet. The battles over table fellowship with Gentiles which rocked the early church at Antioch (cf. Gal 2:11-21) are clearly over by the time Mt writes his gospel.

Commentators who try to maintain that Mt avoids Mk's abrogation of the written law in this pericope cannot explain v.11 and indeed the heightened polemical tone in Mt. The Pharisees have annulled God's word (v.6); now Jesus annuls part of the Pentateuch. The disciples, knowing how Jesus' new rule strikes at the very heart of not only Pharisaism but also Judaism, and knowing what the enmity of the Pharisees might bring, try to caution Jesus. They reflect all too well the hesitations of the early church in putting Jesus' radicalism into practice. But Jesus simply underscores his rejection of the Pharisees and their teaching by using an OT image for Israel and also for the just or evil man (cf. Is 5:1-7; Jer 45:4; Ps 1:3; Wisd 4:3-5). The community of Qumran also considered itself the "planting" of God. The Father has not planted the community formed by the Pharisees (i.e., post-A.D. 70 Judaism); they will be rooted up. Their moral guidance is as worthless as a blind man's directions; they have brought ruin on the Jews who followed them (cf. 23:16; Rom 2:19). Therefore Jesus' disciples must "let them alone" or—as the Greek probably means—"leave them." Thus Mt reflects his church's break with the synagogue.

In Mk the disciples ask Jesus for an explanation of this parable; Mt singles out Peter, who will later be entrusted with the power to make decisions on morality in Jesus' church (16:19; cf. the pivotal role Peter plays in the dispute on levitical uncleanness in Acts 10-11). Although Mt softens the Markan rebuke of the disciples' obtuseness, he shows that he does not consider the disciples' understanding to be perfect during the public ministry. Their understanding, like their faith, is still immature, especially on questions of Mosaic Law and Pharisaic custom. Mt may be charging his own church with the same fault. Still, as opposed to the crowds, the disciples do ask Jesus the explanation of the parable and do receive enlightenment from him (cf. 13:36). Jesus expands on his rule of v.11; notice how "mouth" serves as the key-word. Food entering the mouth is a purely transitory matter of physical processes; it cannot play any decisive role in defiling a man. The sins which come forth from a man's mouth are what defile a man. They make real in the world the defilement which lies in his heart; the "mouth" thus symbolizes the point of contact between man's inner evil and its external manifestation in word and deed. In the catalogue of vices which follows, Mt reworks Mk's rambling list so that, after the internal sin of evil thoughts, all the external sins follow the order of the second tablet of the decalogue (murder—adultery and fornication—theft—false witness). The RSV's "slander" might be better translated "blasphemies"; it sums up sins against the first tablet of the decalogue. As in the antitheses, Mt stresses the basic moral obligations enshrined in the ten commandments. These represent the genuine will of God, and compared to them all ritual and levitical questions become meaningless.

Having finished the second half of the pericope, Mt neatly rounds off the whole with an inclusion; v.20b brings us back to the original problem raised in v.2. This inclusion should not be taken to mean that Mt is trying to ignore or soften what he clearly says in v.11: the food laws are abrogated. The gospel of Jesus frees man from ritual laws, only to bind man more rigorously to his basic moral obligations towards God and neighbor (cf. 22:34-40).

F. THE FAITH OF THE CANAANITE WOMAN.
15:21-28.
[Mk 7:24-30]

> [21]And Jesus went away from there and withdrew to the district of Tyre and Sidon. [22]And behold, a Canaanite

woman from that region came out and cried, "Have mercy on me, O Lord, Son of David; my daughter is severely possessed by a demon." 23But he did not answer her a word. And his disciples came and begged him, saying, "Send her away, for she is crying after us." 24He answered, "I was sent only to the lost sheep of the house of Israel." 25But she came and knelt before him, saying, "Lord, help me." 26And he answered, "It is not fair to take the children's bread and throw it to the dogs." 27She said, "Yes, Lord, yet even the dogs eat the crumbs that fall from their masters' table." 28Then Jesus answered her, "O woman, great is your faith! Be it done for you as you desire." And her daughter was healed instantly.

Jesus has just torn down the wall of laws about clean and unclean which kept Jews and Gentiles apart. Now he acts out his own teaching in one of his rare contacts with a Gentile. The story is very similar to that of the centurion (8:5-13; cf. the comments there). The Gentile, using the title "Lord," comes to Jesus pleading for a sick loved one; in response to great humility and faith expressed in prayer, Jesus heals the loved one from a distance. Both stories indicate that, while Jesus' earthly ministry was restricted in principle to Israel, the church's mission after the death-resurrection will include Gentiles, who will have access to the Lord through faith and humility. Mt follows Mk, but inserts the "particularistic saying" of 15:24, an M-tradition similar to 10:6 (cf. comments on that verse).

Jesus leaves the land of Gennesaret (14:34) and goes to the far northern regions of Galilee, on the border with the region around the southern Phoenician cities of Tyre and Sidon (Mt adds Sidon to Mk's Tyre; cf. 11:21). Probably Mt, unlike Mk, does not intend to portray Jesus as leaving the land of Israel (in v.29 Jesus is already back at the Sea of Galilee). V.22 should probably read: "a Canaanite woman came out *from that region*"; thus she crosses over to Jesus in Israel (an act of humility she later puts into words).

Mk calls the woman a Syrophoenician; Mt changes that to "Canaanite," a name which conjures up the OT image of the pagan enemies of God's people. Yet this Gentile shows she is a believer by addressing Jesus as "Lord." The added title, "Son of David," is spoken by the "no-accounts" of the gospel who nevertheless trust in Jesus' mercy; its use by the woman shows that she believes in the Messiah who has been rejected by his own Jewish people. Jesus at first remains silent. The annoyed disciples ask Jesus to stop her yelling by granting her request (from Jesus' apparent refusal in v.24, this is probably the meaning of "send her away"). Jesus replies that his mission is limited to Israel, which sorely needs his ministrations because it is made up of lost sheep (cf. 9:36). The woman is not to be put off; in Mt, she repeats her request with a heart-rending simplicity reminiscent of the Psalms.

Jesus tests the woman's faith and humility by countering with a harsh parable; Jews often referred to Gentiles as dogs (cf. comments on 7:6). The *bread* of salvation (cf. 14:13-21; 15:32-39) with which Jesus wishes to nourish Israel, the sons of the kingdom (cf. 8:12, and the reference to the banquet in the kingdom), must not be taken from the sons and given to pagan dogs. Mt makes this saying even harsher by dropping Mk's introductory comment, which offers some hope: "Let the children *first* be fed" (Mk 7:27). The plucky woman, however, is capable of a test of wits as well as of faith. She agrees with Jesus' parable and yet turns it to her advantage. "Yes, Lord," your statement of priorities is correct, and as a Gentile I acknowledge the rights and privileges of Israel; indeed, the Jews are admitted to be the "masters" of the pagans. *Yet*, precisely on the terms of your parable I have hope; sooner or later some crumbs will inadvertently fall from the table to the floor, to be snapped up by the dogs. Jesus cannot be swayed by any claims or merit, but he is overcome by the prayer of faith, expressed with humility and humor. As in the story of the centurion, and as opposed to Mk, Mt emphasizes faith as that which gives Gentiles access to healing and salvation (cf. 8:10,13). The possessed daughter, who, like the centurion's servant, has been merely the occasion for the real subject-matter of the pericope, is healed "from that hour" (RSV: "instantly").

G. HEALING AND FEEDING THE CROWD OF FOUR THOUSAND.
15:29-39.
[Mk 8:1-10]

29And Jesus went on from there and passed along the Sea of Galilee. And he went up on the mountain, and sat down there. 30And great crowds came to him, bringing with them the lame, the maimed, the blind, the dumb, and many others, and they put them at his feet, and he healed them, 31so that the throng wondered, when they saw the dumb speaking, the maimed whole, the lame walking, and the blind seeing; and they glorified the God of Israel.

32Then Jesus called his disciples to him and said, "I have compassion on the crowd, because they have been with me now three days, and have nothing to eat; and I am unwilling to send them away hungry, lest they faint on the way." 33And the disciples said to him, "Where are we to get bread enough in the desert to feed so great a crowd?" 34And Jesus said to them, "How many loaves have you?" They said, "Seven, and a few small fish." 35And commanding the crowd to sit down on the ground, 36he took the seven loaves and the fish, and having given thanks he broke them and gave them to the disciples, and the disciples gave them to the crowds. 37And they all ate and were satisfied; and they took up seven baskets full of the broken pieces left over. 38Those who ate were four thousand men, besides women and children. 39And sending away the crowds, he got into the boat and went to the region of Magadan.

Mt replaces Mk's story of the healing of a deaf and dumb man with a summary of Jesus' healing activity. Mt may have omitted this Markan miracle (as he does the healing of the blind man from Mk 8:22-26) because the actions of Jesus smacked of magic, or simply because Mt has already reported the healing of the deaf and dumb in 9:32-34 and 12:22.

Coming back from northern Galilee, Jesus reaches the lake, goes *up the mountain* (RSV: "into the hills") and sits: precisely the actions of 5:1. For the mountain as the place of revelation, see the comments on 5:1 (cf. also 8:1; 14:23; 17:1,9; 28:16). This symbolic geography helps Mt avoid the unintelligible itinerary in Mk 7:31. Mt describes the various kinds of sick persons brought to Jesus, in terms reminiscent of Is 35:5-6; 29:18-19 (cf. comments on 11:5). The allusions to Isaiah explain why the chorus-like finale in v.31 reads: "and they glorified the God of Israel" (cf. Is 29:23: "and they will stand in awe of the God of Israel"). Thus, this title of God does not imply that those healed are Gentiles; the episode of the Canaanite woman was an exception. Mt delights in creating such summaries (cf. 4:23-25; 8:16-17; 9:35; 14:14); here we have the last summary of the Galilean ministry. It is meant to portray the successful climax of Jesus' healing ministry in Galilee. For this crowd is not only healed; it is also fed by Jesus. In v.32, the compassion of Jesus is again mentioned as a motive. In Mk 6:34 it moves Jesus to teach; in Mt 14:14 it moves Jesus to heal; here it moves Jesus to feed the crowd. Mt alters Mk so that the disciples express in a rhetorical question *their* inability (not Jesus'!) to obtain bread for such a crowd. Mt 15:34 adds "a few small fish" to Mk's "seven loaves," and so avoids Mk's awkward addition of a separate blessing over fish later in the narrative. The words "having given thanks" (*eucharistēsas*) instead of "blessed" (14:19) heighten the Eucharistic overtones. Eating, being satisfied, collecting fragments, enumeration of participants (Mt again adds women and children)—all parallel the first multiplication. Mt changes the destination of Jesus' sea-crossing from Mk's Dalmanutha to Magadan; unfortunately, both places are unknown.

Obviously we have here a doublet of the event recorded in 14:13-21. The only notable differences in this second version are the numbers (three days, seven loaves, seven baskets, four thousand men) and the fact that Jesus takes the initiative (cf. 14:15). There is no reason to differentiate Mt's second account by supposing that it symbolizes a Gentile church (contrast Mk 8:3: "and some of them have come a long way"). This doublet of the multiplication is actually part of a larger series of doublets which probably existed before Mk. The whole series was incorporated into Mk's "bread-section" (chaps. 6-8), where there are two series of events in the order: multiplication—crossing of the water—dispute with Pharisees—healings. Since Mt favors doublets, he reproduces most of Mk's "bread-section"; Lk, on the other hand, jumps from the first multiplication of loaves to Peter's confession.

H. JESUS REJECTS THE JEWISH MAGISTERIUM AND WARNS HIS DISCIPLES AGAINST IT. 16.1-12.
[Mk 8:11-21; Lk 11:16; 12:54-56; 11:29; 12:1]

> **16** And the Pharisees and Sadducees came, and to test him they asked him to show them a sign from heaven. [2]He answered them, "When it is evening, you say, 'It will be fair weather; for the sky is red.' [3]And in the morning, 'It will be stormy today, for the sky is red and threatening.' You know how to interpret the appearance of the sky, but you cannot interpret the signs of the times. [4]An evil and adulterous generation seeks for a sign, but no sign

shall be given to it except the sign of Jonah." So he left them and departed.

⁵When the disciples reached the other side, they had forgotten to bring any bread. ⁶Jesus said to them, "Take heed and beware of the leaven of the Pharisees and Sadducees." ⁷And they discussed it among themselves, saying, "We brought no bread." ⁸But Jesus, aware of this, said, "O men of little faith, why do you discuss among yourselves the fact that you have no bread? ⁹Do you not yet perceive? Do you not remember the five loaves of the five thousand, and how many baskets you gathered? ¹⁰Or the seven loaves of the four thousand, and how many baskets you gathered? ¹¹How is it that you fail to perceive that I did not speak about bread? Beware of the leaven of the Pharisees and Sadducees." ¹²Then they understood that he did not tell them to beware of the leaven of bread, but of the teaching of the Pharisees and Sadducees.

Mt tightens the Markan connection between the rejection of the request for a sign and the warning to the disciples. Mt adds the Sadducees and a reference to the sign of Jonah, strikes out the crossing of the sea during the discussion about bread, interprets the leaven in terms of teaching, and turns the blindness of the disciples into little faith. In other words, the pericope bristles with Matthean concepts.

The united front of official Judaism, represented in Mt's mind by the Pharisees and Sadducees, demands a sign from heaven to authenticate Jesus' mission (cf. comments on 12:38). The answer in vv. 2-3 is not contained in some important early manuscripts. If these verses are original, Jesus first draws an unflattering comparison between his enemies' ability to judge indications of the coming weather and their inability to see the indications of the coming of the kingdom in the signs Jesus offers, namely his teaching and miracles, and especially the miracles at the end of chap. 15. If, as seems likely, vv. 2-3 are a later interpolation, Jesus refuses to give to this faithless group, which embodies the persistent unbelief of Israel, any sign—except the sign which will signal the eschatological turning point of salvation history: his own death and resurrection, which he has already compared to the fate of Jonah (cf. comments on 12:38-40). What in Mk is a flat denial of a sign becomes in Mt a positive prophecy of a sign. But even that sign will not convince this evil generation (cf. 28:11-15). And so Jesus acts out their final rejection by leaving them.

Mt apparently thinks Jesus had crossed the lake alone in 15:39. In v.5 his disciples catch up with him; while his mind is still on the false teachers of Israel, their mind is on the food they had forgotten to bring. Two different themes are interwoven in the subsequent misunderstanding and clarification. (1) A subordinate theme is Jesus' rebuke to the disciples for their lack of trust in Jesus, who has proven by two miracles that he can more than supply their physical needs. If their *faith* were not so *little* (cf. comments on 6:30; 8:26; 14:31), they would have known immediately that Jesus was not concerned about material bread, which he can multiply at will. (2) The more important theme is Jesus' warning about the leaven (i.e., the corrupting influence) of the Pharisees and Sadducees. In a verse so typical of Mt, the disciples are said to understand what Jesus means (they remain blind in Mk). The leaven signifies the corrupting *teaching* of the Jewish leaders, which hinders faith in Jesus. Their teaching (and implicitly their teaching office or magisterium) is rejected just before Jesus confers the magisterium on Peter (16:18-19). While the call to obey the Pharisees' magisterium in 23:2-3 seems to stem from an earlier time when Mt's church was still bound to the synagogue, the clearly redactional nature of 16:12 shows that in Mt's own day the church has definitively broken with the synagogue. A curious point is that Mt speaks of *the* teaching common to the Pharisees-and-Sadducees. Such a conjunction reflects neither the time of Jesus (when the Pharisees and Sadducees differed over basic doctrinal questions) nor Mt's day (when the Sadducees had been practically wiped out and their memory was besmirched by the Pharisees). Such a slip about a matter any learned Jew would know may indicate that Mt, our Christian scribe, was a learned *Gentile* Christian.

I. CAESAREA PHILIPPI:
CHRIST AND HIS CHURCH.
16:13-28.
[Mk 8:27-9:1; Lk 9:18-27]

Since Mt drops Mk's messianic secret, he has no need for the gradual healing of the blind man (Mk 8:22-26), which symbolizes the partial healing of Peter's blindness at Caesarea Philippi. Mt may have also omitted the rough story because of its magical overtones. From Mk's two-part pericope placed at Caesarea Philippi, Mt has created a three-part scene which forms the high point of Book Four: (1) Peter's profession of Jesus' greatness and Jesus' prophecy of Peter's greatness (vv. 13-20); (2) Jesus' first prediction of his passion and resurrection, and his rebuke to Peter (vv. 21-23); (3) The passion and resurrection of the disciples (vv. 24-28). The whole pericope, especially the first section, manifests perfectly Mt's desire to join together christology and ecclesiology. As is often the case elsewhere in the gospel, this entails adding a new ecclesiological dimension to traditionally christological material. Notice how Mt both heightens the christological formula addressed to Jesus and the role of Peter as confessor of this high christology.

(1) Peter and Jesus Confer Titles on Each Other.
  16:13-20.

> [13]Now when Jesus came into the district of Caesarea Philippi, he asked his disciples, "Who do men say that the Son of man is?" [14]And they said, "Some say John the Baptist, others say Elijah, and others Jeremiah or one of the prophets." [15]He said to them, "But who do you say

that I am?" [16]Simon Peter replied, "You are the Christ, the Son of the living God." [17]And Jesus answered him, "Blessed are you, Simon Bar-Jona! For flesh and blood has not revealed this to you, but my Father who is in heaven. [18]And I tell you, you are Peter, and on this rock I will build my church, and the powers of death shall not prevail against it. [19]I will give you the keys of the kingdom of heaven, and whatever you bind on earth shall be bound in heaven, and whatever you loose on earth shall be loosed in heaven." [20]Then he strictly charged the disciples to tell no one that he was the Christ.

To the Markan tradition about Peter's confession addressed to Jesus Mt adds from his M-source a "confession" of Jesus addressed to Peter. Having rejected the magisterium of the Jewish leaders (16:1-12) Jesus now confers it on the leader of the Twelve. The M-material in vv.17-19 is probably not a creation of Mt. Many of its phrases reflect an Aramaic background, and the play on Simon's new title is directly intelligible only in Aramaic. Vv.17-19 form a neat unit, since the words of Jesus form three strophes (one for each verse) and each strophe contains three lines (the first line expressing a new theme, and the second and third lines developing the theme in antithetic propositions). The original context of vv. 17-19 may have been the Easter appearance of Christ to Peter.

The momentous scene begins near Caesarea Philippi, the Roman city on the site of the older Paneas. It was a recent foundation of the Tetrarch Philip (hence the name). The importance of the geographical reference is that Jesus is now at the northernmost limits of ancient Israel; in Mt, Jesus' ministry spans most of the Holy Land but never leaves it. Instead of Mk's "who do men say that *I* am?", Mt has "who the *Son of Man* is." The use of this title at the very beginning of the pericope adds solemnity to the question, forms an inclusion with vv.27-28, and creates a clever play on "men"-"Son of Man." The one long pericope of vv.13-28 exemplifies the three meanings of Son of Man: earthly Jesus of the ministry (v.13), suffering servant (implicitly in v.21), and glorious judge of the last day (vv.27-28). The initial use in v.13 plainly refers to Jesus and yet, as always, carries with it an air of mystery, a question which now urgently demands an answer. The answers of the run of mankind are disappointing; they simply recycle great prophetic figures of the past, and so hardly go beyond Herod's superstitious musings in 14:2. Mt adds the suffering prophet *par excellence*, Jeremiah, who points forward to the first prediction of the passion. Jesus, like Jeremiah, will suffer rejection and martyrdom at the hands of his own people even as he predicts the fall of Jerusalem (cf. 23:37-39). Jesus rejects these inadequate christologies of others and demands that his disciples speak for themselves. It is the telling question addressed to every believer: "But *you*—who do *you* say that I am?"

Simon Peter—Mt has anticipated Simon's new title from 4:18 onwards and does so here—acts as spokesman for the disciples, yet he expresses what Jesus praises as an insight given by the Father to Peter in particular. Peter replies with a solemn confessional formula of Mt's church. First he identifies Jesus the Son of Man with the Messiah promised to the chosen people. This forms the complete response in Mk, where no human being confesses Jesus as Son of God before the death on the cross. Even in Mt, no disciple has explicitly called Jesus the Messiah before Caesarea Philippi. But this Son of Man-Messiah transcends all images and hopes from Israel's past. He is also the transcendent Son of God (cf. comments on 11:27; 14:33). The solemn liturgical phrase "living God" is known in both OT and NT, and expresses the truth that God both has life in himself and creates life in others. The Son will do likewise, indeed, by his very death (cf. 27:52-53). Together, Son of Man and Son of God form the highpoint and center of Mt's "Son"-christology.

The first strophe of Jesus' corresponding "confession" to Peter the Son of *Jonah* (perhaps a variant form of *John*, cf. Jn 21:15-17) is a beatitude (v.17). Like certain apocalyptic seers, Peter is congratulated for having been specially chosen to receive the revelation of "my Father," who, of course, can alone reveal the Son (cf. comments on 11:27). "Flesh and blood," i.e., weak, mortal man, could never grasp or communicate this divine mystery of sonship. Peter has received nothing less than an apocalyptic revelation of the end-time. The similarity of the language to Paul's description of the *revelation* of the risen *Son* to him (Gal 1:16) argues for a resurrection appearance as the original context. The second strophe (v. 18) tells what the Son himself will do for Peter on the basis of the Father's gift. To his word of felicitation Jesus adds a word of promise, which takes the form of a conferral of a new title. Peter has addressed Jesus with certain titles; now Jesus reciprocates. But, while Peter was simply acknowledging what Jesus always was, Jesus confers a new title on Peter. Since the title will become a second name, this conferral of title recalls those instances in the OT when Yahweh conferred a new name on some important figure of salvation history, most notably Abraham. Jesus acts with the same sovereign authority as Peter's Lord. It should be stressed that, up to this time in ancient Palestine, "Peter" (*Petros* in Greek, *Kēphâ* in Aramaic) had not been used as anyone's personal name. We should not think of "Peter" as a personal name with the secondary meaning "rock"; the word simply meant "rock" and nothing more. Jesus is not changing one first name to another; he is conferring on Simon a new title, "the Rock." The play on words is lost in English and slightly obscured in Greek. In Aramaic it would run: "You are the Rock (*Kēphâ*; cf. 1 Cor 15:5; Gal 2:9,11; Jn 1:42), and upon this rock (*kēphâ*) I will build my church." The original Aramaic form makes clear that "this rock" refers to the person of Simon, and not to his faith or to Jesus. The significance of the rock is that it is firm, supplying a solid foundation for building (cf. Mt's perfect explanation of the image in 7:24-25). Abraham was considered to be the rock from which the people Israel was hewn (Is 51:1-2), and a rabbinic saying claims that Abraham was the rock on which God built the world. Similarly, Peter will be the human patriarch and foundation-stone of the new people of God. There may also be a reference here to the cosmic rock on which the temple was supposedly built, a rock which gave entrance both to heaven and hell.

On the new rock, Peter, the new temple of Jesus' church will be built. Whether the Semitic background for church (*ekklēsia* in Greek) be *qehālâ*, *kenishtâ*, or *'ēdâ*, the idea is that of the eschatological people which Jesus has gathered together, the holy remnant which is saved. Both the Son of Man and the Messiah (Mt has just made plain that Jesus is both) were corporate personalities; they could not be properly conceived of without the people they saved and led. This community of salvation, the people Jesus will save from their sins (cf. 1:21), will find a firm foundation in Peter. A similar image of building the community of the end-time is found at Qumran. Precisely because it is the congregation of the end-time, the power of death will not be able to defeat it. While "the gates of Hades" might refer to the power of Satan, the more likely reference is to death. The perdurance of the church in and beyond this world is assured, for the church is the expression in the present of the coming kingdom of heaven.

The third and final strophe (v. 19) is a proclamation of Peter's investiture with the power of vicegerent. The image of the keys is taken from Is 22:15-25, where Shebna is removed from his position as major-domo over King Hezekiah's palace and Eliakim is given his powers ("I will commit your authority to his hand . . . and I will place on his shoulder the key of the house of David"). The church built on rock is conceived of as a palace, and in it Peter has the authority to bind and loose (cf. Is 22:22, "he shall open, and none shall shut; he shall shut, and none shall open"). Concretely the power to bind and loose, mentioned in rabbinic sources, refers to (1) the authority to decide what actions are permissible or not permissible according to the teachings of Jesus; and (2) the authority to admit and exclude people from the community. Given the context of chap. 16, teaching authority seems dominant here, while 18:18, speaking of the local church, emphasizes the power to excommunicate. Certainly, one power implies the other. But 16:18 stresses the power to make decisions for the *universal* church ("*my* church"), while 18:18, which does not mention the image of the keys of the kingdom, envisions disciplinary actions by the local community. What Peter "the chief rabbi" decides now on earth will be ratified by God ("bound" and "loosed" are the divine passive) at the last judgment ("in heaven"). The church is therefore not completely identified with the future kingdom; but in Mt the relationship becomes very close. At v.20, Mt rejoins Mk and repeats Mk's command of silence, which Mt pointedly refers to the title Messiah. "Messiah," the new element in the disciples' faith (they already knew to some extent that Jesus was Son of Man and Son of God) was the title which would be most easily misunderstood by the nationalistic crowds. Jesus will now proceed to correct any such nationalistic illusions in his disciples' mind by uttering the first prediction of the passion.

(2) Jesus Predicts the Passion and Rebukes Peter, 16:21-23

> [21]From that time Jesus began to show his disciples that he must go to Jerusalem and suffer many things from the elders and chief priests and scribes, and be killed, and on the third day be raised. [22]And Peter took him and began to rebuke him, saying, "God forbid, Lord! This shall never happen to you." [23]But he turned and said to Peter, "Get behind me, Satan! You are a hindrance to me; for you are not on the side of God, but of man."

Mk, and even more so Lk, bind Peter's confession and the first prediction of the passion closely together. Because he has expanded the confession of Peter with Jesus' praise of Peter, Mt feels the need to separate what follows (Jesus' rebuke to Peter) from what precedes. Mt begins again solemnly in v.21 with "From that time Jesus [some ancient manuscripts add 'Christ'] began to show . . . ." But the need to mark off a new subsection of the Caesarea Philippi pericope should not lead us to the conclusion that we have in v.21 a major structural division of the whole gospel. The opening phrase of v.21 connects as well as divides: from the pivotal moment of Peter's confession that Jesus is the Christ, Jesus Christ must begin to correct and complement that truth with the prediction of his death and resurrection. It is the other side of the Father's secret, apocalyptic plan for salvation; therefore the Son who is revealer "shows" what "must" take place (for this apocalyptic terminology, cf. Rev 1:1). Since Mt has used Son of Man already in 16:13, he does not repeat the title here; but the theme of passion, death, and resurrection naturally conjures up the figure of the Son of Man. In Mt, Jesus has already used Son of Man in a veiled reference to his death (cf. 12:40), and Son of Man will be explicitly used in the second and third predictions of the passion (17:22-23; 20:17-19; cf. the "fourth prediction" in 26:1-2). His passion must take place in Jerusalem (not mentioned here by Mk), the traditional holy-yet-unholy city where the prophets meet their violent fate (23:29-39). There Jesus will suffer at the hands of the highest tribunal of official Judaism: the Sanhedrin, which drew its members from the three groups of elders (lay nobility), leading priestly families, and professional theologians or lawyers (scribes). Then he will be "killed" (*apoktanthēnai*, reflecting the idea of the prophets' martyrdom). Note the lack of any reference here to crucifixion or the role of the Gentiles; it is a purely Jewish affair (contrast the detailed summary in 20:17-19). While Mk, in all three passion predictions, says that the Son of Man will "rise after three days" (Mk 8:31), Mt always substitutes the more precise terminology found also in the early creed of 1 Cor 15:3-5: he will "be raised [by the Father] on the third day."

Peter, who has gladly received and voiced the joyful revelation of the transcendent Son and Messiah, cannot accept this apparently contradictory revelation; the other side of the apocalyptic secret remains hidden from him. Peter dares to take Jesus aside and remonstrate with him. His opening word may mean either: "God forbid" or "God is gracious to you"—and therefore a gracious God could never let any such thing befall his Son! A piety centered on the comfortable words of glory and mercy revolts at the hard word of the cross. Mt, who has expanded Peter's confession and exalted his role, now balances the scale by sharpening Jesus' rebuke. Mk has the harsh "Get behind me, Satan!"; but Mt, unlike Mk, has already recorded a similar dismissal spoken by Jesus to the real Satan at the end of the temptation narrative (4:10). In the third temptation, Satan had tried to deflect Jesus from the way of the cross by a promise of easy glory; now Peter renews the temptation and so takes over Satan's role. With black humor Mt adds that this Rock of the church has just become for Jesus a stumbling-stone (*skandalon*; RSV: "hindrance"). It is a strong temptation, naturally attractive, even for Jesus— hence the verbal violence with which Jesus rejects it. Jesus had begun this whole pericope by appealing to the disciples to transcend the inadequate christologies of *men* in general. Now he finds that the Rock of the church, for all his fine words, is really thinking (*phroneis*) the thoughts and christologies of ordinary men. A christology which revels in divine sonship but which has no room for the cross is no better than the inadequate view of v.14. Peter's heart is still set on the success sought by men, not the goal set by God. Peter must "get behind" Jesus in a deeper sense of learning once again what true discipleship, true following means: a following to the cross. Only then can Peter cease

to be the stumbling-stone and become again the Rock.
Peter represents the tension-filled, paradoxical existence
of every Christian caught between faith and doubt, on the
way of the cross with a promise of glory. In this, too, Peter
is the spokesman for all the disciples. Peter and the whole
church stand subject to both election and danger, grace
and judgment.

(3) Cross and Glory for Both Master and Disciples. 16:24-28

> 24Then Jesus told his disciples, "If any man would
> come after me, let him deny himself and take up his cross
> and follow me. 25For whoever would save his life will
> lose it, and whoever loses his life for my sake will find it.
> 26For what will it profit a man, if he gains the whole
> world and forfeits his life? Or what shall a man give in
> return for his life? 27For the Son of man is to come with
> his angels in the glory of his Father, and then he will
> repay every man for what he has done. 28Truly, I say to
> you, there are some standing here who will not taste death
> before they see the Son of man coming in his kingdom."

Following Mk, Mt presents a series of five sayings which
move from the cost of discipleship in the present to the
reward for discipleship (or the punishment for the lack
thereof) when the Son of Man comes to judge. The first
three sayings (vv.24,25,26) follow Mk closely; vv.24-25
were already used by Mt in a different form in the missionary
discourse (10:38-39); Mk 8:38, which Mt omits here, occurred in a Q-form in Mt 10:33. In the fifth saying, Mt
avoids Mk's new beginning and so ties the final statement,
into which he introduces the Son of Man, more closely to the
other sayings. The introduction of the Son of Man (Mk has
"the kingdom of God") into Mt 16:28 creates a grand
inclusion with 16:13. The christological question about
who Jesus the earthly Son of Man is must receive an answer
in terms of future eschatology and the last judgment.

In v.24 Mt fittingly strikes out Mk's crowd and has Jesus address only the disciples on the cost of discipleship. Discipleship means an affirmation of Jesus which entails a negation of self-centeredness, an immolation of egotism on the cross (cf. 10:38 for comments on the cross). As goes the Master, so goes the disciple. The disciple who has rejected Jesus' prediction of his sufferings in v.21 betrays his illusions about his own future. Not only must the believer accept the Messiah's shattering prediction of v.21; he must accept it as a prophecy of his own destiny, as well as the destiny of his Lord. For, as v.25 drives home, the paradox of temporal loss for eternal gain is *the* law of Christian existence. A truly fulfilled life eludes the grasp of the person who selfishly seeks self-fulfillment. Only those who cease to grasp at life, only those who give up their little projects of a tailored-to-order existence and who surrender their lives to God in imitation of and for the sake of the crucified Jesus will receive the fullness of life, as a gift from God. As v.26 points out, all human conceptions of loss and gain have been turned upside down. Winning the whole world is not success but failure, because this world is passing away, along with anyone who pins all his hopes on a universe under judgment. On the last day, not all the treasures a person has gained on earth will buy the one thing he has lost: his own salvation, his own true, eternal life (cf. Ps 49:5-9). Jesus is going to the cross to give the only acceptable ransom or exchange for man's life (20:28). If a disciple will not accept and imitate Christ's ransom, he will find no other on the last day.

The idea of final judgment, which stands behind vv.25-26, is explicitated in v.27. In a sweeping apocalyptic scene we are presented with a quasi-Jewish "Trinity": the Son of Man, his father, and his angels. The angels, mentioned in Mk 8:38, are pointedly said to be the angels of the transcendent Son of Man in Mt 16:27. And, most importantly for a full appreciation of Mt's "Son"-christology, God the Father is called the Father of the Son of Man ("*his* father"). One must not immediately assimilate all references to

Father and Son in Mt to a "Son-of-God" christology; the figure of the Son of Man may also be meant. It is this Son of Man, coming in and surrounded by "glory," the light proper to and radiating from the divinity, who will hold the last judgment. Being the judge of the whole cosmos, he will reward and punish each person, disciple and unbeliever alike, according to his concrete way of acting (*praxin*, cf. Ps 62:12).

It is under the influence of v.27 that v.28 has been reformulated to introduce the Son of Man. With the solemn Amen-formula of the apocalyptic seer, the earthly Son of Man assures his disciples that some of them will not die until they see the Son of Man coming with his royal power (RSV: "in his kingdom"). While the original saying standing behind Mk 9:1 may have expressed the early Christians' longing for an imminent parousia, such can hardly be the meaning of 16:28 in the mind of Mt, who is writing ca. A.D. 90. Mt's own theology has come to grips with the phenomenon of a second and even a third generation of Christians. As we can see in these verses and throughout the gospel, the stringency of judgment, not its imminence, is the main motive in Mt's moral exhortation. Perhaps Mt makes a distinction between the Son of Man's coming in apocalyptic glory to judge on the last day and his coming to his church in an anticipated "parousia" at the end of the gospel (cf. 28:16-20). It is at that moment, after the turning point of the ages (the death-resurrection), that Jesus the Son of Man can proclaim for the first time that he has received all power over the cosmos (28:18). Then, for the first time, do his disciples see him coming with his royal power.

J. THE TRANSFIGURATION:
SON OF GOD AND SON OF MAN.
17:1-13.
[Mk 9:2-13; Lk 9:28-36]

> **17** And after six days Jesus took with him Peter and James and John his brother, and led them up a high

mountain apart. [2]And he was transfigured before them, and his face shone like the sun, and his garments became white as light. [3]And behold, there appeared to them Moses and Elijah, talking with him. [4]And Peter said to Jesus, "Lord, it is well that we are here; if you wish, I will make three booths here, one for you and one for Moses and one for Elijah." [5]He was still speaking, when lo, a bright cloud overshadowed them, and a voice from the cloud said, "This is my beloved Son, with whom I am well pleased; listen to him." [6]When the disciples heard this, they fell on their faces, and were filled with awe. [7]But Jesus came and touched them, saying, "Rise, and have no fear." [8]And when they lifted up their eyes, they saw no one but Jesus only.

[9]And as they were coming down the mountain, Jesus commanded them, "Tell no one the vision, until the Son of man is raised from the dead." [10]And the disciples asked him, "Then why do the scribes say that first Elijah must come?" [11]He replied, "Elijah does come, and he is to restore all things; [12]but I tell you that Elijah has already come, and they did not know him, but did to him whatever they pleased. So also the Son of man will suffer at their hands." [13]Then the disciples understood that he was speaking to them of John the Baptist.

Mt, though following Mk, uses this narrative as a confirmation of Peter's confession of Jesus as Son of the living God (16:16), as an anticipation of resurrection and parousia, and as a vehicle for developing the connection between Son of God and Son of Man. Six days intervene between Peter's confession and the transfiguration. Such precise time-indications are rare outside the passion narrative. Some have tried to associate the six days with the week-long feast of Tabernacles or the ascent of Moses into the clouds on Mount Sinai, but both references are questionable. The special group of three disciples does not play as large a role in Mt as in Mk; the group as such appears again only in Gethsemane. It is pointless to try to locate the mountain (e.g., Thabor, Hermon); the mountain is a favorite Matthean symbol for revelation (cf. the comment on 15:29). Jesus' appearance is changed ("transfigured"="changed in form"). The radiant face and garments show that Jesus belongs to the heavenly or divine world, the world of light (cf. 13:43 of the righteous in heaven; 28:3, of the angel at the tomb). Commentators refer to the face of Moses after he had spoken with God (Ex 34:29), but here we have rather a common image from apocalyptic literature (cf. the vision of "one like a son of man" in Rev 1:12-16).

The disciples experience a foretaste of the vision of the Son of Man which Jesus promised in 16:28. Reversing and coordinating the names in Mk, Mt depicts Moses and Elijah, the Law and the prophets, speaking with Jesus, the fulfiller of Law and prophets (5:17). In the OT, both figures had received revelation from God on Sinai (Horeb). In Judaism, both were believed to have been taken up to heaven; and one or both were expected to return in the last days. Those days, the time of fulfillment, have arrived. As usual, Peter is the spokesman; and naturally he addresses Jesus not with the Markan "Rabbi" (a sign of unbelief in Mt) but rather with "Lord," the believer's mode of address. Peter is his over-confident self, remarking that it is a good thing that *we* are here to provide for your needs. With a touch of politeness added by Mt ("if you wish"), *he* personally (not the three disciples, as in Mk) will build three tents for the heavenly trio. The RSV and others translate *skēnas* as "booths," with an eye to the Feast of Tabernacles or Booths. But the huts for that feast were used by men, not heavenly beings; "tents," with a possible allusion to the divine dwelling-place, is better. Mt suppresses at this point Mk's reference to Peter's lack of understanding and the disciples' fear.

While Peter is still speaking, the revelation reaches its climax as a radiant cloud, the revealing yet veiling symbol of God's presence, descends upon and envelops the scene. God is perceived not directly by sight but only through his word. Unlike Mk, Mt has the divine voice repeat exactly the revelation spoken at the baptism of Jesus (cf. comments on 3:17): Jesus is the beloved Son, but also the servant on whom the Father's favor rests. The one element not present in the baptismal revelation is the command: Hear him! This probably echoes Moses' prediction that God would raise up a prophet-like-Moses: "him shall you hear" (Dt. 18:15). Listen to him—not only when he confirms the joyful revelation of the glorious Messiah and Son of God, but also when he adds the disturbing revelation of the suffering Son of Man. Listen to him as he explains this mystery to you when you descend the mount. Mt deftly picks up this command in the next verse: when the disciples hear this, i.e., the divine voice announcing the total mystery of the Son, they fall on their faces "and fear greatly." It is the usual reaction of weak, mortal men to an apocalyptic vision (Dan 8:17; 10:9-11; Rev 1:17). The act of Jesus in touching them and encouraging them (present only in Mt) is witnessed in the same apocalyptic texts. Mt has already given examples of the life-giving touch of Jesus (8:3,15; 9:25,29) which raises up the sick and the dead and dispels fear. The Son of the living God, who gives life to the dead, raises up his prostrate disciples and delivers them from fear.

The disciples have been initiated more deeply into the mystery of the final triumph; the passage to that triumph, the passion, is emphasized during the descent from the mount. Jesus specifically labels their apocalyptic experience a "vision" (only so in Mt); they are not to reveal this apocalyptic secret until the turning of the ages takes place, when the Son of Man is raised from the dead. To the disciples it is obvious that the last days are breaking in. Mt typically drops Mk's statement that the disciples do not understand. Instead, they immediately voice a doctrinal objection which probably reflects the polemics of Jews against Jewish Christians in the early church. The scribes, i.e., Jewish theologians, had interpreted Mal 4:5-6 to mean that Elijah would return from heaven before the Messiah came. How can Jesus be the Messiah and the bringer of the end-time when Elijah has not made his appearance? Does Jesus fulfill the prophecies in this case? Jesus first quotes the (Septuagint) text of Mal approvingly (hence the future tense of "he shall restore," RSV: "is to restore"). But then Jesus gives his definitive interpretation of the prophecy: "but I say to you"; we are reminded of the second half of the formula for the antitheses (5:21-48). In fact, Elijah has come in the person of John the Baptist (cf. 11:9-14), but a literal-minded Israel did not recognize the eschatological fulfillment which transcended the letter of the prophecy. They did not *know* him—again Mt emphasizes the role of understanding in believing. And so faithless Israel, in the person of a Jewish king, martyred this prophet, like so many others. (It was no accident that the martyrdom of the Baptist was placed near the beginning of Book Four.) Jesus then drives home the point he tried to impress on the disciples in 16:21, the same point he will inculcate again and again through what remains of the gospel: the Son of Man, the final prophet, must suffer the same violent fate. Triumphant Son of God yet martyred Son of Man—the paradox revealed at Caesarea Philippi has been graphically repeated and confirmed by God on the mount. The Matthean disciples of course understand—at least about the Baptist. The part of the mystery of suffering that touches them more directly will again give rise to little faith.

K. THE EPILEPTIC BOY AND
THE DISCIPLES' FAITH.
17:14-20.
[Mk 9:14-29; Lk 9:37-43]

> [14]And when they came to the crowd, a man came up to him and kneeling before him said, [15]"Lord, have mercy on my son, for he is an epileptic and he suffers terribly; for often he falls into the fire, and often into the water. [16]And I brought him to your disciples, and they could

not heal him." [17]And Jesus answered, "O faithless and perverse generation, how long am I to be with you? How long am I to bear with you? Bring him here to me." [18]And Jesus rebuked him, and the demon came out of him, and the boy was cured instantly. [19]Then the disciples came to Jesus privately and said, "Why could we not cast it out?" [20]He said to them, "Because of your little faith. For truly, I say to you, if you have faith as a grain of mustard seed, you will say to this mountain, 'Move from here to there,' and it will move; and nothing will be impossible to you."

As in the earlier miracle stories (chaps. 8-9) Mt abbreviates Mk, here by more than half. A colorful miracle is turned into a lesson on faith and little faith. As Jesus and the three disciples are descending from the mount, the father of an epileptic boy approaches Jesus. Mt omits the confusing details of the excited crowd and of the debate between the scribes and the disciples. The father kneels and begs for mercy in what sounds like a liturgical formula. That the father is a believer is seen from his gesture and his address of "Lord"—not "teacher," as in Mk. Mt omits the lurid details of the illness and the verbal wrestling between the father and Jesus over faith. Mt alone has the father say of the boy that he is a "lunatic," i.e., affected by the moon (*selēnizetai*, also at 4:24). Mt is the only writer in the NT to use this verb *selēnizomai*; in fact, he is apparently the first to have used it in the whole of the Greek language. Mt reflects here the belief of ancient physicians that the phases of the moon affected the periodic seizures of the epileptic. The only effects of the sickness which Mt mentions is that the boy often falls into fire and water. The father ends his plea by pointing out the inability of Jesus' disciples to cure the boy; this motif will be taken up again in vv.19-20. The father's remark draws from Jesus a lament that goes far beyond the present situation and accuses the whole faithless generation of Israel, which has refused to believe in

Jesus' message and miracles (cf. Moses' complaint in Dt 32:5). Mt probably does not intend the rebuke of "faithless" to apply to the disciples, since their problem is rather "little faith" (v.20). The two rhetorical questions indicate that Jesus' public ministry—and his offer of grace to Israel—are quickly drawing to a close. Omitting the struggle, resistance, and delay in Mk, Mt narrates the miracle in short order; only at this point is the demonic nature of the illness mentioned. Jesus commands the boy to be brought to him, rebukes (the demon within) the boy, and the demon departs. The miracle proper ends with reference to the cure "from that hour" (RSV: "instantly"; cf. 8:13: 15:28).

In private the disciples take up from v.16 the question of their inability to heal the boy. Jesus replies with the favorite Matthean theme of little faith (cf. comments on 6:30; 8:26; 14:31; 16:8). Mt explains the point by adding a Q-saying (cf. Lk 17:6) reworked with a Markan saying (Mk 11:22-23) which Mt himself reproduces at 21:21. The little faith of the disciples is a faith which *understands* and assents, but which does not *trust* God totally. A faith which trusts God can be, in the world's estimation, as small and unimpressive as a mustard seed. Yet such trust can do the impossible, as the hyperbolic image of moving mountains stresses (cf. 1 Cor 13:2). (Some manuscripts add v.21, which reproduces Mk 9:29 and introduces the themes of prayer and fasting; it did not belong to the original text of Mt.) This is the last time in the gospel that Mt will explicitly mention "little faith." Yet it will govern his "yes-but" picture of discipleship up to the final pericope (cf. 28:17).

L. THE SECOND PREDICTION OF THE PASSION.
17:22-23.
[Mk 9:30-32; Lk 9:43-45]

> [22]As they were gathering in Galilee, Jesus said to them, "The Son of man is to be delivered into the hands of men, [23]and they will kill him, and he will be raised on the third day." And they were greatly distressed.

Mt abbreviates Mk and changes the setting. Instead of a secret journey around Galilee (Mk's messianic secret), Mt depicts a large group of people gathering around Jesus, perhaps for the journey up to Jerusalem (cf. 19:1-2). Lest the surging crowds arouse any political or nationalistic illusions about Jesus' messiahship, Jesus again predicts his passion. The first part of the prophecy is a play on words typical of a Jewish *māshāl* or proverb: the Son of *Man* (the one who represents God) will be delivered into the hands of *men* (the faithless generation which opposes God). The passive voice of "delivered" (*paradidosthai*) may indicate that God is the chief agent of the passion (divine passive), just as he is the agent hidden in the passive voice of "he will be raised" (cf. comments on 16:21). This is the vaguest of the three passion predictions, and some hold it to be the earliest; perhaps the *māshāl* of v.22 goes back to Jesus. While Mk says the disciples did not understand, Mt states that they were greatly saddened—a reaction which presupposes basic understanding. By placing the second passion-prediction here, Mt again emphasizes the link between Jesus the Son of Man and the church he will found by his death-resurrection, since all that follows (the final narrative of Book Four and the whole fourth discourse) has a strong ecclesiological slant.

M. PETER QUESTIONED ABOUT THE TEMPLE TAX.
17:24-27.

[24]When they came to Capernaum, the collectors of the half-shekel tax went up to Peter and said, "Does not your teacher pay the tax?" [25]He said, "Yes." And when he came home, Jesus spoke to him first, saying, "What do you think, Simon? From whom do kings of the earth take toll or tribute? From their sons or from others?"

[26]And when he said, "From others," Jesus said to him, "Then the sons are free. [27]However, not to give

> offense to them, go to the sea and cast a hook, and take the first fish that comes up, and when you open its mouth you will find a shekel, take that and give it to them for me and for yourself."

The last pericope in the narrative section of Book Four acts as a bridge to the discourse on church-life which follows it. It also forms an inclusion with 4:13, where Jesus takes up residence in Capernaum as he begins his Galilean ministry. Now Jesus returns to Capernaum for the last time, as he is about to begin his momentous journey to Jerusalem. The idea of the coming visit to Jerusalem is hinted at by the motif of the temple and the possible clash which is avoided. The collectors of the temple tax naturally seek to collect it from Jesus in his hometown. The tax amounted to a half-shekel, which equaled a double drachma in the Attic coinage mentioned in our Greek text. The annual tax was to be paid by all male Jews over 19 (cf. Ex 30:13-15), but priests and sometimes rabbis claimed exemption. Since even the enemies of Jesus considered him a "teacher," the collectors ask whether Jesus will pay the tax; the form of their question indicates that they expect that he will. In keeping with the ecclesiastical theme of Book Four, they instinctively ask Peter for his Master's decision. (This pericope and that of the sinking Peter are the only notable additions of Mt to Mk's material in this section of the gospel; the ecclesiastical interests of Mt are obvious.) Without reflecting, the impetuous spokesman answers yes; after all, Jesus is the one who fulfills the Law. Peter obviously does not understand the full implications of eschatological fulfillment.

When Peter enters the house (his own?), Jesus displays his supernatural knowledge of the situation by taking the initiative and posing a parabolic problem to Peter to bring about a change of attitude (cf. the "what do you think?" in 18:12). As Peter must affirm, kings in general (as in most parables, there is no reference to one concrete system of

government, such as Rome's) collect tolls and taxes not
from their royal sons but from others, namely, their
ordinary subjects. (Some would instead see a reference
to the Roman practice, which exempted Roman citizens—
the "sons"—while taxing subject peoples and allies; but
the tone of the parable is very general.) Jesus draws the
important conclusion, which is the central point of the
pericope: the sons are free. The unspoken further conclusion
is that the sons of God's kingdom—and the temple is God's
palace (cf. 23:21)—are Jesus the Son and his brothers, the
Christian believers in the church (12:49-50), who are sons of
the Father (5:45) and of the kingdom (13:38). Freedom is the
hallmark of such sons: freedom from the temple tax, and
therefore freedom in principle from the temple and from the
Law which imposed the tax. From a theoretical vantage
point, then, the question of the collectors should have
received a negative answer. But Jesus is interested in something more than theoretical rights. If the sons are free
from tax, they are not free from the claims of love, even
love of enemies (cf. comments on 5:43-48). In their freedom
they are obliged to avoid unnecessary scandal (RSV:
"offense"; cf. 18:6-9). From this vantage point of practical
love, Jesus confirms Peter's yes, but for a totally different
reason. Jesus then expresses the true Son's faith in the
Father's loving care (cf. 6:11,25-33) by ordering Peter
to go fishing to obtain the necessary money for both of
them (one shekel or stater=two double drachmas). Since
the final verse hangs loosely onto the rest of the story, and
since the fulfillment of the command is not narrated, we
may have here an instance of a parabolic saying on its way to
becoming a miracle story. Significant in the context of
Book Four is that Jesus provides payment only for Peter
and himself. This close association is not lost on the other
disciples in 18:1.

As for the origin of this pericope, it probably stems
from the earlier days of Mt's church, when the Jewish
Christians were faced with the problem of paying the

temple tax even though they felt exempt. Since the temple tax was converted into a tax for the temple of Jupiter Capitoline after A.D. 70, and since Mt's church has broken its ties with the synagogue by the time of the gospel's composition, Mt retains the pericope not for its specific lesson but because it both underlines the role of Peter (giving answers to problems in the name of Jesus) and stresses the obligation of disciples to avoid giving scandal— a theme prominent in chap. 18.

II. THE DISCOURSE OF
BOOK FOUR:
CHURCH LIFE AND ORDER.
18:1-35.

THE FOURTH of the five great discourses sums up the major concern of Book Four: the connection between Christ and his church. Many divisions of the discourse have been suggested. Easiest is the division into two main sections: care for children and the little ones (18:1-14) and care for the sinful brother (18:15-35). The two sections each have two sub-sections: children (vv.1-5) and little ones (vv.6-14); church discipline with regard to the sinful brother (vv.15-20) and the obligation to forgive the sinful brother (vv.21-35). Each sub-section is composed of a number of sayings grouped around key-words: "child" and "greater"; "little ones" and "scandalize"; "brother" and "sin"; "brother" and "forgive." Each section ends with a parable (vv.10-14; vv.21-35) whose last verse refers to the heavenly Father and repeats the key-word of the whole section: "little ones" (v.14) and "forgive his brother" (v.35).

As can be seen from this overview, this discourse is not on "church order" in the narrow sense of ecclesiastical discipline and hierarchy; hierarchical figures are notably lacking. A more adequate title would be "the discourse on church life and order." The more general aspects of church life are in vv.1-14; more specific questions of church order are in vv.15-35. As the sermon on the mount dealt with the general moral imperatives in every Christian's life, as the missionary discourse dealt with the preaching church's encounter with an often hostile world, as the parabolic discourse dealt with the mystery of the kingdom growing like a hidden seed in a very mixed-up world, so chap. 18 deals with the relations within the church, the conditions necessary for healthy interaction among disciples. The problems of living together are apparent from the keywords; the church must come to terms with scandal, members who easily stray, sinful brothers who resist correction, and the tendency of righteous members to set limits on forgiveness. In other words, the basic problem in church life is sin, and the basic solution is the mercy of the Father. As for sources, in the first section Mt meshes Mk and Q; in the second section he uses mostly M, with a slight touch of Q.

A. BECOMING CHILDREN TO BECOME GREAT. 18:1-5.
[Mk 9:33-37; 10:15; Lk 9:46-48; 18:17]

> **18** At that time the disciples came to Jesus, saying, "Who is the greatest in the kingdom of heaven?" ²And calling to him a child, he put him in the midst of them, ³and said, "Truly, I say to you, unless you turn and become like children, you will never enter the kingdom of heaven. ⁴Whoever humbles himself like this child, he is the greatest in the kingdom of heaven.
>
> ⁵"Whoever receives one such child in my name receives me.

Mt has taken as his cue for the discourse a string of sayings found at the end of Mk 9. Mt creates a new setting by having the other disciples (probably the other members of the Twelve) find Jesus and Peter speaking alone in the house. While in Mk Jesus asks about the quarrel the disciples have had over greatness, in Mt the other disciples (out of jealousy?) pose the question, with a specification: who is greatest *in the kingdom of heaven*? The question may primarily refer to the final stage of the kingdom after the last judgment; but, granted Mt's idea of a number of stages in the coming of the kingdom, and granted the place of the question at the end of Book Four, the question also envisages greatness in the church, the main instrument of the kingdom in this present age. The special position of Peter throughout Book Four makes the question natural. In a parabolic action, Jesus calls a child (Mk's touching mention of Jesus' affectionate embrace is dropped). Jesus then pronounces a statement of a "condition for entrance" into the kingdom (cf. 5:20). As the apocalyptic seer (cf. the Amen-formula), Jesus states that only those who truly repent and are converted, only those who admit their littleness and put all their trust in God their Father can enter the kingdom. We must forget our Christian and romantic views of childhood and realize that, at the time of Jesus, children were pieces of property without any rights; powerless to defend themselves, they had to rely totally on others. Jesus is recommending not childishness but a child-like trust in a loving Father, a trust which awaits everything and grabs at nothing. From this condition for entrance Jesus then draws a conclusion about greatness in the kingdom: greatness belongs to the one who maintains this child-like sense of littleness and so proves he or she belongs to the free children of God (cf. 17:26). He is a brother of Jesus, and therefore whoever receives such a humble person—be that person a child or a child-like Christian—because of Jesus ("in my name") will receive the Son himself (cf. 10:40; 25:31-46). The final verse provides a smooth transition to the second sub-section, where the insignificant disciples are spoken of as "the little ones."

B. SCANDAL OR CARE OF THE LITTLE ONES.
18:6-14.
[Mk 9:42-50; Lk 17:1-2; 14:34-35; 15:3-7]

6But whoever causes one of these little ones who believe in me to sin, it would be better for him to have a great millstone fastened round his neck and to be drowned in the depth of the sea.

7"Woe to the world for temptations to sin! For it is necessary that temptations come, but woe to the man by whom the temptation comes! 8And if your hand or your foot causes you to sin, cut it off and throw it away; it is better for you to enter life maimed or lame than with two hands or two feet to be thrown into the eternal fire. 9And if your eye causes you to sin, pluck it out and throw it away; it is better for you to enter life with one eye than with two eyes to be thrown into the hell of fire.

10"See that you do not despise one of these little ones; for I tell you that in heaven their angels always behold the face of my Father who is in heaven. 12What do you think? If a man has a hundred sheep, and one of them has gone astray, does he not leave the ninety-nine on the mountains and go in search of the one that went astray? 13And if he finds it, truly, I say to you, he rejoices over it more than over the ninety-nine that never went astray. 14So it is not the will of my Father who is in heaven that one of these little ones should perish.

Towards the little ones, i.e., the insignificant disciples who easily go astray because they are neglected, the disciples, especially the leaders, can take one of two possible stances. They can either cause the little ones to sin (literally, "scandalize," "cause to stumble," vv.6-9); or they can actively seek out the straying sheep (vv.10-14). The implication is that church members and leaders can give scandal simply by neglecting or despising the weak members (cf. v.10). Jesus the good shepherd (9:36; 15:24) has scrupulously avoided giving scandal (17:27), and he calls upon his followers to do the same. Mt makes plain that he is thinking here not only of children but also of weak Christians by emphasizing in v.6 that these little ones are those who believe "in me." Those who cause these fragile believers to fall from faith would be better off suffering execution by drowning (v.6); thus they might escape the destruction of body and soul in hell (10:28). The severity of Christ's judgment reminds us that scandals within the church are a sign of the stress of the end-time, the fearful test before the final victory (cf. 7:13; 13:41; 24:10; 26:31). Jesus the apocalyptic prophet then intones a "woe" (a cry of lament over the dead; cf. 26:24) because he knows that this selfish, power-crazed world will necessarily experience fearsome scandals as it hurtles towards its end. The necessity of the apocalyptic plan in no way absolves the individual sinner who causes scandal because of his selfishness and lust for greatness. Jesus warns his disciples not to give into the drive for power, be it expressed through hand, foot, or eye. Better to suffer physical loss than eternal damnation. Mt used a similar exhortation to spiritual rather than physical integrity in 5:29-30. There it forbade sexual lust in the individual; here it forbids lust for power in the church. Ambition is the cleric's lust.

From the negative theme of scandal Mt then turns to the positive theme of how the disciples should care for the little ones who stray. He uses a Q-parable, and frames it with two verses of his own creation (vv.10,14). While Lk applies the parable to Jesus' own astonishing action of seeking out lost sinners and emphasizes the joy in finding what was *lost*, Mt applies the parable to the disciples, who must imitate the good shepherd in seeking out the Christian sheep which has *strayed*. Jesus begins the parable by warning against contempt for these little ones. Jewish theology had developed the idea of the guardian angel; but the rabbis also held that only the highest of angels could see God's face, i.e., have direct access to the divine presence.

Jesus thus declares that it is the highest types of angels who watch over the little ones and who plead their cause before God—who, Jesus pointedly adds, is "my Father." Therefore, the disciples must paradoxically care more for these weak Christians, like the shepherd who acts against all human calculations by leaving the ninety-nine safe sheep and seeking the one sheep which has strayed. The disciples, like the shepherd, should experience more joy in actively saving the endangered sheep than in passively tending the sheep who are safe. As is typical in Mt, even the exhortation to rejoice is traced back to the will of "your Father" that not one of the little ones be lost. Doing the will of the Father, the essence of the Matthean ethic, is not some dreadfully dour duty; it is sharing the redemptive joy of Jesus. Radical demand flows from radical grace. The mention of the "little ones" in v.14 provides an inclusion with the beginning of the sub-section (v.6).

C. CORRECTING THE BROTHER WHO SINS.
18:15-20.
[Lk 17:3]

> [15]"If your brother sins against you, go and tell him his fault, between you and him alone. If he listens to you, you have gained your brother. [16]But if he does not listen, take one or two others along with you, that every word may be confirmed by the evidence of two or three witnesses. [17]If he refuses to listen to them, tell it to the church; and if he refuses to listen even to the church, let him be to you as a Gentile and a tax collector. [18]Truly, I say to you, whatever you bind on earth shall be bound in heaven, and whatever you loose on earth shall be loosed in heaven. [19]Again I say to you, if two of you agree on earth about anything they ask, it will be done for them by my Father in heaven. [20]For where two or three are gathered in my name, there am I in the midst of them."

The second half of the discourse is almost entirely M, with a few traces of Q. While the basic theme of dealing

with sin in the community continues, the theme shifts from
the weak Christian who strays from the community to the
"brother" (i.e., fellow Christian) who sins within the
community and shows no intention of either leaving or
stopping. A carefully ordered procedure for church-
discipline, developed from Lev. 19:17-18 and Dt 19:15 and
paralleled by disciplinary measures at Qumran, is laid down.
Mt proposes a very general case of sin; "against you,"
which the RSV reads along with later Greek manuscripts,
should probably be omitted. Any Christian is empowered to
try to wipe out sin in the community by engaging in fraternal
correction. It must be done privately, to save the sinner's
honor and to maintain the family-atmosphere which is a
hallmark of Mt's conception of church (12:46-50). If the
brother heeds the admonition, the corrector can rejoice that
a member of the family has been won back for the church
and for God. If the correction is rejected, the rule of Dt
19:15 is followed, to support the corrector's viewpoint
and to provide witnesses, if the third step proves necessary.
This third step involves a convocation of the local church
(in Mt, 18:17 is the only verse besides 16:18 which contains
the word "church"). If the sinner rejects the judgment of
the full assembly of believers, he is excommunicated (cf.
1 Cor 5:1-8). He becomes like a Gentile (i.e., a pagan who
is not a member of God's holy people) and a tax collector
(a member of God's people who has turned traitor). The
harsh epithets (cf. 5:46-47) reflect a tradition cultivated
by the stringent Jewish Christianity out of which Mt's
church grew. For Mt, living in a church composed of both
Jews and Gentiles, "Gentile" in v. 17 (*ethnikos*, an adjectival
form which occurs only here and in 5:47 and 6:7) equals
"non-Christian." It betokens Mt's consciousness that
Christians in the church are a new, separate people, neither
Jews nor Gentiles (cf. 21:43).

The church's act of excommunication is ratified by God
("in heaven") and is based on the power from Christ to
"bind and loose." While the phrase in 16:19 referred primarily to Peter's power to teach and solve moral questions
for the *whole church* ("*my* church"), the phrase in 18:18

refers primarily to the *local church's* power to admit or to exclude persons from the community. The church is seen as a group of Christians acting and deciding together; no special leadership role is mentioned. While vv.15-17 speak in the second person singular, v.18, like v.19, is couched in the plural. Apparently vv.18-20 were originally independent sayings which have been woven together to provide a theoretical basis for the church's authoritative actions. Vv.19-20 originally spoke of the power of common prayer; Mt probably interprets the sayings with special reference to the awesome decision to excommunicate, a decision which should be made only after prayer and common consent. V.19 assures the church that, if these conditions are met, the prayer and the decision will be heard and ratified by the head of the family, the Father. The anti-hierarchical tendencies of chap. 18 are reflected in the stipulation that only two people are necessary for the efficacy of communal prayer. V.20 gives the reason for such efficacy by articulating a high christology and a high ecclesiology. Various rabbis claimed that, when two pious Jews sat together to discuss the words of the Law, the *shekinah* (the divine presence) was with them. In the Christian reworking of that idea in v.20, the words of the Torah are replaced by the phrase "in my name," and the *shekinah* is replaced by "*I* am in their midst." The church gathers together not around the words of the Torah but around the person and words of Jesus. The divine presence it experiences in such worship is none other than Jesus himself, Emmanuel, God-with-us (1:23), who has promised to be with his people always (28:20). Obviously it is the risen Jesus who speaks in v.20 to his church.

D. FORGIVING THE BROTHER WHO SINS.
18:21-35.
[Lk 17:4]

> ²¹Then Peter came up and said to him, "Lord, how often shall my brother sin against me, and I forgive him?

As many as seven times?" [22]Jesus said to him, "I do not say to you seven times, but seventy times seven.

[23]"Therefore the kingdom of heaven may be compared to a king who wished to settle accounts with his servants. [24]When he began the reckoning, one was brought to him who owed him ten thousand talents; [25]and as he could not pay, his lord ordered him to be sold, with his wife and children and all that he had, and payment to be made. [26]So the servant fell on his knees, imploring him, 'Lord, have patience with me, and I will pay you everything.' [27]And out of pity for him the lord of that servant released him and forgave him the debt. [28]But that same servant, as he went out, came upon one of his fellow servants who owed him a hundred denarii; and seizing him by the throat he said, 'Pay what you owe.' [29]So his fellow servant fell down and besought him, 'Have patience with me, and I will pay you.' [30]He refused and went and put him in prison till he should pay the debt. [31]When his fellow servants saw what had taken place, they were greatly distressed, and they went and reported to their lord all that had taken place. [32]Then his lord summoned him and said to him, 'You wicked servant! I forgave you all that debt because you besought me; [33]and should not you have had mercy on your fellow servant, as I had mercy on you?' [34]And in anger his lord delivered him to the jailers, till he should pay all his debt. [35]So also my heavenly Father will do to every one of you, if you do not forgive your brother from your heart."

In the final sub-section, the focus shifts again, this time to the brother who is not recalcitrant, but who sins often and therefore needs forgiveness often. Since guilt is readily admitted, forgiveness remains on a one-to-one level (cf. v.15). Peter, as spokesman for the disciples and for all Christians, poses the question, thus creating an inclusion with the first sub-section, which began with the disciples' question (v.1). The mention of Peter introduces into a discourse which sees the church as a fellowship of equals, a

reminder that there are Christian leaders. Jesus' reply to
Peter, which in the Greek can mean either "seventy times
seven" or "seventy-seven times," really means an unlimited
number of times (the perfect number seven, multiplied by
itself and by ten). It is Jesus' reversal of the cry for excessive
vengeance by Lamech in Gen 4:23-24 ("seventy seven fold").

To illustrate this measureless mercy, this forgiveness
without frontiers, and to show the reason for it, Jesus
speaks the parable of the unforgiving servant, which
originally may have existed independent of the question
in v.21 (the parable, strictly speaking, does not illustrate
repeated forgiveness). A king is checking his income from
the taxes collected by his high officials ("servants"). One
servant is found to owe the fantastic amount of ten thousand
talents. A talent was the largest unit of money known to
the Near East, and ten thousand was the largest number
used in counting. To a Palestinian peasant, ten thousand
talents would be equivalent to our "billions of dollars."
The hyperbole of the parable is obvious. To recoup a very
small portion of the money, and more importantly, to
punish the servant and provide a warning to his fellows, the
king orders him and all he has, including his family, to be
sold. The servant's situation is hopeless; his whole existence
is dissolving before his eyes. There is no way to pay the
almost infinite amount owed (so too is sin an infinite
offense against the infinite God, an offense we cannot
possibly undo by ourselves). The desperate state of the
servant is betokened by his abject position and his ridiculous
promise to pay everything if given a little time. The lord
relents, not out of any illusion that the amount will be
paid, but simply out of pity for so wretched a state. The debt
is infinite; there is no point postponing payment. So with
a sovereign act of grace the king wipes out the debt. But the
servant has not learned grace from his experience of it.
As he is coming out from his harrowing audience, he meets
a fellow official who owes him a relatively paltry sum (a
denarius was the daily wage given a laborer). Manhandling
this debtor, who is his social equal, he demands immediate

payment. The debtor takes up the same abject position and, almost word-for-word, the same plea which his creditor has just spoken to the king. Despite the plausibility of the promise this time, the creditor sends him to prison till he pays all (cf. 5:25-26). The creditor does not threaten the debtor and his goods, since the debt is small. The other officials, shocked at the unforgiving nature of a man who has just been forgiven, report the incident to the king. The king denounces the servant as wicked—not because he has mishandled the money given to him but because he has mishandled the forgiveness given to him. The wicked person is the person without pity. Anyone who is forgiven has an obligation to forgive ("*should* not you have had mercy . . . .?"). The king's question is meant to be heard and answered by every one listening to the parable. As punishment, the wicked servant is treated as he treated others (cf. 7:2,12)—the difference being that, since the debt is unpayable, the imprisonment will be eternal (cf. 18:8).

The final verse of the chapter, probably created by Mt, drives home the message. The loving Father will condemn us to eternal punishment if we do not lovingly forgive one another (cf. 6:12, 14-15). Why? Because, although the Father has already forgiven each member of his family, the church, his forgiveness remains conditional and can be revoked at the last judgment, if we have not shared the forgiveness we received with one another. We cannot earn God's forgiveness, but we can lose it—by trying to hoard it instead of passing it on to others. A person who does not forgive others shows he has not really experienced God's forgiveness; otherwise, it would overflow to others. True sons naturally show their resemblance to their Father by acting like him, by forgiving like him—simply out of compassion, with no question of merit (cf. 5:43-45). And the forgiveness must not be grudging or pretended; it must be sincere and effective—"from your heart," the center of the person. Thus does Mt place in perspective the disciplinary measures of vv. 15-20. The final word on church-life and church-order must be forgiveness within the family.

Book Five
The Messiah and His Church on the
Way to the Passion.
19:1-25:46.

Having begun the formation of his church, the Son continues the formation process as he leads his disciples up to Jerusalem for the final clash and break with the leaders of Israel. On the way, Jesus teaches his disciples about the various states of life a disciple can live "under the cross," as well as about some temptations those states involve (chaps. 19-20). Once in Jerusalem, the Messiah brings judgment on the old order and vindicates his authentic teaching authority vis-à-vis the magisterium of Israel in a series of disputes and parables (chaps. 21-22). Having pronounced judgment of the false teachers (chap. 23), Jesus foretells the punishment and rejection of Israel and the reward of those in the church who wait faithfully for the coming of the Son of Man (chaps. 24-25). As for literary sources, Mt resumes the order of the Markan material and will follow it till the end of the Passion.

I. THE NARRATIVE OF BOOK FIVE: JESUS LEADS HIS DISCIPLES TO THE CROSS AS HE CONFOUNDS HIS ENEMIES. 19:1 - 23:29

A. MARRIAGE AND CELIBACY IN THE LIGHT OF THE KINGDOM.
19:1-12.
[Mk 10:1-12]

19 Now when Jesus had finished these sayings, he went from Galilee and entered the region of Judea beyond the Jordan; ²and large crowds followed him, and he healed them there.

³And Pharisees came up to him and tested him by asking, "Is it lawful to divorce one's wife for any cause?" ⁴He answered, "Have you not read that he who made them from the beginning made them male and female, ⁵and said, 'For this reason a man shall leave his father and mother and be joined to his wife, and the two shall become one flesh'? ⁶So they are no longer two but one flesh. What therefore God has joined together, let not man put asunder." ⁷They said to him, "Why then did Moses command one to give a certificate of divorce,

and to put her away?" ⁸He said to them, "For your hardness of heart Moses allowed you to divorce your wives, but from the beginning it was not so. ⁹And I say to you: whoever divorces his wife, except for unchastity, and marries another, commits adultery."

¹⁰The disciples said to him, "If such is the case of a man with his wife, it is not expedient to marry." ¹¹But he said to them, "Not all men can receive this saying, but only those to whom it is given.

¹²For there are eunuchs who have been so from birth, and there are eunuchs who have been made eunuchs by men, and there are eunuchs who have made themselves eunuchs for the sake of the kingdom of heaven. He who is able to receive this, let him receive it."

MARRIED COUPLES and celibates are the first groups in the church considered in this section of the gospel. Mt reorders Mk (cf. 15:1-20): Jesus first excludes divorce by presenting the positive teaching on marriage from Genesis, then explains the reason for the Mosaic permission of divorce in Deuteronomy, and concludes with a statement of casuistic law equating divorce with adultery. Mt adds to Mk a separate teaching on celibacy.

The pericope begins with the stock formula of transition, closing the fourth discourse and providing a change of scene. The Galilean ministry, begun at 4:12-17, is ended; Jesus passes through Perea, the territory east of Judea and the Jordan. To speak of this territory as "Judea beyond the Jordan" is technically incorrect, but Mt is not overly concerned in his gospel with geographical niceties. Crowds are following Jesus up to Jerusalem for Passover, and he continues his healing ministry among them (a foreshadowing of the church?). Curiously, at this point Mk stresses Jesus' teaching, which Mt changes to healing. Perhaps Mt has in mind that, since the parable chapter (chap. 13), Jesus has withdrawn from any extensive teaching of the crowds—though this teaching ministry will resume in Jerusalem.

For all that follows, see first the comments on 5:31-32. Mt emphasizes from the start that the Pharisees come with malicious intent to put Jesus to the test (cf. 22:18,35). They ask about the grounds for divorce. Many commentators presume that "for any cause" refers to the dispute between the schools of Hillel and Shammai. But asking Jesus to side with one of the two famous and revered schools hardly constitutes the type of malicious and dangerous test we see elsewhere in Mt's presentation of the Jewish leaders (cf., e.g., chap. 22). Rather, we should presuppose that the Pharisees already know something of the Law-revoking doctrine of 5:31-32 and seek to force Jesus into an open break with the Torah. Jesus replies disdainfully; his question is a rebuke to those who should know the Law better (cf. 12:3). Jesus appeals to the original will of the Creator, as expressed in Genesis. God made human beings male and female for the precise purpose of lasting union (Gen 1:27 and 2:24). (In Qumran, the first Gen text is used to reject at least polygamy or marriage after one's partner's death, and perhaps even divorce.) From the final phrase "one flesh," indicating the closest personal union possible, Jesus draws the conclusion that no mere human can undo the bond which the Creator himself has cemented.

The Pharisees see that Jesus' exegesis of Gen does away with divorce, and so they counter with the specific rule for drawing up a document of divorce in Dt 24:1ff. Not too much should be made of the distinction between "command" and "allowed" in vv.7-8, since Jesus himself quotes the rule for the certificate of divorce in 5:31 in the form of a command. The main point is the reason for Moses' command/concession: the Israelites' "hardness of heart." This phrase refers not to lack of feelings or a low cultural level, but to Israel's unwillingness to be taught and guided by God's word, a sin excoriated by the prophets. The divorce provisions of the Torah thus reflect the rebellious will of fallen man, not the gracious will of the Creator. Since Jesus is bringing in the kingdom, which is paradise regained, he also reestablishes the original will of the Creator for marriage in paradise. Jesus then adds to his apodictic prohibition of v.6 a casuistic rule ("if-then") in v.9; if any man (notice the male perspective) transgresses Jesus' apodictic rule, he commits adultery, which is what his divorce and remarriage amount to. As in 5:32, Mt has added the provision "except for unchastity (*porneia*)." *Porneia* refers here to incestuous unions contracted by Christians before baptism; Mt's point is that one cannot appeal to the Lord's prohibition of divorce to justify the maintenance of such unions. Thus, the "exceptive clause" does not really weaken Jesus' absolute prohibition of divorce.

That Mt understands the prohibition to be absolute is clear from the disciples' astonishment. If Jesus had simply championed the position of Shammai over that of Hillel, there would hardly be cause for such a shocked exclamation that the unmarried state is preferable. Jesus takes up the disciples' hardly serious judgment about the unmarried state and takes it seriously ("this saying" in v.11 probably refers to the disciples' exclamation). Yes, says Jesus, remaining unmarried is better—but only for some people, who have received a special gift from God (divine passive). These are not those who are eunuchs by birth or castration; rather, they are the voluntary "eunuchs" who embrace celibacy because of the kingdom. This reason for celibacy can mean either "for the sake of," "with a view to" the kingdom which is coming (so RSV) or "because of the kingdom" which has already overtaken one's life, and claimed that life totally for the kingdom's service. While the NT never explicitly states that Jesus was celibate, the veiled invitation to and praise of celibacy because of the kingdom makes sense only if a celibate Jesus is speaking it. But it is not meant for all disciples, only for those who can "receive it" because God has given it to them (v.11; cf. the similar teaching in 1 Cor 7).

One should note, however, that the precise meaning of vv.11-12 in their present context is not unambiguous.

No doubt when vv. 11-12 circulated independently in the oral tradition, they referred to voluntary celibacy in general. Attached as they are now to the question of divorce, they may be intended to speak to the special case of the "innocent partners" who are unwillingly involved in the break-up of a marriage. Such disciples are to express their commitment to Jesus and the kingdom by remaining unmarried. This interpretation does run into one problem, though: the voluntary nature of this celibate state, which is stressed at the beginning of v.11 and at the end of v.12. The more traditional interpretation of this verse is therefore to be preferred. As the true meaning of marriage is to be understood from the original will of the Creator, so too the true meaning of celibacy is to be sought from the future kingdom already breaking into the disciples' lives.

B. THE PLACE OF CHILDREN IN THE KINGDOM. 19:13-15.
[Mk 10:13-16; Lk 18:15-17]

> [13]Then children were brought to him that he might lay his hands on them and pray. The disciples rebuked the people; [14]but Jesus said, "Let the children come to me, and do not hinder them; for to such belongs the kingdom of heaven." [15]And he laid his hands on them and went away.

Mt continues his consideration of "states of life" on the way to the cross. Having used a form of Mk 10:15 in Mt 18:13, Mt omits it here. He creates an inclusion by mentioning the laying on of hands in vv.13 and 15. The dependence of the children is stressed by the passive verb "were brought." As usual, Mt spares the disciples the indignation of Jesus (contrast Mk 10:14); he also omits the colorful, affective detail of Jesus' embrace (Mk 10:16). To come to Jesus is equivalent to entering the kingdom, and the invitation extends even to children, those without rights or status in the ancient world. Indeed, only those who, like children, admit their lack of claim or status and their dependence on the Father can enter the kingdom ("for to *such* . . ."; cf. 18:1-5). Some see in the command "do not hinder" the early church's decision to admit infants to baptism, but this is far from clear.

C. THE RICH AND THE KINGDOM.
19:16-26.
[Mk 10:17-27; Lk 18:18-27]

16And behold, one came up to him, saying, "Teacher, what good deed must I do, to have eternal life?" 17And he said to him, "Why do you ask me about what is good? One there is who is good. If you would enter life, keep the commandments." 18He said to him, "Which?" And Jesus said, "You shall not kill, You shall not commit adultery, You shall not steal, You shall not bear false witness, 19Honor your father and mother, and, You shall love your neighbor as yourself." 20The young man said to him, "All these I have observed; what do I still lack?" 21Jesus said to him, "If you would be perfect, go, sell what you possess and give to the poor, and you will have treasure in heaven; and come, follow me." 22When the young man heard this he went away sorrowful; for he had great possessions.

23And Jesus said to his disciples, "Truly, I say to you, it will be hard for a rich man to enter the kingdom of heaven. 24Again I tell you, it is easier for a camel to go through the eye of a needle than for a rich man to enter the kingdom of God." 25When the disciples heard this they were greatly astonished, saying, "Who then can be saved?" 26But Jesus looked at them and said to them, "With men this is impossible, but with God all things are possible."

The next "state of life" which is confronted with the cross is that of the rich man. Mt does not tell us at the beginning that the eager inquirer is a rich *young* man. His youth (which can range between 24 and 40 years) is mentioned in vv.20 and 22, and his riches are disclosed only at the end of the story. Things do not start off well; the inquirer addresses Jesus as "teacher," the title used by unbelievers. He asks about doing a good deed, perhaps reflecting Jewish piety, which sought to do good deeds beyond the strict demands of the Law to ensure entrance into heaven. The man speaks in very Johannine terms of "eternal life"; as the subsequent verses show, having eternal life is equivalent to entering into life (v.17), being perfect (v.21), entering the kingdom (v.23), and being saved (v.25). In Mk, Jesus answers gruffly: "Why do you call me good?" Mt removes such a scandalous statement from his version, making "good" the object of the inquiry. Reverently, Mt avoids naming God in the allusion to the great Jewish prayer, the *Shema'* ("One there is who is good" alludes to Dt 6:4). In both Mk and Mt, though, the point is not the dogmatic question of Jesus' sinlessness. Rather, Jesus' rebuke aims at deflecting the idle flattery of a superficial admirer and raising the young man's mind to more serious issues. The good God has expressed his will for goodness in the commandments. That the inquirer has to ask *which* commandments does not augur well, though the relative importance of various commandments was a subject of debate among the rabbis. Jesus cites the second table of the decalogue, in the order of fifth, sixth, seventh, eighth, and fourth. Mt then adds the command of love of neighbor from Lev 19:18 (cf. Mt 22:39). Love of neighbor acts as the criterion for interpreting all other commands in the Mosaic Law. And yet, as we shall see, it is still part of the Mosaic Law; it is not the last word on how one enters life.

Half-proud, half-disillusioned, the young man protests that he has kept all these commands (Mt drops Mk's "from my youth," since for Mt the man is still young.) We have no reason to suppose that the young man is lying when he says this. He has observed all, *including* the law of love. Yet he senses that he still lacks something. Jesus' "maieutic" method has brought him to pose the question himself (contrast Mk). At this point, Mt typically omits Mk's moving detail that Jesus looked on the man with love. To the man's question Jesus replies with a phrase that plays on a number of meanings: "if you would be *teleios* [RSV: 'perfect']." *Teleios* can mean *mature* as opposed to *young*; it could also express the *completeness* which the young man says he *lacks*. But Mt, with his OT background, understands *teleios* in terms of whole-hearted, complete dedication to God (cf. 5:48). It does not mean perfection in the sense of some mystic ideal possible only in a cloister, nor does it mean a higher form of morality or evangelical counsel to which only some Christians are called. "If you wish to be perfect" is parallel to "if you wish to enter into life" (v.17) and means the same thing. We are dealing with the basic requirements for salvation (v.25), requirements incumbent on all. Mt is not teaching a two-tier morality of commandments for the masses and counsels for the elite. On this "perfection," this whole-hearted dedication to doing *justice* (5:20), to doing God's will completely, hangs every disciple's salvation. In the case of this particular man, God's good will is that he sell all, express his love for his neighbor by giving the proceeds to the poor (assuring him the heavenly treasure or life he seeks), and then literally follow Christ. Notice: the ultimate demand of God's will, which makes one "perfect," is not even love of neighbor, but a sacrificial following of Christ on the way to his cross. In the last analysis, it is the person of Jesus that is the norm of morality for Mt.

The young man cannot measure up to this standard, because he possesses great riches, or rather, they possess him. Sadly realizing he cannot serve God and mammon (6:24), he decides to maintain his loyalty to the latter (cf. the joyful man who sells everything in 13:44). He proves to be not only young but also spiritually immature. Jesus uses this failure as an example to the disciples of how difficult it is for a rich man to be saved. Indeed, underlining his point, Jesus states by means of a hyperbole (the camel passing through the eye of a needle) that it is impossible that a rich man be saved. Those who try to mitigate the hyperbole miss the point, which is precisely the impossibility, and not just the difficulty, of the rich man's salvation. The astonished disciples understand all too clearly (Mt does not follow Mk here in emphasizing the disciples' amazement and in broadening the question of entrance beyond that of the rich). The disciples had entertained the popular notion that riches were a sign of God's favor; if God's favorites cannot be saved, who can? Mt emphasizes the final statement of Jesus by including the detail of Jesus' glance, a colorful, affective element which Mt usually strikes from his Markan narrative. Salvation *is* impossible, if it must be achieved by human beings, no matter how rich. The good news of Jesus is that salvation is the free gift of the omnipotent God (cf. Gen 18:14; Job 42:2; Zech 8:6).

D. THE POOR DISCIPLES AND THEIR REWARD.
19:27-20:16.
[Mk 10:28-31; Lk 18:28-30; 22:28-30]

27Then Peter said in reply, "Lo, we have left everything and followed you. What then shall we have?" 28Jesus said to them, "Truly, I say to you, in the new world, when the Son of man shall sit on his glorious throne, you who have followed me will also sit on twelve thrones, judging the twelve tribes of Israel. 29And every one who has left houses or brothers or sisters or father or mother or children or lands, for my name's sake, will receive a hundredfold, and inherit eternal life. 30But many that are first will be last, and the last first.

20   "For the kingdom of heaven is like a householder who went out early in the morning to hire laborers for his vineyard. 2After agreeing with the laborers for a denarius a day, he sent them into his vineyard. 3And going out about the third hour he saw others standing idle in the

market place; [4]and to them he said, 'You go into the vineyard, too, and whatever is right I will give you.' So they went. [5]Going out again about the sixth hour and the ninth hour, he did the same. [6]And about the eleventh hour he went out and found others standing; and he said to them, 'Why do you stand here idle all day?' [7]They said to him, 'Because no one has hired us.' He said to them, 'You go into the vineyard too.' [8]And when evening came, the owner of the vineyard said to his steward, 'Call the laborers and pay them their wages, beginning with the last, up to the first.' [9]And when those hired about the eleventh hour came, each of them received a denarius. [10]Now when the first came, they thought they would receive more; but each of them also received a denarius. [11]And on receiving it they grumbled at the householder, [12]saying, 'These last worked only one hour, and you have made them equal to us who have borne the burden of the day and the scorching heat.' [13]But he replied to one of them, 'Friend, I am doing you no wrong; did you not agree with me for a denarius? [14]Take what belongs to you, and go; I choose to give to this last as I give to you. [15]Am I not allowed to do what I choose with what belongs to me? Or do you begrudge my generosity?' [16]So the last will be first, and the first last."

Over against the rich young man, who would not give up his possessions, are set the disciples, who have forsaken all for Christ. As the spokesman for the disciples, Peter asks the blunt question: what will we get for this sacrifice? Peter's question may seem to be on a lower level than what has preceded; but the Matthean Jesus does not hesitate to speak of heavenly reward (5:19; 6:1-18,20), provided it is not understood as a legal claim on God. While Peter's question is taken from Mk and concerns all followers of Christ, Jesus' initial answer is taken from Q (cf. Lk 22:30) and actually concerns only the twelve apostles (cf. the twelve thrones and tribes). The shift is not a great difficulty for Mt, who shows a tendency to equate "the Twelve" with "the disciples." Here no doubt he sees the Twelve as the prime example of what every disciple should be. With an Amen-word which reveals the conditions of the final judgment, Jesus assures the Twelve that on the last day they will have the status of the twelve founding patriarchs of Israel, and indeed will "judge" Israel. Since "judge" can mean rule, the phrase could refer to the Twelve as the rulers of the new people of God, the church. The promise will begin to be fulfilled in the early church and will be completely fulfilled when the whole earth is renewed on the last day ("the new world" is literally "the regeneration," a word which comes from Mt or his tradition). But the picture of the Son of Man on his "glorious throne" (i.e., God's throne) conjures up a picture of judgment instead of ruling (cf. 25:31), and "Israel" in Mt always means the actual OT people Israel, and not the church. More likely, then, the meaning in Mt is that the apostles, poor and persecuted by their own people in this age, will see the tables reversed in the age to come (cf. v.30). Instead of being condemned (cf. 10:17-23), they will judge and condemn an unbelieving Israel (cf. 23:29-39), and thus share in the power and glory of the victorious Son of Man.

In v.29, Mt turns back to Mk and the wider audience ("every one"). The promise touches all those who willingly suffer loss of family or goods for the "name" of Jesus, i.e., for the person of Jesus, especially as known through missionary preaching. While the reward of a "hundredfold" (or, in some manuscripts, "manifold") could be in this life, Mt's omission of Mk's phrase, "in this time," suggests that he places the entire reward in the "new world." The phrase "to inherit eternal life" forms a neat inclusion with the question of the young man in v.16. By throwing away their goods, the disciples will inherit what the young man sought in vain to possess. Thus are all human standards and plans inverted. Many who are first in this world (e.g., the rich man, the Jewish leaders, the powerful, the ostentatiously pious) will be last (probably in the sense of rejected) in the world to come, while the last, the no-accounts (e.g., the apostles, the disciples, the poor) will be first (i.e., admitted to the kingdom). Verse 30 serves as a transition to the parable of the laborers in the vineyard (20:1-16), where it also forms the last verse (v.16). Since the two halves of the verse are reversed in v.16 (thus acting out verbally the reversal it speaks of), 19:30 and 20:16 are examples of both inclusion and chiasm.

Obviously Mt intends the parable which follows to be understood in close connection with Jesus' promise of reward. Yet the parable does not quite fit the context, an indication that Mt is inserting a special tradition into his Markan framework. If the parable goes back to Jesus, the point is the overflowing generosity of God's love, which ignores claims of human merit and works. Like the parable of the prodigal son, it may have been used by Jesus to defend his reception of tax collectors and sinners against the objections of the scandalized Pharisees. The emphasis of the parable is the equal treatment God freely bestows on all, an emphasis which does not fit Mt's concern about eschatological reversal and the reward of the poor in 19:30 and 20:16. At best, Mt could interpret the parable as Jesus' warning that disciples must not fight among themselves over the measure of reward due each of them at the last judgment. An early call to discipleship or even a leadership position does not entitle one to calculate degrees of reward. Often the parable has been taken to refer to the relation of Jews and Gentiles in the church. While that would fit in with a basic concern of Mt, it does not fit the precise redactional framework into which Mt has inserted the parable.

The owner of the vineyard (an OT symbol for Israel, here a symbol of the kingdom, cf. 21:43) hires laborers at 6 A.M., 9, 12, 3 P.M., and finally at 5 P.M. With the first group he agrees on a denarius, the usual daily wage of a laborer. The wages of the others are left to the owner's discretion—though note the key Matthean word: "whatever is *just*" (RSV: "right"). Actually, Mt's interest is focused on the first and last groups (cf. 19:30 and 20:16), which

supply the contrast. At the end of the day's labor payment
is made, as the Law demanded (Lev 19:13; Dt 24:15). The
owner (in v.8, *kyrios*, "Lord") of the vineyard orders that
all be equally paid a denarius. The reversal-theme is sounded
in the command to pay the last first, though the main reason
for the reversal here is to allow the first group to learn about
the payment given to the last group and thus to build up
their hopes. The lord's generosity, which is a pleasant
surprise to the last group, becomes a cruel disappointment
to the first group. They had endured the hot scirocco wind
during the whole day, while the others worked only for an
hour in the cool of the evening. The householder overhears
one of the grumblers and replies with the cooly distant
address, "friend" (cf. 22:12 and 26:50). The lord has done
no *injustice* (RSV: "wrong"; note again the justice theme)
by fulfilling his contract and yet displaying his mercy to
those who had no contractual claim. Since he is lord and
master of his vineyard—the reference to God shines through
clearly now—he can will or choose to do what he wants with
his property. The real problem is that the grumblers harbor
envy (literally, "an evil eye") because the lord is generous
(literally, "good"; cf. 19:17) towards those with no merit
to stand on. His generosity is an expression of a gracious
freedom, not a spiteful arbitrariness, while their complaints
are an expression of their lovelessness.

The parable thus shows that God's justice and right
(cf. vv.4 and 13) are not according to man's calculations.
God's justice bestows mercy on the hapless and rebuffs
the proud claims of merit; one is reminded of Paul's teaching
on God's saving justice and sovereign free choice (cf. Rom
9:14-18). To this extent, the final reminder of eschatological
reversal (v.16) is not totally out of place, even though the
first group in the parable does not suffer the rejection
threatened in v.16. Needless to say, the parable is not
making pronouncements on just employment practices.
Presupposing the immense power of a first-century Palestinian landowner over his own property and workers,
Jesus compares this to the sovereign free choice of God,

who dispenses his gifts with generosity—with degrees of difference, but with no injustice to any rightful claim. Those who think they can calculate exactly how God must act are in for a surprise.

E. THE THIRD PASSION PREDICTION.
20:17-19.
[Mk 10:32-34; Lk 18:31-34]

> 17And as Jesus was going up to Jerusalem, he took the twelve disciples aside, and on the way he said to them, 18"Behold, we are going up to Jerusalem; and the Son of man will be delivered to the chief priests and scribes, and they will condemn him to death, 19and deliver him to the Gentiles to be mocked and scourged and crucified, and he will be raised on the third day."

Talk about rewards is rudely interrupted by Jesus' third passion prediction, yet the basic idea of eschatological reversal is retained: the tortured and crucified Jesus will be vindicated in the resurrection. The disciples must expect a similar pattern of suffering and reward. Typically, Mt omits Mk's theme of the disciples' amazement and fear as they follow Jesus to his death. Jesus speaks this prediction just as he is about to leave Perea and plunge into his final clash with the Jewish leaders in Jerusalem. This is the most detailed of the three predictions made before the entry into Jerusalem (cf. 16:21-23; 17:22-23). Departing from the Markan prediction, early Christian formulas, and even the previous Matthean predictions, Mt replaces "they will kill him" with the exact "to be crucified" (cf. 26:2). The role of the Gentiles in the process is revealed for the first time. As in previous predictions, Mk's "he will rise after three days" is replaced by the more precise "he shall be raised [by God] on the third day." The result is a short summary of the whole passion narrative. Jesus goes to his death knowing what awaits him, even down to the details.

F. A MOTHER'S AMBITION VERSUS JESUS' SERVICE.
20:20-28.
[Mk 10:35-45; Lk 22:24-27]

[20]Then the mother of the sons of Zebedee came up to him, with her sons, and kneeling before him she asked him for something. [21]And he said to her, "What do you want?" She said to him, "Command that these two sons of mine may sit, one at your right hand and one at your left, in your kingdom." [22]But Jesus answered, "You do not know what you are asking. Are you able to drink the cup that I am to drink?" They said to him, "We are able." [23]He said to them, "You will drink my cup, but to sit at my right hand and at my left is not mine to grant, but it is for those for whom it has been prepared by my Father." [24]And when the ten heard it, they were indignant at the two brothers. [25]But Jesus called them to him and said, "You know that the rulers of the Gentiles lord it over them, and their great men exercise authority over them. [26]It shall not be so among you; but whoever would be great among you must be your servant, [27]and whoever would be first among you must be your slave; [28]even as the Son of man came not to be served but to serve, and to give his life as a ransom for many."

While Mt in general omits Mk's statements that the disciples were blind to Jesus' status and message, he does preserve the blindness motif in this pericope as well as in the following one. Jesus has just uttered his most detailed prediction of the passion, and immediately the disciples seek short-cuts to honor in his kingdom. To spare James and John, Mt has their mother (identified by some scholars as Salome, cf. Mt 27:56 and Mk 15:40) present the petition, at first in very general terms and with the proper gesture of worship (v.20). At Jesus' prompting, the mother, reminiscent of Bathsheba pleading with David for her son Solomon (1 Kings 1), asks for the two best seats at the banquet "in your kingdom" (Mk: "in your glory"). Mt then slips back to his Markan model, in which the two brothers had themselves made the request. Jesus says: you (plural) do not understand the implications of what you are asking. Sharing Jesus' kingdom demands sharing his way to the kingdom, namely his cup of suffering which he is about to drink in Jerusalem (for the cup as a symbol of suffering, cf. Is 51:17,22; Jer 25:15,17,28; 49:12; Lam 4:21; Ps 75:8). Mt suppresses the Markan reference to baptism as a symbol of Jesus' death, either because for Mt baptism has become a word which refers only to a water-ritual or because his tradition is aware that John, unlike James (cf. Acts 12:2), did not undergo a martyr's death. While Jesus the Master can promise a share in his sufferings to his disciples, exaltation to the kingdom is something only the Father can give: first to Jesus (cf. Mt's use of the passive "will be raised" [by the Father] in the passion predictions) and then to whomsoever the Father grants it (cf. 25:34). The true Son proves his sonship by always submitting to the Father's will instead of grasping at glory (cf. 4:1-11); his disciples, the true sons, must imitate the Son's humility and obedience. By their indignation, the other ten disciples show they are no less free from ambition than James and John.

In a scene reminiscent of 18:1-5 (cf. 23:11), Jesus uses the occasion of his disciples' pettiness to teach his lofty ideal of service. Hellenistic societies knew all too well the arbitrary exercise of authority on the part of their vain and self-centered rulers. But this world cannot supply the model for leadership in the church. Church leadership is modeled on the paradox of the cross, the inversion of all values and ambitions. Jesus does not reject all desire for greatness and leadership in the kingdom, but the path to that goal dips into the valley of service, even slavery. Jesus first speaks of the servant, the person who freely puts himself at the disposition of others, and then radicalizes his statement with the image of the slave, the non-person who has no rights or existence of his own, who exists solely for others. Only this startling denial of self for the sake of others, and not power-politics, can effectively win mankind to the gospel. Church leaders who derive their tools and signs of power from this world betray the gospel of Jesus. This is the basic rule of church order, summing up everything said in chap. 18.

As usual, this ecclesiological teaching has a christological basis. The "even as" of v.28 has both a comparative and causal sense. The church must be the servant for others just as and just because Jesus the Son of Man, the future judge, has entered this world not as a king in pomp and splendor, but as a lowly servant. He has fulfilled his ministry with the lowliness and care of a servant (cf. 8:17; 12:18-21). And now he will consummate this service by the death of the suffering servant, an atoning sacrifice for the sake of and in the place of "many" (a Semitic way of designating the collectivity, i.e., all who benefit from the service of the *one*; cf. Rom 5:15-19). Precisely because Mt stresses a high christology (Jesus is the Messiah, the transcendent Son of God, and the Son of Man coming to judge), the image of the Son of Man as suffering servant is all the more striking. His power is the power of service; he exalts himself and his authority over others by lowering himself to death. He becomes Son of Man with all power and authority (28:18) by first becoming Son of Man sacrificed on the cross. His death above all is a sacrifice "for the remission of sins" (cf. 26:28), a "ransom" (*lytron*) which buys back, redeems, frees captive mankind from the grip of evil (cf. Ps 130:8; Ex 21:30; Lev 25:24; Num 3:46; Is 45:13; 53:10). Thus does the messianic king "save his people [the church] from their sins" (1:21).

G. THE BLIND SEE AND FOLLOW.
Mt 20:29-34.
[Mk 10:46-52; Lk 18:35-43]

> ²⁹And as they went out of Jericho, a great crowd followed him. ³⁰And behold, two blind men sitting by the roadside, when they heard that Jesus was passing by,

cried out, "Have mercy on us, Son of David!" [31]The
crowd rebuked them, telling them to be silent; but they
cried out the more, "Lord,, have mercy on us, Son of
David!" [32]And Jesus stopped and called them, saying,
"What do you want me to do for you?" [33]They said to
him, "Lord, let our eyes be opened." [34]And Jesus in pity
touched their eyes, and immediately they received their
sight and followed him.

James and John, and indeed, all the Twelve have shown
their blindness with regard to the passion of Jesus. Mt now
presents a symbolic healing of blindness, which foretells
what will happen to all disciples in the light of the death-
resurrection. Mt follows Mk, but abbreviates his account to
highlight the encounter between the believing petitioners
and the healing Son of David. Jesus is on his way up to
Jerusalem from Jericho (the first detailed geographical
reference since 19:1). The crowd, that ambivalent symbol,
is *following*. Mt omits the concrete details of the name
Bartimaeus and the fact that he was a beggar. Various
reasons have been suggested for the doubling of the figure
of the blind man: (1) the two blind men symbolize the two
blind sons of Zebedee; (2) Mt is conflating Mk 10:46-52
with Mk 8:22-26 (which Mt omits); (3) doubling is a stylistic
trait of Mt. The last suggestion is perhaps the best (cf. 8:28-34;
9:27-31).

Three times the blind men speak, beginning each time
(though the Greek text is uncertain in the first case) with
the address of the believer: "Lord." Considering the pleas
to Jesus for mercy here and in 9:27; 15:22; 17:15, one
wonders whether *Kyrie eleison* ("Lord, have mercy") was
not already a liturgical cry in Mt's church. The firm faith
of these lowly men is shown in the fact that they cannot be
silenced by the officious crowd, which prides itself on
following Jesus. The title "Son of David" appeals to Jesus
as the helper and healer of the humble and despised (cf.
comment on 9:27-31). Jesus who has just spoken of lowly
service now practices what he has preached. He gives the

two men the opportunity to express their faith by asking what they want, even though their reply is predictable. The reaction of Jesus is in part typically Matthean: divine pity (cf. 9:36; 14:14; 15:32; 18:27—this is the last mention of it in Mt). But in part it is untypical of Mt, in that Mt retains Mk's concrete detail of touching the eyes. Mt no doubt sees the statement that they "followed him" in a symbolic light: they become disciples of Jesus as he goes to his passion. Perhaps Mt drops Mk's "on the way" to make the symbolism clearer and more universal.

H. THE PROPHET-KING ENTERS HIS CAPITAL.
   21:1-11.
   [Mk 11:1-11; Lk 19:28-38]

   21 And when they drew near to Jerusalem and came to Bethphage, to the Mount of Olives, then Jesus sent two disciples, ²saying to them, "Go into the village opposite you, and immediately you will find an ass tied, and a colt with her; untie them and bring them to me. ³If any one says anything to you, you shall say, 'The Lord has need of them,' and he will send them immediately." ⁴This took place to fulfil what was spoken by the prophet, saying, ⁵"Tell the daughter of Zion,
   Behold, your king is coming to you,
   humble, and mounted on an ass,
   and on a colt, the foal of an ass."
   ⁶The disciples went and did as Jesus had directed them; ⁷they brought the ass and the colt, and put their garments on them, and he sat thereon. ⁸Most of the crowd spread their garments on the road, and others cut branches from the trees and spread them on the road. ⁹And the crowds that went before him and that followed him shouted, "Hosanna to the Son of David! Blessed is he who comes in the name of the Lord! Hosanna in the highest!" ¹⁰And when he entered Jerusalem, all the city was stirred, saying, "Who is this?" ¹¹And the crowds said, "This is the prophet Jesus from Nazareth of Galilee."

The listing of place names in v.1 is from the vantage point of Jerusalem: Jesus is coming from Jericho by way of Bethphage (probably a village on the ascent of the mount of Olives) and then down the mount of Olives to Jerusalem. In Jewish eschatological hopes, the Lord or his Messiah was sometimes depicted as coming to the Holy City from the mount of Olives (cf. Zech 14:4); it will be there that Jesus will pronounce his eschatological discourse (24:3).

The entire narrative, both the command of Jesus and his act of riding, are colored by Mt's intense desire to see prophecy fulfilled *literally* in the life of Jesus. The whole story must therefore be read from its theological center, the formula quotation in vv.4-5. The citation is a composite one. "Tell the daughter of Zion" comes from Is 62:11, a proclamation that "your salvation comes." This command to "tell" Jerusalem is unwittingly fulfilled by the crowds accompanying Jesus in vv.10-11. The rest of the citation comes from Zech 9:9, which stands behind Mk's narrative as well. The original text speaks of only one animal, which is described twice in different words, according to the norms of Hebraic parallelism. Mt has misunderstood the text to be speaking of two different animals; and, even though Mk speaks of only one animal, Mt introduces two animals into both Jesus' command (v.2) and his act of riding (v.7). The RSV obscures v.7 by translating "and he sat *thereon*"; it should read "and he sat on them [the animals]." Mt is more interested in literal fulfillment than historical probability. The fact that so learned a scholar as Mt could misunderstand the literal meaning of a statement set in Hebraic parallelism may indicate that Mt is a Gentile rather than a Jewish Christian. Possible evidence for the theory that Mt was not the sole inventor of formula quotations is the use of the same explicit citation in Jn 12:15.

Besides prophecy and fulfillment, Mt also forms Mk's story according to the pattern of command-and-execution-of-command (cf. v.6 and 1:24). This pattern is more important to Mt than Mk's emphasis on Jesus' foreknowledge;

Mt abbreviates both Jesus' instructions and the disciples' actions. Jesus' self-designation as "the Lord" is unique in the Markan-Matthean narrative of the pre-Easter Jesus; the paschal glory is already shining through the narrative. In v.4, Mt states that the objector will immediately release the animals for Jesus' use, while Mk seems to mean that Jesus promises to send the animal back immediately— another slight change Mt introduces to heighten Jesus' majesty. The act of riding on the ass and colt is a symbolic, prophetic gesture. Jesus is the true messianic prophet-king for whom Jerusalem hopes; and now he comes to lay claim to his capital, even though that capital will prove true to form and murder the prophet (23:37). He comes to conquer not by military means (hence the ass, the symbol of peace). The Septuagint refers to the king as "just and saving" as well as "humble" (or "meek"). So intent is Mt on stressing the humility of this peaceful king, who wins cosmic power (28:18) by his death on the cross, that he omits the first two adjectives, though he certainly would agree with them (cf. 1:21).

Jesus is received with "red-carpet" treatment as the crowds create a festal path of garments and branches (cf. 2 Kgs 9:13; 1 Mac 13:51; 2 Mac 10:7). Actually, the branches and Ps 118 are more reminiscent of the liturgy for the feast of Tabernacles. But no mention is made of either palms or Sunday; both details come from Jn's account. The acclamation Hosanna comes from the Hebrew of Ps 118:25. *Hôshî'ah-nnā,* i.e., "Save [us], we beseech [thee]!" The addition "to the Son of David" indicates that by Mt's time, and probably by Jesus' time, the cry had lost its literal meaning and had become a general shout of jubilation and welcome. The crowds continue with Ps 118:26, which originally meant: "Blessed in [or by] the name of the Lord be he who comes." Mt, like later Christian tradition, may understand the "in the name of the Lord" as modifying "comes." One is reminded of "the one who is to come" in 11:3. At the end of the gospel the Son of Man will come to his church in power, anticipating his final coming in glory. The title Son of David expresses the crowds' belief that Jesus is the eschatological Davidic Messiah, who at the same time fulfills the prophecy of Dt concerning the prophet like Moses (v.11, cf. Dt 18:15,18). The final "Hosanna in the highest" may simply express a heightening of the acclamation, though "in the highest" could be a reverent euphemism meaning "to God," or possibly even something like "God save the king!" The stirring eschatological procession of the Messiah into his capital causes *all* the city to shake as though from an earthquake. The RSV's "stirred" is too weak; the verb is *eseisthē,* the verb describing an earthquake (cf. the noun or verb in 8:24; 24:7; 27:51-54; 28:2-4). In 2:3, *all* Jerusalem is troubled with Herod over the question of the Magi concerning the *king* of the Jews. The question and answer which close the pericope almost remind one of the dialogue in the psalms of entrance (Pss 15 and 24) celebrating the ritual of entry into the temple. While "the prophet" should be taken along with the preceding royal title Son of David, it also hints at the imperfect understanding of the crowds. He who comes is not only prophet-king but also the fulfiller of the Law and the prophets.

I. THE OLD AND THE NEW TEMPLE-COMMUNITY. 21:12-17.
[Mk 11:11,15-19; Lk 19:45-48]

> 12And Jesus entered the temple of God and drove out all who sold and bought in the temple, and he overturned the tables of money-changers and the seats of those who sold pigeons. 13He said to them, "It is written, 'My house shall be called a house of prayer'; but you make it a den of robbers."
>
> 14And the blind and the lame came to him in the temple, and he healed them. 15But when the chief priests and the scribes saw the wonderful things that he did, and the children crying out in the temple, "Hosanna to the Son of David!" they were indignant; 16and they said to

him, "Do you hear what these are saying?" And Jesus
said to them, "Yes; have you never read,

   'Out of the mouth of babes and sucklings
   thou hast brought perfect praise'?"
[17]And leaving them, he went out of the city to Bethany
and lodged there.

Mt rearranges the Markan order by putting the cleansing
of the temple on the same day as the triumphal entry, while
the story of the cursing of the fig tree is unified and placed
on the next day. "Cleansing" is perhaps not the best description of Mt's conception; he sees Jesus' action as one of "over-
turning" the old order, a judgment on the temple which
prefigures its destruction (24:2). Buying and selling were
conducted in the outermost court, the court of the Gentiles.
Pilgrims had to change their various coins into the coinage
of Tyre, the only one allowed in the temple. Animals were
needed for sacrifice; pigeons were used by the poor. Since
these businesses were probably controlled by the priestly
aristocracy, Jesus' action is an attack upon the priesthood,
which is not slow to respond (v.15). Jesus interprets his
prophetic act by citing two prophets, Is 56:7 and Jer 7:11;
"shall be called" means "shall be" (cf. 5:9). Mt omits the
end of the Jer citation, "for all the nations," which Mk has.
Either Mt wishes to preserve his outline of salvation history,
according to which the death-resurrection makes possible
the mission to all nations; or, more probably, Mt, taking
into account the already accomplished destruction of the
temple (A.D. 70), indicates indirectly that the church is the
new temple-community, embracing in itself all the nations.
This theme of a widened community is continued in the
healing of the blind and lame in the temple. The OT (2 Sam
5:6-8 in the Septuagint) and also Qumran barred the
deformed and handicapped from the temple. Jesus rescinds
this barrier in favor of including all types in his eschatological community. As he transcends the Law in the very
act of fulfilling it (5:17-48), so he antiquates the temple in
the very act of fulfilling its true function. To the end he is

the healer of Israel's lowly and outcast, the meaning which Mt attaches especially to the title Son of David (cf. comments on 9:27; 12:23; 15:22; 20:30-31). The children, another embodiment of the poor and lowly whom Jesus receives (cf. 18:1-6; 19:13-15), cry out in the temple itself the truth of Jesus' Davidic messiahship, a truth the Jewish leaders refuse to hear and try to silence.

Over against the new joyful and healed community of the Messiah Mt sets the rulers of the old temple and the old people of God. The "chief priests and scribes" have not spoken in the gospel since 2:4-6, when they indirectly aided Herod in his attempt to kill Jesus. In between, they have been mentioned together only in Jesus' predictions of his passion and death (16:21; 20:18). Their reappearance here, in opposition to Jesus' claim on the temple, is an ominous sign that the proleptic passion story in the infancy narrative is about to become the full-blown passion narrative prophesied by Jesus. Jesus replies to their objections in the style of a rabbinic debate: "Have you never read . . . ," i.e., have you never understood this Scripture passage correctly? The priests and scribes in 2:4-6 knew how to quote Scripture to point out the infant Messiah but now they are blind to Scripture's mature fulfillment in Jesus. The rabbinic debate at the end of this story foreshadows all the debates and clashes over Jesus' authority and teaching down to the end of chap. 22. Quoting Ps 8:2 according to the Septuagint, Jesus indicates once again that the Father's revelation is given to mere babes (11:25-27), while the religious professionals are left in the dark. "Leaving them" anticipates Jesus' final departure from and rejection of the temple and Judaism in 24:1.

J. THE CURSED FIG TREE: A PARABLE IN ACTION. 21:18-22.
[Mk 11:12-14]

> [18]In the morning, as he was returning to the city, he was hungry. [19]And seeing a fig tree by the wayside he went

to it, and found nothing on it but leaves only. And he said to it, "May no fruit ever come from you again!" And the fig tree withered at once. [20]When the disciples saw it they marveled, saying, "How did the fig tree wither at once?" [21]And Jesus answered them, "Truly, I say to you, if you have faith and never doubt, you will not only do what has been done to the fig tree, but even if you say to this mountain, 'Be taken up and cast into the sea,' it will be done. [22]And whatever you ask in prayer, you will receive, if you have faith."

Mt places the cursing and the withering of the fig tree on the same day, uniting what Mk divides over two days. Mt thus heightens the miracle by making it instantaneous. While the words of Jesus in Mk have the form of a wish, they are more like a command in Mt. The miracle, which at first seems spiteful and destructive, is a prophetic parable-in-action, such as Isaiah, Jeremiah, and Ezekiel performed. Judaism, especially Pharisaic Judaism, is covered with the ostentatious foliage of external piety, but truly obedient deeds, the fruit of religion, are lacking. Jesus will therefore reject the old people of God and create a new one, which will produce the kingdom's fruits (so 21:43). This parable-in-action foreshadows the parables of judgment on Israel in chaps. 21-22. This whole story of the cursing of the fig tree may have developed in the pre-Markan tradition out of various parabolic sayings of Jesus (cf. Mt 7:16-20; Lk 13:6-9). To the basic reference to salvation history (i.e., the rejection of the Jews) the pre-Markan or Markan tradition also added a moralizing application (faith expressed in prayer), which fits the instantaneous withering in Mt perfectly. The great enemy of faith in a disciple's life is doubt (cf. Mt's theme of "little faith"). A faith which overcomes such doubt can move mountains or obtain any request. Thus Jesus tells his disciples that they can share his miraculous power and do still greater things, provided they have faith, and express their faith in prayer. Mt has already used a variant of v.21 at the end of the healing of the lunatic boy (17:20).

K. THE BASIC DISPUTE OVER JESUS' AUTHORITY. 21:23-27.
[Mk 11:27-33; Lk 20:1-8]

> 23And when he entered the temple, the chief priests and the elders of the people came up to him as he was teaching, and said, "By what authority are you doing these things, and who gave you this authority?" 24Jesus answered them, "I also will ask you a question; and if you tell me the answer, then I also will tell you by what authority I do these things. 25The baptism of John, whence was it? From heaven or from men?" And they argued with one another, "If we say, 'From heaven,' he will say to us, 'Why then did you not believe him?' 26But if we say, 'From men,' we are afraid of the multitude; for all hold that John was a prophet." 27So they answered Jesus, "We do not know." And he said to them, "Neither will I tell you by what authority I do these things."

Mt follows Mk in presenting an initial clash over Jesus' authority, then parables of judgment (three in Mt), four dispute stories, and, as a conclusion, the woes pronounced against the scribes (and Pharisees in Mt). The initial clash serves as a summation of the whole; more particularly, it "jumps over" the three parables of judgment and forms with the rest of chap. 22 a cycle of five dispute stories.

The adversaries of Jesus are now called "the chief priests and the elders of the people" (cf. 26:3,47, regarding the plot to arrest Jesus and the arrest itself). Their presence sounds an ominous chord. Their struggle with Jesus over the question of genuine religious authority will bring Jesus to the cross. The Jewish authorities ask Jesus about the nature and origin of the authority he claims. "These things" may include the triumphal entry, the cleansing of the temple, the healings, and even his teaching in the temple. In good rabbinic fashion, Jesus answers with a counter-question concerning the origin (and implicitly, the authority) of the Baptist's water-ritual. The Jewish leaders are caught on the horns of a dilemma. To say that John's baptism came from heaven (i.e., God) would be to convict themselves of refusal to repent ("believe him" being equivalent here to "trust him and repent"). Mt apparently does not see the slight tension between this Markan accusation and his own statement in 3:7 (a modification of Q) that the Pharisees *and Sadducees* (the priestly party) did go out to John to be baptized. On the other hand, to claim John's baptism was merely human would be to invite the wrath of the common people, who revered John as a martyred prophet (cf. comments on 11:9; 14:1-12, especially v.5; 17:11-13). Throughout his gospel, Mt has striven to present both John and Jesus as the eschatological prophet-martyrs rejected by a disobedient Israel ("this generation").

Like many time-serving bureaucrats, the leaders refuse to take a clear stand in public. But, by that very fact, they reveal their embarrassment and their inability to teach decisively on a matter of burning importance to their people. They give up their authority by default, and so Jesus feels no obligation to submit his teaching authority to their scrutiny. His act of refusal itself demonstrates his superiority. The true teacher of Israel—one is tempted to say, the teacher of righteousness—has exposed and defeated the false teachers. And they will not forgive that.

L. THE THREE PARABLES OF THE JUDGMENT OF ISRAEL. 21:28-22:14.

At this point in the narrative, Mk has one parable, that of the evil tenants. As so often, Mt takes his cue from Mk and expands on a Markan idea. The three parables of judgment (from three different sources: M, Mk, and Q) hammer away at some of Mt's basic themes: by rejecting and killing the Son, Israel itself has been rejected, and the Gentiles (another "nation") have received the kingdom (the vineyard, the marriage feast) instead. The church, like Israel of old, is now God's son, worker, and table-guest. But, warns Mt, its call likewise stands under judgment. Only obedience can transform initial call into final election.

(1) The Two Sons: Saying and Doing.
21:28-32.

> [28]"What do you think? A man had two sons; and he went to the first and said, 'Son, go and work in the vineyard today.' [29]And he answered, 'I will not'; but afterward he repented and went. [30]And he went to the second and said the same; and he answered, 'I go, sir,' but did not go. [31]Which of the two did the will of his father?" They said, "The first." Jesus said to them, "Truly, I say to you, the tax collectors and the harlots go into the kingdom of God before you. [32]For John came to you in the way of righteousness, and you did not believe him, but the tax collectors and the harlots believed him; and even when you saw it, you did not afterward repent and believe him.

There is great confusion in the Greek text of this parable. Some manuscripts invert the order of the two sons, and some manuscripts have the Jewish leaders identify the son who says 'yes' but does not go into the vineyard as the one who does the Father's will. While some would defend this latter reading as reflecting Mt's emphasis on the hard-heartedness of the Jews, the text in the RSV above seems to be the best reading.

The parable can be interpreted on a number of levels. (1) By itself, apart from vv.31-32, the parable may have had a function similar to the parable of the prodigal son (Lk 15:11-32, another "two sons" parable): the defense of the gospel preached to sinners and outcasts, in the face of sneers from the self-confident religious establishment. (2) Also apart from vv.31-32, the parable echoes a favorite theme of Mt, the split in the religious person between saying and doing (cf. 7:21-23; 12:50; 23:3-4). (3) With the addition of vv.31-32 (be they redactional or M), the parable continues the polemic against the Jewish leaders begun in vv.23-27 and uses the same cudgel: the Baptist. The leaders would not put their trust in (RSV: "believe") the Baptist, even when they saw his effect on the common people. This application is somewhat strained, since vv.31-32 do not explicitly depict a situation in which each group says one thing and then does the opposite. At best, we might imagine that the leaders said yes to God's will in the Law and the sinners said no; but, when the Baptist came, the sinners complied with God's demand as set forth in the Baptist's preaching, while the leaders did not. (4) On the level of Mt's outline of salvation history, the yes-sayers may symbolize the Jews while the no-sayers may symbolize the Gentiles. In Mt, Jesus' welcome to tax collectors and sinners is meant to point ahead to the church's welcome to the Gentiles.

On individual points in the parable, we may note the following. The vineyard signifies either Israel (Is 5:1-7) or better, in Mt's redactional view, the kingdom of God (21:43). The word for "repented" (*metamelētheis*) signifies in the story regret and a change of mind; in the application (v.32) it becomes equivalent to the common NT term *metanoeō*, signifying a change of mind and heart vis-à-vis God. The yes-sayer politely says, "Sir," (*kyrie*, "Lord"), reminding us of those who say "Lord, Lord," but do not "do the will of my Father" (7:21). As in other parables and dispute stories, the adversary or questioner is forced to pass judgment on himself. Vv.31-32 have a slight echo in Lk 7:29-30, but have the literary form of an apocalyptic Amen-saying ("Truly I say to you"), in which Jesus proclaims what will be God's judgment on the last day. The apocalyptic nature of the saying makes it likely that the phrase which the RSV translates as "go into the kingdom before you" means instead: "they go in while you do not." The latter translation is especially probable if there is an Aramaic background to the saying. The fierce judgment expressed by this "exclusive" translation certainly fits the thrust of the two parables that follow. The Baptist came "in the way of righteousness [or 'justice']," which means that the Baptist himself was just (i.e., one who did God's will), or that he taught others a just way of life, or possibly that he fulfilled his appointed role in God's saving plan (cf. comments on 3:15). As with Jesus, so with John, the Jewish leaders continued the sad story of an unfaithful Israel which rejects the prophet sent to call God's people to repentance.

(2) The Evil Tenants: The Transfer of the Kingdom. 21:33-46.

33"Hear another parable. There was a householder who planted a vineyard, and set a hedge around it, and dug a wine press in it, and built a tower, and let it out to tenants, and went into another country. 34When the season of fruit drew near, he sent his servants to the tenants, to get his fruit; 35and the tenants took his servants and beat one, killed another, and stoned another. 36Again he sent other servants, more than the first; and they did the same to them. 37Afterward he sent his son to them, saying, 'They will respect my son.' 38But when the tenants saw the son, they said to themselves, 'This is the heir; come, let us kill him and have his inheritance.' 39And they took him and cast him out of the vineyard, and killed him. 40When therefore the owner of the vineyard comes, what will he do to those tenants?" 41They said to him, "He will put those wretches to a miserable death, and let out the vineyard to other tenants who will give him the fruits in their seasons."

42Jesus said to them, "Have you never read in the scriptures:
'The very stone which the builders rejected
has become the head of the corner;
this was the Lord's doing,
and it is marvelous in our eyes'?
43Therefore I tell you, the kingdom of God will be taken away from you and given to a nation producing the fruits of it."

⁴⁵When the chief priests and the Pharisees heard his parables, they perceived that he was speaking about them. ⁴⁶But when they tried to arrest him, they feared the multitudes, because they held him to be a prophet.

Mt has taken over this parable from Mk. In his redaction he creates an outline of salvation history and adds an ecclesiological message to the christological one (v.43). The motifs of vineyard and son tie this parable to the preceding one. Mt's introduction, "hear another parable," reminds one of 13:18,24,31, and 33. Mk's "man" becomes a "householder," emphasizing ownership and rights to the produce ("*his* fruit" in v.34). The motif of the vineyard comes from Is 5:1-7. The householder becomes an absentee landlord, which helps explain the tension between him and his tenants. At harvest time, the owner wants the entire produce (contrast Mk's "some of the fruit"); the total and exclusive claim of God is clear. The fruits are the good works which God demands of man, the doing of God's will, *justice*. Mt divides the servants into two groups, representing the pre- and post-exilic prophets (cf. the division of Israelite history in 1:1-17 and the Jewish division of prophetic books into "former" and "latter"). The violent fate of the prophets is a common theme in Jewish literature, Q, and Mt's theology (cf. 23:37). Mt drops Mk's description of the son as "the one left, the beloved," though that no doubt agrees with Matthean christology (3:17; 17:5). Perhaps Mt is determined to bring out the ecclesiological dimension of the parable. The periodizing of salvation history is also highlighted; Mt adds "last of all" (better than RSV's "afterward"); the eschatological hour of the Son has struck. The plotting of the tenants is not so outlandish; if a Jewish proselyte died without heir, the tenants would have first claim on the land they worked. The motif of the connection between the Son, the inheritance, and those who wish to share the inheritance, is a common theme throughout the NT (cf. Rom 8:17). Mt changes Mk's order to mirror the events of Christ's passion. The tenants first throw the son outside the vineyard (the image shifts to symbolize Jerusalem) and then they kill him (cf. Heb 13:12).

Jesus' question tears away the veil of symbols: the *Lord* of the vineyard will *come* to pass judgment. The answer in v.41 quotes a classical Greek play on words, seen in Sophocles' *Ajax* and repeated by Josephus. It might be translated: "He will bring those wretches to a wretched end," obviously referring to the destruction of Jerusalem. That Mt imitated a classical Greek pun at this point does not speak well for the idea of a former Jewish rabbi writing a gospel in Aramaic. Mt also specifies in v.41 that the new tenants will differ from the old in rendering the fruits (good works) in their seasons (when God demands them). The idea of giving the vineyard to others will be expanded upon in v.43. The original parable may have ended at v.39; that it comes from Jesus and is not a creation of the church is supported by the strange ending: the death of the son, the last in the train of martyred servants (prophets). There is no mention of the son's vindication or resurrection. That lacuna was remedied by the tradition, which added the citation of Ps 118:22-23, which the early church referred to Jesus' resurrection and exaltation (Acts 4:11; 1 Pt 2:7). Jesus, God's chosen stone (cf. Is 8:14-15; Dan 2:34-35,44-45) has been rejected by the builders of Israel (the leaders who crucified him). But, by the resurrection, God has vindicated him and made him the cornerstone or keystone of a new structure, the new people of God. The connection of the two different images for God's people, vineyard and building, is already found in the OT and Qumran.

All of this leads nicely into Mt's addition in v.43. In Mt's schema of salvation history, Jesus' death-resurrection is the apocalyptic turning point which ushers in the new age of the church. Fittingly, then, right after the text referring to the resurrection, Mt has Jesus announce that after the death-resurrection God will take the kingdom from Israel and give it to a "people" (RSV: "nation") which will produce the harvest of justice, the good works God wills. By introducing this ecclesiological motif, Mt has shifted the imagery and the thrust of the parable. The vineyard no longer symbolizes Israel (v.33) or Jerusalem (v.39), but the kingdom of God, already present and given to Israel in the OT, but now transferred to the new people made up of both Jews and Gentiles, the church. Consequently, what was in Mk a parable aimed solely at the Jewish leaders (so still in Mt 21:45, a reformulation of Mk) really becomes in Mt a parable of salvation history (and damnation history), a parable of judgment on the whole of Israel. One should not restrict the future tenses of "will be taken away . . . and given" to the last judgment. The transfer is being prepared throughout the gospel. It reaches its decisive stage in the death-resurrection, and is announced in the gospel's final pericope (28:16-20). Thus, in Mt, the kingdom of God is a process-reality. Present even in the OT, it is transferred to the church; but it will come in full glory only at the end of the age.

For the moment, the leaders fear to seize Jesus because of the crowd (cf. 26:5). Mt inserts the Pharisees into the group of leaders, since they represent Judaism at the time of Mt. Mt adds a further explanation of the leaders' fear: the crowds revere Jesus as a "prophet" (cf. 21:11,26). Following in the steps of the martyred OT prophets and the Baptist, Jesus approaches his passion. But he does so with full knowledge of what will happen and in full command, because he is totally obedient to the Father's will (cf. 26:2, 42). Mt approaches Jn's idea of "the hour," but he is unique in stressing the nexus between christology and ecclesiology.

(3) The Royal Wedding Feast:
Judgment on Israel and the Church.
22:1-14.
[Lk 14:15-24]

> **22** And again Jesus spoke to them in parables, saying,
> ²"The kingdom of heaven may be compared to a king who gave a marriage feast for his son, ³and sent his servants to call those who were invited to the marriage feast; but

they would not come. ⁴Again he sent other servants, saying, 'Tell those who are invited, Behold, I have made ready my dinner, my oxen and my fat calves are killed, and everything is ready; come to the marriage feast.' ⁵But they made light of it and went off, one to his farm, another to his business, ⁶while the rest seized his servants, treated them shamefully, and killed them. ⁷The king was angry, and he sent his troops and destroyed those murderers and burned their city. ⁸Then he said to his servants, 'The wedding is ready, but those invited were not worthy. ⁹Go therefore to the thoroughfares, and invite to the marriage feast as many as you find.' ¹⁰And those servants went out into the streets and gathered all whom they found, both bad and good; so the wedding hall was filled with guests.

¹¹"But when the king came in to look at the guests, he saw there a man who had no wedding garment; ¹²and he said to him, 'Friend, how did you get in here without a wedding garment?' And he was speechless. ¹³Then the king said to the attendants, 'Bind him hand and foot, and cast him into the outer darkness; there men will weep and gnash their teeth.' ¹⁴For many are called, but few are chosen."

The original parable, represented by vv.1-5,8-10, has a parallel in Lk 14:15-24, and may come from Q. Jesus may have used the original form to defend his table-fellowship with sinners against the pious objections of the Pharisees (cf. Lk 15:1-32). Mt has changed an ordinary meal given by "a man" (so Lk) into a royal wedding feast celebrated by a king for his *son*. Mt has also added the alien theme of the destruction of the murderers and their city (vv. 6-7), possibly a separate parable (vv.11-13, though this addition may have already been made in the tradition), and a final familiar theme (v.14). The motifs of father and son, the sending of two groups of servants, the murder of the servants, the punishment of the murderers, and the transfer of some privilege to a new group all tie this parable to the preceding parable of the tenants, which Mt may have used as a model when he reformulated the parable of the feast. In the process, the periodization of salvation history and the situation of the church come to the fore.

The marriage feast was a well-known Jewish image for the joy of the last days; the NT, taking up the practice of Jesus, often uses table-fellowship or a marriage feast as a symbol of God's fellowship with humanity in heaven (cf. Mt 25:10; Rev 19:7-9). Mt has made the meal a *royal* one; among the evangelists, Mt is especially fond of the images of king and kingdom. The two groups of servants are probably not the former and latter prophets (as in 21:34-36), but rather the prophets of the OT and the apostles of the NT. The unity of the two covenants is the sad history of God's gracious call to the banquet and Israel's violent rejection of the messengers conveying the invitation. One is reminded of the theology of history taught by the Deuteronomistic historian in the OT. God's patience with Israel is underscored by the second invitation, which has become all the more pressing because "everything is ready." In other words, the last days have come; the second invitation brings us into the Christian dispensation. That is why in this parable the son himself is not sent or killed; he is thought of as already with his father in glory. It is the second group of servants, the apostles, who undergo the violent fate of the prophets at the hands of Israel. At best, some Israelites ignore the messengers, while the rest (especially the leaders) kill them. In reprisal, the king sends out his army, kills the murderers, and *burns their city*. The intrusive nature of v.7 could not be clearer. Launching a war after the meal has been prepared but before it is eaten strains even the wide range of probability allowed to parables, and the mention of the burning of the murderers' city comes out of nowhere. The only adequate explanation for this is that Mt is referring to the destruction of Jerusalem as a past event. Yet one does not get the impression from the whole of Mt's gospel that Jerusalem's destruction is an urgent problem from the recent past. Consequently, the gospel should be dated a good while after A.D. 70.

In v.8, which could just as easily follow upon v.5, the king enunciates the theme of the whole parable: who is *worthy* to partake in the (eschatological) banquet? One is reminded of the motif of being "worthy" in 10:10,11,13, 37-38. Since those invited (the Jews) proved they were not worthy by their rejection of both the OT prophets and the NT apostles, a new group is sent out to the world at large (the "thoroughfares" leading out of the city) to invite "whomsoever you find" (the Gentiles). The developing line of salvation history could not be clearer: to the Jews are sent first the prophets and then the apostles. When the Jews reject both, the gospel is offered to the Gentiles. The very words "go therefore" (*poreuesthe oun*) are repeated in slightly different form in the missionary charge of 28:19: "Going therefore . . . ."

The successful but perhaps indiscriminate gathering in of the Gentiles raises a new problem, hinted at in v.10 ("both bad and good") and expanded upon in the addendum of vv.11-13. The church, like the world, is a mixed bag of good and evil (cf. 13:24-30,36-43,47-50); Mt emphasizes the problem by using the order bad and good. Not everyone who receives an initial invitation (call) will remain as a guest (chosen). The great point of division will come at the final judgment, when the king (God) will make his appearance to look at (judge) the would-be guests at the banquet. Oriental courtesy demanded that any guest at a wedding banquet have the proper wedding garment, i.e., clean and neat clothing. In the parable, the wedding garment symbolizes a life lived in keeping with God's call, a life of justice, of doing God's will. One boor has come into the banquet with dirty, rumpled clothing, symbolizing a life that has undergone no basic change, a life that has not produced fruits worthy of repentance (3:8). The king addresses the insensitive person as "friend" (cf. 20:13; 26:50), indicating a cool distance between the gracious benefactor and the recipient who fails to correspond to the kindness shown. The boor's silence shows he has no excuse. In the description of his punishment, the reality signified shines clearly through the parable. Those in the church who have presumed on God's gracious invitation after the rejection of the Jews and who have not corresponded to the demands of the invitation by producing fruit (cf. 21:41,43) will face the same fate. They too will suffer eternal rejection (cf. 8:12, of the Jews; 25:30, of the unproductive servant; also 13:42, 50; 24:51). The church, like Israel, is subject to judgment; and, if the church is not vigilant, it can be rejected just as Israel was.

The final tag in v.14 does not really fit either vv.1-10 or 11-13, since in neither case are only a few admitted to the final banquet. However, the tag fits Mt's general intention, which is to warn church members to take their call to the kingdom seriously. Only this can make them "worthy." Instead of the RSV's translation, a better rendering of v.14 would be: "For the invited (*klētoi*, the called) are many, but the chosen (*eklektoi*) are few." In Paul, Christians can be named either "the called" or "the chosen"; Paul optimistically thinks that, in general, a Christian who is called to salvation will persevere and will be chosen on the last day (cf. Rom 8:28-30,33). Having experienced a second generation of Christianity, Mt's view is more sober; unfortunately, not all those members of the church who are among the "called" will persevere and be found among the smaller group called "the elect." "Enter by the narrow gate" (cf. 7:13-14). Salvation history is a web made up of the interaction between God's gracious invitation and man's free response. If man's response does not take God's invitation seriously, it is already the wrong response. Thus, with consummate skill, Mt has developed a simple parable about a meal into an allegory of the whole of salvation history, from the initial invitation to the Jews to the final judgment of Christians.

M. FOUR DISPUTES WITH THE JEWISH LEADERS. 22:15-46.

Mt follows the Markan order and text closely in the following four clashes with the various representatives of Judaism: the Pharisees (with the Herodians), the Sadducees, a Pharisaic lawyer, and the Pharisees again, but this time on the defensive. The questions range from a concrete problem of conscience concerning taxes to a speculative-dogmatic question on the resurrection, then back to a basic ethical-religious question about the greatest commandment, and finally to the question of the Messiah's true status and relation to David. With the exception of one oblique reference to the Herodians, all of Jesus' enemies are either Pharisees or Sadducees, who symbolize for Mt the Jewish magisterium, united against Jesus.

(1) The Coin of Tribute.
22:15-22.
[Mk 12:13-17; Lk 20:20-26]

15Then the Pharisees went and took counsel how to entangle him in his talk. 16And they sent their disciples to him, along with the Herodians, saying, "Teacher, we know that you are true, and teach the way of God truthfully, and care for no man; for you do not regard the position of men. 17Tell us, then, what you think. Is it lawful to pay taxes to Caesar, or not?" 18But Jesus, aware of their malice, said, "Why put me to the test, you hypocrites? 19Show me the money for the tax." And they brought him a coin. 20And Jesus said to them, "Whose likeness and inscription is this?" 21They said, "Caesar's." Then he said to them, "Render therefore to Caesar the things that are Caesar's, and to God the things that are God's." 22When they heard it, they marveled; and they left him and went away.

Mt changes Mk so that the Pharisees are clearly in command as the instigators of the trap ("entangle" reflects a rare Greek word for snaring animals during a hunt). The Herodians, supporters of the dynasty of Herod, are mentioned only obliquely; having disappeared from the Jewish scene by the time Mt is writing, they are of no concern to the evangelist. The reference to the "disciples" of the Pharisees also reflects Mt's time, when the Pharisaic rabbis became the undisputed teachers of Judaism. The unbelief of the questioners is apparent from the first word out of their mouths; "teacher" is always used in Mt by people who are not true disciples. The adversaries speak the truth without meaning it. Jesus does indeed speak the blunt truth and refuses to tailor his message to fit the desires of his audience; that is what will lead him to the cross.

The trap the Pharisees lay is a dilemma: either Jesus accepts taxation from Rome, and so loses the esteem of the people and the support of almost all Jewish factions except the Sadducees; or he rejects Rome's taxation, and so makes himself liable to arrest and trial for fomenting rebellion a la the Zealots. While the Herodians in principle would want an answer favoring taxation and the Pharisees in principle would want an answer rejecting it, their common, malicious desire is to discredit Jesus, whatever answer he gives. Politics—and religion—make strange bedfellows. Since the questioners are insincere, Jesus feels no obligation to give a direct, detailed answer to guide troubled consciences. Jesus shows that he does not play up to men by calling his adversaries hypocrites to their face; he will excoriate their hypocrisy at greater length in chap. 23. With true Oriental wit, Jesus gives a reply which answers yet does not answer the question. Deftly he asks his questioners for a denarius, the Roman coin used to pay the poll tax. By this apparently simple action, Jesus says: "I do not possess the coin used to pay the tribute; *you*, who seem so troubled about it, do carry and use the coin." And that willingness to use Caesar's money in their business transactions is a tacit acceptance of Caesar's imperial system and the healthy business climate he guarantees. If they are so ready to acknowledge Caesar's sovereignty when it is to their advantage, then they should pay up when Caesar demands his tribute. Jesus gives not a detailed theory of political obligations or church-state relations. His answer is a witty *ad hominem* argument: You willingly carry the coin which bears the image and inscription of Caesar (here, Tiberius); therefore, give back to Caesar what is his. This rule, of course, stands under and is judged by a still greater obligation: to recognize the sovereignty of the supreme Sovereign. How the two obligations are reconciled is not explained by the axiom; such explanations would be useless when the audience is so insincere. There is, however, a final barb in Jesus' words. It has been his constant accusation since he entered Jerusalem that the Jewish leaders have not "rendered" or given God the fruits, the just works, due him (cf. 22:41,43). They should worry less about what is due Caesar and pay more attention to giving God his due!

(2) The Resurrection of the Dead.
22:23-33.
[*Mk 12:18-27; Lk 20:27-40*]

23The same day Sadducees came to him, who say that there is no resurrection; and they asked him a question, 24saying, "Teacher, Moses said, 'If a man dies, having no children, his brother must marry the widow, and raise up children for his brother.' 25Now there were seven brothers among us; the first married, and died, and having no children left his wife to his brother. 26So too the second and third, down to the seventh. 27After them all, the woman died. 28In the resurrection, therefore, to which of the seven will she be wife? For they all had her."

29But Jesus answered them, "You are wrong, because you know neither the scriptures nor the power of God. 30For in the resurrection they neither marry nor are given in marriage, but are like angels in heaven. 31And as for the resurrection of the dead, have you not read what was said to you by God. ³²'I am the God of Abraham, and the God of Isaac, and the God of Jacob'? He is not God of the dead, but of the living." ³³And when the crowd heard it, they were astonished at his teaching.

The Pharisees having failed, the Sadducees, whom Mt sees as the other great party in the united Jewish magisterium (cf. comment on 16:12), attempt to make Jesus look ridiculous. Mt apparently has no clear conception of what distinguished the Sadducees as a party. While Mk and Lk both define the Sadducees in terms of their denial of the resurrection (Mk 12:18; Lk 20:27), Mt says in the Greek: "There came to him Sadducees, saying there is no resurrection" (the RSV is not clear here). In other words, these particular Sadducees are thinking or saying there is no resurrection as they come to Jesus; Mt does not indicate that this was a constant position which defined the whole group. His garbling of the Markan tradition makes one wonder about the supposed Jewish origins of the evangelist "Matthew" (cf. 16:1-12; 21:1-11).

The Sadducees show their unbelief by addressing Jesus as "teacher," the title used by unbelievers. They quote loosely a combination of Dt 25:5-6 and Gen 38:8, the basis of the "law of levirate" (from the Latin *levir*, "brother-in-law"). Behind the Sadducees' question stands a number of presuppositions of Sadducean theology (let us remember that the material of this pericope comes from Mk, not Mt). (1) The Sadducees rejected the Pharisees' placing of oral tradition on a par with written Scripture, and they refused to receive as normative any doctrine which was not taught in the Pentateuch, the five books of Moses. This was why they rejected the idea of the resurrection of the dead. They claimed it was not to be found in the Pentateuch, and they would find many exegetes today who would agree with them. On the basis of their Pentateuch-only approach, they saw in the law of levirate a clear negation of the idea of resurrection. Without any developed idea of an after-life, early Israelites sought a type of immortality in their offspring; it was vital that a man's name continue in his descendants. Hence, the law of levirate stipulated that the children begotten of the new union between in-laws would bear the name of the dead man and continue his line. The Sadducees implicitly argue that, if there were resurrection, there would not be in the Pentateuch this pressing concern to make a man "raise up children for his brother." The very law of levirate, with its concern for "immortality" in this world, presupposes that there is no other form of immortality. (2) For all their disagreements with the Pharisees, the Sadducees agreed upon what resurrection from the dead would involve, if it ever took place. Resurrection from the dead would mean a miraculous return to the conditions and relationships of this earthly life, only bigger and better. Some rabbinic descriptions of the risen life border on the crass. Accordingly, the Sadducees' question presupposes that the resurrected woman will have to resume her marriage relationship—but with whom? The Sadducees choose the number seven, the symbol of fullness and perfection, to underscore the absurdity of the situation.

Jesus' answer in v.29 strikes at the basic, erroneous presuppositions of the Sadducees: they understand (1) neither the Scriptures (in their interpretation of the Pentateuch), (2) nor the power of God (in their conception of what resurrection involves). Jesus then proceeds to treat these two points in reverse order (creating a chiasm). (1) First he explains the true nature of the resurrection. It is not a "coming back" to earthly life; it is a going forward into a totally new type of life in God's presence ("in heaven" may be a reverent periphrasis for "before God"). Like the angels, they are not married; the physical and sexual relationships of this world have been transcended. Jesus does not mean that the saved will have no bodies; the comparison with angels is meant to conjure up the idea of a new kind of bodily existence, somewhat like Paul's paradoxical idea of the "spiritual body" in 1 Cor 15:35-50.

(2) Jesus then corrects the Sadducees' interpretation of Scripture; his argumentation is rabbinic, and may not strike a modern Western mind as cogent. Faced with Jews who accept only the Pentateuch as normative, Jesus seizes upon a famous passage in the Pentateuch, the appearance of Yahweh to Moses in Ex 3. In Ex 3:6, God identifies himself —name expresses essence—in terms of his relationship with the deceased patriarchs Abraham, Isaac, and Jacob. How can the immortal God, the fullness of life and the source of life, be defined in terms of corpses which have long since crumbled into dust? Mt sharpens this point by stressing that God has spoken this definition *to you* and that in doing so he has used the present tense: "I *am* the God of Abraham"—not "I was" or "have been." When the words of the Pentateuch are read today in the hearing of the Sadducees, God continues to define himself in the present by his relationship with the patriarchs. The only conclusion possible is that this relationship continues even today. Death has not broken the living bond, the deep covenant relationship which bound these men to the living God. They live—not because of what they are, but because of who God is—"he is not the God of the dead, but of the living . . . ." He has the power to make all things live in union with himself. One might object that this line of argument proves immortality, not resurrection. But in Jewish thought of the day, the two concepts were usually tied together, either by the Pharisees who accepted them or the Sadducees who denied them. Mainstream Judaism did not conceive of human immortality without some connection with the body. Having been defeated on their own terms, the Sadducees feel astonishment just as the Pharisees marveled (v.22). An unspoken irony of this whole pericope is that the Sadducees, the aristocratic priestly class, will soon precipitate Jesus' own death and resurrection.

(3) The Dispute over the Greatest Commandment. 22:34-40.
[*Mk 12:28-34; Lk 10:25-28*]

> 34 But when the Pharisees heard that he had silenced the Sadducees, they came together. 35 And one of them, a lawyer, asked him a question, to test him. 36 "Teacher, which is the great commandment in the law?" 37 And he said to him, "You shall love the Lord your God with all your heart, and with all your soul, and with all your mind. 38 This is the great and first commandment. 39 And a second is like it, You shall love your neighbor as yourself. 40 On these two commandments depend all the law and the prophets."

In Mk, this pericope is a friendly conversation among scholars; in Mt, it becomes a hostile attack of the Pharisees, who conspire together (cf. Ps 2:2; Mt 26:3-4) and commission a "lawyer" to take up the battle. "Lawyer" occurs only here in Mt; along with other phrases which are closer to Lk than to Mk, it suggests that Mt may have known this story in both a Q and a Markan version. "Lawyer" means the same thing as Mt's frequent "scribe": a professionally trained theologian, whose main source book was the Law of Moses. Since Mt has no sense of the opposition between the Pharisees and the Sadducees, he drops Mk's comment that the scribe approves of Jesus' answer, which has silenced the Sadducees. Instead, the lawyer "tests" or "tempts" Jesus, a word which in the Synoptic gospels (unlike Jn) always has a negative connotation. The lawyer's unbelief is clear from the tell-tale address, "teacher." Mt replaces Mk's "first commandment" with "great commandment"; especially in Greek with a Semitic background, "great" can equal "greatest." In theory, all the commandments were to be observed with equal diligence. But practical necessity forced distinctions to be made within the 613 commandments of the Law between "light"

and "heavy." Knowing Jesus' claim to sovereignty over the
Law, the lawyer may hope to trap him in a damaging
statement.

But Jesus' reply could hardly admit of debate. He first
cites the heart of the *Shema'*, the ancient Hebrew prayer
taken from Dt 6:4-5. Mk includes the initial profession
of monotheism, since he is writing largely for Gentiles; in
a church with a Jewish-Christian background, Mt can
safely omit this. Love of God entails one's whole being:
heart (center of knowing and willing as well as feeling),
mind, and soul (one's whole life and energies). Love is not
so much a matter of feeling as a matter of doing. Keeping a
theocentric outlook, Mt stresses that this commandment
is *first* (taking up Mk's word). But there is a *second* which
is *like* to the first: love of neighbor (Lev 19:18; cf. Mt 5:43;
19:19). Notice the careful balance: God must come first, but
there is no true love of him which is not incarnated in love
of neighbor.

In v.40, Mt adds to Mk: the whole of God's revelation,
the Law and the prophets (a favorite theme of Mt in 5:17;
7:12; 11:13) "hangs upon" these two commandments as
on a double peg. In Jewish usage, commandments were said
to "hang on" a particular passage of Scripture in the
sense that they could be shown to be derived from or implied
in that passage. Therefore, the whole will of God in Scripture is derived from and is summed up in the double command of love. In short, what God wills is love. All individual
commands and obligations must be measured against and
judged by the canon of love. In the Judaism of Jesus' time,
various statements can be found which likewise emphasize
the importance of love of God and/or neighbor (Rabbi
Hillel, the Testament of the Twelve Patriarchs, Philo, and
Rabbi Akiba). But no statement of the period expresses
the absolute and fundamental nature of the double command as does Mt 22:40. The canon of love both binds us to
the heart of the Law as God's will and frees us from the Law
when it degenerates into casuistry. This latter point is

perhaps what leads Mt to present this story as a clash between Jesus and the casuistic Pharisees. In Mk, the scribe repeats and comments on Jesus' answer with approval, and Jesus commends the scribe. The fierce break between Mt's church and the synagogue has made such an irenic scene impossible. Mt says here in a nutshell what he explains at greater length in 5:17-48: Jesus is the true fulfillment of the Law, but in the very act of fulfilling he transcends the letter and frees from casuistry. The complete silence of the adversary at the end of the pericope indicates the total triumph of Jesus. He can now go on the offensive.

(4) David's Son and David's Lord.
22:41-46.
[Mk 12:35-37; Lk 20:40-41]

41 Now while the Pharisees were gathered together, Jesus asked them a question, 42 saying, "What do you think of the Christ? Whose son is he?" They said to him, "The son of David." 43 He said to them, "How is it then that David, inspired by the Spirit, calls him Lord, saying,

44 The Lord said to my Lord,

Sit at my right hand,

till I put thy enemies under thy feet'?

45 If David thus calls him Lord, how is he his son?" 46 And no one was able to answer him a word, nor from that day did any one dare to ask him any more questions.

Mt takes this pericope from Mk, but reformulates it. The rhetorical question in Mk becomes a real question in Mt, answered by the Pharisees. Their "being gathered together" seems to refer back to v.34; they have been standing around Jesus since that point onwards. The Pharisees answer Jesus' question with the opinion common to their party: the Messiah would be David's son (cf. Is 9:2-7; 11:1-9; Jer 23:5; Ezek 34:23; Zech 3:8; 13:1; also the extra-biblical Psalms of Solomon). Jesus' question was not an idle one, since conceptions of the Messiah varied;

Qumran expected two Messiahs, a royal Davidic Messiah and a priestly Messiah of the house of Aaron. Jesus replies to the Pharisees with another question, or rather with two questions (vv.43-45) framing a citation of Ps 110:1, the OT text most frequently cited in the NT. The rabbis considered Ps 110 to have been written by King David under divine inspiration, and possibly at the time of Jesus it was already considered messianic. If David, prompted by the Spirit, refers to the Messiah as "my Lord" when he says that the Lord (=Yahweh) spoke to "my Lord" (=the Messiah), how could this Messiah whom David treats so reverently be David's descendant? There are a number of levels of meaning in this question.

(1) In the context of the dispute stories, Jesus demonstrates for the last time the legitimacy and superiority of his teaching authority vis-à-vis the Jewish magisterium. They have proposed several questions to him and he has always produced a striking answer. He asks one question of them, and they are reduced to silence. They claim to be the authentic interpreters of Scripture, especially messianic texts; and yet they cannot explain this key text. Jesus has conquered the field; moving Mk 12:34 from its place after the question about the first commandment, Mt states that Jesus' enemies dare not risk any further verbal confrontation in public. There remains only the final confrontation of the passion.

(2) In the context of Mt's whole christology, from the infancy narrative onwards, Mt has taught that Jesus is the son of David (1:1) and yet more: he is the son of God (2:15), indeed, God with us (1:23). He certainly deserves to be addressed as Lord—which is just what the believing disciples do, even during the public ministry. The early Christian distinction between the earthly Son of David and the exalted Son of God (or Lord) which is seen in Rom 1:3-4 has been surpassed by Mt. The two distinct stages in the formula of Rom 1:3-4 have become for Mt two facets of the person of Jesus from his conception onwards. The fact that Jesus is Son of God from the beginning of the gospel does

not negate for Mt the importance of his title "Son of David."
Jesus has been hailed as Son of David just yesterday (20:30-
31; 21:9,15). Whatever the dispute of 22:41-46 may have
meant in the mouth of the historical Jesus, Mt certainly
does not mean it as a rejection of Davidic sonship. Jesus
the Messiah fulfills that requirement while transcending it.
The problem with the dogmatic Pharisees is that they are not
open to rethinking their messianic dogma in the light of
the messianic reality standing before them.

(3) In the context of the death-resurrection about to be
narrated, Ps 110:1 would naturally conjure up for any
first-century Christian the exaltation of Jesus to the right
hand of God after his resurrection. It provided a convenient
Scriptural explanation of the time intervening between
the resurrection and the parousia (cf. 1 Cor 15:25). But
this "paschal" reference is at best only alluded to; only
the initial words in Mt 22:44 figure in the questions in vv.43-
45. The lack of any direct reference to the death-resurrection
in the use of the citation may argue for the historicity of
this dispute, however much it may have been reformulated
in the tradition with Christian terms (e.g., the use of "*the*
Messiah" without modifier or further designation).

N. THE JUDGMENT UPON JUDAISM.
   23:1-39.
   [Mk 12:38-40; Lk 11:37-54; 20:45-47]

The disputes are at an end. Jesus alone speaks, and his
words are a frightening indictment of and threat against
the leaders of Judaism. Chap. 23 serves as a bridge between
the disputes and the eschatological discourse. The chief
disputants of chaps. 21-22 are now excoriated in chap. 23.
At the same time, chap. 23 speaks Jesus' judgment upon
Pharisaic Judaism, and so serves as the perfect introduction
to the discourse on cosmic judgment (chaps. 24-25). As
usual in Mt, the large structure of chap. 23 is constructed
out of building blocks of Mk, Q, and M. Chap. 23 is not

counted among the five great discourses of the gospel for two reasons. (1) The five discourses all end with the same transitional formula ("and it came to pass, when Jesus had finished these words, that . . . ."); the formula is lacking at the end of chap. 23. (2) The five discourses have a unified audience. They are addressed exclusively (chaps. 10,18, 24-25) or primarily (chaps. 5-7,13) to the disciples, with the crowds sometimes forming an outer circle. Chap. 23 begins as an address to the crowds and the disciples (vv.1-12), turns to address the scribes and Pharisees (vv.13-36), and concludes with an apostrophe to Jerusalem (vv.37-39). Some commentators, while refusing to count chap. 23 as a separate discourse, join it to chaps. 24-25 as part of the fifth discourse. Yet 23:37-39 seem intended to form a climax. The leaving of the temple (24:1), the narrowing down of the audience to the disciples (24:3), and the change in subject matter and style do not recommend joining chaps. 24-25 to chap. 23.

(1) The Disciples Are to Avoid the Rabbinic Style.
23:1-12.

> **23** Then said Jesus to the crowds and to his disciples, [2]"The scribes and the Pharisees sit on Moses' seat; [3]so practice and observe whatever they tell you, but not what they do; for they preach, but do not practice. [4]They bind heavy burdens, hard to bear, and lay them on men's shoulders; but they themselves will not move them with their finger. [5]They do all their deeds to be seen by men; for they make their phylacteries broad and their fringes long, [6]and they love the place of honor at feasts and the best seats in the synagogues, [7]and salutations in the market places, and being called rabbi by men. [8]But you are not to be called rabbi, for you have one teacher, and you are all brethren. [9]And call no man your father on earth, for you have one Father, who is in heaven. [10]Neither be called masters, for you have one master,

the Christ. [11]He who is greatest among you shall be your servant; [12]whoever exalts himself will be humbled, and whoever humbles himself will be exalted.

Verses 1-12 are a hodge-podge of sayings which come from different traditions in Mt's church. At times a given verse will be contradicted by the verse following or by other passages of the gospel. We must carefully distinguish between Mt's redactional view and traditional material he has taken over. The description of the audience for vv.1-12 and the order of the nouns are unique in Mt: "the crowds and his disciples." In the sermon on the mount, the direct audience is formed by the disciples, while the crowds apparently listen at a distance. In Mt's mind, the two groups may represent the two groups despised by the Pharisaic magisterium of his own day: the crowds equaling the non-observant "people of the land" (*'am hā'āretz*) and the disciples equaling the Jewish Christians expelled from the synagogue as heretics. "Scribes and Pharisees" is Mt's favorite way of describing the Jewish magisterium. In Jesus' time, the scribes were the professional lawyers and theologians; they could be, but were not necessarily, members of the Pharisaic faction. Pharisees were mostly pious laymen who banded together to live out a strict observance of the written Law and oral traditions. For Mt, the two words together have become a code-word for the united front of Judaism which his church faces. The Jewish rabbis claimed to have received divine revelation and the authority to interpret it in an unbroken line from Moses (cf. *Pirke Aboth* [The Sayings of the Fathers] 1,1). "The seat of Moses" is an image of this teaching authority; teachers and judges in Jesus' time usually sat to perform their functions. An actual piece of furniture called "the seat of Moses" was used at a later date, but its use in the first century A.D. has not been proven.

Verse 3 is one of the most difficult to understand in the context of Mt's own theology. Taken with v.2, v.3 acknowledges the legitimacy of the Pharisaic magisterium and urges compliance with *whatever* (literally, "all whatsoever") they teach and command. Such a statement is contradicted not only by the rejection of the Jewish magisterium in 15:1-20 and 16:1-12, but also by the rejection of Pharisaic practices (contrast *practice* in v.3) in vv.5-10 and by the rejection of Pharisaic teaching in vv.16-22. Since verses like 16:12 certainly reflect Mt's own view, we are left wondering why Mt kept 23:2-3, which seem to come from the early, stringently Jewish-Christian stage of Mt's church, perhaps when the church was still struggling to maintain its ties to the synagogue. It may be that Mt understands vv.2-3 within the framework of his view of salvation history: during the public ministry, Jesus pursued his mission only among Israelites and avoided any definitive break with the synagogue and the Mosaic Law. If Jesus was nevertheless rejected and his disciples cast out of the synagogue, the fault lies with the Pharisees, who "say" (RSV: "preach") but do not "do" (RSV: "practice"). On the basic sin of saying and not doing or of doing only to be seen by men, see the comments on 7:21-23 and 6:1-18. The Pharisees and the Christian charismatics of Matthew's church are guilty of the same fundamental sin which afflicts religious people: hypocrisy (cf. "hypocrites" in vv.13-16). The Pharisees' self-centered piety closes them to genuine pastoral concern about others who struggle under the load of Pharisaic interpretations of the Law.

The tone of v.4 is notably different from vv.2-3a. The 613 commandments of the Law, with its Pharisaic interpretations, have become a heavy burden which the ordinary mortal (represented by the crowds) finds hard to bear. Yet the Pharisees offer the weak no help in bearing the burdens the Pharisees have created by their binding and loosing (cf. 16:19; 18:18). This critique is reminiscent of Peter in Acts 15:10. The image of burdens on men's shoulders conjures up by contrast the image of the easy yoke and light burden which Jesus offers the weary (11:28-30).

Verse 5 begins the second form of hypocrisy: what they do, they do only for the sake of ostentation. Three examples are given. First, they broaden the *tephillîn,* the little boxes which contained parchments, on which were written Ex 13:1-16; Dt 6:4-9 and 11:13-21. In literal observance of Ex 13:9; Dt 6:8 and 11:18, they were placed on the left forearm and on the forehead during prayer. Mt calls them "phylacteries" or "amulets," perhaps with polemical intent. The Pharisees also lengthen the tassels (RSV: "fringes") which a pious Jew wore at the four corners of his cloak as a reminder of the Law, in keeping with Num 15:38-39 and Dt 22:12. The second example of ostentatiousness is the love of guest-of-honor seating at feasts (e.g., next to the host) and the seats on the raised podium in the synagogue, facing the people and in front of the ark in which the scrolls were reserved.

The third example of ostentatiousness is the Pharisees' love of greetings and titles, bestowed on them in public. In Oriental etiquette, the inferior had the prior obligation to greet his superior with a salutation whose length indicated the superior's importance. The Pharisees wish to receive salutations and titles, not give them. Three titles are mentioned and forbidden to disciples, though only the first is explicitly said to be used by the Pharisees. "Rabbi," literally "my great one," was a title of respect for Jewish teachers and leaders in the first century A.D., though the NT data suggest that it had not yet been restricted solely to ordained scholars. Christians are not to use the term, for they possess only one true teacher, Jesus. While for Mt the direct address "teacher" is the sign of an unbeliever, this does not mean he rejects the idea that Jesus is a teacher. The problem with the unbelievers is that they recognize in Jesus only *a* teacher, and nothing more. It is noteworthy that the only person in Mt who addresses Jesus with the Hebrew "rabbi" is Judas (26:25,49). Christians know that Jesus is *the* one true teacher precisely because he is Son of God and Son of Man. The Son has made his disciples sons of the same Father and therefore brothers of one another (cf. 5:43-48; 12:46-50); no one in the family must put on airs by assuming the title of teacher.

Likewise, no one should be called Father, for, as Mt stresses more than any other evangelist, all disciples have one common Father in heaven (cf. 6:1). The patriarchs and great Jewish teachers were referred to as "fathers" (hence the tractate in the Talmud, *The Sayings of the Fathers*); there is little evidence, however, that the title was used as a direct address. Some unhealthy practices in Mt's community may be shining through here. Since the form of "Father" in Aramaic would be *Abba*, the sacred cry of early Christians, one could understand Mt's horror at the practice. The third title in Greek is *kathēgētēs* (RSV: "master"), which can mean a philosopher, teacher, spiritual director, or guide of the conscience. The statement in v.10 is simply a more explicit form of v.8, formulated in clearly Christian terms by the early church (as can be seen from the absolute phrase, "the Christ"). Mt's great concern with these three titles indicates that the problem has already arisen in his own church. Leaders are arrogating titles to themselves, thus turning the servants of the brotherhood of Christ into a hierarchy. If Mt's church were at Antioch in Syria, the place where the monarchical episcopate arose around the time of Ignatius of Antioch, we can only conclude that Mt's indignant protests against titles were canonized but not heard. The Catholic Church in particular must reflect on whether these inspired words call it to forsake the ecclesiastical titles which have proliferated in its midst, especially since one of its most common titles, "Father," is specifically forbidden to religious leaders.

It is important to remember that all of Mt's fierce invectives against Pharisaic Judaism reflect a pastoral concern for his own church. The church is in danger of imitating the mistakes of the Pharisees and so falling under the same judgment. Completely contrary to all this haughty "leadership" is the true style of Christian leadership and greatness: humble service (23:11 is a repetition of 20:26 and echoes the theme of 18:1-4). There may be a play on words, "greatest" in v.11 taking up the "rabbi" of v.8. Using a Q-statement (cf. Lk 14:11; 18:14), Mt closes this consideration of false and true leadership by pointing to the final judgment (the future passive verbs referring to God's action on the last day). God's judgment will reverse earthly positions: the humble servant will be rewarded while the self-seeking ruler will be condemned.

(2) The Seven Woes Against the Scribes and Pharisees. 23:13-36.

13"But woe to you, scribes and Pharisees, hypocrites! because you shut the kingdom of heaven against men; for you neither enter yourselves, nor allow those who would enter to go in. 15Woe to you, scribes and Pharisees, hypocrites! for you traverse sea and land to make a single proselyte, and when he becomes a proselyte, you make him twice as much a child of hell as yourselves.

16"Woe to you, blind guides, who say, 'If any one swears by the temple, it is nothing; but if any one swears by the gold of the temple, he is bound by his oath.' 17You blind fools! For which is greater, the gold or the temple that has made the gold sacred? 18And you say, 'If any one swears by the altar, it is nothing; but if any one swears by the gift that is on the altar, he is bound by his oath.' 19You blind men! For which is greater, the gift or the altar that makes the gift sacred? 20So he who swears by the altar, swears by it and by everything on it; 21and he who swears by the temple, swears by it and by him who dwells in it; 22and he who swears by heaven, swears by the throne of God and by him who sits upon it.

23"Woe to you, scribes and Pharisees, hypocrites! for you tithe mint and dill and cummin, and have neglected the weightier matters of the law, justice and mercy and faith; these you ought to have done, without neglecting the others. 24You blind guides, straining out a gnat and swallowing a camel!

[25]"Woe to you, scribes and Pharisees, hypocrites! for you cleanse the outside of the cup and of the plate, but inside they are full of extortion and rapacity. [26]You blind Pharisee! first cleanse the inside of the cup and of the plate, that the outside also may be clean.

[27]"Woe to you, scribes and Pharisees, hypocrites! for you are like whitewashed tombs, which outwardly appear beautiful, but within they are full of dead men's bones and all uncleanness. [28]So you also outwardly appear righteous to men, but within you are full of hypocrisy and iniquity.

[29]"Woe to you, scribes and Pharisees, hypocrites! for you build the tombs of the prophets and adorn the monuments of the righteous, [30]saying, 'If we had lived in the days of our fathers, we would not have taken part with them in shedding the blood of the prophets.' [31]Thus you witness against yourselves, that you are sons of those who murdered the prophets. [32]Fill up, then, the measure of your fathers. [33]You serpents, you brood of vipers, how are you to escape being sentenced to hell? [34]Therefore I send you prophets and wise men and scribes, some of whom you will kill and crucify, and some you will scourge in your synagogues and persecute from town to town, [35]that upon you may come all the righteous blood shed on earth, from the blood of innocent Abel to the blood of Zechariah the son of Barachiah, whom you murdered between the sanctuary and the altar. [36]Truly, I say to you, all this will come upon this generation.

With his love of numerical patterns, Mt composes a series of seven woes, drawn from Mk, Q, and M. While Lk preserves a distinction between the woes addressed to the Pharisees (Lk 11:42-44) and those addressed to the scribes (Lk 11:45-52), Mt typically meshes the two. Well known in prophetic and apocalyptic literature, the word "woe" expresses both the seer's dismay and his threat of punishment. "Woe" may have originated as a cry of lament over the dead; the seer weeps over those who know not that they are already dead within (cf. vv.27-28) and are destined for a swift death without (vv.35-38). Jesus the eschatological prophet had begun his first discourse with the beatitudes (5:3-12), proclaiming final happiness to those who suffer now (23:12b—"whoever humbles himself shall be exalted"). In chap. 23, the transition to the final discourse, the eschatological prophet proclaims eternal woe to those who pride themselves on their own righteousness (23:12a—"whoever exalts himself shall be humbled"). The tone is uncompromisingly bitter, because the painful exerience of Mt's church has colored and developed the polemic. What in the mouth of Jesus was a prophetic critique of Judaism from within Judaism has become a rejection of Pharisaic Judiasm in Mt's gospel and church. We are not to take what follows as a complete and balanced description of Pharisees. The movement produced many good and holy men. Unfortunately, as history shows, the more zealous and puritanical a religious movement is, the more it can produce hypocrites and legalists as a by-product. The constant rebuke of the woes is "you hypocrites." As we have seen (7:21-23; 23:1-12) hypocrisy for Mt is the basic split in "religious" man, the basic split between saying and doing, between appearing and being. A façade without reality is the constant temptation of "religious" man, and Mt is all the more severe with this vice because he sees it endangering the church as well as Judaism. The subsequent history of the church shows that he was not an alarmist.

1. *The first woe:* shutting the kingdom. There could hardly be a severer charge against the the guides and teachers of Israel than that they hinder entrance into the kingdom instead of facilitating it. The definition of a bad religious leader might be the path which has turned into the roadblock. The image of shutting may allude to the rabbinic power to bind and loose: by their casuistic teaching (and perhaps by their practice of excommunication after A.D. 85), the Jewish teachers, having first hardened themselves, proceeded to hinder other people from coming to

Jesus and later to his church. Since the leaders have corrupted their doctrine (16:12), Jesus transferred the power of the keys to Peter (16:19).

2. *The second woe:* Jewish missions. The idea of preventing people from entering the church (the present locus of the kingdom) leads into a condemnation of the Pharisees' zeal for making converts. In the first century A.D., before the Jewish War and the destruction of Jerusalem (66-70), Pharisaic Judaism pursued an energetic campaign among Gentiles, some of whom were persuaded to become full "proselytes," i.e., converts, who accepted circumcision and all the obligations of the Law. To "traverse sea and land" expresses the Pharisees' willingness to go to any lengths and expend any amount of energy to gain just one convert. The charge that the convert becomes twice as damnable ("a child of hell") as the missionaries is extremely harsh. Possibly it reflects the fact that early Christian missionaries encountered more hostility to their law-free gospel from Gentiles who had converted to Judaism than from Jews by birth (cf. Paul's problems in Galatia). The phrase "a child of hell" (literally, "a son of [i.e., one belonging to or deserving of] hell") reminds one of Mt's phrase, "sons of the kingdom" (8:12; 13:38).

3. *The third woe:* casuistry about oaths. At first glance, the third woe seems to contradict Jesus' total rejection of oaths and vows (5:33-37); in 23:16-22 he seems to presuppose that oaths are legitimate. A closer look, however, shows that Jesus is engaging in a mocking, *ad hominem* attack on Pharisaic casuistry. Jesus accepts Pharisaic custom only to attack it as ridiculous on its own grounds. In particular, since Mt specifically rejects an oath "by heaven" in 5:34, he can hardly be accepting it as legitimate in 23:22. The real contradiction is between the rejection of Pharisaic doctrine in 23:16-22 and the apparent acceptance of it in 23:2-3. The latter, as we have argued, makes sense for Mt only in the context of the past ministry of Jesus to Israel. The casuistry of the Pharisees tried to identify

those formulas which made an oath binding. Jesus simply shows that their priorities are topsy-turvy and so their teaching is illogical. Temple and altar were more basic realities of Jewish religion than gold (in the temple building or the temple treasury?) or animals. Although the exact distinctions recorded here are not mentioned in the Talmud, the basic point is clear. The Pharisees' inversion of values, though apparently insignificant here, is a tell-tale symptom of their inability to focus on the "weightier matters of the law" (v.23, in the next woe). Verses 20-22 do not express an approbation of oaths. They are a call to integrity in religion, to a perfection (5:48; 19:21) which gives oneself totally to God, instead of inventing endless distinctions to create secure places in life, where the pious man is safe from the demands of God. By atomizing the Law with their casuistry, the Pharisees have become blind guides ("blind" is used five times in this chapter; cf. Mt 15:14; Rom 2:19). While considering themselves "wise and understanding" (11:25), they have led astray both themselves and others.

4. *The fourth woe:* tithing. The obligation to give a tenth of one's produce to support the temple is found in Num 18:12 and Dt 14:23 (oil, wine, and grain); Dt 14:22 extends the obligation to "all the yield of your seed." The scrupulous Pharisees pushed the obligation to include even small garden plants like mint, dill, and cummin. Jesus does not reprobate what would be admissible as a voluntary sacrifice. On the other hand, Mt does not mean to impose these Jewish practices by saying "these you ought to have done"; the same statement is found in Lk 11:42. The problem Mt is attacking is that preoccupation with trivia has distracted the Pharisees from what really counts in God's sight, "the weightier matters of the Law." Justice and mercy refer to one's covenant obligations toward one's neighbor. "Faith" could mean either a faithfulness and reliability vis-à-vis one's neighbor; or, if Micah 6:8 and the double command of love are in the background, "faith" could mean total surrender to and trust in God. Obsession with trivia and neglect of the essential are likewise expressed by a

metaphor taken from daily usage: cloths were placed over the necks of containers to filter out impurities or insects. The legalistic Pharisees would take extra care to strain out anything which the Law forbade as unclean (according to Lev 11:41-43, anything that swarmed or crept). The camel, the largest animal native to Palestine in Jesus' day, is of course hyperbolic (cf. 19:24).

5. *The fifth woe:* the inner and outer man. The Pharisaic custom of washing vessels becomes, from the beginning of this woe, a metaphor. The starting point of the metaphor may be the Pharisees' fear that any particle of blessed wine or food, falling outside a vessel, could defile the vessel. But, in this woe, the cup and plate immediately become images representing a person who is by all appearances respectable, but whose heart is filled with a desire to rob people (RSV: "extortion") and to be intemperate (Greek, *akrasia*, which could refer to drink or sex; the RSV reads the poorly attested *pleonexia*, "rapacity"). True purity is not a matter of ritual but of a cleansing of the heart (the "inside," cf. 15:17-20); inner purity makes the whole man clean.

6. *The sixth woe:* the white-washed tombs. The split between inner and outer, begun in the fifth woe, is sharpened. Because even unconscious contact with the dead transmitted levitical impurity, tombs were covered with white-wash, especially before Passover, to prevent contamination. The Pharisees are like such tombs, beautiful on the outside (their ostentatious practice) but the very essence of uncleanness on the inside (in their hearts). The contradiction between pretty façade and putrefying flesh is for Mt a perfect symbol of what is for him the essence of sin: hypocrisy, the basic split in religious man, and—surprisingly in an attack on the Pharisees!—lawlessness (*anomia*; RSV: "iniquity"). Lawlessness for Mt does not mean a theoretical, antinomian rejection of Law in principle; there is no antinomian group which Mt is attacking. Rather, lawlessness is that rebellion against God and his holy will which so often expresses itself in hypocrisy; the syndrome can be

found equally in Christian charismatics (7:23, where the RSV's "evildoers" is literally "doers of lawlessness") and in legalistic Pharisees (23:28).

7. *The seventh woe:* murdering the prophets. The last woe reaches a fever-pitch of accusation. Veneration of martyred prophets—whose number grew in popular legend and apocalyptic writings—was widespread in Jesus' time, as many tombs and places of cult witnessed. The mention of both the prophets and the righteous (or "just") in v.29 prepares for the concrete examples of Abel (RSV: "innocent," literally "just") and Zechariah, whom Mt confuses with the prophet of the same name. By their zealous attempts to raise monuments to the martyrs of the past the Pharisees sought to disown the impious murders perpetrated by their ancestors. Yet, says Jesus, using a Semitic play on words, your own statements and actions prove you are the *sons* of murderers. In Semitic usage, "son of" was used metaphorically to describe one who belonged to and shared the characteristics of a group. With grim irony, Jesus intimates that the Pharisees, the physical sons of those who murdered the prophets, are also the spiritual heirs of those murderers. Using apocalyptic language, Jesus affirms that God has appointed a set measure of suffering and martyrdom before the final judgment. Very well, says Jesus, complete the work your fathers began—by murdering me, the eschatological prophet, and all the Christian prophets and sages and teachers I will send you in the church. It is a remarkable vision of salvation history (and damnation history), drawn from the Deuteronomistic historian. Israel, the covenant-people of God, has rebelled again and again against its Lord and has persecuted and murdered the prophets God sent to warn it. As they did to the prophets of old, so they do to the prophetic figures of the new covenant. Jesus roundly consigns this brood of vipers to hell for punishment; thus Jesus confirms the judgment of his martyred prophetic forerunner, the Baptist (3:7; cf. 12:34). The break between synagogue and church could not be clearer.

Verse 34, reminiscent of 10:17,23, reflects the persecution
the early Jewish Christians suffered at the hands of over-
zealous Pharisees—and also of the Romans (crucifixion
was a Roman form of execution). Significant for christology
is the fact that Jesus speaks here as the personified Wisdom
of God, directing the course of salvation history (cf. Lk
11:49, where the parallel reads: "Therefore also the *Wisdom
of God* said: *I will send* unto them prophets and apostles").
The prophets, wise men, and scribes may represent the
various types of leadership roles found in Mt's church.
The persecution of such figures is no small matter. It is the
culmination of the whole fearful history of Israel's apostasy.
Therefore, "upon you," "upon this generation" (i.e., the
unbelieving contemporaries of Jesus) shall vengeance be
taken for all the martyrs of the past—from the first person
to be murdered (Abel in Gen 4:8) down to the last unjustly
killed person mentioned in the Hebrew Bible, which ends
with 2 Chron (Zechariah, 2 Chron 24:20-22). Mt blunders
here, confusing the Zechariah of 2 Chron, who was the son
of Jehoiada, with Zechariah *the prophet*, who was the son
of Berechiah (so Zech 1:1) or the son of Iddo (so Ezra 5:1).
The identification of Zechariah in 23:35 with a Zechariah
the son of Bareis, killed during the Jewish War of A.D. 66-
70, is highly unlikely. This blanket condemnation of the
Jewish leaders must be read in the light both of the church's
experience of persecution and of Jerusalem's destruction
in A.D. 70. The church saw the latter as an apocalyptic
event, a judgment exacted for the death of Christ and his
faithful, and also as an anticipation of the final judgment.
The veiled reference leads neatly into the final section of
chap. 23, the address to Jerusalem.

(3) Jesus and Jerusalem: the Mutual Rejection.
23:37-39.
[*Lk 13:34-35*]

   ³⁷"O Jerusalem, Jerusalem, killing the prophets and
stoning those who are sent to you! How often would I

> have gathered your children together as a hen gathers
> her brood under her wings, and you would not! [38] Behold,
> your house is forsaken and desolate. [39] For I tell you,
> you will not see me again, until you say, 'Blessed is he
> who comes in the name of the Lord.'"

The conclusion of chap. 23 is a highly emotional apostrophe to the holy city, which has proven throughout its unholy history to be an evil city, *the* place in Israel where the prophets have been rejected and murdered (cf. Lk 13:33). The terrible theme of 23:29-36 is now being centered upon Jerusalem. Just as God in the OT is often portrayed protecting Israel, Jerusalem, or the just man "under the shadow of his wings," like a mother-bird protecting its young (cf. Dt 32:10-11; Is 31:5; Pss 17:8; 91:1-4), so too Jesus repeatedly tried to save the capital of Israel from its impending doom at God's hand. The "how often" may be a slight remembrance from the Q-tradition that Jesus' ministry had brought him to Jerusalem a number of times, as Jn—though not the Synoptic traditions—emphasizes. But, as in the past, so now Jerusalem has rejected the prophet of God, as the three parables of judgment have made clear. The difference is that this time she has rejected *the* eschatological prophet; and so she has no future, no further chance. The break between Jesus and Jerusalem is definitive. "Your house is left to you, desolate," says Jesus, with allusions to 1 Kgs 9:7-8; Jer 12:7; 22:5; and Tob 14:4. While "house" could signify Jerusalem or even the whole of Israel, the fact that Jesus is speaking in the temple favors the common OT image of the temple as the house of God. As in Ezek 10:1-22; 11:22-25, the Lord will leave his temple. While the full acting out of this threat was accomplished in A.D. 70, the prophecy already begins to be fulfilled in 24:1, when Jesus leaves the temple, and more fully in 27:51, when the curtain of the temple is rent at the death of Christ. Christians must seek the presence of God in Jesus the Emmanuel (1:23) who is with us all days (28:20) in the midst of his church at prayer (18:20). Once Jesus departs from Jerusalem, Israel will not see its Messiah again until he comes on the last day. Then he will come not as its meek king, as in 21:1-11, but as its dreaded judge. The ritual greeting it will give then will be forced from it, and will be a recognition of its defeat and rejection. Verse 39 is placed by Lk before Jesus enters Jerusalem and therefore receives at least a partially positive fulfillment at the triumphal entry. But Mt's view is unrelievedly pessimistic. Unlike Paul in Rom 11:25-32, there is no consoling vision that "all Israel" will be saved on the last day. While individual Jews may continue to enter the church, Israel as a whole is abandoned to its fate. On this somber note, Mt moves to the eschatological discourse. Since he wishes as direct a connection as possible, Mt drops Mk's story of the widow's mite (Mk 12:41-44).

II. THE DISCOURSE OF BOOK FIVE: THE LAST JUDGMENT. 24-25.

THE ESCHATOLOGICAL discourse falls into two main parts. The first half is taken over from Mark, with some deletions and insertions to highlight Mt's point of view. This first half (24:1-36) is more doctrinal, in the sense that it reveals the succession of events leading up to the parousia. Mt introduces the first half by taking over yet modifying Jesus' prediction of the destruction of the temple (24:1-2). With the help of various words for time, especially "then" *(tote),* Mt proceeds to mark out four major stages of occurrences: (1) the birth pangs (vv.3-8); (2) persecution from without and dissensions within the church (vv.9-14); (3) the great tribulation (vv.15-22); (4) false Christians. The parousia itself is then described with great solemnity (vv.29-31). The certainty of the parousia is emphasized by the concluding parable of the fig tree (vv.32-36). The second half of the discourse, made up mostly of M and Q material, emphasizes parenesis (i.e., moral exhortation) rather than doctrine. Mt's own views come to the fore here. Granted the apocalyptic events just described, the disciples must be ever vigilant and prepared, and vigilance means above all a life of love and mercy. After a transitional section made up of three short parables of vigilance (24:37-44), Mt presents three major parables of vigilance in the face of delay (24:45-51, the good and bad servants; 25:1-13, the ten virgins; 25:14-30, the talents). The entire discourse and the whole public ministry end with the majestic scene (not parable!) of the universal judgment (25:31-46). After this full exposition of the apocalyptic events of the future, nothing remains to be narrated except the pivotal apocalyptic event of the death-resurrection (chaps. 26-28).

A. THE MARKAN HALF OF THE DISCOURSE. 24:1-36.

(1) Introduction: the Destruction of the Temple.
24:1-2.
[*Mk 13:1-2; Lk 21:5-6*]

> **24** Jesus left the temple and was going away, when his disciples came to point out to him the buildings of the temple. ²But he answered them, "You see all these, do you not? Truly, I say to you, there will not be left here one stone upon another, that will not be thrown down."

At 21:23 Jesus entered the Temple; now he departs—an action which begins to fulfill the judgment pronounced in 23:38: "Behold, your house [the temple] is left to you desolate." But there is a further desolation to come. When the disciples point out the magnificent structures in the temple precincts (Herod the Great had begun restoration of the second temple in 19 B.C.), Jesus counters with a solemn prophecy of the end-time ("Amen, I say to you"): this artful symphony of stones will be turned into a field of rubble. Interestingly, nothing is said about the temple's being set on fire—which is what actually happened in A.D. 70 (cf. Mt's addition in 22:7). The basic prophecy may well go back to Jesus himself. As we shall see, though, it is not the destruction of the temple which will be Mt's main concern in what follows. The ecclesiological concern is already clear. Although Jesus had begun chap. 23 by addressing the crowds and his disciples, now only his disciples appear, and only they follow him out of the temple to hear his words on the future. Matthew may be suggesting that following its Master into the future, the church necessarily separates itself from Judaism.

(2) The Birth Pangs Begin.
24:3-8.
[*Mk 13:3-8; Lk 21:7-11*]

> ³As he sat on the Mount of Olives, the disciples came to him privately, saying, "Tell us, when will this be, and what will be the sign of your coming and of the close of the age?" ⁴And Jesus answered them, "Take heed that no one leads you astray. ⁵For many will come in my name, saying, 'I am the Christ,' and they will lead many astray. ⁶And you will hear of wars and rumors of wars; see that you are not alarmed; for this must take place, but the end is not yet. ⁷For nation will rise against nation, and kingdom against kingdom, and there will be famines and earthquakes in various places: ⁸all this is but the beginning of the birth-pangs.

In Mk, only four privileged disciples hear the discourse; in Mt, as usual, revelation goes public—though now only within the full circle of disciples ("the disciples . . . privately"). Mt alters Mk significantly at this point. While Mt retains the setting of the mount of Olives, with its eschatological associations (cf. Zech 14:4), he omits Mk's "opposite the temple." The question of the temple will receive scant notice in the following discourse. Indeed, Mt carefully distinguishes between (1) the destruction of the temple ("when will this be") and (2) the end of the world ("your coming" is equated with "the close of the age," a phrase unique to Mt in the gospels; cf. 13:39,40,49; 28:20). Thus he separates two events which in Mk 13:4 are much more closely connected: "When will this be, and what will be the sign when these things are all to be accomplished?" Mt allows for an interval; and, once the fact of an interval is clearly affirmed, the exact length of the interval becomes theologically irrelevant. Mt speaks of the sign "of your *coming*" (parousia). Parousia (literally, "presence," "coming") denoted the official visit of an Oriental monarch to a city, or the appearance of a savior-god. Early Christians took over the phrase to designate the coming of Christ in glory to judge the world. While it occurs frequently in NT epistles (e.g., 1 Thess 4:15; 5:23; Jas 5:7-8; 2 Pt 3:4; 1 Jn 2:28), only Mt among the evangelists uses it (cf. 24:3,27,37,39). Mt's exclusive use of parousia and "close of the age" within the four gospels indicates how much Mt has pondered the question of the triumphant coming of the Son of Man. It is that question, and not the destruction of Jerusalem, which engages Mt's attention. He even uses the phrase "sign of your coming" to create a neat inclusion with the description of the parousia towards the end of the Markan discourse (v.30: "Then you will see the *sign of the Son of Man*").

Jesus, who is sitting as he teaches (cf. 5:1; 13:2; 26:55), gives no immediate answer to the questions asked. Instead, he begins by warning his community not to be shaken by disasters or led astray by religious pretenders; indeed, warnings punctuate the discourse (e.g., vv.11,23-28). The initial warning develops into a delineation of the various stages of history leading up to "the close of the age." The first stage (vv.5-8) consists in false messianic movements, stirred up by zealots and visionaries, which will result in wars. "Many" will be led astray because most people prefer a clear timetable of salvation to the stringent demands of waiting in hope. Naturally, Mt thinks of the Jewish War of A.D. 66-70, when one nation (the Jews) rose up against another nation (Rome); the language echoes Is 19:2 and 2 Chr 15:6. In apocalyptic writings, however, one specific historical incident is often blown up on a cosmic screen and acts as a type of the gargantuan events to come. Hence the vagueness and generality of Mt's description. While we can identify specific famines and earthquakes between A.D. 30 and 70, we should not imagine that Mt is drawing up a detailed timetable. His point is that all these terrifying events *must* take place according to God's wise plan (cf. Dan 2:28), and therefore the believers must not give way to that panic which betokens "little faith." Mt stresses that all these events constitute *not* the end, but only the beginning of birth pangs. "Birth pangs" and "the woes of the Messiah" are apocalyptic labels for the confusion and suffering which precede the coming of the Messiah.

(3) The Suffering Church.
24:9-14.
[*Mk 13:9,13,10; Lk 21:17-18*]

> 9"Then they will deliver you up to tribulation, and put you to death; and you will be hated by all nations for my name's sake. 10And then many will fall away, and betray one another, and hate one another. 11And many false prophets will arise and lead many astray. 12And because wickedness is multiplied, most men's love will grow cold, 13But he who endures to the end will be saved. 14And this gospel of the kingdom will be preached throughout the whole world, as a testimony to all nations; and then the end will come.

The "then" of v.9 marks the next stage in the process. The strife among nations and natural disasters is matched by the tribulation of the church. The suffering comes from both without (v.9) and within (vv.10-12). At this point, Mt omits the Markan material (Mk 13:9-12) which he has already used in his missionary discourse (Mt 10:17-21). There the emphasis was on Jewish persecution, though the viewpoint opened up to a universal horizon. Here the persecution is, from the beginning, "by all the nations," though the universal sweep of the passage (cf. especially v.14, "throughout the whole world") indicates that the Jews are understood to be included among "all the nations"— hence, *not* "all the Gentiles." The hostile world *hands over* the disciples to death, just as John the Baptist (4:12) and Jesus (17:22) are *handed over*; the Christian community, the successors to the prophets of the end-time, share in their violent fate. Indeed, the Christians are hated precisely because of the "name"—the person and teaching—of Jesus.

But worse than the affliction from without is the upset within. "Many" will commit apostasy (literally: "be scandalized," a favorite word in Mt; cf. 13:21). They will *hand over* (RSV: "betray") their fellow Christians, just as the pagans did. Hated by the nations, Christians will find themselves hated by fellow "Christians" as well (notice the parallels between vv.9 and 10). False prophets will arise within the church, just as they arose outside it (cf. v.5), and the result will be the same: many are led astray. Perhaps, the most poignant aspect of these verses is that they indicate that life in the church will hardly be better or more Christian than life in the pagan world. Wickedness (literally, "lawlessness," the basic revolt against God's will) will spread so far in the church that the idealism and fervor of most Christians' love will wane. Indeed, Mt speaks of the "love of the many"; "the many" is the same phrase used in 20:28 and 26:28 to refer to all who are redeemed by the blood of the Son of Man. It is therefore a ghastly picture of eschatological disruption: the church at large will feel its love grow cold (the noun "love" appears only here in Mt's gospel).

The vast, apocalyptic canvas that is being painted cautions us against taking these verses as an exact portrait of Mt's own church. Yet his insertion of this special material into the Markan discourse may indicate that he is writing for a troubled and deeply divided community. To the mind of an evangelist who stresses Jesus' gospel of love and mercy (5:43-48; 9:13; 12:7), a church which neglects love is a church which has betrayed the gospel. The horrors of the end-time could not be more vividly portrayed. But all is not lost. The Christian who holds fast to the gospel with patient endurance until the bitter end will be saved at the final judgment. Patient endurance, however, must not be thought of in terms of passivity. The courageous Christians must, in the face of betrayal within and without, proclaim Christ's good news in the entire inhabited world (cf. 28:19). It is a testimony which will act for or against "all nations," depending upon how they respond. "This gospel of the kingdom" refers to the joyful message of the triumphant coming of God's kingdom (4:17), as presented throughout Mt's work. This use of "gospel" comes close to, but does not quite reach, the second-century use of "gospel" as a label for a certain type of Christian document. Only when the universal proclamation is completed can "the end" of the world come (cf. v.6); it will be the final "then."

(4) The Great Tribulation in Judea.
24:15-22.
[Mk 13:14-20; Lk 21:20-24]

> [15]"So when you see the desolating sacrilege spoken of by the prophet Daniel, standing in the holy place (let the reader understand), [16]then let those who are in Judea flee to the mountains; [17]let him who is on the housetop not go down to take what is in his house; [18]and let him who is in the field not turn back to take his mantle. [19]And alas for those who are with child and for those who give suck in those days! [20]Pray that your flight may not be in winter or on a sabbath. [21]For then there will be great tribulation, such as has not been from the beginning of the world until now, no, and never will be. [22]And if those days had not been shortened, no human being would be saved; but for the sake of the elect those days will be shortened.

Whatever may have been the origins of this section (an apocalyptic "pamphlet" at the time of Caligula's attempt to set up an image in the temple, directions to the Jerusalem church to flee to Pella at the beginning of the Jewish-Roman war, etc.), Mt no doubt reads it as a prediction of the destruction of the temple in A.D. 70 and the accompanying horrors of the Jewish War. At the same time, Mt can see in these events a paradigm of the great sacrilege and suffering which Christians believed would precede the return of Christ (cf. Rev 12-13; 2 Thess 2:3-4).

The "desolating sacrilege" (literally, "the abomination of desolation") is a phrase taken from Dan 9:27 in the Septuagint (cf. Dan 11:31; 12:11). With his love of the prophets, Mt the scribe, unlike Mk, appends a "footnote" referring to Daniel the *prophet*. The desolating sacrilege in Dan refers to the setting up of an altar to Zeus Olympios in the temple in 168 B.C. by the king of Syria, Antiochus IV Epiphanes; the sacrilege was accompanied by the cessation of the legitimate sacrifices and the offering of pagan sacrifices. Mt makes clear that he, too, is thinking of the temple by changing Mk's vague "standing where it should not" to "standing in the holy place." But Mt is faithful to his pre-A.D. 70 tradition in speaking simply of a desolating sacrilege, and not of the destruction of the temple by fire (contrast 22:7). The intended vagueness of this apocalyptic manner of speaking allows the past historical event to act as a model and forewarning of the greater sacrilege still to come; hence, the admonition to read with understanding. The "great tribulation" of the destruction of Jerusalem foreshadows the great tribulation of the end. That is why Mt can keep this pericope in its present position, even after the announcement in v.14: "and then the end shall come." In the face of such a crisis, one should act decisively and speedily. Those in Judea must flee to the uninhabited mountains of the wasteland near the Dead Sea; this general motif of flight does not match the actual history of the Jerusalem church, which fled to Pella in the northern Jordan valley. Those on the flat roofs of Palestinian houses must flee by the outside staircase, without going back to the house to rescue any earthly possessions. Those working

in the fields must flee without running back to the edge of
the field to pick up their outer garments, laid aside for work.
Mt recounts the various circumstances which could increase
the suffering of fleeing Christians: being pregnant, having to
care for new-born infants, trying to flee amid the chilling
rains and flooded roads of a Palestinian winter, and trying
to flee on the Sabbath, when Christians could easily be
spotted by law-observing Jews, who restricted their movements to 2,000 paces. Some commentators infer from Mt's
insertion of "or on a sabbath" that Mt's church still felt
bound by strict Sabbath observance. But the context speaks
of external circumstances which will make flight difficult,
not impossible. The various dispute stories in Mt do not
favor the view that Mt's church still scrupulously observed
the Sabbath, even when it meant endangering life (cf.
12:1-14)—especially since at least some Jews allowed
flight on the Sabbath to save one's life. So great was—and
will be—the tribulation (cf. Dan 12:1) that unless God (the
divine passive voice) had shortened the period of suffering,
no one would have remained alive ("be saved" in the sense
of "survive"). But God did shorten the time of affliction
for the sake of those in the church who he knew would remain faithful to the end ("the elect," cf. 22:14). The same
loving providence will protect the Christians who must
face the woes of the last days. God will restrict their tribulation, in order that they too may be "saved" in the full,
theological sense. Thus, this pericope on the great tribulation speaks both of the church's past and of its future; in
both cases, church history is a web spun of suffering and
grace.

(5) False Christians and False Prophets.
24:23-28.
[Mk 13:21-23; Lk 17:23-24,37]

> 23Then if any one says to you, 'Lo, here is the Christ!'
> or 'There he is!' do not believe it. 24For false Christs and

false prophets will arise and show great signs and wonders, so as to lead astray, if possible, even the elect.

²⁵Lo, I have told you beforehand. ²⁶So, if they say to you, 'Lo, he is in the wilderness,' do not go out; if they say, 'Lo, he is in the inner rooms,' do not believe it, ²⁷For as the lightning comes from the east and shines as far as the west, so will be the coming of the Son of man. ²⁸Wherever the body is, there the eagles will be gathered together.

The "then" of v.23 introduces a further stage, and a deepening of the affliction, on the church's journey towards the end. Charlatans, claiming to be the Messiah or his prophet, arise. Through diabolical miracles (cf. Dt 13:2-3; Rev 13), they lead astray not only "the many" (cf. vv.5,11) but even—notice the restrictive "if possible"—the elect, those definitively chosen for salvation. The horror of the last days has reached such a fever pitch that it seems as though God's set plan for salvation is being undone and even those confirmed in grace are being wrenched from his hand. But God is not being taken by surprise; Jesus has predicted these events beforehand for the comfort of the elect. Even the frightening catastrophes preceding the end are directed by God's providence. No doubt Mt sees these false Messiahs and prophets as coming at least in part from within the church (cf. the evil wonder-working prophets in 7:21-23). But the allusions to messianic movements in the desert à la Moses (like the Jew Theudas in Acts 5:36; or the "Egyptian" in Acts 21:38) or to esoteric (and gnostic?) movements inviting initiates into the secret chamber suggest that the false revealers could also tempt Christians from outside mainstream Christianity. The "inner rooms" could also refer, however, to the Jewish theory of the hidden Messiah, to be revealed at the proper moment. At any rate, be they zealot or gnostic, such enthusiastic and alarmist movements are not to be believed. Certainly, false messiahs or prophets must have been a serious problem for Mt's church, since to the two references from Mk (Mt 24:5,24) Mt adds a third reference (v.11).

Suddenly switching to Q (vv.27-28), Mt tells how Christians can recognize the falsehood of these claimants. The final coming of the Son of Man (Mt again uses *parousia*, picking up the question in 24:3) will be a brilliant, public, cosmic event, as clear and obvious as the lightning bolt which traverses the whole vault of heaven. What is stressed here is not the sudden and incalculable nature of the event— that will be treated in the parenetic section of the discourse. The stress here is on the open, public character of the parousia, in order to discredit cabals in deserts or closets. We must interpret the curious saying in v.28 in the same way. The saying may be a traditional proverb (cf. Job 39:30), but the point here is again the public and certain nature of the parousia, as visible as vultures circling around a carcass. Because the Greek word *aetoi* can mean not only "vultures" (the best translation here) but also "eagles" (so RSV), some have seen a reference to the Roman legions surrounding Jerusalem. But since Mt is now speaking of the parousia of the Son of Man, which is carefully distinguished from the fall of Jerusalem, the allusion to Rome is unlikely. Note, by the way, that the parousia is mentioned in this pericope dealing with the horrors preceding the end only to point out that the false messiahs and prophets can be detected by their non-public nature. The real discussion of the parousia belongs to the following pericope.

(6) The Coming of the Son of Man.
24:29-31.
[*Mk 13:24-27; Lk 21:25-28*]

> [29]"Immediately after the tribulation of those days the sun will be darkened, and the moon will not give its light, and the stars will fall from heaven, and the powers of the heavens will be shaken; [30]then will appear the sign of the Son of man in heaven, and then all the tribes of the

earth will mourn, and they will see the Son of man coming
on the clouds of heaven with power and great glory;
[31]and he will send out his angels with a loud trumpet
call, and they will gather his elect from the four winds,
from one end of heaven to the other.

The question asked in 24:3 ("the *sign* of your coming")
now receives a direct answer. "Immediately after" the
horror of the last days reaches its fever pitch (vv.23-28),
the "end of the age" (24:3; 28:20) will come. The spiritual
disasters are now matched by cosmic disasters (cf. Is 13:10;
34:4). The old world passes away completely, just as it
passed away proleptically at the death of Christ (cf. 27:45,
51-54). Both Jews and Gentiles thought that the celestial
bodies were controlled by angelic or divine beings ("the
powers of heaven") who governed the destinies of men.
All such powers are swept away as the true cosmocrator,
the Son of Man, comes to claim the universe as his own.
"Then," when the fabric of the old creation is rent, will the
Son of Man appear, riding the clouds of heaven like a
chariot, as Dan 7:13 had predicted. "The sign of the Son of
Man" probably means simply "the sign which *is* the Son of
Man" (cf. Mt 12:38-42; 16:4; 24:3), surrounded by heavenly
light (cf. 16:27).

The latter half of v.30 contains an intriguing combination
of Dan 7:13-14 with Zech 12:10-14 ("when they look upon
him whom they have pierced, they shall mourn for him, as
one mourns for an only child . . . and the earth shall mourn
by tribes"). The same combination is seen in the NT only
in Rev 1:7, though the connection exists more loosely in the
fourth gospel (cf. Jn 19:37; 3:13-15; 8:28; 12:34). The Son
of Man who was pierced, i.e., put to death by crucifixion,
will be the same Son of Man who comes in glory to judge.
All the tribes of the earth who have refused to become
disciples (cf. 28:19)—and not just the Jews—will bewail
their imminent condemnation. Compared with 16:27, what
is striking here is the total absence of God the Father. The

Son of Man acts completely on his own authority, sending out *his* angels to gather in from all the earth *his* elect (cf. 13:41-43, where the Father is mentioned; cf. also the "chosen" [i.e., "elect"] in 22:14). The trumpet is a traditional symbol of the last judgment (cf. Is 27:13; 1 Thess 4:16; 1 Cor 15:52; Rev 8:2-11:15). Mt raises the divine majesty of the Son of Man to the greatest heights imaginable.

(7) The Conclusion of the Markan Section: the Fig Tree. 24:32-36.
[*Mk 13:28-32; Lk 21:29-33*]

> [32]From the fig tree learn its lesson: as soon as its branch becomes tender and puts forth its leaves, you know that summer is near. [33]So also, when you see all these things, you know that he is near, at the very gates. [34]Truly, I say to you, this generation will not pass away till all these things take place. [35]Heaven and earth will pass away, but my words will not pass away.
> [36]"But of that day and hour no one knows, not even the angels of heaven, nor the Son, but the Father only."

The first or doctrinal part of the discourse ends with an affirmation that the end is certain and near, yet sudden and incalculable. A bridge is thus created to the more "parenetic" or exhortatory half of the discourse. The stress on the nearness of the parousia in this pericope comes from Mk and is kept by Mt because of its usefulness for exhortation. But it must be balanced by Mt's stress on the delay in the three great parables of the second half of the discourse.

To the disciples' initial question of "when" (v.3), Jesus replies indirectly, with a parable. During the rainy winter season in Palestine, most trees do not lose their leaves; but the fig tree does. Hence, the reappearance of leaves on the fig tree signals the approach of the dry summer season. Since a good part of the Palestinian harvest takes place during the summer, it is a very apt sign for the final judgment (cf. 13:39). Like the budding fig tree, the occurrence of all the predicted events of vv.4-28 will indicate that the consummation is certainly at hand—yet no precise date can be given. Indeed, a word like "consummation" might be the understood subject of "is near" in v.33, though the RSV is probably correct in taking the Son of Man ("he") as the subject.

V.34 creates a great problem. In the mouth of Jesus, and possibly even in Mk, it affirms that the end of the world will take place within the lifetime of Jesus' generation. That is difficult enough to interpret, but the greater difficulty for us is to understand how Mt, writing ca. A.D. 90, would understand a prophecy which obviously had not taken place in its literal sense. Possibly Mt applies it to his own generation, which he sees enduring the pangs of the end-time. But this involves taking "this generation" in a sense not usual in Mt (cf. e.g., 23:36). One is tempted to reinterpret the verse in the light of Mt's presentation of Jesus' death-resurrection as a "proleptic parousia"; but the reference to "*all*" these things" makes such an interpretation difficult. Perhaps Mt lets the Markan statement stand for the sake of conveying a sense of urgency; in what follows, Mt will correct any misconceptions by his stress on delay. V.35 reminds us of 5:18. Heaven and earth, and indeed, even the Mosaic Law, will pass away; but the words of Jesus, like the word of God (cf. Is 40:8) stand forever, across all cosmic catastrophes. When even the foundations are shaken, the disciples can still put their trust in the teaching of Jesus.

V.36 acts as something of a counterbalance to v.34. The nearness of the parousia must not tempt Christians to indulge in speculation and calculation about precise dates. The motifs of "day" and "hour" will be repeated in 24:42, 44, 50 and in 25:13, along with the theme of uncertainty. The Father alone knows the precise time of the parousia; neither the angelic servants nor even the Son of Man knows that. A number of points should be noted here. The verse restores the Father to the picture of the consummation, thus balancing vv.29-31. The verse contains the "apocalyptic trinity" of Father, Son of Man, and angels, which we see elsewhere in Mt (e.g., 16:27). As the whole context of chap. 24 makes clear, "the Son" means the Son of Man; the absolute title should not be automatically equated with "Son of God." The saying is so astounding, not to say offensive, to Christian ears, that it most likely comes from Jesus himself. A large number of manuscripts omits the phrase "nor the Son," and some have claimed that the omission is original in Mt, vis-à-vis Mk, since the statement offended Mt's high christology. More likely, though, it is an omission by later Christian scribes. The clash with Mt's high christology reminds us that in chap. 24 we are dealing mainly with Markan material, only lightly retouched. Chap. 25 is more typically Matthean in approach.

B. THE PARENETIC HALF OF THE DISCOURSE. 24:37-25:46.

(1) Introduction: Three Parables of Vigilance. 24:37-44.
[*Mk 13:35,33; Lk 17:26-36; 12:39-40*]

> ³⁷As were the days of Noah, so will be the coming of the Son of man. ³⁸For as in those days before the flood they were eating and drinking, marrying and giving in marriage, until the day when Noah entered the ark, ³⁹and they did not know until the flood came and swept them all away, so will be the coming of the Son of man. ⁴⁰Then two men will be in the field; one is taken and one is left. ⁴¹Two women will be grinding at the mill; one is taken and one is left. ⁴²Watch therefore, for you do not know on what day your Lord is coming. ⁴³But know this, that if the householder had known in what part of the night the thief was coming, he would have watched and would not have let his house be broken into. ⁴⁴Therefore you also must be ready; for the Son of man is coming at an hour you do not expect.

While most of chap. 24 tried to calm excessive eschatological fervor and calculation, the rest of the discourse tries to stir up a proper eschatological fervor (i.e., watchfulness) in those who have become too immersed in the flow of this world's events. Three parables from Q (the generation of Noah, the two pairs of workers, and the thief in the night) announce the major theme of the second part of the discourse: vigilance and preparedness for the "coming [*parousia*] of the Son of Man" (a motif which forms an inclusion in vv.37 and 39 and harks back to v.3). Mt is so intent on his key-word *parousia* that he breaks the original Q-parallelism seen in Lk 17:26 ("the days of Noe . . . the days of the Son of Man"). Although Jewish and Christian tradition emphasized the wickedness of the contemporaries of Noah, that is not the point here. Rather, the problem with the flood-generation was that it was so immersed in ordinary, everyday pursuits that it was blind to the imminent disaster of the flood.

The second parable stresses that the final judgment will bring to light distinctions between persons which lay hidden in this age; this theme of division will continue through chap. 25 (cf. especially 25:31-46). The two men working in the field or the two women grinding meal with a hand-mill look alike to the human eye. But at the parousia (the "then" of v.40) one will be "taken" into the kingdom while the other will be "left" to reprobation. The parable itself does not state the grounds for the distinction, but the context indicates that vigilance or lack thereof is the reason. The reason for this vigilance is enunciated by the concluding warning in v.42 (note the equivalence of the titles "Lord" and "Son of Man") and by the third parable: ignorance of the date of the parousia. A thief does not telegraph ahead his timetable, and so the only protection against theft is watching throughout the night (i.e., this present age). The symbol of the thief, used to express the sudden, unexpected "break-in" of the parousia, is found in 1 Thess 5:2-4 (the thief=the day of the Lord); 2 Pt 3:10 (the thief=the day); Rev 3:3 (the thief=Jesus); 16:15 (the thief=Jesus). The Q-document's daring equation of the thief with Jesus—reminding us that a parable is not to be pressed beyond the point of comparison—is thus closer to the imagery of Rev, a datum which makes sense, since in both cases we are dealing with a Christian apocalypse. The emphasis on the uncertainty of the time of the parousia (repeated in each of the three subsequent parables) corrects and stands in tension with the listing of signs and the affirmations of the parousia's imminence in the rest of chap. 24.

(2) The First Parable of Vigilance During Delay: the Prudent or Profligate Servant. 24:45-51. [Lk 12:41-46]

> [45]"Who then is the faithful and wise servant, whom his master has set over his household, to give them their food at the proper time? [46]Blessed is that servant whom his master when he comes will find so doing. [47]Truly, I say to you, he will set him over all his possessions. [48]But if that wicked servant says to himself, 'My master is delayed,' [49]and begins to beat his fellow servants, and eats and drinks with the drunken, [50]the master of that servant will come on a day when he does not expect him and at an hour he does not know, [51]and will punish him, and put him with the hypocrites; there men will weep and gnash their teeth.

Mt ties together three long parables of vigilance by underlining in each the theme of delay (24:48; 25:5,19). This emphasis on delay gives us Mt's modification of the Markan stress on imminence (24:34). Other themes also connect the three parables: being faithful or prudent, the reward of greater responsibility, the punishment of the wicked who do not watch, eating and drinking, ignorance of the day or hour, weeping and gnashing.

With his ecclesiastical interests, it is not surprising that Mt addresses the call to vigilance especially to church leaders. While this application is underlined even more by Lk (cf. the question of Peter in Lk 12:41), the reference to the servant's being "set over his household" to take care of his fellow servants' needs makes the allusion to church leaders clear enough. Watchfulness is thus interpreted concretely as prudence and dependability in fulfilling one's obligations towards the community of believers "at the proper time," and not at one's own convenience. The servant who proves faithful is declared truly happy; his reward on the last day will be still greater responsibility. But if the church leader forgets that all his power is derivative and is conferred only for a time and for the good of others, the "servant" will turn into a "cleric." The delay of the parousia becomes his great temptation (cf. 2 Pt 3:4). He begins to give himself airs as though he were the master and to abuse the authority entrusted to him. Losing a proper sense of others, he tyrannizes his *fellow* servants (an emphasis of Mt) as though they were slaves. Losing a proper sense of self, he lapses into excessive eating and drinking with the worst of companions. Over the gaping chasm of two thousand years, some clerical patterns remain remarkably consistent.

The servant has forgotten that he is subject to recall, and his recall is precisely the sudden, unpredictable return of his "master" (*kyrios*, "Lord," i.e., the Son of Man) after the delay. Although the original Aramaic form of the parable may have spoken simply of a severe beating as punishment, Mt depicts the gruesome Persian punishment of dismemberment (the Greek for the RSV's "punish" in v.51 is *dichotomēsei*, "cut in two"). At first glance, the next phrase, "put him with the hypocrites," seems hopelessly anti-climactic, until we remember that for Mt the hypocrites are primarily the Jewish leaders, the scribes and the Pharisees (cf. chap. 23). The unfaithful Christian leader is no better than the Jewish leaders, and he will receive the same punishment: eternal damnation, symbolized by the

Matthean tag of weeping and gnashing (cf. 8:12; 13:42,50; 22:13).

(3) The Second Parable of Vigilance During Delay:
the Prudent and Thoughtless Virgins.
25:1-13.

> **25** "Then the kingdom of heaven shall be compared to ten maidens who took their lamps and went to meet the bridegroom. ²Five of them were foolish, and five were wise. ³For when the foolish took their lamps, they took no oil with them; ⁴but the wise took flasks of oil with their lamps. ⁵As the bridegroom was delayed, they all slumbered and slept. ⁶But at midnight there was a cry, 'Behold, the bridegroom! Come out to meet him.' ⁷Then all those maidens rose and trimmed their lamps. ⁸And the foolish said to the wise, 'Give us some of your oil, for our lamps are going out.' ⁹But the wise replied, 'Perhaps there will not be enough for us and for you; go rather to the dealers and buy for yourselves.' ¹⁰And while they went to buy, the bridegroom came, and those who were ready went in with him to the marriage feast; and the door was shut. ¹¹Afterward the other maidens came also, saying, 'Lord, lord, open to us.' ¹²But he replied, 'Truly, I say to you, I do not know you.' ¹³Watch therefore, for you know neither the day nor the hour.

This parable occurs only in Mt; it is tied to the larger context by the themes of delay, division within a group, prudence, and being prepared for an arrival. In the preceding parable, the evil servant realized his master would be delayed; unfortunately, the realization led to his failure to be responsible and watchful. Here, on the contrary, five of the virgins do not reckon with the possibility of a delay, and their failure to anticipate the delay leads to their lack of preparedness. Mt therefore rejects both a sense of irresponsibility arising from the delay of the parousia and also a frivolous enthusiasm which does not take the length of the delay seriously.

The "then" in v. 1 again refers to the parousia. The kingdom is not directly compared with the ten virgins. The introductory formula means that the final coming of the kingdom may be compared to the whole situation about to be described. Wedding customs in first century Palestine are not fully known, and commentators argue over the meaning and even the possiblity of the events described in this parable. The ten virgins are an escort of honor appointed to greet the bridegroom when he comes. Probably the virgins are stationed at the bridegroom's own house and are waiting to welcome the groom after he returns from the house of his bride's parents with his newly acquired bride. It also is possible that the bride has already been escorted to the groom's house, and that the groom has been delayed by Oriental haggling over the marriage contract and gifts for the bride's relatives. Since the wedding celebration is being held at night, the virgins are equipped with lamps (or torches) for the joyful procession. As often in parables, we encounter round numbers: a group of ten virgins, divided evenly into five who are foresighted ("wise") enough to bring extra oil, and five who do not reckon with a delay ("foolish") and therefore lack any provisions for the future.

The delay causes all the virgins first to nod and then to sleep. Then a voice pierces the midnight silence, announcing the bridegroom's approach. (There is no need to see here an allusion to the night of Passover, when the Messiah was expected to come.) All the virgins awake and hastily set about putting their neglected lamps in order. The foolish see that their lamps are nearly extinguished, but their request to borrow some oil is brusquely rejected by the wise virgins. The latter know that any attempt at sharing the oil will mean that all the lamps will go out and the whole ceremony will turn into a debacle. While the wise virgins carry on with the escort of honor, the foolish run off to buy more oil. The wise virgins, who are pointedly called "those who were ready" escort the groom to the wedding banquet (cf. 9:15 and 22:1-14 for the wedding feast as a symbol of the consummation of the kingdom). When the foolish return, the cumbersome mechanism for bolting the door is already in place. Significantly the foolish maidens address the bridegroom as "Lord" (*kyrie*), confirming that he is the Son of Man (cf. 24:39,42), the bridegroom who comes at the parousia to claim his bride, the people of God. The double cry "Lord, Lord" reminds one of the charismatics in 7:21, who are likewise refused entry into the kingdom. In both cases Jesus declares his rejection of the unfaithful disciples with the formula: "I never knew you," or "I do not know you," thus breaking all supposed ties with those who claim his fellowship. The parable ends with a warning which meshes the admonition of 24:42 with the assertion of 24:36. At first glance, the call to "watch" does not seem to fit the parable, since all ten fell asleep. But the verb "to watch" (*grēgoreō*) is so common in NT apocalyptic passages that its original sense probably was reduced to a general "be ready." The verse could thus be an original part of the parable.

The parable obviously interprets being awake as being prepared for the parousia; this in turn means living soberly in the present with one's gaze directed towards the future, while at the same time reckoning with the space of time in between. But the concrete content of this preparedness is not spelled out. Likewise, what precisely foolish unconcern about delay of the parousia means concretely is not said. The cross-reference to 7:22-23 makes possible an allusion to enthusiasts who rejoice over the miraculous powers of the kingdom but who are not interested in the dull work of doing the Father's will over the long haul of history. They lack the "oil" of the good works of love, works which the wise disciples perform and which shine before men (5:16). The distinction between wise and foolish also reminds one of the distinction between the wise man who does the words of Jesus and the foolish man who does not do them (7:24-27). This interpretation is strengthened by the following parable and especially by the scene of final judgment in 25:31-46. There, too, the Son of Man divides mankind into two camps, the saved and the reprobate, according to the criterion of the works of mercy.

(4) The Third Parable of Vigilance During Delay:
the Talents.
25:14-30.
[*Lk 19:12-27*]

14"For it will be as when a man going on a journey called his servants and entrusted to them his property; 15to one he gave five talents, to another two, to another one, to each according to his ability. Then he went away. 16He who had received the five talents went at once and traded with them; and he made five talents more. 17So also, he who had the two talents made two talents more. 18But he who had received the one talent went and dug in the ground and hid his master's money. 19Now after a long time the master of those servants came and settled accounts with them. 20And he who had received the five talents came forward, bringing five talents more, saying, 'Master, you delivered to me five talents; here I have made five talents more.' 21His master said to him, 'Well done, good and faithful servant; you have been faithful over a little, I will set you over much; enter into the joy of your master.' 22And he also who had the two talents came forward, saying, 'Master, you delivered to me two talents; here I have made two talents more.' 23His master said to him, 'Well done, good and faithful servant; you have been faithful over a little, I will set you over much; enter into the joy of your master.' 24He also who had received the one talent came forward, saying, 'Master, I knew you to be a hard man, reaping where you did not sow, and gathering where you did not winnow; 25so I was afraid, and I went and hid your talent in the ground. Here you have what is yours.' 26But his master answered him, 'You wicked and slothful servant! You knew that I reap where I have not sowed, and gather where I have not winnowed? [27]Then you ought to have invested my money with the bankers, and at my coming I should have received what was my own with interest. [28]So take the talent from him, and give it to him who has the ten talents. [29]For to every one who has will more be given, and he will have abundance; but from him who has not, even what he has will be taken away. [30]And cast the worthless servant into the outer darkness; there men will weep and gnash their teeth.

This is a Q-parable, with a slight echo in Mk 13:34. Mt has preserved the original lines of the parable, while Lk has complicated the parable with allusions to the ethnarch Archelaus of Judea, allusions which may come from a different parable. On the other hand, Lk may be original in his smaller sums of money (minas instead of talents) and in the more realistic reward and punishment. The themes of good and bad servants, final division within a group, reward and punishment, and the return of the master after delay help anchor this parable in the larger context.

Having warned those who do not reckon with the parousia (24:48-51) and those who do not reckon with its delay (25:1-13), Mt now explains what he means by being watchful or ready during the delay. Being awake means being faithful to God's instructions and acting upon them with all the energy we can muster, with all the abilities God has entrusted to us. Watching for the Lord does not mean self-centered idleness or pusillanimous inactivity during the period of the delay. This "in-between time" must be filled up and made meaningful by our deeds of love, as the final scene of judgment (vv.31-46) will make clear. How we act during this apparent "lull" in salvation history will actually determine the denouement of that history.

The parable begins abruptly, without the initial comparison being complete (the Greek reads: "For just like a man going on a journey . . . ."). No doubt the comparison is with the "kingdom of heaven" (25:1). A wealthy business-man (not a nobleman who becomes king, as in Lk) is going abroad on some commercial venture. Lest business at home lag while he is away, he entrusts the capital he will not be using on the trip to three servants. The wealth is distributed in proportion to each one's capability. The cash amounts are expressed in talents. The talent was originally a measure of weight; here it denotes a form of currency, indeed the largest single unit of currency known in the Hellenistic world (cf. 18:24). We must remember that in NT Greek "talent" means only money; its metaphorical meaning (one's native ability) developed later, precisely because of this parable. The modern idea of "talent" is expressed in the parable by the phrase "to each according to his ability" (v.15). With the high interest rates of the time, the first two servants are able by dint of effort and keen trading to double their respective amounts. The third servant, a mouse-minded man paralyzed by a fear of taking any risk, carefully hides the money in a way traditional in chaotic Palestine (cf. 13:44).

After a long time (Mt's addition to denote the delay of the parousia) the master (*ho kyrios,* i.e., the Lord, the Son of Man) returns and demands a reckoning (the final judgment; cf. 18:23). The first two servants are praised for their industry and courage in having doubled their amounts, and for their fidelity in returning everything to their master. Fidelity in small things leads to much greater reward, a reward which consists in still greater responsibilities (cf. 24:47) and intimate friendship with one's master ("enter into joy" may refer to table-fellowship at a feast; cf. 8:11; 22:1-14; 25:10). The fact that both servants receive the same reward shows that what is valued is not one's accomplish-ments in a quantitative sense but the fidelity of one's com-mitment, as mirrored in one's whole-hearted activity. The anxiety-ridden servant is condemned as evil and inactive— indeed, evil precisely because he is inactive. With a crazy sort of logic, he puts forward the demanding nature of the master as the reason for doing nothing. Out of fear of failure he has refused even to try to succeed.

The master's reply in v.26 ("you knew . . .") could be taken either as a statement or a question, but the question-form must not be taken to mean that the master denies that he is a demanding person (as expressed by the servant in the proverb of v.24). All the parables of Mt's eschatological discourse—indeed, all the moral teaching in Mt's gospel (cf. 7:13-14)—stress the fierce demands of Jesus, demands which we must meet if we are to pass the stringent judgment on the last day. The stringency of judgment replaces the imminence of judgment as the main motive in Mt's moral exhortation. One can be unfaithful to these stringent demands either by positively evil actions (24:49), by lack of foresight (25:3), or by sheer inactivity, as is the case here. Consequently the inertia-ridden servant loses the little he had received. This punishment is explained by a wisdom-saying in v.29, which may originally have been a pessimistic comment like "the rich get richer and the poor get poorer." In the context of the parable it refers rather to the basic law of the interaction between God's free gift and man's response. A disciple who "gives himself" fully to the gift God has given him (note the divine passive) will receive greater grace still. The spiritual life is not unlike the stock market; nothing is gained without risk and effort. The person who is stingy in his expenditure of self will receive nothing further and will lose what he has. God's grace is like our physical limbs and intellectual talents: exercise brings greater strength; neglect brings atrophy. The "atrophied" disciple, the useless Christian, will be punished exactly like the dissolute and the thoughtless—with eternal damnation (v.30; cf. 13:42,50; 22:13; 24:51). For the supposed Christian, laziness comes at a high price. The parable has a special bite if Mt intends a particular reference here, as in 24:45-51, to church leaders. A Christian leader who does not lead is damned.

(5) *The Conclusion: the Great Scene of the Last Judgment. 25:31-46.*

³¹"When the Son of man comes in his glory, and all the angels with him, then he will sit on his glorious throne. ³²Before him will be gathered all the nations, and he will separate them one from another as a shepherd separates the sheep from the goats, ³³and he will place the sheep at his right hand, but the goats at the left. ³⁴Then the King will say to those at his right hand, 'Come, O blessed of my Father, inherit the kingdom prepared for you from the foundation of the world; ³⁵for I was hungry and you gave me food, I was thirsty and you gave me drink, I was a stranger and you welcomed me, ³⁶I was naked and you clothed me, I was sick and you visited me, I was in prison and you came to me,' ³⁷Then the righteous will answer him, 'Lord, when did we see thee hungry and feed thee, or thirsty and give thee drink? ³⁸And when did we see thee a stranger and welcome thee, or naked and clothe thee? ³⁹And when did we see thee sick or in prison and visit thee? ⁴⁰And the King will answer them, 'Truly, I say to you, as you did it to one of the least of these my brethren, you did it to me.' ⁴¹Then he will say to those at his left hand, 'Depart from me, you cursed, into the eternal fire prepared for the devil and his angels; ⁴²for I was hungry and you gave me no food, I was thirsty and you gave me no drink, ⁴³I was a stranger and you did not welcome me, naked and you did not clothe me, sick and in prison and you did not visit me.' ⁴⁴Then, they also will answer, 'Lord, when did we see thee hungry or thirsty or a stranger or naked or sick or in prison, and did not minister to thee?' ⁴⁵Then he will answer them, 'Truly, I say to you, as you did it not to one of the least of these, you did it not to me.' ⁴⁶And they will go away into eternal punishment, but the righteous into eternal life."

As one comes down the center of the Sistine Chapel in Rome, one draws closer to Michelangelo's gargantuan depiction of the Last Judgment. So too, as one approaches the conclusion of Mt's eschatological discourse, one is confronted with this solemn, overpowering scene of the last judgment, found only in Mt. It is not a parable but the unveiling of the truth which lay behind all the parables in chaps. 24-25. The emphasis is no longer on the theme of delay, nor even on the continued motifs of the Son of Man, final reckoning, and separation of good and bad. The central point now is: what is the criterion of judgment? Or, put in the terms of chap. 25, what does it mean to be watchful and ready and faithful? The answer is that to be watchful means to be able to recognize the Son of Man in all those in need; to be ready means to be loving towards the Son of Man in these people; and to be faithful means to translate this love into active service, into concrete deeds of mercy. This is the criterion by which one enters into or is rejected from eternal life. Therefore we are not dealing with supererogatory works, performed to get "extra points." On these works of mercy, which most would not consider their strict duty, hangs their salvation or damnation.

The christology of this passage, is intriguing. Within the one scene we find the title King, Lord, implicitly the Shepherd-Messiah, and implicitly the Son ("my Father"). "Son of David" is lacking, probably because the judgment is universal, and not just for Israel. But the christology which dominates is that of Son of Man. A Son-of-Man christology has suffused the whole of the eschatological discourse. Besides the times that the Son of Man is explicitly said "to come," all sorts of parabolic figures "come" as symbols of him (cf. 24:30,42,43,44,46; 25:10,19,27). Now, for the last time, we hear: "The Son of Man comes." The picture is one of divine majesty. The Son of Man comes in *his* glory, with all the angels escorting *him*, and he sits on *his* glorious throne (compare 19:28 and 24:29-31, and contrast 16:27: *"his* angels," but "in the glory of *his Father"*). It is fitting that the divine cosmocrator and judge presides over the final reckoning with all mankind (RSV correctly translates *panta ta ethnē* as "all the nations," not "all the Gentiles"). The nations are gathered like a flock by its shepherd; vv.32-33 contain the only "parabolic" element in the scene. The motif of gathering recalls the parables of the wheat and the tares and the fish net, but here the picture is taken from Palestinian pastures. While sheep and goats would graze together during the day, they would be separated at night or when a change of pasture was necessary. Being more valuable animals the sheep naturally symbolize the good, placed on the right hand, the side of favor. The goats are placed on the left, a sign of disfavor. The King (not the most usual designation for Jesus in Mt, though cf. 2:2 and 21:5) welcomes those blessed (i.e., predestined) by his Father into his kingdom. While Jesus is clearly the divine instrument of the Father and has even here become King of the kingdom in place of the Father (cf. 5:35), it is still the Father who, according to apocalyptic views, prepared the good things of the last day from all eternity in heaven and who reveals them to the elect at the proper time.

The good and the bad are being separated by a final blessing and curse. Just as Israel inherited an earthly promised land, the new people of God inherit the heavenly kingdom (cf. 5:3, 5, and 20), ruled by the King who is Son of Man. The King welcomes the blessed and then explains the reason for the blessing: they took care of him when he was hungry, thirsty, a foreigner, naked, sick, and imprisoned. Here we have a list of the traditional "corporal works of mercy," as known to Judaism, Christianity, and other religions. It is not the commendation of works of mercy that is the surprising element here. The elect know they have performed such works, and know that such works are pleasing to God. Fittingly, they are designated "the righteous" or "just," i.e., those who do God's will. What astounds them, however, is that the King claims that they did all this "to me." When? How? The King replies by revealing a mystery not even the just comprehended: Jesus has fully identified himself with the poor and outcast and oppressed. Jesus is indeed Emmanuel, God-with-us. He is with his people, his church, but he is most especially with the no-accounts of this world, all those in desperate need of the basic necessities of life. The Son of Man, the crucified King who judges all men, is encountered in every one who suffers. His association with the poor in the beatitudes and in his healing activity is broadened here to cosmic scope.

The stunning universalism of this revelation must not be blunted by restricting "the least of my brethren" to Christians, to poor or insignificant Christians, or to Christian missionaries. The phrases used in such passages as 10:42 ("little ones" . . . "because he is a disciple") and 18:6 ("these little ones who believe in me") are different, and the context in such places is clearly ecclesiastical; they lack the sweeping universalism of this scene. Earlier in the gospel, in an Israel-versus-the disciples context, Jesus identified his brothers as those disciples "who do the will of my Father" (12:50); and this will was interpreted in terms of mercy (9:13; 12:7). Now, in the broader context of the last judgment, he calls all men in need his brothers. And so he rewards deeds of love, wherever they are performed, for they have been done to him. It is not that he considers these works "as though" they were done to him; in virtue of his mysterious presence in all who suffer, they *were* done to him. These deeds for others are the criterion of judgment because they define a person's essential behavior and relation to the Judge, not just to other men.

Judgment according to works of mercy is therefore a judgment based on christology, on the centrality of the person of Jesus Christ. Jesus is the criterion of judgment as well as the judge. That is why those who have neglected such works are "cursed"—the only time the word appears in Mt—and damned (cf. 7:23). Neglect of the poor is the decisive not-doing of the will of God which marks one as fit company for the devil. The second group is guilty of evil by default—which is just as serious as positive wrong-doing (cf. the servant with the buried talent in 24:24-30). The condemned do not deny their neglect of the suffering; they do, however, object that they never saw Jesus in need. But that is just the point, and the reason for their condemnation. Failing to understand Jesus' identification with the needy, they failed to *minister* to or *serve* him (note the introduction of this key concept in v.44). Jesus has already demanded that his disciples be servants (20:26; 23:11). Here it becomes clear that "servant" cannot evaporate into another hierarchical title; service means the concrete performance of the loving acts listed (cf. 16:27). Because the second group has neglected such acts, it neglected the Son of Man; and so its neglect has become fatal. No matter what good they may have done or evil they may have perpetrated, the decisive question is: did you love the poor in concrete acts of mercy? Christ's teaching on the twofold love of God and neighbor (22:34-40) thus undergoes a profound transformation: love of (the poor) neighbor is practically identified with love of God and receives a christological basis.

The final verse describes the execution of the King's judgment, though in reverse (chiastic) order, so that the joyful element comes last: irrevocable punishment and incorruptible life. Mt has noted that not all those invited to the banquet of life (the *klētoi*) will finally be among the chosen (the *eklektoi*, 22:14). What makes the invited the chosen is love, incarnated in practical, daily living. The eschatological discourse thus ends on a somber as well as a triumphant note. The sensibilities of some may be offended by the emphasis given to the possibility of damnation, even as regards members and leaders of the church (cf. 13:40,42,50; 18:8-9; 24:51). But the possibility of damnation simply means that God takes man seriously and calls man to respond to his offer of life with supreme seriousness. Eschatology means that, in the end, we are responsible for our free decisions. Only a child playing a game keeps crying: "That was only a practice-shot; it didn't count!"

Eschatology says it does count. These last words of Jesus to his disciples in a lengthy address bear an interesting resemblance to the Last Supper discourses of Jesus in Jn's gospel. In both places, the final message of Jesus is love. Now that Jesus has spoken this message, now that the Son of Man who is judge has identified himself fully with the suffering in his teaching, he has nothing left to do except act out his teaching by becoming the crucified Son of Man in the passion.

The Climax:
The Death-Resurrection.
26-28.

It has been said, with some exaggeration, that the gospels are passion narratives with extended introductions. While the length of Mt's gospel obscures this fact, it is true that, for all the long discourses and parenetic material, Mt's gospel remains a paschal proclamation. Its ultimate thrust is the good news that, by his death-resurrection, Jesus has defeated the powers of sin and death, has entered upon his rule over the universe, and on the basis of his cosmic power has commanded a mission to all nations—thus breaking down the barriers of race, nation, and Law which restricted his public ministry. Mt binds together the two events of death and resurrection into one earth-shaking, apocalyptic event, the beginning of a new age, the age of the church. In this apocalyptic drama, Mt centers his attention on the person of Jesus and noticeably heightens the christology of Mk. Jesus knows everything that is to take place in the passion and purposefully moves towards his death with the desire to fulfill all the prophets (cf. 5:17-18). Mt emphasizes the dignity of Jesus as Son of Man, Son of God, Messiah, and King. Around this dominant christological motif Mt musters a number of secondary themes: the responsibility of the people Israel for the blood of the innocent Jesus, the "founding" of the church by the crucified and risen Jesus, the weakness of Peter and others as a foil to the strength and majesty of Jesus, and all the moral examples or counter-examples given to Christians by Jesus and the other actors in the drama. *Especially for Mt.'s church, rent by persecution and apostasy, the suffering and death of the Son, the fall of Peter, the fate of the betrayer, and the failure of the Jewish leaders all speak comfort or warning to later Christians, struggling under their cross.*

Since there are so many cross-references among the various pericopes in Mt's closely knit passion narrative (e.g., the denial of Peter and the suicide of Judas, the apocalyptic signs at the cross and at the tomb, the setting of the guard at the tomb and the report of the guard), it is somewhat arbitrary to introduce major divisions into the narrative. For the sake of the reader, the narrative will be divided into three major chronological sections, which coincide with the three chapters: (A) from Wednesday to Thursday night (26:1-75); (B) from Friday morning to Saturday (27:1-66); (C) from Sunday to the end of the age (28:1-20). For all the material, Mt has only Mk as a continuous source. Mt may have had some stray individual traditions at hand (the addition to the consecration of the cup, the fate of Judas, Pilate's wife), but his narrative is mainly the product of his creative redaction of Mk.

I. FROM WEDNESDAY TO THURSDAY NIGHT.
26:1-75.

A. THE PROLOGUE TO THE PASSION.
26:1-16.

(1) Jesus Foretells and Unleashes the Passion.
26:1-5.
[*Mk 14:1-2; Lk 22:1-2*]

> **26** When Jesus had finished all these sayings, he said to his disciples, [2]"You know that after two days the Passover is coming, and the Son of man will be delivered up to be crucified."
>
> [3]Then the chief priests and the elders of the people gathered in the palace of the high priest, who was called Caiaphas, [4]and took counsel together in order to arrest Jesus by stealth and kill him. [5]But they said, "Not during the feast, lest there be a tumult among the people."

Out of Mk's short notice about the time of the plot against Jesus, Mt creates a double scene which emphasizes Jesus' knowledge and control of all that is to come upon him. In Mt's passion Jesus is not only the central figure but also the central actor, the agent who guides the events of the passion instead of just enduring them.

The first part of the double scene begins with the formula which has marked the end of all five discourses (7:28; 11:1; 13:53; 19:1). While all the other formulas ran, "and it came to pass when Jesus had finished these words [instructions, parables]," this time Mt explicitly notes that Jesus has spoken his last discourse to the disciples: "And it came to pass when Jesus had finished *all* these sayings . . . ." It was fitting that the last discourse should be the apocalyptic discourse. Nothing now remains for Jesus to do except to precipitate the apocalyptic events of the death. It is these he foretells in his *fourth* passion prediction, unique to Mt. Since the events are only two days away, the "delivered up" (divine passive, with God as the understood agent) is put into the present tense in Greek: "is being handed over" (contrast 17:22-23; 20:18-19). "After two days" seems to indicate that Jesus is speaking on Wednesday, the thirteenth of Nisan, since, in Mt's chronology, Jesus dies on Passover, the fifteenth of Nisan, which falls on a Friday that year. By preserving Mk's mention of the Passover and by placing it in Jesus' mouth, Mt creates a connection between the sacrifice of the Passover lamb and Jesus' prediction of his death, a connection which does not appear in any of the three traditional passion predictions. For Mt, the death of Jesus and its symbolic celebration in the Eucharistic meal form the true Passover sacrifice of the new people of God. The one to be sacrificed is, naturally, the Son of Man who has come to serve and give his life as ransom (cf. 20:28). Thus the whole passion is put under the rubric of Son of Man.

"Then" (v.3)—that is, only when Jesus has freely set the course of events in motion—the Jewish leaders gather in the second part of this double scene to plot Jesus' death. The gathering together of "the chief priests and the elders of the people" [i.e., the lay nobility who sat in the Sanhedrin] recalls the gathering of "the chief priests and the scribes of the people" around Herod in the infancy narrative (2:4), a gathering which likewise resulted in a plot against Jesus' life. The mention of this hostile "gathering" may allude to Ps 2:2 in the Septuagint ("the kings of the earth rose up and the rulers were gathered together against the Lord and against his Christ"; cf. Acts 4:26). Mt is the only Synoptist to mention Caiaphas in the passion narrative; in this, he parallels Jn. Joseph Caiaphas, the son-in-law of Annas, who controlled the high priesthood after he lost it by having various relatives appointed, held the office from A.D. 18 to A.D. 36. The wily politicians plot to avoid arresting Jesus during Passover, when Jerusalem was bursting with pilgrims and a riot was an easy thing to start. All their planning, however, will avail nothing. The prophetic word of Jesus has already set the course of events in motion and has connected the Passover with the passion; nothing his enemies will do can prevent his arrest on the night of Passover. (Another interpretation is that the phrase "not during the feast" should be translated "not while he is in the crowd gathered for the feast." In that case, the plot does succeed. But does such a translation correspond to Mt's redaction in setting up this double scene and stressing Jesus' control?)

(2) Jesus Receives His Anointing for Burial.
26:6-13.
[*Mk 14:3-9; Lk 7:36-50*]

> [6]Now when Jesus was at Bethany in the house of Simon the leper, [7]a woman came up to him with an alabaster flask of very expensive ointment, and she poured it on his head, as he sat at table. [8]But when the disciples saw it, they were indignant, saying, "Why this waste? [9]For this ointment might have been sold for a large sum, and given to the poor." [10]But Jesus, aware of this, said to them, "Why do you trouble the woman? For she has done a beautiful thing to me. [11]For you always have the poor with you, but you will not always have me. [12]In pouring this ointment on my body she has done it to prepare me for burial. [13]Truly, I say to you, wherever this gospel is preached in the whole world, what she has done will be told in memory of her."

The tradition of an anointing occurs in all four gospels, and there has been a mutual contamination of two different events: the tearful repentance of a sinful woman (Lk) and the loving act of an unnamed woman (Mk-Mt). Jn 12:1-8 represents the most confused state of the tradition (*Mary* of Bethany applies the ointment to Jesus' *feet* and then wipes the feet with her hair).

Mt has the love and devotion of the woman (unnamed, and not a sinner) contrast sharply with the plot of the officials which precedes and the offer of Judas which follows. Mt, as usual, abbreviates Mk's narrative, omitting the concrete details of "pure nard," the "reproach" of the woman, and the mention of the price (300 denarii).

Simon the leper is otherwise unknown; perhaps his leprosy had been healed by Jesus. Bethany is a village about 1 and 5/8 miles east of Jerusalem. To prevent the evaporation of expensive perfume, an amount sufficient for one application would be sealed in a jar, which had to be broken to release the ointment. The pouring of oil on the head was customary at a banquet (cf. Ps 23:5); there may also be a secondary allusion here to the anointing of a king's head at his coronation. Mt specifies that it is the disciples who are annoyed at this prodigality. Their insensitivity to the deeper meaning of this prophetic sign contrasts with the woman's insight and prepares for their desertion of Jesus. Jesus, knowing with his divine knowledge what the disciples are saying, defends the woman on two grounds. (1) Jesus is soon to die and therefore deserves this special honor, while the poor will always be available as objects of charity. (2) More importantly, Jesus, again displaying his foreknowledge, interprets the anointing as preparing for his imminent burial. This explanation fits especially well with Mt's presentation, which does not have the women coming to the tomb on Sunday morning to anoint the body (contrast Mk 16:1) and does not introduce Nicodemus with his spices at Jesus' burial (contrast Jn 19:39-40). Jesus solemnly promises the woman that her deed of love amid so much hatred and ignorance will be proclaimed just as widely as "this gospel," namely, throughout the world (cf. 24:14; 28:19). "This gospel" probably means for Mt the message proclaimed in the book he is writing.

(3) Jesus Is Betrayed by Judas.
26:14-16.
[Mk 14:10-11; Lk 22:3-6]

> [14]Then one of the twelve, who was called Judas Iscariot, went to the chief priests [15]and said, "What will you give me if I deliver him to you?" And they paid him thirty pieces of silver. [16]And from that moment he sought an opportunity to betray him.

Judas now becomes a tragic parallel-yet-contrast to Jesus, as both men move purposefully towards Jesus' arrest. "Then," when Jesus has displayed his contempt for concern about money, Judas goes to the priests and asks for money. Mt thus introduces a motive for the betrayal (greed) which is lacking in Mk. The taking of silver stands in ironic contrast to Jesus' prohibition of silver in 10:9, in his instructions to the twelve apostles. The precise amount of money, which is mentioned only by Mt, comes not from some eye-witness account but from prophecy. Verse 15b, "and they paid him thirty pieces of silver" is actually a quotation from Zech 11:12, the payment for the rejected shepherd. Zech, in turn, is alluding to Ex 21:32, where the price of thirty shekels of silver is the payment given in reparation to the master of a slave who is gored by an ox. In Zech, the amount is meant to be demeaning: it is a paltry sum. All the more would this be the case in Mt, since thirty shekels were worth at the time of Jesus perhaps one-tenth of what they were worth when Ex was written. Mt has already cited Zech at the triumphal entry (21:5), and the explicit citation of Zech 11:12 will occur at the death of Judas (27:9).

"From that moment" of betrayal (cf. 4:17; 16:21) Judas hurtles unwittingly towards his own death as well as Christ's. Everything that follows will be simply a playing-out of the prologue (26:1-16). This apparent tragedy proceeds from a subtle interaction of God's will, foretold in prophecy, and man's sinful heart. Both are expressed by the same Greek verb *paradidōmi*, "to hand over" or "betray." Jesus is "handed over" (passive voice) to death by the salvific will of the Father, while Judas "betrays" (active voice) Jesus for the sake of money.

B. THE PASSOVER MEAL.
26:17-29.

(1) Jesus Commands that the Passover Be Prepared.
26:17-19.
[Mk 14:12-16; Lk 22:7-13]

> 17Now on the first day of Unleavened Bread the disciples came to Jesus, saying, "Where will you have us prepare for you to eat the passover?" 18He said, "Go into the city to a certain one, and say to him, 'The Teacher says, My time is at hand; I will keep the passover at your house with my disciples.'" 19And the disciples did as Jesus had directed them, and they prepared the passover.

Mt abbreviates Mk sharply and emphasizes the theme of Jesus' command and the disciples' obedience, instead of the Markan theme of Jesus' foreknowledge. Mt takes over from Mk the inexact phrase "the first day of Unleavened Bread." As the narrative shows, Mt is thinking of Thursday, the 14th of Nisan, when the old leavened bread was thrown out of Jewish houses. Strictly speaking, the first day of Unleavened Bread coincided with the first day of Passover, the 15th of Nisan. Mt strikes out Mk's story about Jesus' foreknowledge of the disciples' meeting a man with a jar on his head. Instead, Jesus sends his disciples directly to "a certain main" (RSV: "to such a one"; no doubt there is no name because Mk supplies none and, since Mt drops the story of the man with the jar, there is no other way to identify the host). While "teacher," used as an address, always implies unbelief in Mt, the evangelist has no problems about the word in the mouth of Jesus, who knows its proper meaning (cf. 23:8,10).

Instead of asking a question, as in Mk, Jesus makes a solemn affirmation, another expression of his knowledge of the plots around him: "My time is near." This statement, added by Mt, conjures up memories of prophetic and apocalyptic promises in both the OT and the NT that "the day of the Lord" is near. The apocalyptic event of the death-resurrection, the true "day of the Lord," is imminent. The majesty of Jesus is expressed in his flat statement that he will celebrate the Passover at "such a one's" house. No questions are asked, no favors are requested. The obedience of the disciples is narrated with the same words as in 21:6.

(2) Jesus Foretells His Betrayal.
26:20-25.
[Mk 14:17-21; Lk 22:21-23]

> 20 When it was evening, he sat at table with the twelve disciples; 21 and as they were eating, he said, "Truly, I say to you, one of you will betray me." 22 And they were very sorrowful, and began to say to him one after another, "Is it I, Lord?" 23 He answered, "He who has dipped his hand in the dish with me, will betray me. 24 The Son of man goes as it is written of him, but woe to that man by whom the Son of man is betrayed! It would have been better for that man if he had not been born." 25 Judas, who betrayed him, said, "Is it I, Master?" He said to him, "You have said so."

Mt follows Mk more closely here. Omitting any reference to the group's coming to the house, Mt begins immediately with the reclining at table. Originally the Passover meal was eaten standing; but, by the time of Jesus, Jews had adopted the Hellenistic custom of reclining. It is interesting to note that there is no mention of the Passover in this or the following pericope. This may be an indication that originally the Last Supper was not designated as a Passover meal; such is the case in Jn's gospel. It may be that the Synoptic tradition has made the Last Supper a Passover meal for theological reasons (e.g., the Eucharist is portrayed as the Passover sacrifice and meal of the new covenant). Strange to say, Mt drops Jesus' designation of the betrayer in Mk as "the one who eats with me," a possible allusion to Ps 41:9. The announcement of Jesus should not be thought of as a sad premonition. Jesus, the Lord of the situation, is prophesying what will necessarily take place. That is why the shocked disciples are forced to ask whether they might be marked out to play the fateful role. Jesus does not identify the betrayer directly, but it is the person who has (just?) dipped his hand into the common bowl with Jesus (compare Mk's "one of the twelve, he who *is dipping* into the bowl with me"). Manifesting his foreknowledge once again, Jesus reaffirms the necessity that he, the Son of Man, go to his death, according to the prophecies of Scripture. Yet this inevitable fulfillment of prophecy does not absolve his betrayer of responsibility. God's saving action and man's sinful action are intertwined in the passion; the dialectic is brought out by the play on words: "Son of man . . . that man."

The punishment prepared for the betrayer is unimaginably horrible; non-existence would be preferable to it (27:3-10). The church's horror at the betrayal by one of Jesus' inner circle rings clear in this verse, just as the troubled questions of the disciples remind Mt's church that no one is above such temptations. One must examine oneself, especially as one comes to table-fellowship with the Lord in the Eucharist. Mt then adds a final, dramatic touch to Mk. Judas, no doubt wishing to hide the truth, joins the other disciples in asking: "Is it I?" (a better translation of all these questions would be: "It isn't I, is it?"). But his very speech betrays Judas. While the others address Jesus with the title of believers (*kyrie*, Lord), Judas uses the title employed by unbelievers (Rabbi). Indeed, Judas "has said it"—an ambiguous phrase which throws the responsibility for the question back on the questioner: "You said it, not I." In this case, unfortunately, both Jesus and Judas know how the ambiguity is to be resolved.

(3) Jesus Institutes the Eucharist.
26:26-29.
[*Mk 14:22-25; Lk 22:15-20*]

> [26]Now as they were eating, Jesus took bread, and blessed, and broke it, and gave it to the disciples and said, "Take, eat; this is my body." [27]And he took a cup, and when he had given thanks he gave it to them, saying, "Drink of it, all of you; [28]for this is my blood of the covenant, which is poured out for many for the forgiveness of sins. [29]I tell you I shall not drink again of this fruit of the vine until that day when I drink it new with you in my Father's kingdom."

There are two major forms of the Eucharistic words of Jesus recorded in the NT: the Pauline-Lukan and the Markan-Matthean. The earlier form is found in 1 Cor 11:23-25 and Lk 22:19-20. In this form, the words over the bread and over the cup are explicitly separated by a whole meal, and the word over the cup ("this cup is the new covenant in my blood") does not provide a perfect parallel to the word over the bread ("this is my body"). Yet even Paul and Luke show influences from liturgical traditions, traditions which manifest themselves in explanatory statements and in attempts to balance the two "consecrations."

Mt follows the Markan tradition, which is more developed in that there is no mention of a meal between the two actions and in that the two consecratory formulas have become parallel ("this is my body" . . . "this is my blood"). The Markan tradition, however, retains some primitive traces: there is no command to repeat the actions and the phrase "which is [given] for you" is not attached to the word over the bread. While Mt basically follows the Markan tradition, he revises it somewhat to make it coincide with the liturgical traditions of his church. Note, by the way, that 26:26-29 is a self-contained unit which would fit perfectly into a larger Eucharistic prayer; it is easily detachable from the narrative framework around it.

The successive actions of taking bread, giving thanks or pronouncing a blessing (addressed to God, not the bread), breaking, and distributing are the common form of Jewish grace-at-table; Jesus recycles them to create two parabolic and prophetic actions. These actions are reflected both in the narratives of the multiplication of the loaves (14:19; 15:36) and the consecrating prayers of the Christian Eucharist. Mt underlines the fact that Jesus gives this sacred food to the disciples (Mk: "to them"). Mk's stark command, "take," is balanced in Mt: "take, eat." "This is my body" identifies the bread with the whole person of Jesus, in all its corporeal reality, vulnerability, and mortality. Following Mk, Mt uses *eucharistēsas* ("giving thanks") with the cup, while he used *eulogēsas* ("pronouncing a blessing") with the bread. Mk narrates that "they all drank" of the cup before he has Jesus speak the words of interpretation. Mt turns the narrative into a command of Jesus which precedes the words of interpretation: "Drink of it, all of you."

The words over the cup, especially in the expanded Matthean form are much more sacrificial in tone than the words over the bread. "The blood of the covenant" recalls the covenant sacrifice of Ex 24:8. After the animals are slain, Moses takes half of the blood and throws it against the altar (the symbol of Yahweh). After reading the Law to the people and receiving their acceptance of it, Moses throws the other half of the blood upon the people, saying: "Behold the blood of the covenant." By a solemn sacrifice, a common bond of life (symbolized by the blood, the seat of life) has been forged between God and his people. This bond of life, this covenant, demands a new mode of action from the people who now enjoy a special fellowship with God. "*My* blood of the covenant" may also allude to Zech 9:11, where God says: "Because of the blood of my covenant with you, I will set your captives free." Jesus declares the wine in the cup he shares with his disciples to be his blood, i.e., his life poured out in sacrifice to create a bond of life, a community of life, a covenant between God and his new people, the church. While Mk uses the Greek preposition *hyper* to express "for," "for the sake of," Mt uses the preposition *peri*, which echoes more closely the sacrificial language of the song of the suffering servant in Second Isaiah (Is 53:4,10; cf. 1 Pt 3:18; 1 Jn 2:2; also often in the Epistle to the Hebrews). This sacrificial blood is poured out "for the many"; "many" does not mean some as opposed to all, but rather, according to Semitic usage, the mass of mankind as opposed to the one who is making the sacrifice.

Mt pointedly adds to the Markan formula "unto the remission of sins"—no doubt reflecting the liturgical usage of his church. But Mt himself certainly thinks of Christ's death as an atoning sacrifice. In 1:21 he has the angel predict that Jesus "will save his people [the new people of God] from their sins." In his description of John the Baptist's baptism, he carefully avoids calling it a baptism "unto the remission of sins" (Mt 3:11; contrast Mk 1:4)—the very words Mt appends to the word over the cup. Mt definitely does see Jesus' death as a vicarious sacrifice for sin; he preserves Mk's saying about "a ransom for many" (Mk 10:45=Mt. 20:28), a saying which stands out all the more because Lk omits it. For the most part, the Jewish sacrificial system dealt with ritual and legal transgressions, not with what we understand today as personal sin. Jesus' sacrifice forgives all sins; Mt probably sees here the fulfillment of God's promise of a "new covenant" in which Israel's iniquity would be forgiven (Jer 31:31-34). By sharing the one bread and drinking the one cup, the disciples share in the saving effects of Jesus' atoning sacrifice. For Mt, the Christian receives forgiveness of sins neither through baptism (which aggregates one to the life of the Trinity) nor through the "binding and loosing" of the church (which refers to excommunication and readmittance) but rather through the Eucharist.

After the words of institution, Jesus concludes with a solemn affirmation that this is the last cup of wine he will drink before his death, a death which will break the table-fellowship he has enjoyed with his disciples and which will apparently destroy his life's work. But Jesus affirms his faith that the Father will see him vindicated beyond death and will bring both him and his disciples to a new table-fellowship, the messianic banquet in the kingdom "of my Father" (Mk: "of God"). Jesus therefore will not drink "from this time on" (*ap' arti*, not well represented in the RSV)—that is, from this critical turning point of the death-resurrection, until he drinks wine *anew* "with you" (an addition by Mt, stressing Jesus' union with his church through the Eucharist). Indeed, while the ultimate thrust of the saying is the heavenly banquet on the last day, Mt no doubt also thinks of the anticipation of that banquet in the Eucharistic meal, which both recalls the Son of Man sacrificed on the cross and awaits the Son of Man coming in glory.

C. JESUS PREDICTS PETER'S DENIAL.
26:30-35.
[Mk 14:26-31; Lk 22:31-34]

> [30]And when they had sung a hymn, they went out to the Mount of Olives, [31]Then Jesus said to them, "You

will all fall away because of me this night; for it is written, 'I will strike the shepherd, and the sheep of the flock will be scattered.' [32]But after I am raised up, I will go before you to Galilee." [33]Peter declared to him, "Though they all fall away because of you, I will never fall away." [34]Jesus said to him, "Truly, I say to you, this very night, before the cock crows, you will deny me three times." [35]Peter said to him, "even if I must die with you, I will not deny you." And so said all the disciples.

Mt follows Mk closely, placing the prediction of the denial on the way to Gethsemane, rather than during the supper, as do Lk and Jn. The Passover meal is concluded by the singing of Psalms 114 to 118, the second part of the so-called *Hallel* ("Praise") collection of psalms, recalling God's redemption of Israel from Egypt and of the individual from death. This is the only time that the gospels record that Jesus sang—on the night before his death. This joyful note is rudely broken by Jesus' announcement to the disciples that all of them will fall away from faith, will stumble into sin (literally: "be scandalized") because of Jesus. Precisely because Jesus does not fulfill ordinary human expectations of a Messiah or Savior, he can be a stumbling stone for prospective believers (cf. 11:6; 13:57; 15:12). The cross in particular is what causes the half-hearted to fall away (13:21; 24:10). With his foreknowledge, Jesus sees that scandal, the greatest woe of the end-time, will engulf even his inner circle: *all* will fall, and indeed "in this very night," because what is going to befall Jesus does not fit into their childish messianic hopes. Jesus is not shattered by this knowledge; he knows it is part of God's saving plan, mapped out beforehand in the prophets. Zechariah, who has been prominent in the scenes of the triumphal entry, the betrayal by Judas, and the Last Supper, is now freely cited by Jesus (Zech 13:7). Jesus, the true shepherd of Israel (Mt 9:36; 15:24), is about to be struck down, by the very people he sought to shepherd. Even the sheep he had safely led into his flock will now be scattered, as the disciples abandon him after his arrest (26:56). Yet this will not be the end. For the first time in chap. 26, Jesus prophesies not only his death but also his resurrection. Once the slain shepherd is raised up, he will go like a shepherd before his sheep into Galilee. The angel at the tomb will repeat this message to the women (28:7), and the rehabilitated disciples will go into Galilee to receive from the Son of Man their definitive founding as a church and their universal mission (28:16-20).

Peter, as usual, does not want to hear this talk of death and resurrection (16:21-23), and even more, he refuses to contemplate the possiblity of *his* failure, even though the rest of the disciples succumb. His affirmation is underlined by Mt: "*never* will *I* fall away." Jesus replies to Peter's arrogance with a further display of his prescience. With a solemn Amen-word, he assures Peter that "in this very night" (cf. v.31), before daybreak (before the rooster crows) Peter will deny his master three times. The rebellious Peter still refuses to accept the fact that Jesus foresees everything. *Even if*—something Peter does not really concede—even if he must die with Jesus, he will not deny Jesus. It is a splendid profession of what the personal bond between disciples and master should be (10:32-33,37-39; 16:24-28); but the reader knows that Jesus' foreknowledge, not Peter's boasting, will be vindicated in the end (27:69-75). Peter has acted as spokesman for the foolish confidence of all the disciples, who now echo his profession of loyalty.

D. PRAYER AND ARREST IN GETHSEMANE. 26:36-56.

(1) Jesus Prays in Gethsemane.
26:36-46.
[*Mk 14:32-42; Lk 22:39-46*]

   36Then Jesus went with them to a place called Gethsemane, and he said to his disciples, "Sit here, while I go

yonder and pray." ³⁷And taking with him Peter and the two sons of Zebedee, he began to be sorrowful and troubled. ³⁸Then he said to them, "My soul is very sorrowful, even to death; remain here, and watch with me." ³⁹And going a little farther he fell on his face and prayed, "My Father, if it is possible, let this cup pass from me; nevertheless, not as I will, but as thou wilt." ⁴⁰And he came to the disciples and found them sleeping; and he said to Peter, "So, could you not watch with me one hour? ⁴¹Watch and pray that you may not enter into temptation; the spirit indeed is willing, but the flesh is weak." ⁴²Again, for the second time, he went away and prayed, "My Father, if this cannot pass unless I drink it, thy will be done." ⁴³And again he came and found them sleeping, for their eyes were heavy. ⁴⁴So, leaving them again, he went away and prayed for the third time, saying the same words. ⁴⁵Then he came to the disciples and said to them. "Are you still sleeping and taking your rest? Behold, the hour is at hand, and the Son of man is betrayed into the hands of sinners. ⁴⁶Rise, let us be going; see, my betrayer is at hand."

While Mt takes over most of the two scenes in Gethsemane from Mk, both the length of these scenes and the changes Mt makes in them set them off as a key part of the passion narrative.

Mt highlights both the person of Jesus and his fellowship with his disciples by saying "Jesus went with them" instead of Mk's "they come." Gethsemane ("oil press") was an estate with olive trees on the western slope or at the foot of the mount of Olives. As the inner three disciples were allowed to see his glory at the transfiguration, so now they are invited to witness and share his suffering. Instead of speaking of Jesus' great alarm or fear, as Mk does, Mt mentions his sorrow, which leads nicely into his confession of sorrow—a citation of Ps 42:6, to which is added the phrase "even to death" from Jonah 4:9. The sense is: Jesus could easily die of the sorrow which now overwhelms him.

Even the majestic Son must plead for human companionship and comfort as the hour of his passion approaches. He appeals to his three followers to spend some time in prayer with him. The command "watch" carries a deeper meaning. It was the warning of Jesus to his disciples in the apocalyptic discourse (24:42; 25:13; cf. 1 Pt 5:8). Now, in the night of this world, as the apocalyptic events of the passion draw near, Jesus exhorts his disciples to keep awake not only physically but also spiritually. The more Jesus feels distant from God, the more he seeks the closeness of his followers ("with me" in v. 38 is a Matthean addition). He offers them fellowship in prayer, which they in effect refuse. In a gesture of distress and supplication, Jesus falls *on his face* (a Matthean addition, taken from the OT). Unlike Mk, Mt reports the whole of Jesus' prayer in direct address. Mt renders Mk's Aramaic *Abba* with a touching "my Father" (cf. "Our Father" in 6:9). Mk's flat statement, "all things are possible to you," is changed to the impersonal proviso, "if it be possible." Mk's sweeping affirmation may have seemed awkward to Mt, in light of the fact that the Father does not answer Jesus' request. The cup (Mt drops Mk's mention of the "hour") is the OT symbol of one's fate as prepared by God, be it reward or punishment. Drinking a cup could in particular be a symbol of undergoing suffering or punishment (cf. Ps 11:6; Lam 4:21; Is 51:17,22).

Jesus returns *to his disciples* (a Matthean addition, stressing the union which should exist at this moment between Jesus and his chosen ones), only to find them sleeping—a symbol of being unprepared in the eschatological crisis (cf. 1 Thess 5:6-7; Eph 5:14). Although the rebuke (softened vis-à-vis Mk) speaks in the plural to all three, Mt aims it explicitly at Peter, the leader. After a sad, ironic question Jesus renews his exhortation, pointedly adding prayer to vigilance. Without both, they will fall prey ("enter into") the overpowering test ("temptation") of the eschatological crisis. Another part of the Our Father is thus echoed (6:13). Jesus then explains why they—and anyone else—can be so easily overwhelmed by the final test.

The "spirit" (either God's Spirit given to the human spirit, or the human spirit as fortified by God's Spirit) is willing to overcome the challenge of evil, but the "flesh" (the concrete human person in all his fragility, mortality, and proclivity to sin) is too weak to follow through on the resolution of the spirit. The anthropological dualism expressed in v.41 reflects Persian or Hellenistic influence, and is found at Qumran. The human person is a battlefield between two forces, God's spirit and fleshy desires; and, without prayer and vigilance, Satan will breach the battlements at their weakest point, the flesh.

While Mk simply reports that Jesus repeated the words of his prayer, Mt gives the direct address again, in a slightly altered form, which hints at the inner progress of Jesus' struggle. Now the condition is "if this cannot pass unless I drink it"; the failure of his disciples to accompany him in prayer seems to signal the failure of his own petition. He receives a negative reply from the divine as well as the human audience. His reaction to the Father's refusal to set aside the necessity of the cross is not Petrine rebellion; Jesus practices the obedience he has preached to others: "Thy will be done" is an exact citation of the third petition of the Our Father (6:10). Mt is making Jesus a model of prayer and obedience for the suffering church. The Son proves his sonship and reverses the sin of disobedient man by obeying the Father in all things; it is this inner spirit of obedience which gives the outward tragedy of the crucifixion its saving value.

A second visit to the sleeping disciples confirms the necessity of the path of suffering; in Mt, contrary to Mk, Jesus does not even bother to awaken them. Also contrary to Mk, Mt explicitly mentions a third session of prayer, though this time without a direct quotation. His first words to the disciples in v.45 could be either an ironic command ("sleep on and take your rest") or an ironic question (so RSV; the latter fits better with the commands which follow in v.46). Solemnly ("behold") Jesus announces a double "is at hand": his hour to be handed over to the passion is approaching (v.45), in that his betrayer is approaching (v.46). The verb for "is at hand" was also used to express the nearness of the kingdom (e.g., 4:17); by Jesus' death, the kingdom will break into this world in a new and definitive way. Judas may be the human agent who is betraying him (*paradidous*, active participle), but he is only an instrument in the deeper mystery: the Son of Man, the earthly yet heavenly figure, the lowly yet powerful man, is being handed over by the Father into the hands (i.e., the power) of sinners (perhaps the Gentiles in particular are meant) to save his people from their sins (1:21; 26:28). The disciples, who have slept through Jesus' struggle in prayer, must at least arise to witness the outcome of that prayer: Jesus freely and obediently accepts God's will, even in the form of arrest and death. The Son triumphs by filial obedience, while the disciples fail to obey him and so find themselves unprepared for the eschatological crisis. They enter into temptation and flee.

(2) Jesus Is Arrested in Gethsemane.
26:47-56.
[Mk 14:43-52; Lk 22:47-53]

47While he was still speaking, Judas came, one of the twelve, and with him a great crowd with swords and clubs, from the chief priests and the elders of the people. 48Now the betrayer had given them a sign, saying, "The one I shall kiss is the man; seize him." 49And he came up to Jesus at once and said, "Hail, Master!" And he kissed him. 50Jesus said to him, "Friend, why are you here?" Then they came up and laid hands on Jesus and seized him. 51And behold, one of those who were with Jesus stretched out his hand and drew his sword, and struck the slave of the high priest, and cut off his ear. 52Then Jesus said to him, "Put your sword back into its place; for all who take the sword will perish by the sword. 53Do you think that I cannot appeal to my Father, and he will at once send me more than twelve legions of angels? ⁵⁴But how then should the scriptures be fulfilled, that it must be so?" ⁵⁵At that hour Jesus said to the crowds, "Have you come out as against a robber, with swords and clubs to capture me? Day after day I sat in the temple teaching, and you did not seize me. ⁵⁶But all this has taken place, that the scriptures of the prophets might be fulfilled." Then all the disciples forsook him and fled.

Mt follows Mk closely, with the exception of two expansions (in v.50 and vv.52-54). Jesus' knowledge of the inevitable course of events is again verified by the arrival of Judas while Jesus is still speaking about him (vv.46-47). The "great" crowd (Mt's addition) is said to come from "the chief priests and the elders of the people," which repeats the phrase Mt uses in describing the initial plot (cf. comment on 26:3). To prevent confusion in the garden at night, Judas has arranged to identify Jesus to the crowd by a hypocritical kiss. Judas again shows that he is no true disciple by greeting Jesus as "Rabbi" (cf. comment on 26:25). Mt adds the Greek form of greeting, "Hail" (*chaire*, literally, "rejoice"; cf. 27:29; 28:9). Knowing the true state of affairs, Jesus answers Judas coolly with a distant "friend" (cf. comments on 20:13; 22:12). The next statement of Jesus, the first insertion of Mt into the Markan story, is elliptical and ambiguous in Greek. The RSV takes it as a question; other suggestions are: "it is for *this* [or, is it for *this*] that you have come?"; or, "it is a kiss of betrayal for which you have come." Since Mt emphasizes Jesus' sovereign control of the flow of events in chap. 26, the best translation is perhaps the imperative: "Do what you have come for!" As in 26:2, the words of Jesus unleash all that follows.

When the crowds begin to lay hands on Jesus, "one of those with Jesus," i.e., one of his disciples (which is clearer than Mk's "one of the bystanders") cuts off the ear of the slave of the high priest. The fourth gospel names Peter as the disciple and Malchus as the slave; it is hard to believe that Mt, with his great interest in Peter, would not have mentioned him if he had known the Johannine tradition. This act of violence introduces Mt's second insertion into the Markan pericope. Mt first has Jesus majestically order the return of the sword to its scabbard. Then Jesus gives three reasons for the order. The first reason is a general proverb (with a chiastic structure) which speaks a truth going far beyond the present situation: violence is self-destructive and futile. There is an inherent law or nemesis in human affairs which always makes brute force return like a boomerang to the one who unleashes it. In this rejection of violence Jesus again practices what he preaches (5:38-48; contrast the scribes and Pharisees in 23:3). The second reason Jesus rejects violence is that he is confident of his Father's protection. If it were the Father's will to save Jesus by force, the angelic army would be sent to the rescue. But that is not the will of the Father, as the third reason makes clear. With a rhetorical question, Jesus indicates that "it must happen this way" in order that "the Scriptures" might be "fulfilled." Jesus freely and obediently submits himself to the will of the Father as expressed in OT prophecy. This statement draws upon many of the words used by Mt to introduce his formula quotations (cf. v.56).

After this second insertion into the traditional story, Mt rejoins the Markan thread with the phrase "at that hour." Jesus' reaction to his arrest is thus divided into two statements, the first to his disciples, and now the second to the crowds. With sovereign disdain he rebukes them for acting as though he were some guerrilla bandit who had to be taken by surprise and dragged away by force. He purposely placed himself in the public view by teaching daily in the temple (typically, Mt notes that Jesus "sat" as he taught; cf. 5:1; 13:1-2; 24:3). But Jesus consoles himself with the knowledge that, however wrong their action, it is no mere meaningless accident. Citing Mt's set phrase for introducing the formula quotations (contrast Mk's laconic "but let the Scriptures be fulfilled"), Jesus states that *all* this has taken place, that the writings of the *prophets* might be *fulfilled* (cf. e.g., 1:22). Mt views the whole of the Law and the prophets as prophetic; indeed, turning the canon of the OT on its head, he has spoken of "all the prophets and the Law" as prophesying (11:13). Now, as the passion in the more restricted sense begins, he places the whole series of eschatological events under the rubric of the fulfillment of prophecy. While Mk speaks simply of "the Scriptures," Mt purposefully says "the Scriptures *of the prophets.*" With the exception of the suicide of Judas, no event in the passion narrative is accompanied by a formula quotation (and even the suicide of Judas has a modified introduction). This is especially strange, when one considers both Mt's interest in the fulfillment of prophecy and the many events in the passion which would easily lend themselves to formula quotations (e.g., 27:35, reflecting Ps 22:18). The reason for the omission of formula quotations in the passion seems to be that Mt conceives of the death-resurrection of Jesus as one great eschatological event which fulfills not this or that prophecy, but all prophecy. Hence, instead of individual citations inserted at various points, the whole of the passion is put under the rubric of 26:54,56. *All* this has taken place that the Scriptures of the prophets as a whole might be fulfilled. Heaven and earth (the old creation) shall not pass away, and the smallest part of the Mosaic Law shall not pass away, until all things prophesied come to pass—in the death-resurrection, the apocalyptic turning of the ages (cf. 5:18).

Now that Jesus has expressed his free acceptance of this plan of the Father, outlined in prophecy, the events of the passion can proceed rapidly, with a minimum of explanatory statements from Jesus. "Then," almost as though Jesus had given his leave, all the disciples flee. Mt naturally omits the enigmatic story of the young man who flees naked.

E. THE JEWISH TRIAL.
26:57-75.

(1) Setting the Stage.
26:57-58.
[Mk 14:53-54; Lk 22:54]

> ⁵⁷Then those who had seized Jesus led him to Caiaphas the high priest, where the scribes and the elders had gathered. ⁵⁸But Peter followed him at a distance, as far as the courtyard of the high priest, and going inside he sat with the guards to see the end.

Verse 57, mentioning Jesus, prepares for vv. 59-68; v. 58, mentioning Peter, prepares for vv. 69-75. Mt again names Caiaphas (cf. comment on 26:3). The priestly families, represented here by Caiaphas, the scribes (lawyers and theologians), and the elders (the lay nobility) made up the Jerusalem Sanhedrin, the highest court and legislative body in Judaism. Mt follows Mk in presenting the hearing before the Sanhedrin as a legal, full-dress trial. Lk and Jn seem to think only of a hearing, leading to the trial before Pilate; in this, they may be closer to the historical truth. Mt does not place Peter by a fire, warming himself, as in Mk. Peter simply enters the courtyard and sits with the guards (or attendants) "to see the end"—i.e., to see what results the arrest and trial of Jesus would have. Perhaps, granted Peter's agitated state, "the end" carries the deeper connotation of death. Peter already expects the worst.

(2) Jesus Before the Sanhedrin.
26:59-68.
[Mk 14:55-65]

> ⁵⁹Now the chief priests and the whole council sought false testimony against Jesus that they might put him to

death, ⁶⁰but they found none, though many false witnesses came forward ⁶¹and said, "This fellow said, 'I am
able to destroy the temple of God, and to build it in three
days.'" ⁶²And the high priest stood up and said, "Have
you no answer to make? What is it that these men testify
against you?" ⁶³But Jesus was silent. And the high priest
said to him, "I adjure you by the living God, tell us if you
are the Christ, the Son of God." ⁶⁴Jesus said to him, "You
have said so. But I tell you, hereafter you will see the Son
of man seated at the right hand of Power, and coming on
the clouds of heaven." ⁶⁵Then the high priest tore his
robes, and said, "He has uttered blasphemy. Why do
we still need witnesses? You have now heard his blasphemy. ⁶⁶What is your judgment?" They answered, "He
deserves death." ⁶⁷Then they spat in his face, and struck
him; and some slapped him, ⁶⁸saying, "Prophesy to us,
you Christ! Who is it that struck you?"

The innocence of Jesus, a theme struck also in the trial
before Pilate, is made clear from the start of the Jewish
trial. Despite the deadly intent of the authorities and their
complete unscrupulousness (Mt emphasizes from the
beginning that they seek *false* testimony), no convincing
witnesses can be found. All the false witnesses who come
forward trip over one another's testimony. Finally, however, *two* witnesses (two is the minimum number required
for probative testimony) arise who claim that Jesus said
he could destroy the temple of God and build it in three
days. Interestingly the only place in the gospels where
Jesus says something like this is Jn 2:19 ("Destroy this
temple and in three days I will raise it up"). Mt changes
Mk's wording of the statement to make it perfectly true and
to focus upon the power of Jesus (instead of Mk's "I shall
destroy," Mt has "I *can* destroy"). Therefore, Mt, unlike
Mk, does not call the two witnesses "false" or say that
their witness did not agree. Though their motives may be
evil, they are speaking the truth about Jesus; the irony is

almost Johannine. Jesus will precipitate judgment on the temple, beginning at his death (27:51) and culminating in A.D. 70 (22:7; 24:2).

When the high priest asks Jesus' reaction to this testimony, Jesus, like the suffering servant (Is 53:7) remains silent. But the high priest insists; he places Jesus under oath, adjuring him solemnly with the liturgical-sounding title "of the living God" (recalling 16:16). The question, "are you the Christ, the Son of God" (contrast Mk's reverent "Son of the Blessed One") likewise recalls Peter's profession of faith in 16:16. What Peter affirmed with partial faith, the high priest now asks in total disbelief. Taking into account the disbelief and the erroneous political conception of the titles "Christ" and "Son," Jesus does not answer directly, but rather gives a veiled "yes" with the ambiguous phrase, "you said it—not I" (cf. comment on the same answer, given to Judas in 26:25; cf. also Mk's more straightforward "I am"). The indirect answer may also be connected with Jesus' rejection of all oaths (5:33-37). Jesus then explains why the conceptions of the high priest are inadequate and what titles and concepts he prefers. "But I tell you [*plēn*, 'but,' a strong adversative; the whole introductory phrase is added by Mt], hereafter [*ap' arti*, i.e., from the decisive and imminent moment of the death-resurrection] you will see [this is primarily addressed to the believing church, not the Sanhedrin] the Son of Man seated at the right hand of Power [i.e., in the place of favor beside God and sharing his rule; cf. Ps 110:1] and coming on the clouds of heaven [Dan 7:13-14]." As at Caesarea Philippi, someone addresses the titles Christ and Son of God to Jesus; and Jesus, while not rejecting those titles, emphasizes that they need to be completed by another title, Son of Man. With Peter, the title is meant to supply the missing element of the cross. With the high priest, who is quite sure Jesus will die, the title supplies the missing element of exaltation out of death, cosmic rule, and coming as final judge. All this will be realized, at least proleptically, in 28:16-20. The captive who stands bound and powerless before the supreme tribunal of Israel claims that soon he will be exalted to divine, omnipotent status. This scene's close connections with the temptation narrative, the Caesarea-Philippi pericope, and the final pericope of the gospel should remind us that we have here not a newspaper report of a trial, but a theological statement by the evangelist about the ultimate meaning of Jesus' condemnation and death.

Jesus' claim causes the high priest to state immediately, before he even consults his confreres, that Jesus has committed blasphemy (contrast Mk). The rending of garments, originally a sign of sorrow, became in Judaism a sign of indignation at blasphemous words or acts. The Sanhedrin agrees that he deserves the death penalty (cf. Jer 26:1-19, where Jeremiah is said to deserve death for prophesying that the temple would be destroyed). Ill treatment (spitting, striking, slapping, mocking; cf. Is 50:6) immediately follows at the hand of, ostensibly, the Sanhedrin (contrast Mk). Since Mt mentions no blindfold, the demand that Jesus prophesy is apparently a challenge to identify the names of the individuals who strike him. Mt uses this scene of mockery to show that the Jews as well as the pagans (27:27-31) mistreated Jesus.

(3) A Disciple Denies and Repents.
26:69-75.
[Mk 14:66-72; Lk 22:56-62]

> 69Now Peter was sitting outside in the courtyard. And a maid came up to him, and said, "You also were with Jesus the Galilean." 70But he denied it before them all, saying, "I do not know what you mean." 71And when he went out to the porch, another maid saw him, and she said to the bystanders, "This man was with Jesus of Nazareth." 72And again he denied it with an oath. "I do not know the man." 73After a little while the bystanders came up and said to Peter, "Certainly you are also one of them,

for your accent betrays you." [74]Then he began to invoke a curse on himself and to swear, "I do not know the man." And immediately the cock crowed. [75]And Peter remembered the saying of Jesus, "Before the cock crows, you will deny me three times." And he went out and wept bitterly.

Mt follows Mk, with some minor changes. Mk lists the accusers as a maid, the same maid, and the bystanders. Mt distinguishes between two different maids; the second maid points out Peter to the bystanders in the large gateway (RSV: "porch"), and then the bystanders make the third accusation. Mt begins the pericope with Peter sitting in the courtyard in front of the room in which the trial is taking place. The contrast between Jesus who openly proclaims the truth about himself and Peter who denies the truth about his relationship with Jesus is obvious. The first maid articulates the basic point at stake in the denials: being *with* Jesus, belonging to him as a disciple. Mt introduces the mention of Jesus the *Galilean*, to prepare for the accusation in v.73. Peter denies his fellowship with Jesus before all (cf. 10:32-33) by claiming that he does not know what the girl is talking about. The second accusation, which again speaks of "being *with*," designates Jesus as the "Nazorean" (RSV: "of Nazareth"), thus harking back to the end of the infancy narrative (2:23). This time, Peter violates Jesus' prohibition of oaths (5:33-37) by strengthening his denial with an oath. He claims he does not even know the man. Notice the more serious form of denial here: from claiming he does not understand what the first maid was saying, Peter now explicitly states that he does not know Jesus. The bystanders make the final accusation: Peter obviously belongs to the group of Jesus' disciples, since he too is a Galilean, as is plain from the type of Aramaic he speaks (Galilean Aramaic differed from Judean Aramaic in some word-formations and also in pronunciation). Peter's denial reaches a crescendo; his denial that he knows Jesus is strengthened not only with an oath but also with a curse (most probably on himself, though possibly on Jesus). Immediately Jesus' prophecy is verified: a cock crows (cf. 26:34). Over against Mk's puzzling ending, Mt agrees with Lk: Peter goes outside the gateway and weeps bitterly, indicating immediate repentance.

While this scene of weakness and sin is meant to be a warning to all disciples, and especially church leaders, it also contains a word of encouragement. Despite the grave warning of final rejection in 10:32-33, God's mercy is always ready to forgive the weak denier, if he repents (cf. 9:12-13). While Peter's weakness contrasts unfavorably with Jesus' courage, it contrasts favorably with Judas' despair (27:3-10).

II. FROM FRIDAY MORNING TO SATURDAY. 27:1-66.

A. THE ROMAN TRIAL. 27:1-31.

(1) Jesus Delivered to Pilate. 27:1-2. [Mk 15:1; Lk 23:1]

> **27** When morning came, all the chief priests and the elders of the people took counsel against Jesus to put him to death; ²and they bound him and led him away and delivered him to Pilate the governor.

EARLY IN THE MORNING on Friday (note the inclusion with v.57, "when it was evening"), the whole Sanhedrin "reached an official decision" to put Jesus to death (this is a better translation than the RSV's "took counsel"). This may mean that, more clearly than Mk, Mt distinguishes the questioning and preliminary decision of the night session from a final decision reached at a separate morning session. More likely, however, Mt means that the lengthy trial extended through the night into the early morning, when the final decision was reached. The first verse of chap. 27 thus resumes the story of the trial, after the aside about the denial of Peter. The members of the Sanhedrin hand Jesus over (*paredōkan*) to Pilate, just as Judas "handed over" Jesus (the same verb is translated as "betrayed") to them. The third passion prediction is thus literally fulfilled: "the Son of Man will be *handed over* to the chief priests and scribes, and they will condemn him to death, and they will *hand him over* to the Gentiles" (20:18-19). Mt describes Pilate here and throughout chap. 27 with the general term *hēgemōn* (RSV: "governor"), a word which puts the emphasis on his military power. A recently discovered inscription from Caesarea Maritima shows that Pontius Pilate held the title of prefect, not procurator; he governed from A.D. 26 to 36.

(2) A Disciple Despairs and Commits Suicide. 27:3-10.

³When Judas, his betrayer, saw that he was condemned, he repented and brought back the thirty pieces of silver to the chief priests and the elders, ⁴saying, "I have sinned in betraying innocent blood." They said, "What is that to us? See to it yourself." ⁵And throwing down the pieces of silver in the temple, he departed; and he went and hanged himself. ⁶But the chief priests, taking the pieces of silver, said, "It is not lawful to put them into the treasury, since they are blood money." ⁷So they took counsel, and bought with them the potter's field, to bury strangers in. ⁸Therefore that field has been called the Field of Blood to this day. ⁹Then was fulfilled what had been spoken by the prophet Jeremiah, saying, "And they took the thirty pieces of silver, the price of him on whom a price had been set by some of the sons of Israel, ¹⁰and they gave them for the potter's field, as the Lord directed me."

In this pericope, the first major insertion by Mt into the passion narrative, Mt develops a number of themes: the prophetic knowledge of Jesus is confirmed (cf. 26:24); the transfer of the blood money to the leaders emphasizes their responsibility for Jesus' death; and, even in the tragedy of

Judas' acts of betrayal and suicide, God's will as expressed in the OT is mysteriously fulfilled.

Mt alone among the evangelists speaks of the fate of the betrayer. Acts 1:15-20 contains a somewhat similar tradition, though with a number of variations: Judas himself buys the field and dies on it, apparently by some accidental fall; the "field of blood" in Acts thus refers to Judas' blood. The similarities in the two stories suggest that Mt has not simply invented his version; rather, he has reformulated a legend from the oral tradition with an eye to certain passages of the OT prophets. A clear contrast is intended between Peter and Judas. As the night session occasioned Peter's denial and then his repentance, so the final decision in the early morning occasions Judas' regret and suicide (v.3 harks back to v.1). Judas is thought of as remaining near the scene of the trial; when he hears of the outcome, he "feels remorse" (Greek: *metamelētheis*, not the usual NT verb for repent, *metanoeō*). Trying to undo his crime and its results, he brings back the money and proclaims his sin and Jesus' innocence (the latter being a theme of chap. 27; cf. v.19).

Judas' confession would result in at least a new trial, if justice were of interest to the leaders. But it is not; they wanted to get Jesus, not justice. They tell Judas that his guilty conscience does not concern them; it is his affair (cf. Pilate's reiteration of these sentiments to the Jews in v.24). Judas throws the money in the temple (Zech 11:12-13 is already having its effect on the narrative) and then hangs himself. The allusion is probably to Ahithophel, who betrayed King David for Absalom and then hanged himself when he lost favor with Absalom (2 Sam 17:23). Judas thus fulfills the command of Scripture which the Sanhedrin refuses to observe: a false accuser must suffer the same fate as the falsely accused. The hypocritical priests, having engineered a major miscarriage of justice, suddenly become very scrupulous about the use of the money (cf. 23:23-24). Although various forms of ill-gotten gain were prohibited from use in the temple (cf. Dt 23:18), nothing in the OT covers this exact case. But, to be on the safe side, they use the money to buy a field as a cemetery for "strangers" (probably Gentiles visiting Jerusalem); the unclean money is used to bury unclean people in an unclean place. Mt then tells us that there is a field called the Field of Blood even at his time (Acts 1:19 supplies the Aramaic name, Hakeldama). Later tradition locates this field to the southeast of Jerusalem, at the eastern end of the valley Hinnom ("Gehenna").

Mt then appends the last of his formula citations. Like the one attached to the story of the slaughter of the innocents (2:17), it avoids appealing to the direct intention of God ("in order that . . .") and instead narrates the brute fact ("then was fulfilled . . ."). As in 2:17, Jeremiah, the prophet of national tragedy and judgment, is named, even though the bulk of the citation is from Zech 11:12-13 (cf. Mt 26:14-15). The mention of the potter and the buying of a field may be allusions to Jer 19:1-13 or 32:6-9, or less likely, 18:2-3. In view of Mt's sovereign freedom in reworking and combining OT citations to make them fit NT events, an appeal to a lost apocryphal work of Jeremiah is unnecessary.

(3) Jesus on Trial before Pilate.
27:11-26.
[Mk 15:2-15; Lk 23:1-25]

> [11]Now Jesus stood before the governor; and the governor asked him, "Are you the King of the Jews?" Jesus said, "You have said so." [12]But when he was accused by the chief priests and elders, he made no answer. [13]Then Pilate said to him, "Do you not hear how many things they testify against you?" [14]But he gave him no answer, not even to a single charge; so that the governor wondered greatly.
>
> [15]Now at the feast the governor was accustomed to release for the crowd any one prisoner whom they wanted.

¹⁶And they had then a notorious prisoner, called Barabbas. ¹⁷So when they had gathered, Pilate said to them, "Whom do you want me to release for you, Barabbas or Jesus who is called Christ?" ¹⁸For he knew that it was out of envy that they had delivered him up. ¹⁹Besides, while he was sitting on the judgment seat, his wife sent word to him, "Have nothing to do with that righteous man, for I have suffered much over him today in a dream." ²⁰Now the chief priests and the elders persuaded the people to ask for Barabbas and destroy Jesus. ²¹The governor again said to them, "Which of the two do you want me to release for you?" And they said, "Barabbas." ²²Pilate said to them, "Then what shall I do with Jesus who is called Christ?" They all said, "Let him be crucified," ²³And he said, "Why, what evil has he done?" But they shouted all the more, "Let him be crucified."

²⁴So when Pilate saw that he was gaining nothing, but rather that a riot was beginning, he took water and washed his hands before the crowd, saying, "I am innocent of this man's blood; see to it yourselves." ²⁵And all the people answered, "His blood be on us and on our children!" ²⁶Then he released for them Barabbas, and having scourged Jesus, delivered him to be crucified.

The scene before Pilate can be divided into three parts: (1) the interrogation (vv.11-14); (2) Jesus and Barabbas (vv.15-23); (3) the condemnation (vv.24-26). Mt follows Mk, but makes three important insertions: the dream of Pilate's wife, Pilate's washing of his hands, and the cry of "all the people." The whole scene emphasizes the innocence of Jesus and the guilt of his people.

In v.11, Mt resumes the main line of narrative after the interlude of Judas' suicide. Before the Sanhedrin Jesus had confessed in a veiled fashion that he was the Christ (26:63-64). This title, equivalent to King of Israel (27:42), becomes in the mouth of a non-Jew, "King of the Jews" (2:2; 27:29,37). It also heightens the political overtones of the title, a useful point as the case is brought before the Roman prefect; to claim political kingship was treason, a capital offense. As in the case of Judas and Caiaphas, Jesus refuses to answer directly; the ambiguous "you said it—not I" both affirms Jesus' true messiahship and denies the worldly, political connotations. Jesus will say nothing further to the charges of the Jewish leaders. Both his silence and Pilate's amazement may echo the fourth song of the suffering servant (Is 53:7; 52:15). Just as Jesus has previously directed the course of the passion by his words, so now he directs its course by his silence.

Mt obviously means to contrast Jesus the true Son with Barabbas, whose name in Aramaic means Son of the Father. Some later scribes carried the contrast further by giving Barabbas the name of Jesus as well, but the manuscript evidence is too weak and the desire to heighten the parallel too obvious to accept the reading as original. Since Pilate knows that Jesus' only crime is arousing envy in the religious leaders, he seizes the initiative (contrast Mk 15:8) and invokes a custom of amnesty supposedly practiced at Passover. No proof of such a custom in Palestine can be found outside of our gospels, though similar customs are attested elsewhere. Barabbas was "notorious" to the Romans, "famous" (the same Greek adjective can have both meanings) to the Jews. Though Mt omits Mk's explanation that Barabbas was an insurgent and murderer, he probably presupposes the information as known to his audience. Mt conceives Judaism standing at the crossroads of its history; will it choose the genuine spiritual Messiah or the illusory promise of political liberation?

Mt inserts an interlude at this point, both to give the leaders time to persuade the crowds and to emphasize the innocence of Jesus. The insertion may come from an oral legend which circulated in Mt's church. Pilate's wife has had a disturbing dream "today" (i.e., last night) which warned against becoming involved with this "just" (RSV: "righteous") man. In the mouth of Pilate's wife, "just" may simply mean "innocent"; Christian readers, however, would be reminded of the psalms of the suffering just man, one of the main OT backgrounds to the passion narrative. The motif of the monitory dream (1:20; 2:12,13,19,22) together with the title King of the Jews (2:2) and the adjective "just" (1:19), harks back to the infancy narrative, the proleptic passion narrative. With these motifs Mt has created still another contrast: while Pilate is admonished (ultimately by God) to see justice done by saving Jesus, the Jewish leaders urge the crowds (*not* "the people" of the RSV) to pervert justice by destroying Jesus. The flow of the narrative is resumed in v.21, with Pilate posing the choice and the crowds choosing Barabbas. When Pilate asks about the fate of their supposed Messiah, they call for the brutal Roman form of execution, crucifixion. While Mk has them commanding Pilate to crucify Jesus, Mt puts the command in the passive voice, emphasizing the responsibility of the crowds. When Pilate asks for reasons, the crowds give him louder screams.

Seeing that his attempts to rescue Jesus are only inciting to riot, Pilate caves in, preferring peace to justice. In an attempt to transfer all responsibility to the crowds, Pilate washes his hands and solemnly declares his innocence as regards the taking of Jesus' life ("blood"). The hand-washing ritual recalls the strange rite of Dt 21:6-8, prescribed in the case of homicide when the perpetrator is unknown (cf. also Ps 26:6-10; Is 1:15-17). The fact that a Roman prefect voluntarily undertakes the rite makes the historicity of the incident doubtful. With the same words that the priests addressed to Judas (27:4) Pilate tells the crowds that the crucifixion of Jesus is their business, not his. At this point, Mt suddenly stops speaking of chief priests, elders, and crowds; "all the people," i.e., the whole people of Israel, the covenant-people of God, take upon themselves and their children forever the responsibility for Jesus' death. One must read this verse, of course, as a reflection of the debate between Pharisaic Judaism and Mt's church over the question of who constituted the true people of God. What Jesus had prophesied in 21:43 is now beginning to take place. The death-resurrection marks the end of Israel as the people of God and the founding of the church as the new people of God, the people whom Jesus will save "from their sins" (1:21). Writing after A.D. 70, Mt sees the self-inflicted curse of 27:25 visibly fulfilled in the disaster of the Jewish War and the destruction of Jerusalem. The Jews choose Barabbas and the Zealot party instead of Jesus the meek and lowly King; Mt sees in the destruction of Jerusalem the ultimate result of that fatal choice. What Jesus had foretold in 23:35-36 has proven true: "upon you shall come all the *righteous blood* shed on earth . . . . Amen I say to you, all this will come upon this generation."

As soon as the people express their willingness to accept responsibility, Pilate releases Barabbas. Jesus he has scourged—a normal procedure prior to crucifixion (notice how the evangelists do not dwell on the brutal elements of the passion for their own sake). Then Pilate hands Jesus over (*paredōken*) to the Jews for crucifixion. The third passion prediction (20:18-19) is thus fulfilled, although Mt adds an extra "handing over," which shifts responsibility for the crucifixion back to the Jews. No doubt Mt does not consider the weak Pilate to be absolved of all guilt; his dereliction of duty is damnable in its own way. But Mt is more concerned with the implications of the scene for salvation history and ecclesiology.

(4) Jesus Mocked by Gentile Soldiers.
27:27-31.
[*Mk 15:16-20*]

> [27]Then the soldiers of the governor took Jesus into the praetorium, and they gathered the whole battalion before him. [28]And they stripped him and put a scarlet robe upon him, [29]and plaiting a crown of thorns they put it on his head, and put a reed in his right hand. And kneeling

before him they mocked him, saying, "Hail, King of the Jews!" [30]And they spat upon him, and took the reed and struck him on the head. [31]And when they had mocked him, they stripped him of the robe, and put his own clothes on him, and led him away to crucify him.

Mt tightens up Mk's scene, and provides a few changes and additions. The emphasis is neither on the agony of the scourging (which is not even mentioned here) nor on the pain caused by the crown of thorns, but rather on the mockery, which ironically proclaims the truth of who Jesus is: King, not only of Jews, but of Gentiles as well. The soldiers take Jesus into the interior of the praetorium, the official residence of the Roman prefect. The prefect normally resided at Caesarea Maritima, on the Mediterranean coast; he took up residence in Jerusalem only during the great feasts, when there would be a danger of riot from the large crowds. Whether Pilate's praetorium was the Palace of Herod in western Jerusalem or the fortress Antonia to the northwest of the temple area, is still disputed. Mt, like Mk, speaks of the whole cohort or battalion, which at full strength numbered 600 men; no doubt only a portion of it is meant here. Instead of Mk's unlikely "purple" cloak (the color worn by the emperor), Mt has the soldiers use a scarlet cloak, such as any soldier would have available. The crown of thorns was intended not so much to cause physical pain as to mock Jesus' royal claim. The thorns were meant to imitate the rays of light which radiated from the head of a divinity, symbolized in the pointed edges of a king's diadem. Mt adds a reed in Jesus' right hand as a mock-scepter. They kneel as suppliants and greet him with the same *chaire* ("hail") that Judas used (26:49). The Gentile soldiers, who had fought and deeply hated Jews, can think of no more derogatory title for this helpless, tortured prisoner than King of the Jews. Yet it will be Roman soldiers who will be shaken into faith by the apocalyptic events at the cross (27:54), and it will be to such Gentiles that the crucified and risen Jesus will send the eleven (28:16-20). The theme of Gentiles coming into contact with the King of the Jews again harks back to the infancy narrative. Mt's church sees in this scene of mockery a deeper, ironic truth: by his death-resurrection, Jesus indeed becomes divine cosmocrator, receiving the worship of both Jews and Gentiles. At the end of the pericope, two facts are mentioned in preparation for the scenes at the cross. The soldiers clothe Jesus in his own garments, thus preparing for the dividing of his garments in v.35. And, despite the fact that Pilate has handed over Jesus to the Jews, the actual execution is carried out by Gentile soldiers, thus preparing for their confession of faith in v.54.

B. THE CRUCIFIXION OF THE SON OF GOD. 27:32-44.
[Mk 15:21-32; Lk 23:33-43]

> [32]As they went out, they came upon a man of Cyrene, Simon by name; this man they compelled to carry his cross. [33]And when they came to a place called Golgotha (which means the place of a skull), [34]they offered him wine to drink, mingled with gall; but when he tasted it, he would not drink it. [35]And when they had crucified him, they divided his garments among them by casting lots; [36]then they sat down and kept watch over him there. [37]And over his head they put the charge against him, which read, "This is Jesus the King of the Jews." [38]Then two robbers were crucified with him, one on the right and one on the left. [39]And those who passed by derided him, wagging their heads [40]and saying, "You who would destroy the temple and build it in three days, save yourself! If you are the Son of God, come down from the cross." [41]So also the chief priests, with the scribes and elders, mocked him, saying, [42]"He saved others; he cannot save himself. He is the King of Israel; let him come down from the cross, and we will believe in him. [43]He trusts

in God; let God deliver him now, if he desires him; for he said, 'I am the Son of God.'" [44]And the robbers who were crucified with him also reviled him in the same way.

Mt skillfully weaves together in this section the title "King" which has occupied the first half of chap. 27, with the transcendent title Son of God, which again harks back to the infancy narrative, and even more so, to the temptation narrative.

The soldiers are said to "come out" of the city, thus fulfilling Jesus' prophecy in the parable of the tenant farmers (21:39—first they cast the son *out of* the vineyard, then they kill him). Since Simon of Cyrene was not especially known to Mt (contrast Mk, who can name Simon's two sons), Mt mentions him only in passing. Simon would have carried only the transverse bar of the cross; the vertical pole would have remained fixed in the ground at Golgotha. Why the place of execution is called Golgotha, "skull-place," is never explained by the evangelists. Perhaps it is a general reference to death and corpses. Possibly it refers to the shape of the hill, but Golgotha is never said to be a hill in the NT. Instead of Mk's wine mixed with myrrh (a narcotic to kill the pain), Mt alludes to Ps 69:21 ("they gave me poison [in the Greek: gall] for food, and for my thirst they gave me vinegar to drink"). The second half of this verse is alluded to in v.48; the whole of the crucifixion is thus framed with the themes of the fulfillment of Scripture and of the suffering just man. After he tastes the drink, Jesus refuses it, either because he rejects the mockery intended or because he does not wish to be drugged by a narcotic. In either case, Jesus retains control of events— even the events of his execution.

As with the scourging so with the crucifixion, the brutal event itself is narrated only in passing, with a participle. Crucifixion was originally a Persian form of punishment; the Romans adopted it, not for Roman citizens, but for rebels, slaves, and bandits. It was the most shameful as well as the most painful of deaths. The garments of an executed man fell to the executioners as booty, but Mt naturally sees the fulfillment of Ps 22:18. Although Mt uses the very words of the psalm, he does not make of it a formula quotation, a reminder that the whole passion lies under the quotation-like statements of Jesus in 26:54,56: "*All of this* has taken place that the scriptures of the prophets might be fulfilled." Mt adds at this point that the executioners also act as the soldiers standing watch over the crucified. While this may indicate an apologetic desire to guarantee the real death of Jesus, the major point is that the sinful Gentiles who scourged, mocked, and crucified Jesus also become the first Gentile believers in Jesus as the Son of God (v.54). Mt follows Mk in mentioning the inscription proclaiming the crime which is being punished; to Mk's bald "King of the Jews," Mt prefixes, "this is Jesus." The derisive proclamation speaks an ironic truth: Jesus *is* King, and becomes so fully by his death-resurrection. The two robbers are placed on either side of Jesus, perhaps as mock royal attendants, perhaps to make of Jesus the head robber.

The Jews quickly react to their crucified King. First the passersby imitate the mocking gestures recorded in Ps 22:7 and hurl in Jesus' face the mighty claim attributed to him during the Jewish trial—although they omit the "I *can*" (26:61). The powerful Messiah has no power to save himself. Mt adds to the challenge in Mk: "if you are God's Son." This condition echoes the challenge of the devil in the temptation narrative (4:3,6). In both cases, unbelievers interpret sonship to mean a power which guarantees painless success, power which can be exploited for one's own advantage, not the advantage of others. In both cases, Jesus shows that true sonship is a matter of trust in and obedience to the Father, even when faced with the mystery of suffering and death. The whole Sanhedrin (Mt adds the elders to the priests and scribes of Mk) takes up the insulting chant, though in the third rather than the second person.

The one who healed so many others and even raised the dead cannot save himself from death. Instead of King of the Jews the Jews naturally speak of the King of Israel. Typically, the leaders demand a miracle (12:38; 16:1) to authenticate this King and to make belief in him a reasonable act.

The derisive reference to Jesus' trust in God and vain hope of deliverance is a literal citation of Ps 22:8. The addition of "for he said, 'I am the Son of God,'" probably reflects Wis 2:11-20, which is something of a reflective reinterpretation of Ps 22. In Wis 2, the just man is felt to be a reproach to the wicked, who therefore condemn him to a shameful death to test him. For, if the just man be truly God's son, God will rescue him. The weaving together of the suffering just man with Son of God fits Mt's theology perfectly. The enemies of Jesus see his sufferings as a proof that he is not God's Son; Mt sees them as a proof that he is. It would have been human to come down from the cross; it was divine to hang there. The Jewish leaders do not realize that they are only the tools of the great Adversary of Jesus, who tested Jesus' sonship in the same way in the temptation narrative. They are taking part in "the last temptation of Christ." Unwittingly, they are playing Satan to Jesus, as did Peter (16:23), who likewise rejected the idea of a crucified Son of God. Completing the group of mockers, and emphasizing Jesus' total isolation, the robbers also "revile" their comrade in pain; the word "reviled" probably alludes to Ps 69:9. Even in the abyss of suffering and abandonment, the will of God, as foretold in Scripture, is being fulfilled.

C. JESUS DIES TO RAISE HUMANITY TO LIFE. 27:45-54.

(1) Prayer and Death.
27:45-50.
[Mk 15:33-37; Lk 23:44-46]

> ⁴⁵Now from the sixth hour there was darkness over all the land until the ninth hour. ⁴⁶And about the ninth hour

Jesus cried with a loud voice, "Eli, Eli, lama sabach-thani?" that is, "My God, my God, why hast thou for-saken me?" [47] And some of the bystanders hearing it said, "This man is calling Elijah." [48] And one of them at once ran and took a sponge, filled it with vinegar, and put it on a reed, and gave it to him to drink. [49] But the others said, "Wait, let us see whether Elijah will come to save him." [50] And Jesus cried again with a loud voice and yielded up his spirit.

Mt follows Mk fairly closely. While he has omitted Mk's statement that the crucifixion took place at the third hour (nine A.M.; Mk 15:25), Mt keeps the darkness "over all the land" from noon to three P.M. The darkness is a prophetic and apocalyptic motif, expressing God's wrath on his great day of judgment (cf. Amos 8:9). There may also be a reference to the plague of darkness "over the whole land of Egypt" (Ex 10:22). Around three P.M. it seems as though the darkness has encompassed Jesus' soul as well. Using the initial words of Ps 22, which has supplied a number of motifs in the previous scenes, Jesus expresses his sense of abandonment by God, despite the fact that he will not abandon hope in God. One must avoid two extremes here. On the one hand, we should not indulge in the pulpit rhetoric or contemporary existentialistic interpretation which sees Jesus as falling into momentary atheism. Ps 22 is typical of those psalms of lament in the OT which begin on a note of desperation and end on a note of joy and thanksgiving. The psalmist dares to protest so vehemently to God precisely because he trusts his basic relationship with God; the psalms end with a vindication of that trust. Ps 22 would be especially well known to pious Jews and would readily come to their lips in moments of great distress. Knowing as they would the way the psalm ends, they would not mistake its initial cry for the despair of an atheist. On the other hand, we should not think of Jesus as though he were disinterestedly saying the breviary on the cross. His pain and anguish are real, and his use of the psalm is heart-felt. It is by holding fast to the mysterious will of his Father even in the midst of such terrible suffering that he proves his sonship.

Mt cites the initial word *Eli* ("my God") in Hebrew, though the citation then continues in Aramaic. Mk has the more Aramaic form of *Eloi, Eloi*. Some of the bystanders mistakenly understand *Eli* to be an appeal for help from the prophet Elijah. Elijah was taken up to heaven in a whirlwind (2 Kings 2:9-12) and Jews believed he would return before the end-time to aid Israel. One of the bystanders, trying to keep Jesus alive in case Elijah does miraculously come to save him (cf. the theme of "save" in vv. 40,42), attempts to offer Jesus a sop of cheap sour wine or vinegar. Mt no doubt sees the fulfillment of the second half of Ps 69:21 (cf. comment on Mt 27:34). The other bystanders discourage their companion, telling him not to give the drink until they see Elijah coming. (Mk's version of the offer of vinegar is somewhat different. The man offering the drink says to the bystanders, "Wait, let us see whether Elijah will come." In Mk, the "wait" means not "do not do that," as in Mt, but rather "do not hinder me" in preventing his death and giving Elijah an opportunity to come.) In the midst of this puerile argument, Jesus cries out again and "yields up his spirit" (*aphēken to pneuma*, a more refined phrase than Mk's *exepneusen*, "expired"). As in Mk, the loud cry is unusual, since crucified people usually died slowly of asphyxiation. Perhaps Mt intends to say that, even in his death, Jesus exercised sovereign control over the flow of events; the cry is a cry of victory, not of defeat.

(2) The Apocalyptic Events at the Death of Jesus.
27:51-54.
[*Mk 15:38-39; Lk 23:45,47*]

> 51And behold, the curtain of the temple was torn in two, from top to bottom; and the earth shook, and the

rocks were split; [52]the tombs also were opened, and many bodies of the saints who had fallen asleep were raised, [53]and coming out of the tombs after his resurrection they went into the holy city and appeared to many. [54]When the centurion and those who were with him, keeping watch over Jesus, saw the earthquake and what took place, they were filled with awe, and said, "Truly this was the Son of God!"

As so often in his redaction of the passion narrative, Mt takes his cue from Mk. Mk had already invested the death of Jesus with apocalyptic tones by mentioning the darkness at noon and the rending of the temple veil. Mt expands upon these motifs; in fact, in Mt, we should not speak of apocalyptic "signs" but apocalyptic events, which proclaim that the turning-point of the ages, the definitive breaking-in of the kingdom, has occurred.

The astounding events in vv.51-54 make four basic affirmations. (1) Mt 27:51a repeats Mk 15:38. The exact significance of the rending of the curtain in the temple is disputed. In fact, it is not clear which curtain is meant—the one before the Holy Place or the one before the Holy of Holies—though the second is more likely. The rending of the veil may mean that all people (cf. 28:19) now have free access to God through the sacrifice of Jesus (cf. Heb 9:3; 10:20). In addition, there may be an allusion to the destruction of the temple in A.D. 70 as punishment for the death of Jesus, or the cessation of temple cult precisely as a result of Jesus' death. All these suggestions have one thing in common: the death of Jesus in some way puts an end to the sacrificial cult of the temple. According to a rabbinic saying, the world was built on three foundations: on Law, on (cultic) worship, and on deeds of kindness. Now one of the props of the old world is being pulled out, at least in principle, at the death of Jesus.

(2) Mt 27:51b is a Matthean addition. The earthquake, a common theme of theophany in OT (Judg 5:4; 2 Sam 22:8;

Ps 68:8), the later apocalyptic literature, and the rabbis, is inserted into Markan material in a number of places by Mt (cf 8:24; 28:2; 21:10). This "shaking of the foundations" of the old creation signifies God's judgment on the old age and the powerful breaking-in of his kingdom. The earthquake in 27:51 sets off a chain reaction: the earthquake splits the rocks, the splitting of the rocks opens the tombs, and the opening of the tombs allows the dead to come forth. The passive voice of the verbs indicates that God is the agent.

(3) Mt 27:52-53 depicts the resurrection of the dead as taking place proleptically at the death of Christ. Some commentators suggest that, in the oral tradition, this scene was connected with the resurrection of Jesus and that, when Mt moved this general resurrection back to the death of Jesus, he inserted the awkward phrase "after his resurrection" (to be read probably with "went into the holy city") to keep the primacy of Christ as the "first fruits of the dead" (cf. 1 Cor 15:20). Be that as it may, the fact is that Mt presents the death of Jesus as life-giving; the dead rise at the cross of Christ, thus fulfilling the promise of God in Ezek 37:12: "O my people, I will open your graves and raise you from your graves." Mt carefully connects the death of Jesus with his resurrection by the twin motifs of earthquake (28:2) and resurrection. We may speak of the death-resurrection in Mt as one great eschatological event which ushers in a new age, the age of the church (28:16-20).

(4) Mt 27:54 rejoins Mk 15:39, but with a significant addition. Mk has only the centurion confessing Jesus as Son of God, and he does this when he sees how Jesus dies. Mt says that the centurion and *those with him standing guard over Jesus* see the apocalyptic events and are moved with holy fear to make the Easter confession of faith: "Truly this [omitting Mk's 'man'] was the Son of God." This is the same confession of faith that the disciples make in 14:33. The missionary mandate of the risen Lord in 28:16-20 is thus proleptically realized: the Gentiles are becoming disciples—the very Gentiles who mocked Jesus as King of

the Jews, crucified him, and divided his garments. They
believe in that sonship which a few minutes ago was being
mocked. There *is* a wideness in God's mercy (cf. 9:10-13).

D. BURIAL AS PREPARATION FOR RESURRECTION.
27:55-66.

(1) The Women as Witnesses.
27:55-56.
[*Mk 15:40-41; Lk 23:49*]

> ⁵⁵There were also many women there, looking on from
> afar, who had followed Jesus from Galilee, ministering
> to him; ⁵⁶among whom were Mary Magdalene, and Mary
> the mother of James and Joseph, and the mother of the
> sons of Zebedee.

This pericope and the following two are not so much a
continuation of the narrative of the death of Jesus as a
preparation for the resurrection narratives of chap. 28.
All the male disciples of Jesus had abandoned him in
Gethsemane. In contrast to them and to the jeering crowds,
faithful women who had followed Jesus *from* Galilee (contrast Mk's *in* Galilee) and had served him on the road up
to Jerusalem and his cross attend him even at the cross. All
they can do is "look on from afar," a phrase expressing
their helplessness and his isolation, and also perhaps
alluding to Ps 38:11 ("My friends and my companions . . .
and my kinsmen stand afar off"). Yet their "looking" or
"seeing" (*theōrousai*) serves a deeper function, especially
in the case of Mary Magdalene and Mary the mother of
James and Joseph. They are the witnesses who see not only
the death, but also the burial in the tomb (27:61), the empty
tomb on Sunday morning (28:1), and finally the risen Jesus
(28:8-10). We should note in particular that in 28:1 the same
verb is used as in 27:55: they come to "see" (*theoresai*) the

tomb. Thus, the short pericope of 27:55-56 not only rounds off the narrative of Jesus' death but also, and more importantly, prepares for the good news of the resurrection.

The names of the women differ slightly in the various Greek manuscripts. The situation becomes more complicated if, with some commentators, we read four women in Mk 15:40: Mary Magdalene, Mary (the daughter or wife?) of James the Small, the mother of Joses, and Salome. If Mt understood Mk in this way, he consciously conflated the references to the second and third women. If, however, one follows the RSV in reading only three women at Mk 15:40, the problem disappears. Mt also replaces the obscure Salome with the mother of the sons of Zebedee (cf. Mt 20:20); despite the opinion of some commentators, there are no solid grounds for identifying the two women.

(2) Jesus Is Buried by Joseph of Arimathea.
27:57-61.
[*Mk 15:42-47; Lk 23:50-56*]

> 57When it was evening, there came a rich man from Arimathea, named Joseph, who also was a disciple of Jesus. 58He went to Pilate and asked for the body of Jesus. Then Pilate ordered it to be given to him. 59And Joseph took the body, and wrapped it in a clean linen shroud, 60and laid it in his own new tomb, which he had hewn in the rock; and he rolled a great stone to the door of the tomb, and departed. 61Mary Magdalene and the other Mary were there, sitting opposite the sepulchre.

Mt follows Mk, with some abbreviations and additions. With a time designation simpler than Mk's ("when it was evening" forms an inclusion with "when morning came" in 27:1), Mt indicates that the sabbath, which began at sundown, was fast approaching. To a Jewish mind, corpses, especially the corpses of the crucified, were ritually unclean.

Dt 21:22-23 specified that the corpse of a man hanged on a tree should be buried before sundown. To this end Joseph of Arimathea (possibly a site ten miles northeast of modern Lod) is introduced in v.57, only to depart in v.60, after his task is completed. His quick appearance and disappearance remind us of the unnamed woman who anointed Jesus at the beginning of the passion narrative (26:6-13). Mt does not follow Mk in calling Joseph a respected member of the council (i.e., Sanhedrin), lest he be associated in any way with the sentencing of Jesus to death (contrast the explanation given by Lk 23:51). Joseph instead is called a rich man, a designation which may allude to the fourth song of the suffering servant: "they made his grave with the wicked, and with a rich man in his death" (Is 53:9). While Mk says that Joseph was "waiting for the kingdom of God," and was hence a pious Jew, Mt brings him clearly into the camp of Jesus' followers by making him a disciple of Jesus (cf. the interesting parallel in Jn 19:38).

Mt drops various details of Mk's story (the daring of Joseph, the surprise of Pilate, the summoning of the centurion to certify the death). In narrating Pilate's release of the body to Joseph, Mt avoids Mk's word for corpse (*ptōma*) in favor of "body" (*sōma*). Joseph "took" the body, probably from the soldiers who took it down from the cross; nothing in Mt suggests that Joseph himself removed the body from the cross. Mt adds the details of a *clean* linen shroud and a *new* tomb (i.e., in which no one had yet been laid; cf. Lk 23:53; Jn 19:41); perhaps these elements of ritual purity are meant to offset the ritual impurity of the corpse of a crucified person. Also operative, though, is an apologetic desire to defend the reality of the resurrection. There were many tombs carved in the hillsides around Jerusalem, and a confusion among tombs might be claimed by adversaries of the resurrection. Mt replies that the tomb was that of a well-known rich man, no other body had lain in it, a *great* stone (Mt's addition) was rolled before it, and two women who had seen Jesus die (27:56), and would see the empty tomb (28:1) and the risen Jesus (28:8-10), also saw the precise place where the body was laid. In fact, in the traditional Jewish posture of mourning, they *sat* opposite the tomb to begin the period of grieving for the dead. When they return on Sunday to resume their mourning, they will instead find cause for great joy. The Jesus they saw die will be the same Jesus whom they can once again see, and hear, and feel.

(3) The Jews Set Guards and Seal the Tomb. 27:62-66.

> [62]Next day, that is, after the day of Preparation, the chief priests and the Pharisees gathered before Pilate [63]and said, "Sir, we remember how that impostor said, while he was still alive, 'After three days I will rise again.' [64]Therefore order the sepulchre to be made secure until the third day, lest his disciples go and steal him away, and tell the people, 'He has risen from the dead,' and the last fraud will be worse than the first." [65]Pilate said to them, "You have a guard of soldiers; go, make it as secure as you can." [66]So they went and made the sepulchre secure by sealing the stone and setting a guard.

This story, unique to Mt, reflects the arguments over the resurrection which raged between Jews and Christians in the first century. Apparently the Jews explained the resurrection of Jesus by charging that the disciples had stolen Jesus' body from the tomb. An intriguing point here is that it never occurred to the Jews to claim that the body was still in the tomb on Easter Sunday morning; both sides in the debate agreed that the tomb was empty. Mt's church— the core of the story probably existed before Mt—replied with a charge of its own: that Jewish and Roman military might had conspired to prevent any resurrection and *a fortiori*, any grave-robbery; but God's might defeated men's arms by raising Jesus anyway. The story is therefore a product of Jewish polemics and Christian apologetics, and should not be taken as an eyewitness report of what happened in A.D. 30. In the framework of Mt's gospel, this story, preparing as it does for the resurrection, belongs more with chap. 28 than chap. 27. Indeed, from 27:55 onwards, there is a forward thrust and something of a "leap-frog" effect. The pericope of the women at the cross (27:55-56) leaps over the pericope of the setting of the watch (27:62-66) to introduce the empty tomb story (28:1-8) and the two appearances of Jesus (28:9-10, 16-20). The setting of the watch leaps over the empty tomb story to introduce the story of the lie of the priests and the elders (28:11-15). The reference to the guards at the empty tomb (28:4) provides the linchpin uniting the two blocks of narratives.

The awkward time-reference in v.62 arises from Mt's taking over of "the day of Preparation" from Mk's burial story (Mk 15:42). The circumlocution may also indicate that Mt does not want to stress that the "next day" is the Sabbath, on which all this activity by the priests and the Pharisees would be highly unlikely. Since the Sabbath is not explicitly mentioned here (contrast 28:1), it is questionable whether Mt intends to underline the hypocrisy of the Pharisees in breaking the Sabbath, after they hounded Jesus for that very "crime." The joining of high priests and Pharisees is unusual; perhaps because the denouement of the story will contain a reference to the Judaism of Mt's own day (28:15)—a Judaism controlled by the Pharisees—Mt wishes to place them at the origin of the lie. Some commentators suggest that the Pharisees are placed here so that they can recall the prediction of the resurrection they heard in 12:40. But this is to look for historical probability in a pericope that is noticeably lacking it. When they come to Pilate, the Jewish leaders hide their deeper fears by claiming they fear a grave-robbery and subsequent fraud. This last fraud (the claim of resurrection) will be worse than the first (belief in Jesus' messiahship during his earthly ministry).

The leaders unconsciously echo Jesus' sad prediction about themselves and their contemporaries in 12:45: "and the last state of that man becomes worse than the first; so shall it be also with this evil generation."

As Pilate gave the order in v.58 to bury Jesus, so now he gives the order to set a guard. More likely Pilate assigns the Jews a detachment of Roman soldiers (RSV margin: "take a guard"), though the Greek could also mean: "you have your own guard; use it." The Christian story hints that Pilate doubts whether the Jews will succeed in their effort; note that he adds "as best you know how" (or RSV: "as you can"). The sealing of the stone is reminiscent of the measures taken by the King when Daniel is thrown into the lions' den (Dan 6:17); Jesus can no more be held captive in death by the Jewish leaders than Daniel was by his enemies. Perhaps we have here the origins of the use of the figure of Daniel in the lions' den as a symbol of the crucified and risen Christ; such representations can be seen in the early Christian catacombs of Rome.

III. FROM SUNDAY TO THE END OF THE AGE. 28:1-20.

A. THE APOCALYPTIC EVENTS AT THE TOMB. 28:1-8.
[Mk 16:1-8; Lk 24:1-12]

28 Now after the sabbath, toward the dawn of the first day of the week, Mary Magdalene and the other Mary went to see the sepulchre. ²And behold, there was a great earthquake; for an angel of the Lord descended from heaven and came and rolled back the stone, and sat upon it. ³His appearance was like lightning, and his raiment white as snow. ⁴And for fear of him the guards trembled and became like dead men. ⁵But the angel said to the women, "Do not be afraid; for I know that you seek Jesus who was crucified. ⁶He is not here; for he has risen, as he said. Come, see the place where he lay. ⁷Then go quickly and tell his disciples that he has risen from the dead, and behold, he is going before you to Galilee; there you will see him. Lo, I have told you." ⁸So they departed quickly from the tomb with fear and great joy, and ran to tell his disciples.

The *fact* that Jesus was raised from the dead stood at the center of early Christian preaching (1 Cor 15:4-5; Rom

1:3-4; 4:25). The *manner* and *circumstances* of the resurrection and of the resurrection appearances were not described in the earliest preaching, and so it is not surprising that the evangelists describe the event differently. In the form we have it, the gospel of Mk really ends with the discovery of the empty tomb and the message of the "young man" (Mk 16:1-8). The fact that, after this point, Mt and Lk go their separate ways, as does Jn and the later endings of Mk, shows that there was no normative description of the resurrection appearances. The situation is close to that of the infancy narratives, which also lay outside of the normative pattern of the earliest preaching: certain basic facts were known, but beyond those facts the evangelists were free to pursue their own theological interests. That is why the resurrection appearances, like the infancy narratives, offer a fine opportunity to understand the particular message of each evangelist. In the empty tomb story, Mt basically follows Mk. Nevertheless, he changes the women's reason for coming to the tomb; he omits Mk 16:3-4 as not relevant; he inserts a mention of the guards to tie together two blocks of material (the burial tradition and the guard tradition); he adds various apocalyptic elements; and he changes the women's reaction at the end of the story.

The time designation in v.1 could also mean twilight on Saturday evening, after the Sabbath had ended, but the RSV's translation is probably correct. It would not make much sense for two women to go alone to a tomb outside the city at night, simply to "see" the tomb in the dark and to sit all night in mourning. Mt has reduced the three women of Mk to two, to have the witnesses coincide with those of 27:61. Since the tomb is sealed and guarded by soldiers, Mt cannot say, as Mk does, that the women come to anoint Jesus' body. Rather, resuming the theme of 27:55, they come "to see" the tomb, no doubt to resume their posture of mourning (27:61). They are probably thought of as witnessing the apparition which follows.

In v.2, Mt begins to color the empty tomb tradition with apocalyptic hues. This was no easy task, since it seems to have been an unwritten rule in the early Christian tradition that the resurrection of Jesus was never itself described — probably because no one had seen it. Mt therefore seizes upon the "young man" of Mk as his vehicle for introducing apocalyptic motifs. (For all that follows, one should first consult the comments on 27:51-54, since the apocalyptic motifs in chap. 28 serve to tie together the resurrection with the death as one great eschatological event, the turning of the ages.) Mk's young man becomes "the angel of the Lord," a figure which harks back to the infancy narratives (1:20; 2:13,19). The angel's descent from heaven (not in Mk) is accompanied by an earthquake (cf. 27:51), which announces the shaking of the old world to its foundations as Jesus breaks the bonds of death (cf. 27:52; also Ps 114:7; 76:5-9; Ex 19:18; 1 Kings 19:11). The angel of the Lord — actually, God himself in visible form — performs the mighty act of rolling back the "great" stone (27:60). Then he sits upon the stone in triumph, a perfect symbol of God's triumph over death in the resurrection of Jesus. While this action might be thought of as opening the way for the risen Jesus to leave the tomb invisibly, probably Mt thinks of the tomb as already empty. The rolling back of the stone simply reveals the emptiness of the place of death. The description of the angel in terms of lightning and white confirms him as a stock-figure of apocalyptic (cf. Mt 17:2; Mk 9:3; Dan 7:9; Rev 1:14-16; 10:1).

In v.4 Mt turns to the theme of the guards, but he uses the Greek word which occurs in 27:54 (*tērountes*), not the word used in 27:65 (*koustōdia*). An ironic constrast is thus created. The guards at the cross saw the earthquake and other apocalyptic events, feared with a salutary fear, and came to faith. The guards in 28:4 are shaken (same verb as 27:51) with the fear of unbelievers and become as dead men. The angel addresses his glad tidings not to them but to the women. First, as in any OT theophany, he speaks the consoling words: "Fear not" — all the more fitting, since the resurrection of Jesus has freed the believer from fear of death. The angel knows what the women are seeking: Jesus the crucified. But that description, "crucified," is a designation even an unbeliever could give Jesus. The good news is that Jesus the crucified is also Jesus the Risen One — hence, the prison room of death is empty. For Jesus has been raised by God the Father (better than RSV's "he has risen"), "just as he said" — harking back to the three predictions in 16:21; 17:23; and 20:19, to say nothing of other passages like 12:40 and 26:32. Thus, for the last time, Mt underlines Jesus' foreknowledge of the events of his passion. The angel invites the women to "come" and "see" the emptiness of the prison of death. But then he urges upon them a pressing mission ("go quickly") to announce the gospel of the resurrection to the disciples, who are thought of as remaining in Jerusalem, despite their flight from Jesus in 26:56. In addition to the good news of the resurrection, the women are to remind the disciples of Jesus' prophecy in 26:32: he goes before them into Galilee, the Galilee of the Gentiles where he began his public ministry, called his first disciples, preached, and taught. The angel adds to Jesus' prophecy a more specific promise: *there*, in Galilee, not here in Jerusalem or here in the tomb, the disciples will see the risen Lord (cf. v. 17).

The angel then majestically dismisses the women with an indication that he has finished his prophecy and command (Mt substitutes, "Lo, I have told you" for Mk's "just as *he* said," since Mt has already used Mk's phrase in 28:6, when the angel reminds the women of Jesus' prediction of his resurrection). Strange to say, Mt omits Mk's special mention of Peter (Mk 16:7), despite Mt's great interest in Peter throughout the gospel. Perhaps Mt feels that Mk's special mention of Peter heralds a unique appearance to Peter (as in 1 Cor 15:5). Since Mt has other plans for the scene of Jesus' appearance to the disciples (and since, perhaps, he has already used the traditions about Jesus' resurrection appearance to Peter in 16:16-19), Mt drops the reference to Peter. While Mk ends the pericope with the women disobeying the young man's order and telling no one of their experience because of their fear, Mt has the women departing *quickly* (in obedience to the angel's message) with a fear that is more than overcome by "great joy" (cf. 2:10, of the Magi). The women become the first apostles to the unbelieving disciples.

B. THE RISEN JESUS MEETS THE WOMEN. 28:9-10.

> [9]And behold, Jesus met them and said, "Hail!" And they came up and took hold of his feet and worshiped him. [10]Then Jesus said to them, "Do not be afraid; go and tell my brethren to go to Galilee, and there they will see me."

This small scene is unique to Mt, though it has intriguing parallels to Jesus' appearance to Mary Magdalene in Jn 20:14-18 (Magdalene is common to both; Jesus appears to a woman before he appears to the disciples; this takes place in the vicinity of the tomb; Jesus seizes the initiative and appears unexpectedly; the woman shows great love and reverence by touching the risen body; Jesus brings this touching to a halt by sending the woman to the disciples with the announcement of the resurrection; the disciples are called "my brothers"). Jesus encounters the women with the usual Greek term of greeting, *chairete* (RSV: "hail"). The word literally means "rejoice"; and, since the attitude of the women has just been described as one of "great joy" (*charas megalēs*), Jesus' greeting may carry the deeper meaning of conveying the joy of Easter (cf. 2:10 for the same juxtaposition of the verb and the noun). In a gesture of reverence the women "seize" his feet (to kiss them?); then they adore him, as do the eleven in v. 17.

Surprisingly, Jesus' message seems to be simply a repetition of the angel's words in vv. 5a and 7b; some have therefore concluded that Mt's addition of vv. 9-10 is superfluous. But in two verses Mt is making three important points.

(1) Jesus' risen body is a real body which can be touched. Mt thus emphasizes the identity of the earthly Jesus with the risen Lord. Hence, just as Son of Man was *the* dominant christological title in chaps. 24-26, and just as Son of God was *the* dominant title in chap. 27, so the simple name Jesus is the dominant "title" in chap. 28. Instead of piling up in his final chapter all the titles he has developed throughout the gospel, Mt refers to the Risen One throughout chap. 28 as Jesus (vv. 5, 9, 10, 16, 18). (2) Jesus had called his disciples his brothers during his public ministry because they did the will of his Father (12:49-50). By abandoning him in Gethsemane they had ceased to do his Father's will and so had ceased to be his brothers. But by his death-resurrection Jesus has defeated the power sin had over his disciples, and so now he mercifully restores the renegade disciples to full fellowship by calling them once again "my brothers" (why the RSV uses "brethren" in 28:10 but "brothers" in 12:46-50 is a mystery; the same word, *adelphoi*, is used in both pericopes). Jesus again calls sinners to be forgiven and therefore to be the church. The merciful act prepares for and makes possible the founding of the church (28:16-20). (3) The third point remains implicit in the Matthean narrative (contrast Jn 20:17): Jesus does not indulge the women in their tender gestures of love. He abruptly breaks off this reunion to send them on an Easter mission to the still ignorant disciples, who are insistently directed to Galilee of the Gentiles. *Only* there will the eleven see him. The risen Jesus appears to people not to satisfy personal needs but to send them on mission—even to all nations (28:19). The disciples cannot cling to their old relationship to Jesus. They encounter the same Jesus, but receive a new mission.

C. THE FALSE TEACHING ON THE RESURRECTION.
28:11-15.

> [11]While they were going, behold, some of the guard went into the city and told the chief priests all that had

taken place. [12]And when they had assembled with the elders and taken counsel, they gave a sum of money to the soldiers [13]and said, "Tell people, 'His disciples came by night and stole him away while we were asleep.' [14]And if this comes to the governor's ears, we will satisfy him and keep you out of trouble." [15]So they took the money and did as they were directed; and this story has been spread among the Jews to this day.

The narrative of the setting of the guards at the tomb followed the narrative of the burial in chap. 27; so now, in chap. 28, the narrative of the report of the guards and its consequence follows the narrative of the discovery of the empty tomb. As the women rush to announce the good news to the disciples, the guards go to the chief priests and elders (Mt's usual code name for the Jewish leaders in the passion narrative), who think up a lie to counter the good news. One is reminded of Herod gathering together the chief priests and scribes when he is informed of the threat stemming from Jesus' birth (2:4); lies and a "military solution" proved equally ineffectual then. One should take 28:11-15 as a paradigmatic scene of the conflict between Christian missionary activities and Jewish anti-missionary activities in the first century. As in 27:62-66, we have a product of polemics and apologetics, not of eyewitness reporting.

The solution of the Jewish leaders is to bribe the soldiers; as with Judas, their favorite problem-solver is a sum of *silver coins* (*argyria*, also used in 26:14-16 and 27:3-10). The ironic outcome is that they are left propagating a lie which they first presented to Pilate as a sober estimation of a clear and present danger (27:64). They, not the disciples, become guilty of fraud. Having failed to prevent the resurrection, they are reduced to trying to render it unbelievable. No doubt Mt intends the lie to be seen as patently ridiculous: how could the soldiers testify to what had happened while they were asleep? And how could the theft have occurred when the soldiers were posted with the precise intent to prevent such a theft? Despite the holes in the story, the Jews assure the guard that they will "take care" of Pilate. With almost a parody of his customary command-execution formula, Mt states that the soldiers did as they "were directed" (*edidachthēsan*, literally, "were taught"). We are told that the false teaching of the Jewish officials concerning the resurrection has been spread abroad among the Jews even "to this day" (i.e., the time of Mt's writing). Mt speaks of "this story," literally "this word," which is meant to counter "the word" of the gospel. The false teaching on the resurrection, carried out by the rejected Jewish teachers (cf. 16:1-12), is thus contrasted with the true and legitimate preaching and teaching of the disciples, who are sent by the risen Jesus to all nations (28:19-20). Mt, of course, is convinced that lies will impede the Risen One and his gospel no more than did military might, unjust trials, a cruel death, a great stone, and an ineffectual guard. It may be no accident that Mt, who has always spoken of "Israel" during his gospel, and who has placed "Jews" only in the mouths of pagans, now refers to the people of the old covenant simply as "Jews." The kingdom of God has been taken away from them and given to a people bearing its fruit, i.e., the church (21:43). They have lost their privileged status as the chosen people; Israel is no more. A new period of salvation history and mission has been born out of the death-resurrection. The Jews are no longer coterminous with the people of God; they are simply one of the "nations" or "peoples" to which the disciples are sent (28:19). Needless to say, one must read Mt in the light of the polemics between church and synagogue in the first century A.D. and not naively transfer his statements into later, sometimes bloody and shameful contexts.

D. PROLEPTIC PAROUSIA: THE SON OF MAN COMES TO HIS CHURCH TO COMMISSION IT.
28:16-20.

> [16]Now the eleven disciples went to Galilee, to the mountain to which Jesus had directed them. [17]And when

they saw him they worshiped him; but some doubted.
[18]And Jesus came and said to them, "All authority in
heaven and on earth has been given to me. [19]Go therefore
and make disciples of all nations, baptizing them in the
name of the Father and of the Son and of the Holy Spirit,
[20]teaching them to observe all that I have commanded
you; and lo, I am with you always, to the close of the age."

This final pericope, unique to Mt's gospel, has been
called the key to the understanding of the whole gospel.
We have here an extraordinarily rich statement on Christ,
church, and salvation history, along with secondary themes
of faith and doubt, baptism and morality, Jewish past and
Gentile future. After his death-resurrection, the pivotal
turning point of history, Jesus comes as the Son of Man
to found and commission his church. While he sent his
apostles only to the land and people of Israel during his
public ministry (10:5-6), he now sends the eleven to all
nations, with baptism, not circumcision as the initiation rite,
and with *his* commands, not the Mosaic Law, as the final
norm of morality. Thus, the present form of the pericope
definitely comes from Mt's hand and reflects his theology,
although we can discern traces of earlier traditions, perhaps
even a tradition about an Easter appearance, which Mt is
adapting for his purposes. As for the literary genre or
category of the pericope, many suggestions have been made
(missionary command, a hymn of royal enthronement, OT
pattern of divine speech, a royal decree, a rule for church
order, a concise resurrection narrative, or an apostolic
commissioning based on an OT pattern). The reason why
none of these suggestions is satisfactory is that the pericope
is stamped too much with Mt's creativity; the pericope is
too unique to be placed in any category defined by what is
typical, i.e., shared by many texts.

The pericope is divided into two halves: the introductory
narrative (vv. 16-18a) and the words of Jesus (vv. 18b-20); the
theological accent lies on the latter half. The words of Jesus
may be divided into three sayings: the announcement of

exaltation (v.18b), the consequent commissioning (with the three stages of making disciples, baptizing, and teaching, vv.19-20a), and the final promise of Jesus' sustaining presence (20b).

For the only time in his gospel Mt speaks of the inner group of disciples as "the eleven," a sad reminder of the fate of Judas (27:3-10). In obedience to Jesus' command (28:10), they, the restored "brothers," go to Galilee. The place of Jesus' "exile" during his earthly life will now become "Galilee of the Gentiles" (4:15) in a much more salutary sense: the place from which the universal mission will go forth. The mention of the mountain should not surprise us, since the mountain has been the special place of revelation throughout the gospel (5:1; 8:1; 14:23; 15:29; 17:1,9). On a mountain the Son had refused to receive all kingdoms and their glory from the devil at the cheap price of idolatry (4:8); now the Son of Man has received all power from the Father at the cost of the cross. The phrase "to which Jesus had directed them" does not correspond to anything in the preceding narrative, and may reflect a pre-Matthean story of a resurrection appearance. The phrase "when they saw him" is the only actual reference to a resurrection *appearance*. This seems strange when one remembers that the message of the angel and of Jesus culminated in the promise: "There you will see him/me." Perhaps we have here a sign of tension between tradition and Mt's redaction.

The details of what the eleven saw are not related; Mt is moving swiftly to the words of Jesus. As in the whole of chap. 28, so too here, "Jesus" is the only "title" used of the Risen One in the narrative; thus does Mt inculcate the identity of the Risen Lord with the earthly Jesus. In Mt, adoration is properly given only to God or Jesus; the temptation narrative reached its height of horror when Satan asked Jesus for adoration (4:9). It is interesting to note that adoration of Jesus occurs notably in the infancy narrative and in the Easter stories. The disciples had also adored Jesus during the earthly ministry (14:33); now they resume their posture of true disciples by adoring the Risen Jesus. Yet "some doubted"; in fact, the Greek might also be translated "*they* [i.e., all of the eleven] doubted." We are not to ask why they doubted or how the doubt was overcome. Mt is giving us a paradigm of what discipleship will always mean until the close of the age: believers caught between adoration and doubt. "Doubt" here means hesitation or practical oscillation rather than speculative difficulties over doctrine; it is Mt's last reference to the problem of "little faith" (cf. 14:31). Jesus graciously approaches his prostrate disciples; the only other time Jesus is said to "approach" (better than the RSV's "came") anyone is at the end of the transfiguration, when he likewise approaches his three prostrate disciples (17:7). Before the majestic, glorified Jesus, men can only bow low; Jesus must bridge the distance by drawing near and speaking his words of comfort and commission. The words divide into three key statements, which enunciate a past event, a present command, and a future promise.

The first saying, in v.18b, proclaims that, by his death-resurrection, Jesus has received from the Father ("was given," i.e., by God) total power over the *universe*; this is what enables him to initiate a *universal* mission (notice the "therefore" in v.19). This conferral of cosmic authority constitutes Jesus as that all-powerful Son of Man of whom Daniel spoke: "Behold, upon the clouds of heaven there came one like a son of man ... and *to him was given power*, and *all nations* ... shall serve him" (Dan 7:13-14 in the Septuagint). The exaltation of the Son of Man to power is a past event ("has been given," the aorist in Greek); for Mt, who has no separate narrative of an ascension or exaltation, the exaltation of Jesus is equivalent to the death-resurrection. The exalted Jesus now comes in a "proleptic parousia" to his church, anticipating his final coming in glory to all (cf. 24:29-31). What all, believers and unbelievers alike, will see and experience at the end of time, the believing church sees and experiences from the death-resurrection onwards: the exaltation and coming of the Son of Man (cf. Jesus' "from now on," *ap' arti*, in his prophecy of 26:64). The church alone experiences this anticipated coming in the present moment, for the church is the only place where the kingdom of God is not only an objective reality but also a subjectively appropriated experience, the only place where the Son of Man not only rules but also is acknowledged, obeyed, and praised.

Mt thus has a highly developed sense of realized eschatology with regard to the present time of the church, a time which is qualitatively different from the time of Jesus. The death-resurrection has ushered in a period when Jesus as Son of Man is lord of the cosmos. Mt describes this present situation plainly in his allegorical explanation of the wheat and the tares (Mt 13:36-43). The earthly Jesus indeed exercized authority or power (*exousia*), and "all things" (*panta*, in the sense of all truths to be revealed) were given to him (11:27). But only the exalted Son of Man has *all authority* given to him (*pasa exousia* occurs only here in the gospel). The death-resurrection means a new situation, not only for the church, but also and first of all for the church's Lord. Because his status is different, she can act differently.

The "different" action of the church is explained in the great commission of vv.19-20a, which divides into three parts. First and fundamentally, the eleven *disciples* (v.16) are sent forth into the world ("Go!") to make *disciples* of all nations. It has taken Mt a whole gospel to explain what being a disciple means. In short, it means following Jesus by obeying his teaching, by accepting his fate of death and resurrection in one's own life, and by proclaiming him as Son of Man, Lord of the universe. Those who do this are doing the will of the Father and hence are brothers and sisters of Jesus; his true disciples are his true family (12:46-50; 28:10). This call to discipleship is no longer restricted to Israel. Since the death-resurrection has smashed the barriers of the old age, and since it was a sign of the last days that the Gentiles would stream to Zion in pilgrimage, the eschatological mission is to all nations. While the RSV is correct in translating *panta ta ethnē* as "all nations" (*not* "all Gentiles"), the new element here is obviously the inclusion of the Gentiles among the people who are the object of the disciples' mission. The severe restrictions of the missionary mandate of 10:5-6 (*not* to Gentiles and *not* to the Samaritans, but only to Israel) are explicitly rescinded by the very person who gave the previous commission. Jesus died "for the many" (26:28), i.e., for the whole mass of mankind, and therefore it is to all mankind that the fruits of his death are now offered. The Jews are not excluded from this offer, although they no longer enjoy a privileged status as the chosen people Israel (cf. comment on 28:15). All peoples are invited to submit themselves freely in faith to the Son of Man's rule now, lest they fall under his punitive power on the last day. Mt's gospel began by recalling that Jesus was the son of Abraham, in whose descendants "all the nations of the earth shall be blessed" (Gen 22:18 in the Septuagint).

The second part of the commission explains how one passes from the state of unbeliever to the state of disciples: baptism in the name of Father, Son, and Spirit. At first, one is surprised by this "trinitarian" formula, which does not seem anticipated by anything previous in the gospel. Indeed, some scholars have tried to show that the trinitarian formula is not the original text of v. 19b, but to no avail; it is present in all the Greek manuscripts. When one considers the high christology of Mt's gospel, the emphasis on the personal relationship between Father and Son, the share the disciples have in this relationship, and the "trinitarian" scene at Jesus' own baptism (3:16-17), the formula seems less surprising than at first. Certainly, one could hardly imagine a more forceful proclamation of Christ's divinity — and, incidentally, of the Spirit's distinct personality — than this listing together, on a level of equality, of Father, Son, and Spirit. One does not baptize people in the name of a divine person, a holy creature, and an impersonal divine force. To be sure, this formula was not the original one used by the early church, which rather baptized candidates "in the name of Jesus" (Acts 2:38; 10:48). The trinitarian formula arose at some point in the liturgy of Mt's church; no doubt, Mt no more invents it than he invents the Our Father or the words of consecration over the cup.

One is baptized, washed, plunged, "into the name" of the Trinity—i.e., one is plunged into and immersed in the bonds of "family love" which bind together not only Father, Son, and Spirit, but also the members of the church, the family of God. Mt thus conceives of baptism as incorporation into the life of God and his church; nothing is said about baptism's power to remit sins (contrast the Eucharist in 26:28). The fact that baptism, not circumcision, is the initiation rite by which all nations enter into the new people of God underlines the breaking down of the limitations surrounding Jesus' public ministry. A gospel which ends with a universal mission and with baptism as the only initiation rite can hardly be called "Jewish" or "Jewish-Christian" in any strict sense.

The third and final part of the commission (v. 20a) involves the teaching of all of Jesus' commands. In the missionary discourse, Jesus commissioned the disciples to imitate him in preaching and performing miracles (10:1,7), but not in teaching. Only after Jesus has completed his teaching, and only after the new age has been inaugurated, does Jesus send his disciples to teach. This teaching of Jesus indeed encompasses much of what was in the Mosaic Law. But the church teaches these commands not because they come from Moses but because they come from Jesus. And, as we saw in the antitheses (5:21-48), wherever the Law of Moses and the word of Jesus clash, the Law of Moses must give way. The command of Jesus—one might almost say Jesus himself—is the ultimate norm of morality, the criterion for deciding what is the will of God. This teaching no doubt precedes and follows baptism, but Mt may have in mind here the particular order of conversion and instruction followed by his church: first the proclamation of the basic good news of the kingdom (make disciples), then the conferral of baptism on those who accept the good news, finally detailed instruction in the various commands of the Lord. Proclamation of the saving act of God in the gospel and communication of that saving act of God in baptism must precede and make possible the moral response of the individual Christian.

The final word of revelation in v.20b looks to the future, to the period which spans the time from proleptic parousia to the parousia in glory (the close of the age, *synteleia tou aiōnos*, a phrase unique to Mt in the NT; cf. 13:39-40,49; 24:3). Mt's realized eschatology by no means makes him forget the need for the final separation of good and evil in the church and in the world, a separation which will take place only at the close of the age. In the meantime, the universal mission poses a staggering task, before which the original eleven disciples—and later church leaders—might easily shrink. The Son of Man therefore ends his threefold word of revelation with a consoling and strengthening promise. Jesus is not an absentee landlord. Just as Yahweh, appearing to and commissioning the patriarchs and prophets of old, would issue his bracing "Fear not! I am with you!", the Son of Man promises to his nascent church his abiding presence to strengthen her in her world-wide mission. He who was from birth God-with-us (1:23), he who promised his presence to two or three gathered in prayer (18:20), now promises his continual presence to his church on the move. This is not a static presence, as might be the case with regard to the local community in 18:20. In 28:20, the all-powerful Son of Man promises his dynamic, energizing, enabling presence to his pilgrim church as it moves ever farther into time and space. When the missionary disciples come to a new people, it is the triumphant Son of Man who "comes" in proleptic parousia. This will be true until he comes in final glory "at the close of the age"—an open-ended expression which shows how Mt has come to terms with the "delay" of the parousia by means of his realized eschatology. Unlike Lk-Acts, there is no departure or ascension. Jesus does not ascend *from* his church; he comes to it, to remain with it all days.

One final point: notice the repeated use of *all* in vv. 16-20 to convey a sense of fullness of power, mission, teaching, time, and space. By his death-resurrection, the cosmocrator has already conquered the universe in principle. It remains for the reader of this gospel to actualize and spread the Son of Man's victory by observing *all* his commands.

SUGGESTED READING LIST
FOR MATTHEW

The list is divided according to topics.

A. CHRISTOLOGY AND SALVATION HISTORY
1. J.D. Kingsbury. *Matthew: Structure, Christology, Kingdom.* Philadelphia: Fortress, 1975.

    The heart of this work deals with the various christological titles of the gospel; Son of God is seen as the central title.
2. J. P. Meier. *The Vision of Matthew: Christ, Church and Morality in the First Gospel.* New York: Paulist Press, 1979.

    The specificity of Mt's gospel is the nexus between Christ and his church; on this nexus Mt builds his vision of morality. The title Son of Man is just as important as the title Son of God.

B. MATTHEW AND JUDAISM
1. W. D. Davies. *The Setting of the Sermon on the Mount.* Cambridge: Cambridge University Press, 1966.

    Davies sees Mt's gospel as a Christian answer to the Pharisaic reform movement of Jamnia after A.D. 70. Mt's church has not yet broken with the Jewish synagogue. Only for the advanced student.—A popular, paperback version is published by the same publisher: *The Sermon on the Mount,* 1966.
2. D. R. A. Hare. *The Theme of Jewish Persecution of Christians in the Gospel according to St Matthew.* Cambridge: Cambridge University Press, 1967.

    Mt's church has already broken with the Jewish synagogue.

C. THE INFANCY NARRATIVE
1. R. Brown. *The Birth of the Messiah*. New York: Doubleday, 1977.

   The book contains an exhaustive study of both Mt 1-2 and Lk 1-2.

D. THE FORMULA QUOTATIONS (all three books are only for advanced students)
1. K. Stendahl, *The School of St. Matthew* (2nd edition). Philadelphia: Fortress, 1968.

   The author examines all the uses of the OT in Mt, with an eye to parallels at Qumran.
2. R. H. Gundry. *The Use of the Old Testament in Matthew's Gospel*. Leiden: Brill, 1967.

   Gundry examines all OT citations in Mt, direct or indirect.
3. G. Soares Prabhu. *The Formula Quotations in the Infancy Narrative of Matthew*. Rome: Biblical Institute Press, 1976.

   The author investigates the nature and function of Mt's formula quotations, especially in chaps. 1-2.

E. THE LAW IN MATTHEW (cf. W.D. Davies, above)
1. G. Barth, "Matthew's Understanding of the Law," in G. Bornkamm, G. Barth, H.-J. Held, *Tradition and Interpretation in Matthew*. Philadelphia: Westminster, 1963.

   Barth tries to avoid any programmatic revocation of Law in Mt.
2. J. P. Meier. *Law and History in Matthew's Gospel*. Rome: Biblical Institute Press, 1976.

   Mt's theology of fulfillment does leave a place for revocation of individual laws.

F. MIRACLES IN MT
1. H.-J. Held, "Matthew as Interpreter of the Miracle Stories," in Bornkamm-Barth-Held, *Tradition and Interpretation in Matthew*.

   Held shows how Mt reinterprets Mk's miracle stories for his own theological purposes.

G. THE PASSION NARRATIVE.

1. D. Senior. *The Passion Narrative according to Matthew*. Louvain: Leuven University Press, 1975.

    Senior examines Mt's creative redaction of Mk's passion narrative line-by-line. Only for the advanced student.

H. THE RESURRECTION APPEARANCE IN MT 28:16-20.

1. G. Bornkamm, "The Risen Lord and the Earthly Jesus," in *The Future of Our Religious Past* (ed. J.M. Robinson). New York: Harper and Row, 1971.

    Bornkamm sees Mt as a Hellenistic-Jewish Christian, open to a Gentile mission, yet fighting those who would use a law-free gospel as an excuse for moral license.

2. J. P. Meier, "Nations or Gentiles in Matthew 28:19?," CBQ 39(1977) 94-102.

3. J. P. Meier, "Two Disputed Questions in Matt 28:16-20," JBL 96(1977) 407-424.

I. OTHER TOPICS

1. J. P. Meier, "John the Baptist in Matthew's Gospel," *JBL* 99 (1980) 383-405.

2. D. Garland. *The Intention of Matthew 23*. Leiden: Brill, 1979.

3. B. Przybylski. *Righteousness in Matthew and His World of Thought*. Cambridge: Cambridge University Press, 1980.

GALILEE FROM ALEXANDER THE GREAT TO HADRIAN, 323 B.C. TO 135 A.D.

by Sean Freyne

- "The subject of Freyne's most recent book is Galilee, and more particularly Galilean Judaism, during the period from 323 B.C. to 135 A.D. His treatment is comprehensive, including chapters dealing inter alia with the geography of Galilee, the rise of Hellenism, Roman administration, the cities, social stratification, the attitude of Galilean Jewry towards the Jerusalem temple and halakhah, and the early development of Christianity.

  Theological Studies

- "It is a detailed, documented study that will probably be definitive on the subject."

  Christianity Today

$27.50

Old Testament Message

A Biblical-Theological Commentary

Editors
CARROLL STUHLMUELLER, C.P. and MARTIN McNAMARA, M.S.C.

Michael Glazier, Inc.

1723 Delaware Avenue,   Wilmington, Delaware 19806

NEW TESTAMENT MESSAGE
A Biblical-Theological Commentary

Editors: Wilfrid Harrington, O.P. & Donald Senior, C.P.

"A splendid new series . . . The aim is to mediate the finest of contemporary biblical scholarship to preachers, teachers, and students of the Bible . . . There are treasures to be found in every volume of it."

George MacRae, S.J.

"The stress is on the message, the good news, the *'God-Word'* of the Christian Scriptures."

The Bible Today

"An excellent series of biblical commentaries."

The Catechist

"This series offers new insights and rewards."

Sisters Today

"A sane and well-informed series of commentaries which draws on the best of the Catholic tradition and on a wide range of modern biblical scholarship."

Henry Wansbrough, O.S.B.

(See list of titles on back cover.)